ATLA Monograph Series
edited by Don Haymes

1. Ronald L. Grimes. *The Divine Imagination: William Blake's Major Prophetic Visions.* 1972.
2. George D. Kelsey. *Social Ethics among Southern Baptists, 1917–1969.* 1973.
3. Hilda Adam Kring. *The Harmonists: A Folk-Cultural Approach.* 1973.
4. J. Steven O'Malley. *Pilgrimage of Faith: The Legacy of the Otterbeins.* 1973.
5. Charles Edwin Jones. *Perfectionist Persuasion: The Holiness Movement and American Methodism, 1867–1936.* 1974.
6. Donald E. Byrne Jr. *No Foot of Land: Folklore of American Methodist Itinerants.* 1975.
7. Milton C. Sernett. *Black Religion and American Evangelicalism: White Protestants, Plantation Missions, and the Flowering of Negro Christianity, 1787–1865.* 1975.
8. Eva Fleischner. *Judaism in German Christian Theology Since 1945: Christianity and Israel Considered in Terms of Mission.* 1975.
9. Walter James Lowe. *Mystery & the Unconscious: A Study in the Thought of Paul Ricoeur.* 1977.
10. Norris Magnuson. *Salvation in the Slums: Evangelical Social Work, 1865–1920.* 1977.
11. William Sherman Minor. *Creativity in Henry Nelson Wieman.* 1977.
12. Thomas Virgil Peterson. *Ham and Japheth: The Mythic World of Whites in the Antebellum South.* 1978.
13. Randall K. Burkett. *Garveyism as a Religious Movement: The Institutionalization of a Black Civil Religion.* 1978.
14. Roger G. Betsworth. *The Radical Movement of the 1960s.* 1980.
15. Alice Cowan Cochran. *Miners, Merchants, and Missionaries: The Roles of Missionaries and Pioneer Churches in the Colorado Gold Rush and Its Aftermath, 1858–1870.* 1980.

16. Irene Lawrence. *Linguistics and Theology: The Significance of Noam Chomsky for Theological Construction.* 1980.
17. Richard E. Williams. *Called and Chosen: The Story of Mother Rebecca Jackson and the Philadelphia Shakers.* 1981.
18. Arthur C. Repp Sr. *Luther's Catechism Comes to America: Theological Effects on the Issues of the Small Catechism Prepared in or for America prior to 1850.* 1982.
19. Lewis V. Baldwin. *"Invisible" Strands in African Methodism.* 1983.
20. David W. Gill. *The Word of God in the Ethics of Jacques Ellul.* 1984.
21. Robert Booth Fowler. *Religion and Politics in America.* 1985.
22. Page Putnam Miller. *A Claim to New Roles.* 1985.
23. C. Howard Smith. *Scandinavian Hymnody from the Reformation to the Present.* 1987.
24. Bernard T. Adeney. *Just War, Political Realism, and Faith.* 1988.
25. Paul Wesley Chilcote. *John Wesley and the Women Preachers of Early Methodism.* 1991.
26. Samuel J. Rogal. *A General Introduction of Hymnody and Congregational Song.* 1991.
27. Howard A. Barnes. *Horace Bushnell and the Virtuous Republic.* 1991.
28. Sondra A. O'Neale. *Jupiter Hammon and the Biblical Beginnings of African-American Literature.* 1993.
29. Kathleen P. Deignan. *Christ Spirit: The Eschatology of Shaker Christianity.* 1992.
30. D. Elwood Dunn. *A History of the Episcopal Church in Liberia.* 1992.
31. Terrance L. Tiessen. *Irenaeus on the Salvation of the Unevangelized.* 1993.
32. James E. McGoldrick. *Baptist Successionism: A Crucial Question in Baptist History.* 1994.
33. Murray A. Rubinstein. *The Origins of the Anglo-American Missionary Enterprise in China, 1807–1840.* 1996.
34. Thomas M. Tanner. *What Ministers Know: A Qualitative Study of Pastors as Information Professionals.* 1994.

35. Jack A. Johnson-Hill. *I-Sight: The World of Rastafari: An Interpretive Sociological Account of Rastafarian Ethics.* 1995.
36. Richard James Severson. *Time, Death, and Eternity: Reflections on Augustine's "Confessions" in Light of Heidegger's "Being and Time."* 1995.
37. Robert F. Scholz. *Press toward the Mark: History of the United Lutheran Synod of New York and New England, 1830–1930.* 1995.
38. Sam Hamstra Jr. and Arie J. Griffioen. *Reformed Confessionalism in Nineteenth-Century America: Essays on the Thought of John Williamson Nevin.* 1996.
39. Robert A. Hecht. *An Unordinary Man: A Life of Father John LaFarge, S.J.* 1996.
40. Moses Moore. *Orishatukeh Faduma: Liberal Theology and Evangelical Pan-Africanism, 1857–1946.* 1996.
41. William Lawrence. *Sundays in New York: Pulpit Theology at the Crest of the Protestant Mainstream.* 1996.
42. Bruce M. Stephens. *The Prism of Time and Eternity: Images of Christ in American Protestant Thought from Jonathan Edwards to Horace Bushnell.* 1996.
43. Eleanor Bustin Mattes. *Myth for Moderns: Erwin Ramsdell Goodenough and Religious Studies in America, 1938–1955.* 1997.
44. Nathan D. Showalter. *The End of a Crusade: The Student Volunteer Movement for Foreign Missions and the Great War.* 1997.
45. Durrenda Onolehmemhen and Kebede Gessesse. *The Black Jews of Ethiopia: The Last Exodus.* 1998.
46. Thomas H. Olbricht and Hans Rollmann. *The Quest for Unity, Peace, and Purity in Thomas Campbell's* Declaration and Address, Text and Studies. 2000.
47. Douglas W. Geyer. *Fear, Anomaly, and Uncertainty in the Gospel of Mark.* 2002.

Fear, Anomaly, and Uncertainty in the Gospel of Mark

Douglas W. Geyer

ATLA Monograph Series, No. 47

The Scarecrow Press, Inc.
Lanham, Maryland, and London
2002

SCARECROW PRESS, INC.

Published in the United States of America
by Scarecrow Press, Inc.
4720 Boston Way, Lanham, Maryland 20706
www.scarecrowpress.com

4 Pleydell Gardens, Folkestone
Kent CT20 2DN, England

British Library Cataloguing-in-Publication Information Available

Library of Congress Cataloging-in-Publication Data

Geyer, Douglas W.
    Fear, anomaly, and uncertainty in the Gospel of Mark / Douglas W. Geyer.
        p. cm. — (ATLA monograph series ; no. 47)
    Includes bibliographical references and indexes.
    ISBN 0-8108-4202-5 (alk. paper)
        1. Bible. N. T. Mark—Criticism, interpretation, etc. I. Title. II. Series.

    BS2585.2 .G49 2002
    226.3'06—dc21   2001049549

To Melanie,
my wife and partner in this journey

Contents

Preface

The ideas now developed in this book first came to mind when I worked as a psychiatric social worker for the Veterans Affairs Medical Center in North Chicago, Illinois, in their Stress Disorder Treatment Unit. This is a treatment facility for veterans who are diagnosed with post-traumatic stress disorder. The patients there have their own vivid stories to tell about the anomalous, the frightening, the disgusting, and the outrageously violent. While in this context, I pondered the crucifixion of Jesus, especially as the story is found in the Gospel of Mark. It occurred to me that in order to interpret the crucifixion vividly, I would need to uncover what it fully represents. Blood violence is no trivial thing, not now and especially not then. How could I bring this to light, especially from the Gospel of Mark?

My training in biblical research has been overseen by teachers who have done their best to make me a better student. Their admonitions guided me at Bethany Theological Seminary and at The Divinity School of the University of Chicago. I had brilliant and expert readers who helped develop the ideas now expressed in this book: Arthur Droge, Adela Collins, and Michael Murrin. Don Haymes, my reader and editor for this series, has been a friend. He saw the merits of this project when others did not and invited it to be part of the American Theological Library Association Monograph Series.

I hope that this book saves time for future students of the Gospel of Mark, especially those who are interested in what can be ascertained of the historical and cultural context of the Gospel. It is truly worthwhile to learn how to use a well-stocked theological library and the primary sources buried therein, and to marshal these various resources into a coherent argument. If done properly, this kind of argumentation can lead to a much improved reading ability. Through it we end up with more to say, have better problems to solve, and discover that making theology out of Mark is an exhilarating and comprehensive experience. I hope to demonstrate this in this book, even if only in a fledgling and halting way, given my limitations. May every reader who tries her or his hand at this approach excel past what little I am able to do.

1

Mark and Violent Death:
Crucifixion as Horror and Riddle

Everything in Mark's Gospel leads up to the cross, and the crucifixion of Jesus is the story that best correlates all other stories in Mark.[1] Although this is perhaps a simple observation, it leads us to ask questions about the meaning of this central story and Gospel event. Crucifixion was a horrible death, meant to fill anyone who saw it or heard about it with terror and dread. It made for an impure and anomalous death. It was cruel and unusual punishment, and Mark's contemporaries agree in their perception of it as an exquisite violence. Such violence is surely anomalous as a central textual event. Indeed, outside of Christian Gospels there is no precedent for such a composition. So why did an author create an expansive narrative around it? Crucifixion is so rarely discussed or even described in ancient narratives that we must ask why and how it could serve the Gospel of Mark as a foundation for a literary presentation from which broader theses are argued. This kind of violent death was anomalous and not conducive to rhetorical aptness. Yet here it is in Mark, precisely the main event, to which every other detail in Mark is directed and around which the whole story is composed.

Why had ancient authors before Mark not expanded on themes of crucifixion, expostulating values or philosophies from it or developing characters through description of it? Its violence and contemptible meaning seem to have prohibited this. What was so unusually uncanny about the violence of crucifixion? We find examples and narratives of other violent deaths in ancient mythography and history. Sometimes authors claim that these deaths produced favorable results for others. Yet no one expected death by crucifixion to be favorable, or to be a benefaction, an *exemplum*, a model for good, or a "saving" event. No one interpreted crucifixion as a just or vicarious suffering, like those deaths recounted about characters as different as Eleazar and the seven brothers,

Philoctetes, and Aesop (see appendix A, "Redeeming, Violent Death in Hellenistic Literature"). Instead, crucifixion was a brutal, state execution, accomplished through torturous, violent death in a fully public spectacle; it was an overwhelming demonstration of the power of Nemesis. Literature and religious writings avoided it. Even in early Christian art and symbolism, crucifixion does not appear.[2]

Many witnesses from the time of Mark predict a variety of severe troubles after a violent death, from impurity to unresolved injustice to unquiet ghosts of the deceased wandering about in nefarious desire for revenge. By making crucifixion central, Mark presents to us just this set of themes about violent death and miasmic wrongs, with primary priority. If we remain sensitive to ancient meanings of these themes, then we will recognize the difficulty in correlating violent death by crucifixion to other, very different stories. We may try to interpret scenes of healing and deliverance as benefactions, but overshadowing the whole is an ostensibly anti-salvific, anti-beneficent violent death. As we make statements about the literature that we now recognize as the Gospel of Mark, these interpretive problems become literary problems. How are we to read Mark's stories about the sage and parable maker who subsequently suffers a scandalous death? How are we to read Mark's stories about the healer who later suffers anomaly and utter abjection through state-sanctioned violent death? What literary sense are we to make of a mix of promise and horror, of hope and anomaly?

As we awaken to these dichotomies in Mark, we become aware of a problem that cannot easily be ignored. What interpretive principles can be applied to interpret these dichotomies? Possibly we might interpret the other stories in Mark as trivially correlated to the crucifixion, saying "That's just what happens in the story," even acknowledging the three occasions (8:31, 9:31, 10:34) when Jesus predicts his death. Yet I should argue that the central problem is indeed just this, that the story goes in exactly this way. Violent death was too volatile a topic then for us now to settle for an explanation like "the story just goes like that." Given the gravity of the subject, we cannot assume that there is a trivial relationship between crucifixion and the other stories in Mark. How does this help us to understand what we read?

We begin to understand when we begin once again from the beginning, looking for clues that may help us to ascertain the dimensions of the literary problem at hand. The Gospel of Mark starts with fulfill-ment, satiety, blessing, and gathering. People gather from every direction, coming to John the Baptist at the river. From the first sentence, ἀρχὴ τοῦ εὐαγγελίου ' Ιησοῦ Χριστοῦ (beginning of the Gospel of Jesus Christ), the course of fulfillment begins. The gospel (εὐαγγέλιον) seems the thing that will bring old times to a close and initiate better times long since foretold.[3] Conflated lines from Malachai and Isaiah depict a messenger and a preparation in the wilderness for a reunion of people with God. This promise is linked to John the Baptist through the carefully crafted opening composition.[4] Then John speaks of Jesus as ὁ ἰσχυρότερός μου (one stronger than I), a bold and positive assessment implying good things to come. In water baptism Jesus joins everyone in what they are doing, receiving the highest accolade from heaven: he is ὁ υἱός μου ὁ ἀγαπητός (my son, the beloved) who brings pleasure to God. This is a representation of certainty, security, and hope. These opening scenes close when there is a transfer from John the Baptist to Jesus, and Jesus moves off to Galilee. The future still looks promising, with Jesus now the herald (κῆρυξ) of the gospel (εὐαγγέλιον). Everything vital seems right at hand: open access to the Kingdom of God and effective ritual purification to end anomalies or fearful separations from God's blessing.

In light of this, we look at the shorter ending of Mark's Gospel in 16:1-8, as found in the oldest tradition.[5] Much belabored in exegetical theory because of its brevity, this ending befits the anomaly and terror of violent death. The opening themes of satiety and security have disappeared. After the violent death, this ending does not undo the violence of the cross. There are no stories about reappearances of Jesus, comforting to those who knew him, bringing fulfillment, reunion, security, or renewal. As has been argued by others, there is no reason to think that this ending is due either to Mark's *strict use* of earlier sources (that have no postmortem appearances) or to Mark's *ignorance* of other traditions (that indeed do have stories about meetings and conferences with Jesus after his resurrection).[6] In the shorter ending, a thematic consistency with violent death emerges. Mark hands off intact the uncanny and frightening aspects of crucifixion and does not assuage them with resurrection appearances. A total disaster is not reported, since although the ending includes no reunion of the disciples with Jesus it does include a hope that Jesus is alive, that he has survived violent death, and that he is not angry and vengeful but instead is beckoning a reunion in Galilee. Yet no explanation of the violent death is offered. There is no removal of the scandal of the crucifixion. At the empty tomb an unexpected νεανίσκος (young man) greets the women, and he makes brief and cryptic statements: ἠγέρθη οὐκ ἔστιν ὧδε (he is raised, he is not here). In a manner opposite the Gospel's opening themes of fulfillment and blessing, the women run away in fear and say nothing. Instead of a progression into blessing, there is a regression into fear. With the crucifixion as the primary event, the Gospel starts with the good, peaks with the bad, and ends with the ugly. Little is explained, little is taught. The weightiest of matters go by with the lightest apparent concern, as in fact happens earlier in Mark. As readers, it will us take some time to understand how bizarre all of this is and how we can begin to make sense of it.

Given the general outline of Mark, it is unlikely that there is a trivial relation between the crucifixion and everything else in the Gospel. Once this is acknowledged, a question promotes itself to us. What is the relationship between earlier parts of Mark and this unlucky, uncanny, atypical, impure, violent death of Jesus? Do they have anything in common? I seek to show that, indeed, before the crucifixion story there are already in the Gospel stories of fear, indeterminacy, perplexity, and uncertainty. These stories not only stand in the shadow of the Gospel's culminating death, but their themes also foreshadow that death and its terror, ghastliness, hopelessness, and revenge. These stories represent the anomalous and the frightful, and they are found in Mark 4:35-6:56, a literary cycle that focuses on anomaly, uncertainty, indeterminacy, impurity, violence, revenge, the demonic, fear, and loss of place and community.

Understanding the Anomalous Frightful

I seek to develop a method for interpreting Mark that allows for a firmer grasp of the anomalous and the uncanny in it, or what I call "the anomalous frightful." If the Gospel of Mark compels us to correlate blessing with violence, safety with terror, and certainty with uncertainty, then we need ways to read it that will keep these elements all simultaneously alive in our thinking. My approach remains committed to redaction analysis, a type of criticism that is highly developed in studies of Mark. Indeed I find it overly developed and, usually, fraught with guesswork. I therefore use redaction analysis in its most general form: (a) discovery of how two things, (b) deliberately juxtaposed together, (c) create a third meaning. This is what readers everywhere have always done while reading and discerning how elements of a whole create the meaning of the whole. In redaction analysis an interpreter deduces the way a text appears to have been put together. This deduction is based on the abstraction or hypothesis that a reader senses may be coordinating the various elements of the text. It is best if the interpreter's deduction has, today, at least the appearance of significance. Fear, death, impurity, horror, hopelessness, the uncanny, and anomaly each have significance, as also does hope for survival through any of them.

My approach to Mark also depends on comparisons to other ancient evidence. I will describe many things and discern similarities between them. Such similarities include words, themes, genres, or ideas, and they all stem from a great variety of sources, mostly external to Mark. It is rewarding to compare phenomena in Mark with what elsewhere appear similar, and comparisons like this are a way of developing evidence. But since there is no such thing as evidence without a theory of evidence, and one thing is not evidence about something else unless it is so assumed or hypothesized to be, my comparisons become evidential only when they are based on some logic of observations. Under these circumstances, propositions about relationships between variables can be stated. For example, stories about a stormy ocean in Mark and a stormy ocean in *The Odyssey* can be compared, depending on what variables are construed as evidential and how those variables are stated. I should attempt to articulate variables that appear common elements between two reports: fear evoked by the storms, rituals done in proximity to storms, explanations about storms. I should not state that these variables represent an "Ur-Storm" myth or some type of archetype. Instead, I should state aspects of fear, supplication, and aetiological explication linked to each occasion of storm in these stories. These aspects are represented in many different accounts of storms at sea. They are identifiable variables. Measuring them can tell us much about what the stories about storms mean, individually and comparatively.[7]

Mark 4:35-6:56 as a Cycle of Uncertainty

Developing a method to interpret Mark in such a way as to allow us a better grasp on the anomalous frightful in it requires redaction and comparative analysis. With these techniques I discern in Mark 4:35-6:56 a cycle, based on some rudimentary observations.

    A.   Comparison to what comes before and after this cycle.
    B.   Analysis of what uniquely occurs within the cycle.

   C. Comparison of specific elements in the cycle to elements like them elsewhere.
   D. Analysis of the ways stories begin and end within the cycle.

Mark 4:35-6:56 is notable for the absence of explanations of what Jesus does or asks others to do in the stories. This absence is critical, and it should dismay our expectations because in matters of the anomalous frightful explanations were, almost always, sought and sought fervently. We know this because responses to the anomalous frightful in antiquity ranged from vigorous, proactive magical rituals to robust, reactive interpretations of omens, portents, or signs. But in Mark 4:35-6:56, just the opposite occurs. Here we find painfully little response, emphasizing absence of explanation as an integral feature of this cycle. I should argue that absence of explanation functions as a *paralepsis*, drawing attention to itself as an absence and thereby thematically highlighting the anomalous frightful. The characters in the stories are not distanced from things, places, events, or other characters that evoke uncertainty, frighten, create impurity, or introduce the inopportune. Without pause or digression, the stories present critical incidents that are:

   A. Strange: occluded benefactions (εὐεργεσία), truly radical autonomy from ethnic homelands (πάτρις) and household (οἰκία).
   B. Frightening: the storm, wind, sea, and night (Λαῖλαψ, Ἄνεμος, Θάλασσα, Νύξ).
   C. Harbingers of dreadful uncertainty: violent death, untimely death (βιαιοθανασία, ἄωρος θάνατος).
   D. Tokens of utter disaster: the Roman Legion and a demonized man (Λεγιών and ὁ δαιμονιζόμενων).

All these thematic elements are stitched together in this cycle, culminating in the final story about Jesus walking on the ocean (θάλασσα) as a ghost (φάντασμα). None of these things are explained, and this lack of explanation increases the bizarre sense effected by the stories.

Details that make my literary analysis plausible come later. I want to generalize just a bit further and note that the anomalous frightful works as a literary theme because of the way it engages its audience. One is invited to feel alien to the events reported. This kind of alienation is not due to chronological or cultural distance from the text. The first readers targeted for this experience would have felt it also. Alienation is a permanent part of the text, and the cycle means to evoke an experience of uncertainty and unsure subjectivity, based very much on its content. It draws a reader into a search for a meaning of its fast-paced irresolution of so many strange and unfortunate situations.

Ancient Readings of Violent Death

Being drawn into a text in this way is not a modern phenomenon. Ancient readers also felt the need to resolve the literary problems I have outlined (see appendix B, "Ancient Reading of Narrative and Plot"). Origen felt called to answer critical objections to Christianity during his time. He built a career on close reading, and the scrutiny of plot and close examination of narrative details such as he employed were widely known and utilized. By the time of Mark, these had become cultivated studies, later to become only more so. This kind of close examination was occasionally focused on texts that bore a meaning of misfortune, terror, or awful outcome.[8] It is misfortune, terror, misery, and their apparent reversal by a savior who does not properly seem a savior that turn out to be exactly what some ancient readers puzzled over in reports about Jesus. For them, there was a basic flaw at the heart of a story such as Mark's, since it reported a painful outcome, telling how Jesus was subjected to the anomalous frightful through untimely, violent death. These readers wanted to know why Jesus was implicated in such things, and specifically, why he submitted to such a horrible fate as crucifixion. Ancient readers such as these show us how bizarre it seemed that Christians reported violent death by crucifixion as a part of the history of their savior.

Celsus, a second-century reader of Mark, attacked Christian theology because Jesus seemed weak and impotent, providing no beneficent works for humankind.[9] He argued that the gospel highlights a Jesus who does not fight back against violence done to him, seems unable to help himself, and seems subject to chthonic, infernal powers that everybody knows are dangerous, impossible to overcome, and deadly. Celsus wondered, Did not Christians realize that there is an insurmountable problem at the heart of their proclamation of the disgraceful violence of the cross? Did not Christians realize that their gospel story about Jesus has the suspicious and nefarious character of Bacchic mysteries with their "ghosts and terrors?" Did not Christians realize that Jesus, violently killed, appeared only as a dreadful ghost after his death, so in reality is utterly demonic?[10]

Origen's response is complex. He suggested that Celsus did not comprehend the "divine enigmas" of Scripture and also misunderstood the violence in Greek traditions of divine conflict as found in Heraclitus, Pherecydes, and Homer. Traditions about divine conflict were long in mythographical and philosophical discussion, the discussion furthered along by Hellenistic intellectuals.[11] In light of this, Origen argued that there is nothing unusually troubling in the gospel traditions. He did not reject the violence done to Jesus, and interpreted it neither as weakness nor failure. After all, he argued, stories about violence inflicted on other divine figures circulated freely among Hellenistic readers, and posed no stumbling blocks to interpretation. Both Origen and Celsus were clearly aware of the problems involved in interpretation of stories about gruesome violence. Celsus detected in the reports about Jesus abundant evidence for what I should call the anomalous frightful. Pointedly, he concluded that Christians are gullible and stupid for not recognizing the extremely bizarre nature of the gospel anomaly.[12] Origen didn't deny the facts as ascertained by Celsus; he simply interpreted them differently

The impact of the violent death of Jesus is detected elsewhere, in other explanations of the gospel anomalies. The *Martyrdom of Pionius* states that some people had a misunderstanding about Jesus. They argued that ὁ χριστὸς ἄνθρωπος ἦν καὶ ἀνεπαύσατο ὡς βιαιοθανής (Christ was human and died as a violently killed person). Subsequently, they claimed that the violently killed Jesus was useful to Christians for their suspected rituals of necromancy.[13] These critics identified the cross (ὁ σταυρός) as the chief necromantic ritual tool and implement, since it is representative of the manner of violence done to Jesus.[14] A necromantic theory like this testifies to opinions then held about violent death. The inauspicious nature of this kind of death made it dreadful and highly suspect, and these kinds of perceptions formed the basis for apotropaic rituals used to keep similar violence from happening to others.

I mention these cases to outline the reality that violent death was not a neutral subject for people in the ancient Mediterranean world. Types of death were important, and they were noted and interpreted. Violent death (βιοθανής) contrasted with death that was good (ἰδιοθάνατος). An ἰδιοθάνατος death was a natural death (κατὰ φύσιν), a βιοθανής death unnatural (παρὰ φύσιν).[15] Violent death signified a death of dreadful character and inauspicious destiny, and it is a flourishing of the anomalous frightful. Linked to this was the belief that those killed violently are denied a blessed afterlife.[16] Whether their souls (ψυχαί) were thought caught in an intermediate space, anchored to their tomb and available for one ritual or another, or snatched away into the retinue of a Hekate or some similar monstrous entity, their destiny remained a pressing question. It seemed their lives were cut off, and that the death was sudden and inopportune. In light of the *Martyrdom of Pionios*, Bowersock comments on how such deaths came to be reinterpreted as holy benefactions. On the Christian development of the term μάρτυς (witness), it must be remembered how "an aura of the unnatural, the inhuman, and the diabolical attached to the victim of violent death."[17] Unnatural, yes, and anomalously frightful. The violently dead were thought angry and bearing μήνιμα (wrath at the blood-guiltiness of the living). In this condition, some considered them restlessly wandering, seeking ways to assault the living.[18]

Tertullian, speaking about the fate of souls if left unburied after death, brings up the topic in *De Anima* 57. He refers to *biaeothanatos,* claiming this idea and the concepts behind it stem specifically from *magia.*[19] He describes how the violently killed were not infrequently invoked in many types of magic rituals, just as the *ahori* (too early dead) were invoked. In such magic rituals, when invoked, these dead appear as *phantasmata.* For Tertullian, all of this is real, but deceit. He insists that in actuality there were demons behind all such appearances of the dead. "In exorcisms the demon at first passes himself off for an ἄωρος [untimely dead] or βιαιοθάνατος [violently dead], but ultimately he is forced to admit defeat and to confess that in reality he is an evil spirit."[20] Tertullian hypothesizes that souls of the *ahori* and *biaeothanatoi* are actually demons who were active in such people while they were alive (*sed daimones operantur sub ostenu earum* [but daimōns operate under cover of them]). These demons drove these poor victims toward their unfortunate and violent end (*quique illas in huiusmodi impegerant exitus*). Here, as in his *Apology* 22.2,[21] Tertullian's demonology explicitly attempts to account for the evil consequences commonly believed to result from sudden and unfortunate death. In this way, he acknowledges the reality of the anomalous frightful that many of his contemporaries perceived in such events. True, he interprets such consequences as the outcome not of actual spirits of the dead, but of entities somehow "behind" the dead or pretending to be the dead. But Tertullian's bit of apologetic footwork does not obscure the fact that when it comes to violent and untimely death, many questions were raised by those who heard about it. So it was with the violent death of Jesus. For those not willing to accept Christian beliefs about the matter, Jesus was frightening, anomalous, and disgraceful, and his violent death was not adequately explained. Definitions, word studies, or narrative examination did not alleviate this problem.

Crucifixion can be plainly seen for the inauspicious and terrible event that it was. It is from Origen's description of crucifixion as *mors turpissima crucis* (utterly vile death of the cross) that Martin Hengel would sort through ancient evidence about the practice.[22] Though Hengel did not specifically link crucifixion to contemporary beliefs about the crucified fated to be a wandering soul (ψυχή), he did conclude that crucifixion was considered the worst of fates. It is an utterly unpleasant event that was scrupulously avoided by most authors.[23] Compared to crucifixion as practiced in Persian, Greek, and Carthaginian cultures, in Roman contexts this mode of violent death was an especially favored punishment for sedition, often reserved especially for rebels and slaves in revolt. It was considered the worst of fates for certain traitors, and even a *summum supplicium*, the most terrible of retaliatory tortures.[24] State vengeance in this way was the imposition of Nemesis over official enemies. It is not unlike καταποντίσμος, or the violent act of snuffing out enemies in the ocean and exposing them to the boundless emptiness of chthonic destruction. Crucifixion is an ideal expression of the anomalous frightful. In accordance with ancient evidence about types of death and the destinies of those killed violently, it is terrifying, ghastly, and laden with uncertainty. It is a violent and abrupt end of mortal life, and it remained this volatile problem for the ancient audience of the gospels. The tenacity of this problem for early Christianity is not to be underestimated.

In this context, we can glimpse the dimensions of anomaly and fright that the Gospel of Mark employs as its major narrative focus. The event of the crucifixion begins to make its appearance in the Markan narrative through prophetic predictions attributed to Jesus in 8:31, 9:31, and 10:34, the first of which includes the statement by Jesus about following and "taking up the cross." It then fully appears in the stories about the last meal, betrayal, arrest, adjudication, and execution of Jesus (14:1-15:47). Part of Mark's strategy in dealing with this kind of material is to link Jesus with the anomalous frightful already in Mark 4:35-6:56, where there is evocation of both the experience and descriptions of the anomalous frightful. This evocation and description serve as a narrative preparation for the final, catastrophic event of the definitive anomalous frightful: the apparent, total collapse of divine benefaction at the crucifixion.

What is safe or dangerous, maleficent or beneficent is encountered already in Mark 4:35-6:56. In this cycle we find odd occurrences of strange benefactions by a figure who questions why his disciples are terrified when, by common expectation, they should be terrified. Jesus relates to the Hellenistic πόλις (city) at mysterious places and in unusual ways. He cannot easily be comprehended. Although his largesse is tangible, there is nothing here that properly leads to a consensus about him as a savior, or even as an ἀγαθὸς ἀνήρ (good man). The Λαῖλαψ, Ἄνεμος, Θάλασσα, and Νύξ (Storm, Wind, Sea, Night) seemed easily navigated by him, and overpowered, but this navigation and overpowering are of no comfort to those with him, and these feats are never acclaimed. Jesus moves from the ἥμερος (civilized) to the θηριώδης (wild), a direction antithetical to contemporary expectations for εὐεργεσία (benefaction). With no explanation given, Jesus freely interacts with those thought trapped in the world of the dead or with those thought plagued by infernal disabilities. As in the end of Mark in 16:8, we are not sure what to make of these things because we are given no explanation.

What We Learn from Mark

I want the reader to discover that bewilderment and uncertainty are valid and even expected outcomes of reading Mark. These outcomes are not well-handled by interpretations that remove them and their scandal. Even so, we do well to discover what it is *exactly* that seems bewildering or uncertain. Interpretation that remains good enough, appropriate, relevant, and satisfying will identify and clarify relations between elements in a text: signified objects, signifiers, evocations, and illustrations.[25] In so doing, interpretation need not eliminate from texts what seems incomplete or uncertain. It can respect any evocation of indeterminacy, or that which is like the gray area between dreaming and consciousness. It can respect evocation of fear, fright, lack of hope in a good end, disgust, violence, or contempt. It is possible to identify elements of a text that either directly report about the anomalous frightful or evoke feelings of the anomalous frightful. Much of my identification is accomplished by comparing Mark to other sources. Furthermore, elements that create and promote fear or uncertainty in Mark come to light when we recognize certain aspects of Mark's style: the way that stories begin and end, unfinished or interrupted story lines, and strange turns of events. Applied to Mark, such interpretation can be done well, allowing for the discovery of the anomalous frightful in Mark: uncertainty, fear, strange events, occluded benefaction, indeterminate help, and danger at the heart of the Gospel.

Notes

1. Readers of Mark often make this assessment. Willi Marxsen (*Mark the Evangelist: Studies in the Redaction History of the Gospel*, trans. by J. Boyce and others [Nashville, Tenn.: Abingdon Press, 1969; orig. German publ. 1959], 126-38) developed this point of view through examination of Mark's use of the apostolic term εὐαγγέλιον for the whole compilation. He argues that the apostolic term early came to indicate the death and resurrection of Jesus, and its use at the beginning of Mark maintains this meaning. I admire the work of Johannes Schreiber (*Der Kreuzigungsbericht des Markusevangeliums: Eine traditions-geschichtliche und methodenkritische Untersuchung nach William Wrede*, Beiheft zur Zeitschrift für die neutestamentliche Wissenschaft und dies Kunde der ältern Kirche 48 [Berlin: Walter de Gruyter, 1986]), who suggested that the story of the crucifixion seemed *very odd*, especially to Christians. He outlined a reception of this strange story by early Christians, suggesting that the early story can be identified in the Markan crucifixion narrative. To eliminate the discomfort they produced, these early stories were modified by additional tradition. The crucifixion was perceived as an "abgrundtiefe Paradoxie" (p.159), and a later assimilation of apocalyptic and Scriptural materials into the early stories attempts to resolve the paradox. Already from the arrest of John the Baptist (Mark 1:14), the crucifixion of Jesus is brought into view ("ist im Anfang des Evangeliums schon das furchtbare Geheminis der Kreuzigung Christi" [p.189]), mostly because of use of the verb παραδίδωμι here and in Mark 14:21.

2. Graydon F. Snyder, *Ante Pacem: Archaeological Evidence of Church Life before Constantine* (Macon, Ga.: Mercer University Press, 1985), 26.

3. The use of ἀρχή in 1:1 may not be exactly that suggested by Ronald F. Hock ("Why New Testament Scholars Should Read Ancient Novels," pp. 121-38 in *Ancient Fiction and Early Christian Narrative*, ed. by Ronald F. Hock and others, Society of Biblical Literature Symposium Series 6 [Atlanta, Ga.: Scholars Press, 1998], 127): "Mark's use of ἀρχή (1:1) to signal 'the beginning' of the fulfillment of Isaiah's prophecy (vv.2-3) in the preaching of John the Baptist matches the use of ἀρχή in the romances. Early in Xenophon's story, Habrocomes and Anthia receive an oracle from Apollo (1.6.2), whose dire predictions, however, do not find immediate fulfillment. But later in the story, when the sailors on board the ship they are on become drunk and allow a pirate ship to attack, Xenophon notes that this incident represented the 'beginning' (ἀρχή) (1.12.13) of the oracle's fulfillment (cf. also Chariton, 1.6.5; Achilles Tatius, 1.3.1)." There is no indication in Mark that the whole gospel story is the fulfillment of a specific oracle or prediction. However, themes of the general fulfillment of a long line of promises by God to Israel do open the work. Alas, were it so that ἀρχή here paralleled its use elsewhere, in the beginnings of Greek hymns, whose lines emphasize the fullness and brilliance of the subjects being praised. See William

H. Race, "Aspects of Rhetoric and Form in Greek Hymns," *Greek, Roman, and Byzantine Studies* 23/1 (1982): 5-8.

4. On the protasis and apodosis of a periodic prœmium in 1:2-4, including reinforcing use of a comparative clause ("*as* it stands written . . . *so* there occurred John the Baptist in the wilderness."), as well as use of citation, see Heinrich Lausberg, "Minuscula philologica (III): Die prœmial Periode des Evangelium nach Marks (1, 2-4)," in *Nachrichten der Akademie der Wissenschaften in Göttingen: I, Philologisch-historische Klasse*, Nr. 3, Jahrgang 1979, 1-11. The hypotactic syntax of this pœmium (εἰρωμένη λέξις) is in contrast to the paratactic of the rest of Mark (διηρημένη λέξις). See Aldo Scaglione, *The Classical Theory of Composition, From Its Origins to the Present: A Historical Survey* (Chapel Hill: University of North Carolina Press, 1972), 27. Lausberg's analysis shows that the ἀρχή of the opening is not simply a title for the Gospel as a whole. It is a κῶλον, linked without copulative to the protasis of vv.2-3.

5. Review of the tradition history found in Paul Rohrbach, *Der Schluss des Markusevangeliums, der Vier-Evangelien-Kanon und die Kleinasiatischen Presbyter* (Berlin: Verlag von Georg Nauck, 1894), who on his way to outlining the tradition history of the longer ending, notes that both Jerome and Eusebius reported their copies of Mark to end at 16:8. Besides study of the different dates and provenances of the manuscript traditions, there has also been an intense source-critical discussion of the traditions about the death, burial, and tomb of Jesus. Parallels between Mark, the Gospel of John, and the Gospel of Peter have been discussed at length, though the guesses about historical processes presented as conclusions by the exegetes have not always been convincing. For review, see F. Neirynck, "The Apocryphal Gospels and the Gospel of Mark," in *The New Testament in Early Christianity*, ed. Jean-Marie Sevrin Bibliotheca Ephemeridum Theologicarum Lovaniensium 86 (Leuven, Belgium: University Press, 1989), 123-76.

6. The various points of view are now refreshed in a review found in W. R. Teleford, *The Theology of the Gospel of Mark*, New Testament Theology (Cambridge: Cambridge University Press, 1999), 137-51, though still here both the meaning of "Galilee" and the meaning of the women who do not tell the (Jewish) disciples is interpreted as a Markan statement validating missionary activity among the Gentiles. I admire the work of Andreas Lindemann ("Die Österbotschaft des Markus: Zur theologischen Interpretation von Mark 16.1-8," *New Testament Studies* 26 [1980]: 298-317), who suggested that there is a unique theological point of view about the resurrection maintained by Mark, and that Mark's expression of this point of view takes place through the brief narrative ending that lacks a resurrection appearance. Lindemann proposed a theological view promoted by Mark, that the resurrection is properly believed when it is based on a future-oriented expectation, and improperly believed when it is based on historical reports of the disciples encountering a resurrected Jesus. In contrast to him, I believe that the point of not reporting resurrection appearances is to emphasize the uncanny death and its similarly uncanny resolution. In so reporting, anomaly and fear are aggrandized.

7. Comparisons between Mark and something else from its contemporary world create a temptation to infer wrongly causation or influence between one and other. Comparisons can falsely seem evidence of "what happened" when Mark was composed. Statements that something in Mark is a certain way because of some previous cause generally turn out to be trivial, primarily because they over-simplify the problems of comparison so much that the circumstantial evidence they claim to provide is worthless. Circumstantial evidence cannot suggest circumstances; it is relevant only when motive or opportunity is clear and when the actual circumstances are confirmed by other evidence. As for Mark, we do not have reliable information about the circumstances, or the motive; we do not know who the author is or what the author knew, nor even what the author knew but decided not to use, or forgot, or liked, or disliked. We do well to avoid believing the illusion that our comparisons produce evidence about what caused the Gospel of Mark.

8. Roughly at the same time as Mark, in another part of the world Heliodorus Homericus wrestled with the uncertain meaning of the Greek word ἀδευκέϊ (cruel, unexpected), as found in *Odyssey* 4.489. See Andrew R. Dyck, "The Fragments of Heliodorus Homericus," in *Harvard Studies in Classical Philology* 95 (1993): 11. Considerable philological observations were made, which Dyck summarizes: the word could be used "as a description of the death which Menelaus darkly suspects may have befallen some of his comrades on the expedition to Troy during their voyage home and about which he asks Proteus (*Od* 4.489), or as the kind of reputation that Nausicaa shuns (*Od* 7.273), or of the fate of Eurylochus' unlucky companions, changed to swine by Circe (*Od* 20.245), [then] ἀδευκής clearly had an unpleasant meaning. The ancient interpreters, agreeing on an alpha-privative formation, divided between (a) those who thought the basic meaning 'unexpected' (to δεύχω, a posited by-form of δέχομαι) and (b) those who derived it from γλεῦκος and hence found the sense 'harsh, unpleasant.' Heliodorus' interpretation 'unconjectured' arrived at a result not dissimilar to (1), but was probably based on a different etymology." In general for details of ancient practices of Homeric interpretation, see Rudolf Pfeiffer, *History of Classical Scholarship: From the Beginnings to the End of the Hellenistic Age* (Oxford: Clarendon Press, 1968), 105-122. Later, on a different note, Agatharchides (*De Mari Erythraeo* §21) comments on how many orators had attempted, with various styles and thematic emphases, to articulate the past tragedies of history. See Karl Müller, *Geographi Graeci Minores* (Hildesheim: Georg Olms, 1965; orig. published 1853), 1:119-23. Specifically, τὸ δείνον (the terror) and τὸ πάθος (the suffering) was created by the razing of the cities of Olynthus (destroyed by Philipp) and Thebes (destroyed by Alexander). The rhetoricians attempted to exegete and investigate the events, trying to signify (σημαίνειν) the cause (αἴτιον) for the wretched gloominess of these events (τὸ δὲ σκυθρωπὸν τῆς πράξεως ἄρρητον). Portentous events like the destruction of capitols are a dreadful suffering, and the suffering became a topic for exegesis.

9. Origen, *Contra Celsum* 1.67.

10. For the Bacchic φάσματα καὶ τὰ δείματα see *Contra Celsum* 4.10, with comments by Robert J. Hauck (*The More Divine Proof: Prophecy and Inspiration in Celsus and Origen*, American Academy of Religion Academy Series, 69 [Atlanta: Scholars Press, 1989], 87). For Jesus as a φάντασμα after his death, see *Contra Celsum* 3.22. In *Contra Celsum* 6:34 Origen reports how Celsus poked fun at the Christian traditions he knew, suggesting that the violent death of Jesus was foolishness apprehended by Christians for less than the disastrous defeat it truly was: "They have further added one on top of another saying of prophets, and circles upon circles, and emanations of an earthly Church, and of Circumcision, and a power flowing from a certain virgin Prunicus, and a living soul, and heaven slain that it may have life, and earth slain with a sword and many men slain that they may have life, and death in the world being stopped when the sin of the world dies, and a narrow descent again, and gates that open of their own accord. And everywhere they speak in their writings of the tree of life and of resurrection of the flesh by the tree—I imagine because their master was nailed to a cross and was a carpenter by trade. So that if he had happened to be thrown off a cliff, or pushed into a pit, or suffocated by strangling, or if he had been a cobbler or stonemason or blacksmith, there would have been a cliff of life above the heavens, or a pit of resurrection, or a rope of immortality, or a blessed stone, or an iron of love, or a holy hide of leather. Would not an old woman who sings a story to lull a little child to sleep have been ashamed to whisper tales such as these?" (Trans. from Henry Chadwick, *Origen Contra Celsum* [Cambridge: Cambridge University Press, 1953].

11. For Origen's criticism of Celsus in this regard, see *Contra Celsum* 1.54; 6.42-43. On the Hellenistic heritage, see Philo of Byblos, *Phoenician History* 4.47; text and translation in Harold Attridge and Robert Oden, *Philo of Byblos: The Phoenician History: Introduction, Critical Text, Translation, and Notes*, CBQ Monograph Series 9 (Washington: Catholic Biblical Association, 1981), F 4.47. In this passage, writings by Pherecydes of Syros are cited, about the battle between Kronos and Ophioneus. This ancient tradition about the snake enabled Philo to make his own points. The same happened later in Celsus and Origien (Origen *Contra Celsum* 6.42). See Kirk and Raven (*Presocratic Philosophers*, 65-68) for material there collected on "The Fight between Kronos and Ophioneus." Pherecydes is a somewhat ambiguous name, referring to at least two authors: one from Syros who wrote a "Theology" (traditions about Zeus and Kronos) and one from Athens who wrote a "Genealogy." Distinguishing them was of concern to Eratosthenes, another Hellenistic intellectual; see Felix Jacoby, "The First Athenian Prose Writer," in *Abhandlungen zur griechischen Geschichtschreibung von Felix Jacoby zu seinem achtzigsten Geburtstag am 19. März 1956*, ed. Herbert Bloch (Leiden, The Netherlands: E. J. Brill, 1956), 100-143.

12. See Origen, *Contra Celsum* 1:9, where Celsus is quoted comparing Christians to "begging priests of Cybele and soothsayers, and to worshipers of Mithras and Sabazius, and whatever else one might meet, apparitions of Hecate or of some other daemon or daemons. For just as among them scoundrels frequently take advantage of the lack of education of gullible people and lead them

wherever they wish, so also . . . this happens among the Christians." Why did
Celsus compare Christians to Hekate and the ghosts in her retinue? *Contra Celsum*
6:22 speaks of the mysteries of Mithra and the mysteries of Hekate as celebrated
at Aegina. Pausanius (Περιήγησις 2.30.2) commented on the annual celebration
of mysteries for Hekate at this location. Cybele and Sabazius also received a
variety of ecstatic worship in mystery rites; see Dodds, *Greeks and the Irrational*,
193-194. In *Contra Celsum* 1:9, the quotation from Celsus implies that he thought
that Christians reveled in perceptual uncertainty (the dubious nature of orgiastic
experiences) and fear (the dubious nature of the violence involved with myths).
Celsus suggested that Christians are indistinguishable from those who deal with
ghosts and spirits.

13. *Martyrdom of Pionius* 13.3. According to Auguste Bouché-Leclercq
(*Histoire de la Divination dans l'Antiquité* [Bruxelles: Culture et Civilization,
1879], 3:365) necromancy was always directly motivated by desire for revenge.
The living would manipulate the dead for purposes of revenge. The dead didn't
appear to mind, as they often had died violently and unhappily and therefore were
particularly amenable to intentions of revenge. The view in the *Martrydom of
Pionius* was that the violent death of Jesus implicated Christians in rituals
specifically of retaliation and revenge.

14. *Martyrdom of Pionius*, 13.8. The author countered this idea, arguing that
a reputation of such a necromantic figure in no way could compel the gathering
of so many disciples from so many places, who were in fact calling Jesus teacher
(διδάσκαλος). The argument continues that furthermore, a mere necromantic
figure cannot have worked through his followers such a successful number of
exorcisms as the Christians accomplished on a regular basis.

15. Ptolemy *Tetrabiblos* 4.8 (Περὶ ποιότητος θανάτου); similar material in
Vettius Valens, τὴν τοῦ θανάτου ποιότητα; see Wilhelm Kroll, *Vetti Valentis
Anthologiarum Libri*. (Berlin: Weidmann, 1908), 128 line 8. On the natural
aspects, see Auguste Bouché-Leclercq (*L'Astrologie Grecque* [Paris: E. Leroux,
1899], 423), who refers to comments made in *scholia* on Ptolemy's definitions.
Franz Cumont (*Lux Perpetua* [Paris: Librarie Orientalise Paul Geuthner, 1949],
309) argued that ideas about βιαιοθάνατος (violent death) developed out of
astrological theory that considered good or bad births, deaths, destinies. See J. H.
Waszink ("Biothanati,"*RAC* Bd. 2 col.392) for an overview of these developments, especially of how violent death was linked to ἀναιρέτης (Anareta, a planet
that cut short a life). Louis Robert (*Le Martyre de Pionios, Prêtre de Smyrne*, ed.
Glen W. Bowersock and C. P. Jones; Greek text trans. André Vaillant [Washing-
ton, D.C.: Dumbarton Oaks Research Library and Collection, 1994], 84) wrote
about the types of death, that "c'était [βιαιοθάνατος] une catégorie de morts ayant
une grande importance dans la pensée ancienne . . . le contrarie . . . c'est
ἰδιοθάνατος" (this is a category of the dead having a great importance in ancient
thought . . . the contrary . . . is a good death).

16. J. H. Waszink ("*Mors immatura*," in *Opuscula Selecta* [Leiden: E. J.
Brill, 1979], 108) writes that "from the fifth century B.C. onward, an ever-growing
number of passages testify to the existence of a belief that the souls of those who

had found a premature death were forbidden to enter the Underworld."

17. Glen W. Bowersock, *Martyrdom and Rome*, Wiles Lectures, Queen's University of Belfast, 1993 (Cambridge: Cambridge University Press, 1995), 71.

18. This was thought a problem that developed within family histories, as a result of incomplete purifications badly undertaken for family members. This type of family problem has widespread witnesses, found in culturally diverse sources. See Walter Burkert, *Orientalizing Revolution: Near Eastern Influence on Greek Culture in the Early Archaic Age*, Revealing Antiquity 5 (Cambridge, Mass.: Harvard University Press, 1992), 66. Burkert refers to Plato *Phaedrus* 244d, which mentions the μηνίματα (wraths) who manifest themselves through great sufferings in certain, unfortunate families. Purifications were divinatory, accomplished by a μάντις (prophet).

19. Magical texts with instructions for revivifying the bodies of the dead to perform a task willed by an enchanter can be viewed in *PGM* 13.277-282 ("I conjure you, spirit coming in air, enter, inspire, empower, resurrect by the power of the eternal god, this body; and let it walk about in this place, for I am he who acts with the power of Thayth, the holy god" [trans. Morton Smith in Betz, *Greek Magical Papyri*, 180]) and *PGM* 19b.5-15 ("Onto a cutting of hieratic papyrus write with myrrh and dedicate it to one who has died a violent death: 'I adjure you by . . . you, who are able, raise your body and go to her, NN, until she is willing.'" [trans. by E. O'Neil in Betz, *Greek Magical Papyri*, 258]). Morton Smith (*Jesus the Magician* [San Francisco: Harper and Row, 1978], 118) commented that "magical papyri contain a few directions for resurrections . . . but these profess to make the revived body perform a specific function, in other words, they originate from exaggerations of the necromantic claim to call back and utilize the spirit of a dead man." Smith did not comment here on the specific nature of these deaths, but typically they are violent; see Theodore Hopfner, *Griechisch-ägyptischer Offenbarungszauber*, *2 Bd.*, Studien zur Palaeographie und Papyruskunde, Bd. 21, Bd. 23 (Amsterdam: Verlag Adolf M. Hakkert, 1921; repr. 1974), 2§371-372 on *Totendaemon* in *PGM* 4.2145-2151, 2186-2205, 2205-2240, 2146-2186. This magical material is a complex of formulas for various *lamellae* to be used specifically in deadly situations of risk and danger. The situations were: (1) the interrogation of criminals just before they are executed; (2) the interrogation of prisoners while being tortured to death; (3) the violent battle of gladiators; (4) the deadly competition between charioteers; (5) the seditious danger of runaway slaves in revolt. The spell is based on three distinct lines of Homeric poetry that emphasized battle, violent death, and purification: "After saying this, he drove the solid-hoofed horses through the ditch [*Iliad* 10.564] . . . And men gasping out their lives amid the terrible slaughter [*Iliad* 10.521] . . . And they washed off in the sea the sweat that covered them [*Iliad* 10.572]." These are lines depicting violent death and purificatory washing in the salt water of cleansing Ocean.

20. J. H. Waszink, *Quinti Septimi Florentis Tertulliani De Anima: Edited with Introduction and Commentary* (Amsterdam: J. M. Meulenhoff, 1947), 579.

21. Included in this passage is discussion of Socrates' δαίμων (daimon) as well as δαιμόνες (demons) in general; of the latter Tertullian noted that they are invoked through cursing by "ignorant people and the congeries of material on demons and angels available through magic's mountebanks."

22. Origen, *Commentary on Matthew* 27.22. See Martin Hengel, *Crucifixion in the Ancient World and the Folly of the Cross*, trans. John Bowden (Philadelphia: Fortress Press, 1977), xi.

23. Hengel, *Crucifixion*, 14.

24. Hengel, *Crucifixion*, 64. See Livy 30.43.13 and Valerius Maximus 2.7.12, on how the older Scipio punished Roman deserters at the end of the Second Punic War more harshly than others; Hengel, *Crucifixion*, 29-30.

25. Tzvetan Todorov (*Introduction to Poetics*, trans. Richard Howard, Theory and History of Literature 1 [Minneapolis: University of Minnesota Press, 1981], 14) wrote, "a certain signifier *signifies* a certain signified, a certain phenomenon *evokes* another, a certain episode *symbolizes* an idea, another *illustrates* a psychology."

2

The Anomalous Frightful:
What It Is and What It Means

"The Anomalous Frightful" admittedly appears to be a modern designation, perhaps reminiscent of a psychological category. Rather than starting from psychology, however, I begin from literary observations about the Gospel of Mark, noting that the report of the violent death of Jesus seems to determine the composition of the remaining narrative and our understanding of how to read it. With this observation in mind, I seek out ways to read Mark well, because we must interpret the crucifixion and other anomalous matters in it. "Anomalous frightful" is a designation meant to facilitate identification and interpretation of several types of evidence and themes, and to assist in their organization into an explanation that is both satisfying and reasonably accurate to the time period of Mark. The contextual accuracy of this effort is of extremely high value to me. But before all this unfolds, I must further develop a working idea about the anomalous frightful by exploring two of its aspects: perplexing uncertainty and fear.

Anomalies and Strange Events

Terms used in ancient descriptions of anomalous and strange phenomena are θαυμάσιος (wonderful), παράδοξος (marvel), and *mirabilis* (miracle). The adjective most pertinent to my interests, ἀνόμοιος (strange), does not occur in the literature of paradoxography, one of the most organized and well known ancient descriptions of phenomena thought anomalous. Pollux, a lexicographer roughly contemporary to Mark, lists ἀνόμοιος with only a brief citation, showing its synonym to be ἀπεοικώς (unlikely). I use the term "anomalous" to indicate what the ancient term παράδοξος (marvel) indicates: that which is unusual, strange, not like anything else, and therefore inexplicable. The accent here is on the quality of something being without explanation or unexplainable. What is anomalous has its roots in strange events that occur without benefit of a satisfactory consensus about what happened.

Events like this are not unusual in human experience, and it comes as no surprise that they were discussed in antiquity. What may come as a surprise is that, in the Hellenistic world, there grew a fondness for detailed reports about such experiences. In order to find out about anomalous events in the Hellenistic context, we should examine reports of them in their most focused source, collections of *paradoxa*. We should find them there in abundance, but the thematic effect of the anomalous influenced far more than this simple literary genre. Aelius Aristides, in the five *Sacred Discourses*, used παράδοξος (marvel) as one term for describing his experiences of divine healing. He wrote about his experiences, that "the god helped me much, continuously and unexpectedly" (παρὰ τοῦ θεοῦ βοηθείας πολλῆς καὶ συνεχοῦς καὶ παράδοξα ἐχούσης).[1]

Such personal expectations of divine assistance in these anomalous ways developed elsewhere, in a variety of settings. Within early Christian theology and apologetics, the term παράδοξος is prominent in debates about miracles and supernatural activity. The rumor that Simon Magus could fly (something that the Holy Apostle Peter was reported to have witnessed) was identified as a rumor about a marvel (παράδοξον).[2] Origen suggested that a report that Jesus was the son of Mary and Pantherus, was an anti-Christian myth attempting to remove τῆς παραδόξου ἀπὸ ἁγίου πνεύματος συλλήψεως (the anomalous conception by the Holy Spirit; *Contra Celsum* 1.32). Early Christian witnesses not infrequently refer to the miracles of Jesus generally as τὰ παράδοξα.[3] We also have reports of discussions sustained in the Classical, Hellenistic, and Roman worlds about the criteria used to distinguish the ordinary from the extraordinary. This material is reviewed by Raymond Bloch and Harold Remus, from whose work we know that anomalous events were labeled with terms like τέρας (wonderful sign), σημεῖον (signficant indicator), and φάσμα (sign [from heaven]).[4] Although they were considered to be generally inexplicable, the uncertainties of anomalous events were thought to bear symbolic meaning. Anomalous events were conceded by all to be strange, but after that concession the meaning of their strangeness was debated. Experiences of anomalies create a need to discern what the anomalies probably mean, and the conundrums created by critically important anomalies were experienced as riddles in desperate need of solution.[5]

In the Roman world, παράδοξα were perceived as *prodigia* or *portenta*. Some were predictions of terrible events to come, calling for interpretation and response. Resolving *prodigia* (anomalous events taken as portents) was not unique to Romans. There is a long and varied history of *apotropaic* rituals (rituals and practices used generally to ward off bad outcomes from anomalous phenomena) and omen collection (gathering and analyzing data about anomalous phenomena).[6] Included in Livian historiography, by the fourth century C.E. collections of *prodigia* are well indexed in formatted tables.[7] They served as a road map to past critical events, as had like collections elsewhere. Such anomalous events from the past no longer seemed immediately frightening and puzzling, but were instead taken as important indicators now open to interpretation. The activity of identifying portents and interpreting them was so popular that Klaus Berger rightfully points out their regular use in biblical materials.[8] We should note that portents were never simply mild, unusual events that might be ignored. In the Roman world, official responses developed to them, ranging from consultations of Sibyls/Sibyllene texts to rituals of *expiatio, propitio*, and *gratulatio*.[9] Requests for benefaction from the gods through these very rituals were the standard responses to anomalous or hurtful events, and they were celebrated with ceremonies of *supplicatio*. A request for benefaction from a god indicates how unclear it seemed that anomalous events could be contained by human interpretation alone. Invocation of divine power seemed mandatory in order to move beyond the deep uncertainties initiated by anomalous events and to prevent their recurrence.

There are more reports of public rituals of *expiatio, propitio*, and *gratulatio* from the time of the Republic than from the time of the Empire.[10] Models of divine benefaction, with tandem models of how to resolve prophecies and portents, began to change in the Hellenistic kingdoms at least by 150 B.C.E., when there is evidence that political leaders themselves usurp various divine roles. The Hellenistic dynastic development influenced later Roman conceptions of authority, and it bloomed definitively in 27 B.C.E.. during the tenure of Augustus. At this time, political authority absolutely is linked to divine benefaction. A decree from 9 B.C.E., about the recalibration of a sacral calendar for the provinces of Asia, gives the emperor's birthday an importance equal to festival dates for ancestral gods.[11] The Halicarnassus version of this decree marks the ὑπερβαλλούσας εὐεργεσίας (abundant benefactions) by which humans are graced (χαρίζω), specifically because of the emperor, who is imagined now as one who satisfies human needs and resolves any troubles caused by anomalous events.[12] Here the royal person of the Roman emperor is the focus for resolution of the unexpected and unusual, and this ability and gifting is a sign of divine benefaction. Simultaneously, the properties and public buildings of emperors begin to represent this ability, and building programs in Rome and the provinces symbolize the gradual ascendancy of these men to divine power.[13] Appending divine power to human authority like this seemed a reasonable idea that was manageable politically and religiously. The propaganda is that these fortunate men embody the power necessary to resolve the deep uncertainties created by anomalous events. Unfortunately, as in all places at all times, proximity to divine power inherently had its risks. Uncertainty and terror struck mercilessly. Deaths of emperors and kings were said to be terrible and ghastly if their negotiations with divine power went awry.[14]

These historical developments in human authority and divine benefaction served as literary themes. In the *Acta Hermaisci* (*P.Oxy.* 1242) a dramatic reversal of the Emperor's power to settle the anomalous frightful is effective because of the audience's cultivated expectation of such power from an emperor. In this report of adjudication, when Hermaiscius makes his defense: "the bust of Sarapis that they carried suddenly [αἰφνίδον] broke into a sweat, and Trajan was astounded [ἀπεθαύμασεν] when he saw it. And soon tumultuous crowds gathered in Rome and numerous shouts rang forth, and everyone began to flee to the highest parts of the hills."[15] The emperor's own authority is overshadowed as we see the mighty supplier of benefaction now quivering before a strange and marvelous stone bust, an object suddenly more uncanny than his own royal person. The *Acta Hermaisci* story is an example of how literary themes grew with use of these ideas, and include the development of a narrative vocabulary of verbs and adverbs that illustrate the strange ways of the anomlaous.[16] Here in the *Acta Hermaisci*, Trajan is amazed (ἀπεθαύμασεν) at an anomaly, instead of his subjects being amazed at him.

Paradoxographers long made it their special focus to describe anomalous people, places, and things. Pliny, like writers before him, has several notices about strange humans, plants, animals, and strange natural phenomena. Writers of various kinds found the work of these paradoxographers useful for framing their own points of view about strangers, enemies, or exotic foreigners. The historian Lycus of Rhegium quotes frequently from a work entitled ' Ἀντιγόνου ἱστοριῶν παραδόξων συναγωγή (*Strange Stories Collected by Antigonus*).[17] With literary technique a writer could try to direct the anomalous toward his own ends. An orator could present himself as experienced and well-traveled by manipulating amazing insights into unusual, strange, and anomalous aspects of foreign and exotic people. The uses were boundless. Tacitus placed motifs from paradoxography in his own historiography, in one instance portraying Nero to be a truly odd and strange character who is anomalously anti-Roman. So also Plutarch, whose account of Sertorius has a strange and marvelous tale about a journey to, of all places, the Isles of the Blessed.[18] Whereas Tacitus crafts a negative depiction, Plutarch uses the unusual and marvelous to identify the truly noble character and good intentions of his Sertorius. In Plutarch's description, the unusual conditions on the Isles of the Blessed appear just they are in writings of the paradoxographers. These most strange and blessed isles have moderate rainfall, gentle breezes, healthful air, little seasonal change, fertile soil, abundant crops, and no need of agricultural toil.[19] We can see that the anomalous is intriguing, colorful, and persuasive, especially under proper control of a clever author, an orator, or a storyteller. In contrast to such literary possibilities, compendiums of the anomalous are not always vivid. Paradoxographers' catalogs sometimes simply list strange phenomena, each statically introduced by the verbs φασί, ἱστορεῖ, or λέγει (it says, it reports, or it states).[20] There is little sense of drama in the catalogs. Information about the strange contained in these catalogues might be employed as a type of peripheral historical or ethnographical detail by other writers. Effective and dramatic use of παράδοξα (marvel) requires narratives in which liveliness is created with verbs of movement or with tales of travel—as in the Gospel of Mark.

The same also happens in Aelius Aristides. Perhaps due to his own personal involvement with divine manifestations, he writes about intriguing and exciting events as he depicts the marvelous. He is emotionally braced and physically healed by his not-so-secret epiphanies. Rarely does he describe himself as personally agitated or troubled by them. Rather, the anomalies are comforting and bring him continual experiences of physical relief. With a focus like this on vividly described medical cures, the anomalous and the marvelous could become literary themes in autobiographies. Perhaps Aristides' milieu was really that of a literary salon, in which he spent time with a group of like-minded littérateurs,

in interpreting dreams, in comparing them, or in watching the performances the god had imposed on someone or other of their company; and
all this is combined with visits to the temple, with conversations with
the priest or the sacristans, and also with literary discussions. For this
small society is a cultivated one; its members write, show each other
what they have written, encourage and flatter each other."[21]

Such a setting offered the chance to experiment with the oral and
written expression of ideas about the strange and irregular. The men who
experimented were not themselves inexperienced in the anomalous. Their
mutual flattery was focused through personal religious experience. This
setting allowed Aristides to declaim his allegiance to his saving divine
power, Asclepius, and deliberately to cultivate his experiences of the
marvelous and the anomalous. For him, what is anomalous is truly
engaging. It is ever an indication of divine favor and benefaction in his
somewhat sickly existence, and anomalous events are healing events.

The contributions of Aristides and the vivid narrative material in the
Acta Hermaisci provide a novelistic presentation of the wonderful and
unusual. In such Hellenistic and Roman presentations, themes of the
anomalous and their literary development in fiction reach an apex, all of
this to be trumped by the later novelists. Antonius Diogenes writes about
the travels of Dinias, of Demochares (the son of Dinias), and of Dercylla
(the mistress of Dinias). In the account, Dercylla already has her own
marvelous tales to tell, about an ascent from Hades and a meeting with the
Sirens. At one point in the narrative, the story grows thick with the
remembrance of tales. Diogenes reports that Dinias says that Dercylla
reported that her brother Mantinias once "wandered much and seen many
wondrous sights concerning men and other creatures and concerning the
sun itself and the moon and the planets and especially islands."[22] The
layers of source citation, the descriptions of the wonders, and the
complexity of the characters each present what is unusual and strange in
a remarkably successful set of themes. Travel, love lost, and love regained
each constitute moments of wonder in this narrative frame. Diogenes
himself claims that his discovery of this remarkable ancient text is itself
a most mysterious, anomalous, and bizarre event.[23] Through such writers
and tales as these the anomalous grew in its literary and narrative impact.
In these new applications it retains its usefulness as commentary on and
description of historical, political, or ideological concerns (witness
Tacitus *Annals*, Plutarch *Sertorius*, and the *Acta Hermaisci*). It remained
ideal for novelists and storytellers, especially when they wrote about
matters concerning healing, love, or adventurous travel.

Yet not every reader was enchanted, and here we find another interpretation of the uncertainty created by anomalous events. Lucian (*Verae historiae* I,2) scoffs at such anomalies and stories about them, complaining that the stories are ψεύδεα ποικίλα (cunning lies). Lucian suggests a literary history of such falsities, mentioning the πολλὰ παράδοξα (numerous oddities) in Ctesias of Cnidos (*Verae historiae* I,3), and blames accounts about Odysseus for initiating the development of such fictional deceptions. According to Lucian, the unusual events and creatures in *The Odyssey* appeal only πρὸς ἰδιώτας ἀνθρώπους (to simple folk; *Verae historiae* I,3). In *Philopseudes* 1 he suggests that an audience with a taste for these stories and tales like them had what he derides as an ἐπιθυμία τοῦ ψεύδος (hunger for deception). In so commenting, Lucian is well within Greek traditions of critical reading. Plots, characters, and events that seem anomalous, marvelous, or just plain fanciful were long subjected to criticism in accordance with principles of philosophy and rhetoric.[24] But even given its negative estimate of the phenomenon, the development of such criticism shows that, by the time of the Gospel of Mark, the anomalous was recognized as a literary theme and a topic at many levels of reflection.

What exactly is there to discuss about anomalous phenomena? One focus then was on how the anomalous creates perceptual problems. This is well displayed in comments by Apuleius. In the *Metamorphoses*, he writes that at the time Pamphile turns into an owl, "I was greatly astonished, and although I was enchanted by no kind of charm [*nullo decantatus carmine*], yet I thought I seemed not to have the likeness of Lucius, for so was I vanished from my senses [*sic exterminatus animi*], amazed in madness, that I dreamed waking [*attonitus in amentiam vigilans somniabar*], and felt mine eyes to know whether I were asleep or no."[25] When confronted by the anomalous, uncertainty in perception and judgment may very well lead to what seems to be an induced deception. This whole experience is described as a type of intoxication, stupefaction, or flight of mind.[26] Not surprisingly, there is already a history behind this kind of observation. In the Platonic dialogue *Meno*, Socrates' interlocutor complains that the doubts (ἀπορεῖς) raised in his mind by Socrates seem the result of magic (γοητεύω) or sorcery (φαρμάττω). Corresponding to this idea, the *Phaedrus* offers a perspective on the experience of rhetoric and, in particular, on how a presentation of *likely* or *unlikely* stories affects a listener. When a listener is moved to belief by these stories, it is a ψυχαγωγία, a "leading-away of the soul."[27] In Plato, such leading is intangible and is compare to Bacchic reveling (that is, anomalies associated with divine epiphanies). After exposure to such rhetoric or argumentation, conclusions are reached, but it is not clear how. Jumping to conclusions about improbable, new, strange, or anomalous phenomena is as if the soul becomes airborne, flies, and then lands.

This kind of perceptual experience was developed further by Aristotle, who theorized about similar experiences among audiences of tragedies. The role of uncertainty and anomaly in perception are specifically discussed in relation to rhetoric, stories, storylines, and audiences. The tragedy's storyline, sudden change in fortune, and denouement are psychagogic (ψυχαγωγεῖ) (*Poetics* 1450a33.). Something intangible and wonderful seems to happen to audiences at these very dramatic moments. Aristotle postulated that a dramatic ἀναγνώρισις has the same effect on an audience as has all fiction in general: the effect of pretense through the use of tricky illusions.[28] I should note that these perceptual states, induced by exposure to what appears anomalous, were of concern to critics as well as to religious believers. Various beliefs or states of mind come into question after exposure to the anomalous.

Many agreed that the anomalous, if witnessed or heard reported in πλάσματα or *fabulae* (fictions), is bewildering, confusing, and uncertain. Cultivated by some, such uncertainty was not well-received by others. Both cultivation of the anomalous and its rejection show the persistence of this theme among all types of readers and audiences. Dionysus of Halicarnassus once comments about an anomalous and improbable (ἀπίθανον) assertion, that "it [was] a violent attempt (βιαζόμενος) to commend the wretched paradox: 'it is likely that the unlikely may at times occur' " (τὸ κακουργάτατον τῶν ἐπιχειρημάτων ποιεῖν πιθανώτερον).[29] Resolution of uncertainty was a demanding experience. Whether a critic, a religious believer, or a storyteller, one had to know how to resolve questions of the anomalous. Uncertainty, then as now, leads into a shadow land between objectivity and subjectivity, producing an experience parallel to that state between waking and dreaming. Remaining unconvinced while exposed to uncertainty can induce powerfully negative feelings of coercion and discomfort. In order to avoid such negative results, development of proper conviction in audiences is a vital step in the presentation of the anomalous. Ancient sceptics and believers both needed to be handled correctly. The uncertainty of the anomalous could be resolved rationally (that couldn't have happened) or ritually (now that it happened, let us supplicate). Whether rationally or ritually, uncertainty needed to be resolved plausibly. Need for plausibility and belief is not infrequently played out as a literary theme, appearing in tales about how one character might believe or disbelieve another. This reality could also focus on the readers themselves, or on those who heard such stories. Evidence or tales presented to audiences make claims on their conviction and belief. The experience of what is anomalous is to be identified by this very dynamic: the extension of belief or the suspension of disbelief. No matter what the religious or intellectual orientation, it was necessary that there be some sort of mental conclusion about perceptual uncertainty, indeterminacy, or objects that seemed vaguely attested. Those who decided in favor of παράδοξα (marvels), that they most likely contain *important* information *in need* of interpretation, discerned meanings in anomalies that often implicate an engagement of divine benefaction, as either given or withheld. From emperors, to literary presentations of heroes, to stories about personal encounters with divine figures, to portents and omens, what is anomalous evokes perceptual uncertainty within a context of matters held to be of great or even divine importance. Uncertainty makes for the very real problem of inadequately discerning anomalies. Quite often the stakes in discerning are critically high.

Fear and Danger

What is anomalous was experienced not only with perceptual difficulty but also with the conviction that a meaning for what is dimly perceived must be temporarily occluded. Often matters that kindled this experience pertained to death and dying. The manner in which a person dies might convey anomaly, especially if the death is violent, since it is believed that violent death leads to dismal prospects in the afterlife. Anomalous, strange, or unsettling deaths did lead to interpretations of those deaths as terrifying. The pattern both of one's living and of one's death were believed to influence what would happen to an individual after death. Anomalies in this sensitive and crucial arena brought into focus broader human concerns of safety *versus* danger, blessing *versus* curse, and final salvation *versus* final destruction.

Some deaths called for scrutiny and attention. Given this, some death reports appeared anomalous, stirring up horror as they reported outrage, anger, or terror due to an improper treatment of the deceased. On these matters we can learn much from the work of Jean-Pierre Vernant and Charles Segal.

The dismemberment of the corpse, whose remains are scattered here and there, culminates in the practice described in the first verses of the *Iliad* and recalled throughout the poem: leaving the body as food for dogs, birds, and fish. This outrage carries horror to its height. The body is torn to pieces and devoured raw instead of being consigned to the fire that, in burning it, restores it to wholeness in the world beyond. The hero whose body is surrendered to the voracity of wild animals is excluded from death while also having fallen from the human condition. (Vernant)

The theme of the mutilation of the corpse was doubtless well-imbedded in the epic tradition. It was a useful device which could be added to intensify a battle scene. It also has moving affective possibilities. From the rich shaft graves and the great *tholoi* tombs of Mycenae to the geometric burials and *prothesis*-scenes on the Dipylon amphoras down to the elaborately sculpted *stelai* of the Kerameikos cemetery in the classical age, all of Hellenic culture displays an extraordinary solicitude for the remains of the deceased. (Segal)[30]

Ideas of terrible death due to mistreatment of the bodies of the deceased persist into the Hellenistic period, especially in narratives intending to create a sense of how odd, bizarre, and cruel are foreigners. Quintius Curtius Rufus (*Historia Alexandria Magni* 7.5.36-43) reports how Alexander had Bessus cruelly mutilated and then handed over to Oxathres, Darius' own brother. Alexander gave orders that Bessus should be crucified and pierced with arrows; then by keeping carrion-eating birds away from his corpse, Alexander meant to defile the deceased by refusing his body a purification thought to be accomplished by such nibbling. Onesicritus (Strabo, *Geography* 11.11.3.) reports a strange, eastern Iranian practice. He thought that Iranians expelled aging members from their communities, thereby handing them over as prey for dogs, animals whom Onescritus supposed were called ἐνταφιάσται (undertakers) by these anomalous Iranians. Through this tale a legend grows about how Sogdians murdered their parents anomalously and horribly, and then left their bodies exposed. The story is meant to be horrifying as well as informing, for the ethnographic idea presented here reaffirms suspicions about barbarians, that they are bizarre and beyond explanation.[31] Writers of such descriptions of death and dying intended their readers to perceive these strange subjects with their foreign ways as ghastly, strange, and horrible.

In matters of death and dying, anomaly and indeterminancy were construed as chthonic. Ancient evidence about theories of the chthonic dimensions of the cosmos, especially in regard to death and the dead, brings to the fore a singularly important aspect of the anomalous frightful: fear. Although the term φόβος is not always mentioned in each and every reference to matters of the underworld, it often is, or a related term is employed. In Plato (*Phaedo* 81d) Socrates reminds his interlocuter of a popular theory that dead people sometimes maintain a φόβος τοῦ ἀιδοῦς (dread of Hades), with the result that their ψυχαί (souls) do not leave this world but, instead, dwell in it, especially around their tombs. A hymn from the third century C.E. expresses life in the underworld as φόβος γόνυ δεῖ ΄κ φόβου (fearful submission).[32] The *Apocalypse of Peter* 8 speaks of a λίμνη τις μεγάλη (a certain great lake) in which the dead are tormented by ἄγγελοι βασανισταί (avenging angels). This passage can be compared to Lucian, *De Luctu* 6, with its description of the divine personnel who join with Pluto and Persephone to bring torment to deceased humans: ᾿Ερινύες καὶ Ποιναὶ καὶ Φόβοι (Avengers and Punishers and Fears).[33] The Φόβοι are personified as a set of assaultive agencies, and they are like Christian ἄγγελοι βασανισταί (tormenting messengers). Typically, protection against such post-death torments was sought,[34] since terrors were everywhere in the underworld. Even Olympian gods shudder at the sights therein (Homer, *Iliad* 20.65). Should a human being venture into the chthonic underside of the cosmos, and return alive, stories about the journey and the many παράδοξα (marvels) there encountered are vivid. And so Pausanias describes the oracle of Trophonius, where a man, after descending into the oracle's chthonic cave, returns to the upper world. After his exposure to the divine in its chthonic setting, he is brought again to his family members who have to care for him since he is κάτοχόν τε ἔτι τῷ δείματι καὶ ἀγνῶτα ὁμοίως αὑτοῦ τε καὶ τῶν πέλας (paralyzed with terror and unconscious both of himself and of his surroundings).[35] Chthonic zones and territories were large, invisible, and immeasurable spaces abutting upon immense powers. In some Jewish traditions, what is chthonic is considered an abyss, the *tehôm*. Some said that this chthonic anomaly was sealed up with a stone, closed off from the orderly creation by means of "The Name of the Lord." A seal like this has much the character of a magical incantation, through which the anomalous frightful with its chthonic terrors is kept at bay in underground chasms.[36] Tradition- ally, it was only by the intervention of some divine power that the nether regions could be controlled for good or ill, which all goes to show how intense were underworld entities. All of these chthonic elements are linked to φόβος (fear), and especially to underworld παράδοξα (marvels), horrors of punishment after death, including assaults from δαίμονες (demons).

Pollux (*Onomasticon* 5.122) gathers together synonyms to describe the word φόβος as it was then used, in chthonic contexts or not. His lexicon demonstrates how versatile was Hellenistic Greek for depicting fear: "ὄκνος, δέος, ὀρρωδία, εὐλάβεια, δειλία, ἀθυμία, ἀνανδρία, ἔκπληξις, φρίκη, τρόμος, πτοία, πτόησις, συστολή, θόρυβος, ταραχή [cowardice, alarm, shuddering fright, fearful awe, timidity, fainthearted-ness, unmanliness, panic fear, chilling shiver, trembling, terror, vehement emotion, pusillanimity, public panic, public confusion]." As it happens, Pollux fortuitously stands as a scholarly witness to many important terms in Mark 4:35-6:56.[37] In particular, he produces an encyclopedic set of metaphors for fear, demonstrating the vivacity of the language then in use for the emotion. Not only could an encyclopedic philologist elaborate on φόβος, but so also could, and so also did, religious practitioners, especially practitioners attuned to aspects of fear in close proximity to strange activities of divine power. In one magical text, the god Typhon is addressed as δεινὸν ἄνακτα . . . φοβερὸν καὶ τρομερὸν καὶ φρικτόν (dreaded sovereign . . . fearful, awesome, threatening).[38] This is a hymn to a deity in the context of magical operations invoking the performance of a supernatural task. As such, it points to a part of φόβος (fear) quite relevant for this study: negotiations with divine power that are laced with fear, in which the divine power is asked to undertake an action meant to benefit whomever makes the request. This is the type of φόβος that compels the requesting party to perform ritual activities to prevent the dangers and troubles that any invocation might inaugurate. Similarly, one might seek magical protection against *nocturnos pavores* (night terrors) and *umbrarum terrorem* (dreadful ghosts). If one were to traffic in divine powers, one would need protection, especially if the divine powers threaten very intrusive, untimely, agitating intrusions into human affairs. Such is epitomized by Hekate, who "instills fear among mortals" (φόβον θνητοῖσι φέρουσα), not an infrequent result of her appearance as a ἀμαιμάκετον βασίλειαν . . . ψυχαῖς νεκύων μέτα βακχεύουσαν (mon-strous queen . . . reveling in the souls of the dead).[39] A late piece of evidence contains a special plea that Hekate punish disturbers of a tomb, or those who would disturb the balance between the living and the dead, the chthonic and the world above. Her punishing hand is called βαρύφθονος (intensely jealous), indicating that horrible jealousy of divine power whose aim is retaliation and which is invoked to bring harm to others.[40] It is this kind of power that made divine proximity utterly and unbearably terrible. Pan is hymned as one φαντασιῶν ἐπαρωγέ φόβων ἔκπαγλε βροτείων (who induced fantasies of dread into the minds of mortals).[41] Hermes is similarly addressed: γλώσσης δεινὸν ὅπλον τὸ σεβάσμιον (you wield the dreaded and respected weapon of speech).[42]

Φόβος (fear) and divine power are also linked together in the very different tradition of scriptural epiphanies, those times when the God of Israel is depicted as especially near. This tradition has not gone unstudied. Albrecht Scriba lists *Schreckreaktionen* as an essential part of a motif-complex related to the genre of "epiphany" in the Old Testament. In suggesting a pattern of thirty-three motifs typically found in miracle stories, Gerd Theissen proposed that "characteristic motifs of an epiphany are extraordinary visual and auditory phenomena [and] the terrified reaction of human beings." Franz Annen earlier supported this, considering φόβος in scriptural accounts to be one of the *Anschauungshorizonte* (basic ideas) of the most developed Markan miracle accounts. Barry Blackburn examined the same material and placed this tradition within its wider context, suggesting that, out of some twenty elements by which were fashioned Hellenistic miracle accounts about activities of a θεῖος ἀνήρ (divine man), the theme of "Fear and Distress" ranked high in frequency. His analysis focuses particularly on the epiphanies of God that displayed God's destructive capabilities. Frequently, themes of chaos, sea, and the underworld (subterranean violence) prevail in these vignettes.[43]

When faced with anomalies of divine power, fear is a common theme and an oft-reported experience. Such response to Yahweh's epiphany is reported in Psalm 18:7-15, and one sees why fear might ensue.

> Then the earth reeled and rocked;
>> the foundations also of the mountains trembled.
>> and quaked, because he was angry.
> Smoke went up from his nostrils,
>> and devouring fire from his mouth;
>> glowing coals flamed forth from him.
> He bowed the heavens, and came down;
>> thick darkness was under his feet.
> He rode on a cherub, and flew;
>> he came swiftly upon the wings of the wind.
>> He made darkness his covering around him,
>> his canopy thick clouds with water.
> Out of the brightness before him
>> there broke through his clouds
>> hailstones and coals of fire.
> The Lord also thundered in the heavens,
>> and the Most High uttered his voice.

And he sent out his arrows, and scattered them;
    he flashed forth lightening, and routed them.
Then the channels of the sea were seen,
    and the foundations of the world were laid bare
at your rebuke, O Lord,
    at the blast of the breath of your nostrils (NRSV).

This epiphany of the God of Israel comes with displays of power over enemies.[44] It is the close presence of this power that created problems for spectators.

In Josephus' reworking of biblical narratives about epiphanies, themes of anomaly and benefaction are expanded. He clearly labels the epiphanies as such: in *Antiquities* 2.339, the ἐπιφάνεια of God at the Exodus; in *Antiquities* 1.225, the wondrous finding of Rebecca for Isaac is the blessing of the marriage by an ἐπιφάνεια; in *Antiquities* 8.119, the fire which comes down to consume Solomon's sacrifices is an ἐπιφάνεια. Josephus expanded the history of epiphanies past the time line of the biblical chronology, as in *Antiquities* 18.286, on how it rains miraculously when Petronius, governor of Syria, agrees to intercede for Jews with Caligula, and in *Antiquities* 15.425, on how no rain falls during daytime hours while the (Herodian) temple is being built (miraculously, to benefit the builders, rain falls only at night). About this latter account, Josephus comments that this is a believable story, given the marvelous abundance that was repeatedly bestowed through ἐμφανείας τοῦ θεοῦ (epiphanies of God).[45]

Yes, proximity to divine power was thought to be advantageous. But proximity was also dangerous: some won and some lost. The battles of pious Jews in 2 Maccabees are accompanied by divine appearances.[46] Heaven displays ἐπιφάνειαι when Judas Maccabeus and his family fight against Antiochus Epiphanes and Eupator (2:21). God creates an ἐπιφάνειαν μεγάλην in order personally to fight against Heliodorus at the entrance to the temple treasury (3:24). Appropriately, sheer terror is the result. In the battle of Maccabeus against Timothy and his Asian mercenaries, a terrifying sign from heaven appears (ἐφάνησαν): five horsemen on beautiful horses with golden bridles are seen leading Maccabeus and his men (10:29). Subsequently, more than 26,000 opponents are reported massacred. The army of Judas itself, as a terrifying mass of warriors, is likened to an ἐπιφάνεια, and it is said to have created a great φόβος (12:22). It is also said that the God of Israel had always protected the chosen people with ἐπιφανείας, and would continue to do so (14:15). The troops of Judas, having killed more than 35,000 of the troops of Nicanor, are glad at heart because the slaughtering is considered an ἐπιφάνεια of their god (15:27, 34). In all of these incidents, danger and fear are the results of proximity to divine power. This danger is celebrated and acclaimed, especially when people thought it benefitted them. This belief in the beneficence of divine power is a key to these situations of terror. The ones who survive closeness to divine power are the ones who believe themselves benefitted by it. Even so, a hypothetical question persisted: "When near God, who benefits and who not?"

Accounts about violent and terrifying divine power are found elsewhere also. A hymn points to a similar, fearful phenomeon: Οὔρεα σὺν πεδίοις εἰς θεὸς ἀθάνατος τρέμουσιν (the singular, immortal god caused the mountains together with plains to tremble in fear).[47] Poseidon is the "Royal Earth Shaker" who races across a battlefield with a single shout at the volume of ten thousand warriors yelling simultaneously (Homer, *Iliad* 14.133). Elsewhere in mythographic cosmology, Poseidon (named Pontus) is called Θυῖον (frenzied) (Hesiod, *Theogony* 131). In Euripides (*Hippolytus* 1200), Poseidon is responsible for the death of Hippolytus, having stirred up the ocean into a strange and deadly tidal wave. He retains his noisy verve throughout antiquity. Poseidon and Ocean frequently are depicted as divine powers in direct relation to the monstrous creatures that are agents of Poseidon's vengeance, creatures frequently the object of divinatory practice. Poseidon is acclaimed Ποντομέδων, ἀλίδουπε, βαρύκτυπε, ἐννοσίγαιε (deep-roaring ruler of the sea and shaker of the earth). He is a fighter, and represents divine powers assaulting one another as well as assaulting humans. Aelius Aristides claimed that it was Poseidon who granted safety to humans traveling the seas, and that until Poseidon's benefaction the oceans were a "terrible and frightening beast" filled with δαιμόνες θαλάττιοι (conflicting, watery divine powers; *Oration* 46.42). Aristides also asserted that, thanks to Poseidon, prayers could be made effectively for the safety of sailors and passengers at sea. And indeed, many thought it mandatory to offer such prayers, given the imminent danger from being too close to the domain of Poseidon's frightening power while helplessly floating on it in a small vessel.[48]

Danger was perennial in proximity to divine power, felt most acutely when the benevolence or malevolence of divine power effected the safety of humans. Vivid depictions represent these ways in essential and important texts. The *ekphrasis* of the shield of Achilles in *Iliad* 18 is a depiction of human life with the divine *not* at war with it. Within a broad cosmic context of earth, sky, sea, sun, moon, and constellations (Pleides,

Hyads, Orion, The Bear), various symbols of a blessed human life are
etched. These symbols include two cities with "beautiful" people in them,
one city celebrating banquets and festivals, the other happily and
honorably at war with besiegers. Also depicted are scenes of fertility:
abundant harvest and fat livestock. The whole picture is surrounded by
symbols of the mighty "Stream of Ocean," or symbols depicting a
balanced totality of divine rulership over the known universe.[49] The
shield, reportedly made by Hephaestus and delivered by Hera, depicts
blessed life in proximity to divine power. It is a view of Olympian
benevolence. It illustrates how a good, satisfying life was a divine
benefaction, or a kind of life due to divine power whose proximity did not
put humans at risk or create anomaly.

This *ekphrasis* of Achilles' Shield can be compared to very different
material in Scripture. Although in Ugaritic traditions the home of El and
of the Divine Council is placed at the "springs of the Two-Rivers (the
meeting place of the Double-Deeps,)"[50] a different perspective is
presented in the Bible. The Bible testifies to a new development in Syria-
Palestine: the idea that the One God provides for all needs, from healthy
births, to long count of days, to success in war, to prosperity.[51] Instead of
a mighty "Stream of Ocean" and a temporary peace between a divine
mother and her son (Hera and Hephaestus), the One God alone is the
divine giver, bestowing basic benefaction. In Deuteronomy 32:8-9, it is
divine will and not sundry cosmic powers that is assigned a cosmogonic
role: "When the Most High ('elyon) gave to the nations their inheritance,
when he separated humanity, he fixed the boundaries of the peoples
according to the number of divine beings. For Yahweh's portion is his
people, Jacob his allotted heritage."[52] The separation of earthly and
cosmic territories as accomplished by the will of God creates a balance
and interplay between each place within a cosmic geography. A Yahwist
view of this creative benevolence is expressed in Exodus 23:25-26:

> You shall worship the Lord your God, and I will bless your bread and
> your water and I will take sickness away from among you. No one shall
> miscarry or be barren in your land; I will fulfill the number of your
> days. I will send my terror in front of you, and will throw into confusion
> all the people against whom you shall come (NRSV).

Blessed life in proximity to divine power in Homer and Moses shows
considerable overlap. In both, satiety and safety are the goals of security.
Yet divine benefaction in such a vision is always a risk; that is, the risk of
the wager to attain it is always high. In a later Deuteronomic view,

disobedience of covenant stipulations (the covenant promised benefits of satiety and safety) creates dangerous responses from Yahweh's divine power: early and latter rains will be withheld (Deut. 11:14). Although abundance and security in both Homer and Moses are the result of proximity to divine power, it must not be forgotten that such beneficence is always presented as a gamble. Reliance on divine power is a wager on the goodwill of the divinity, a wager that is attended by fear, especially fear that what is truly needed might, anomalously, not be provided.

Divine Benefaction, or Not

In epiphanies divine power is intensely proximate to humans, and epiphanies are vivid and vividly different one from another. Events depicted as part of the worship of the Thracian Dionysus are vividly epiphanic.[53] Diodorus suggested that these worship events were actual ἐπιφάνειας of the hero, since participants believed that Dionysus himself initiated (raised up [ἐγείρῃι]) this festival or epiphany at the appropriate time, every third year.[54] In this case Dionysus is present in and through the liturgical events and ritual characters. Proximity to the divine in cases like this one can become a wild and maddening experience. In other cases, proximity is not like this, and initial bewilderment at epiphanies is meant to pass. Dio Chrysostom describes initiation into mysteries as a truly life-changing event; any bewilderment in these august and mystic settings is meant to transform into wonder for the initiate.[55] In another example, Sarapis appeared (παραφανείς) at night to a simple man of no special stature (κοινὴν συναστρίαν ἔχων), in no cultivated ritual setting, creating no special madness or wildness in the least. Often it is in dreams that such appearances occur. Chaeremon reports how Isis appeared to Amenophis κατὰ τοὺς ὕπνους (while sleeping), correcting Amenophis for allowing the destruction of an Isis temple during war. In an inscription, Asclepius is described as philanthropic: δαίμονι φιλανθρώπῳ Νέῳ ᾿Ασκληπιῷ ἐπιφανεῖ μεγίστῳ (to the very great, philanthropic daimon New Asclepius who appeared).[56] The accounts of healings at the Epidaurus Asclepium have a refined vocabulary for the hero's appearance in dreams as he brings aid to suffering clients.[57] It was said that the sanctuary had a *tholos,* in which was a painting of a somnific Eros depicted with lyre and not bow or arrow (Pausanias Περιήγησις 2.26.4). Other iconography there symbolized sleepiness and drowsy intoxication. These are hardly depictions of revelry or fear, or wildness and terror.

Still, proximity to divine power did not lose its dangerous quality, even here in these sleepy healing rituals. However framed, the dangerous risk persists that divine favor might be withheld. Absence of divine benefaction in this way was interpreted as the divine *purposefully* withholding benefaction. Willful extension or withholding of benefactions, originally assigned to divinities and heroes, came to be extended to some humans. Ptolemy XII used a benefactor-title similar to the Ascelpius form Νέος ᾽Ασκληπιός, when he was acclaimed Νέος Διόνυσος. Hellenistic emperors took the epithet ᾽Επιφανής, thereby representing themselves with the ability to provide divine benefactions.[58] This propaganda is an attempt to domesticate the vagaries of divine favor and disfavor for political purposes. This idea of benefaction expanded through levels of society, as both political and nonpolitical ideas of the θεῖος ἀνήρ (divine man) spread. These ideas demonstrate how some humans were assigned the power to give or withhold benefactions. The powerful presence of such humans, rumored to be able to bestow favors and graces, was demonstrated by public acclamation of their ἐπιφάνειαι (divine manifestations). This idea is not confined to the Hellenistic period, but it is in this period that there is a massive dissemination of it.[59]

Extension or withholding of benefaction was taken quite personally. Individuals, families, cities, or nations stood to suffer much if benefaction were not forthcoming. Such suffering is a terrible fate, sometimes due to the poor disposition of the divine toward humans. Among Greeks, this disposition was explained by the idea of divine φθόνος (jealousy), and Greeks had to live with this aspect of their divinities.[60] This idea was vibrant, changing and developing from archaic to classical periods, and once divine jealousy came to be linked to ideas of justice, φθόνος was personalized as Νέμεσις. This is idea extended into the Roman world, where the goddess Nemesis is associated with violent sporting spectacles. These violent events symbolically represent a distribution of punishments through an ἀγών (contest). Such symbolism emerged from traditions about divine retribution and divine wrath. The ἀγών became a powerful symbol of the struggle between favor or loss, salvation or destruction. The depiction of φθόνος as Evil Eye, common in popular beliefs and in the iconography in homes throughout the Hellenistic world, shows what kind of trouble jealousy could stir up. Φθόνος is a kind of portable power of destruction, and victims of φθόνος experience another's malice. They were imagined bitten, choked, wasted away, forced into gnashing their teeth, and experiencing torturous pain of their viscera, with trembling lips.

The Evil Eye is linked to strange and anomalous events, and horrible pain could result from wretched human jealousy. Even so, human jealousy is one thing, divine jealousy another.[61]

So, indeed, is divine jealousy in the Bible. In the Song of Moses, Yahweh is jealous (Deut. 32:19), and this jealousy is dangerous and punishing.

> The Lord saw it and was jealous;
>   he spurned his sons and daughters,
> He said: I will hide my face from them,
>   I will see what their end will be;
> for they are a perverse generation,
>   children in whom there is no faithfulness (NRSV).

Exodus 20:5 articulates a reason for the command to honor only the One God: "I the Lord am a jealous God, punishing children for the iniquity of parents" (NRSV). This is but one way that God's divine jealousy overflows quite easily into retribution. This jealousy seems an urge generated by the exclusive and personal interests of the God of Israel. In Ezekiel 39:25 the prophet announces, "Therefore thus says the Lord God: Now I will restore the fortunes of Jacob, and have mercy on the whole house of Israel; and I will be jealous for my holy name" (NRSV). Conditions after exile were attributed to the jealousy of the God, who is quoted in Zechariah:

> The word of the Lord of hosts came to me, saying: Thus says the Lord of hosts: I am jealous for Zion with great jealousy, and I am jealous for her with great wrath. Thus says the Lord: I will return to Zion, and will dwell in the midst of Jerusalem (NRSV).

The dangerous jealousy and retribution of the God of Israel are clearly depicted in Baruch 1:18, where the punishments of Jerusalem are explained as the result of an unpleasant truth: οὐκ ἠκούσαμεν τῆς φωνῆς κυριου θεοῦ ὑμῶν (we did not obey the voice of the Lord our God). Here and in many other examples, not listening to a jealous god is genuinely risky behavior.

These ideas permeate all ancient religious thought. In the Septuagint, Psalms 13:3 and 35:1 exhort the maintenance of a proper φόβος θεοῦ (fear of God). Proverbs 1:7 teaches that access to divine wisdom occurs only if there is the requisite fear of God. The theme of access to wisdom in this manner is magnified in Sirach 1:11-12, 18, 26-27, 30. Fear of God

in these cases is respect for the overwhelming superiority of God. Lack
of respect is dangerous, and it leads to divine retribution as expressed in
one's debauched life. Wisdom, that sphere of human life where one acts
well or poorly, wisely or foolishly, is thematically utilized in this way,
both within and without Scripture. The *Instruction of Ankhsheshonq*
begins its wise sayings with a warning acclamation about the dangerous
power of Pre. In it, a quest for wisdom seems based on a singular
motivation: prevarication from Pre's wisdom placed one at risk of Pre's
anger.[62] Proximity to divine power means negotiating risk and danger; in
wisdom literature, it means negotiation between foolishness and wisdom.
Attainment of wisdom, just like survival of an epiphany, depends on
benefactions granted by divine power. Benefaction withheld because of
jealousy or anger means trouble, if not destruction, and is a theme found
in all manner of ancient sources. The *Oracle of Hystaspes* predicts
overthrow of cities, civil discord, and cosmic collapse if divine power
becomes angry and turns against humanity. The *Oracle of the Potter*
predicts the sun's darkening and the ground's rejection of seeds because
of evil done, and subsequent removal of divine benefaction from the land
of Egypt.[63] The list could go on. Fear and threat color narratives and
predications about every human negotiation with divine power.

Indeterminate Perception and Uncertainty

Indeterminacy and perplexity create a sense of the unusual and strange.
A strange event that causes fear kindles what I call the anomalous
frightful. It is anomalous if the event and its report is perceived as
irregular, without apparent explanation, perplexing, and uncertain. It is
frightful if it evokes fear and seems repugnant, unclean, horrible, violent,
or ghoulish.[64] At the time of the Gospel of Mark, there is no singular
event that alone accomplishes all of this. Yet experiences of direct
encounters with divine power and, as a unique subset, with death or with
the (un)dead, are events that produce these very things.

I want to emphasize that the anomalous frightful consists of
perplexing uncertainty and fear, each reinforcing the other. Indeterminacy
of perception is vital in this pairing, perhaps because of the sense of
uncanny that it incites and sustains. Such indeterminacy can very well be
likened to the experience of dreaming, a phenomenon observed by ancient
and modern authors alike. Dreaming provides an unusual similarity

between ourselves and our ancestors, and taking note of such a similarity may allow for interpretation of our ancient evidence that makes robust sense to us and keeps us from becoming bored modern observers of antiquity's minutiae.

In our modern traditions, dreaming has been an ideal metaphor for the experience of the anomalous. Gérard de Nerval wrote,

> The dream is a second life. I have not been able to penetrate those ivory and horned gates which separate us from the invisible world without shaking. The first moments of sleep are the image of death; a nebulous enervation seizes our thought, and we are not able to determine the precise moment when the *I*, under another form, carries on the work of existence.[65]

A hypnagogic reverie preceding sleep may not be unlike standing consciously baffled and bewildered by apparently objective facts, but having no workable idea of what they might mean. Dreaming is part of an ongoing internal conversation, taking place between our states of mind. Our senses of the subjective and objective are fabricated and forged through the rhythm of waking and sleeping states, and Nerval, exemplary in his literary explication of these matters, comments on this rhythm throughout his *Aurélia*.[66] Dreaming, falling in love, being confused, or being strangely frightened are all experiences that overlap in perceptual vagaries. Famously, a father of the Symbolist movement exercises a poetic conceit based of these vagaries, charming us with a dream (or not a dream): "I would perpetuate these nymphs; so clear, the glow of them, so nimble in the air. Drowsiness encumbers—did I dream that love?"[67] Each of us, and, I should suggest, also our ancestors, when in an unusual situation and when emotionally compelled through love or fear, question ourselves: Did what we see really take place? Did what we sense really happen? Is it what we think it was? The oscillation between poles of belief and doubt, certainty and confusion, or clarity and occlusion, is an oscillation whose influence over us never comes to an end. At certain times, it makes us acutely aware of our limitations, perhaps even terrifying us with the way it inhibits us from deciding what's what.

The world of the Gospel of Mark also knows this uncertainty in these very ways. Aelius Aristides reports how Asclepius apparently appeared to him one night. But, had it really been the true Asclepius, or had it only been a dream image? This was the critical choice as described in Aelius Aristides *Orations* 48:18, as translated by Charles Allison Behr:

> When we arrived at Smyrna, [Asclepius] appeared to me in some such
> form. He was at the same time Asclepius, and Apollo, both the Clarian
> and he who is called the Callitechnus in Pergamum and whose is the
> first of the three temples. Standing before my bed in this form, when he
> had extended his fingers and calculated the time, he said, "You have ten
> years from me and three from Sarapis," and at the same time the three
> and the ten appeared by the position of the fingers as seventeen.
> [Asclepius] said that "this was not a dream, but a waking state."

When in the darkness of night divine epiphanies occur, of gods forecasting fate, then a dreamlike uncertainty might very well prevail. Dreams and other nighttime phenomena were taken quite seriously, and various meanings contingent on *kinds* of dream phenomena were given considerable examination in the ancient world.[68]

Exposure to things that seem improbable, paradoxical, uncanny, or anomalous tends at first to evoke chaos. Our perception alternates between the certainty of wakefulness and the uncertainty of dreaming. We might refer to the resolution of this chaotic process as "achieving abstract sets, coping with novelty and uncertainty, responding to feedback . . . searching through a lexicon of problem-solving strategies, as well as [activating] working memory." Or, we might speak as literary critics and develop an idea about the *fantastic*, which is that "hesitation experienced by a person who knows only the laws of nature, confronting an apparently supernatural event." Or, we might speak as anthropologists about *cosmography*, "the creation, development, and persuasive use (by some particular agent or group of agents) of a discourse concerning anomalies for the purpose of promoting, refining, confirming, or challenging a belief-system, worldview, or ideology." There are many different facets of perceptual difficulties, and therefore many different explanations.[69] In a tradition of American westerns, stories may have as their setting an isolated place with events depicted as an intrusion "of one or more mysterious strangers who are potential saviors, potential destroyers, or ambiguous combinations of both."[70] Depending on the frame of reference, many different explanations might aid in understanding, especially when life and death are at risk and the story is populated with ambiguous figures who may be either saviors or dangerous characters.

The anomalous frightful, in this aspect of perceptual strangeness and uncanny dimensions, is well compared to the paranormal or the supernatural. Uncertainty prevails in these domains as well, often accompanied by fear. E. R. Dodds set a precedent for the historical study of such phenomena from classical Greece,[71] and later I shall present much more historical material of similar themes. But for now, it is worth reviewing other recent studies on similar phenomena within very different contexts, in order to help clarify issues and topics associated with the anomalous frightful. I seek to discover possible ways to read texts like Mark, texts that not only report the anomalous frightful but intend to stir up that very response in readers.

Linked to violent death, the anomalous frightful has a sense of threat and unfortunate fate. David Hufford, in a study about beliefs in night-roaming and supernatural violence, highlights some basic questions raised by interpreters of such anomalous events. He interviews individuals who told stories about their experiences of such violence, then poses a theoretical question about whether such beliefs are "cultural" or some part of human experience "independent of culture."[72] For cultural constructivists, the question is incendiary, since they are apt to think that there is no reality that is not "culturally constructed." Hufford looks for a broader understanding and explanation and does not assume that individuals do or say something because of environmental stimuli. He notes that research of experiences such as night terrors typically gravitates toward the first theory, being based on what he calls a "cultural source hypothesis." Use of such a hypothesis is based on the assumption that "the experiences are either fictitious products of tradition or imaginary subjective experiences shaped (or occasionally even caused) by tradition."[73] The alternative that Hufford offers to the cultural source hypothesis is what he calls an "experiential source hypothesis." In this theoretical formation, fear of attack at night needs no link to some known tradition to be coherent as a human experience. Names like "Old Hag" or stories about any similar nighttime creatures have freely circulated in many cultures, and may even have become traditional in them, but these traditions are not shown to manufacture the nighttime experience of fright.

Hufford's subjects typically did not interpret their experience of supernatural and violent entities with others' explanations. They did not use traditions about such violence (the "Old Hag"). Instead, they frequently reported sensations in their bodies (pressure on the chest and inability to move) that aroused primitive, negative emotions. In their perception, the apparitions typically took on vague humanoid forms in the darkness. The perceptual uncertainty that prevailed during the course of their experiences of night-roaming attackers was vividly recalled.[74] Hufford discovered, I suspect to his surprise, that the individual narratives about these experiences could not be explained on the basis of commonly known legends or traditions. Furthermore, similar experiences are reported by subjects elsewhere, in very different cultures, who could not recall ever having heard about night-time creatures like the "Old Hag" or similar legends. Hufford shows that explanation and interpretation of uncanny or supernatural events must account for unique elements that are not attributable to influence from a context of circulating stories, traditional legends, or religious affiliations. I take this to mean that the anomalous frightful, though approachable through analysis as a literary theme, is not merely a matter of literary theme or tradition. It is not only a theme about which a narrative might be composed (a reader reports, "I see that one character frightens another in the story). It is also an experience that the reader might have (a reader reports, "This story seems eerie to me).

James McClenon's results support Hufford's work. He argues that subjects often experience anomalies, or unexplained events in general, with "wonderment." Subsequently, individuals attribute explanations to these wondrous experiences that often do not agree with traditional explanations, even those from their own dominant cultures.[75] Committed Buddhists, Christians, or atheists who were interviewed all gave similar narratives about anomalous events, and then gave similar interpretations of what the anomalous events meant to them. All groups typically did not use their religious or philosophical affiliations to explain what they thought had happened to them. Experiences identified as anomalous in McClenon's study include extrasensory perception, encounters with apparitions, out-of-body experiences, near-death experiences, spiritual possession, pain and heat immunity, psychokinesis, encountered poltergeists, miraculous healings, and contact with the dead. He broadened his field of study beyond interviews and sociological data to include an analysis of ancient Chinese "Records of Anomalies." These 'Records' are a genre of Chinese literature stemming from the Six Dynasties (317-589 C.E.) and T'ang Eras (618-906 C.E.), and McClenon interprets them as proof of the historical universality of anomalous experience in general. With far more detail, Robert Ford Campany outlines with precision the types of redactional logic, categorization, and classification exhibited in these Chinese texts.[76] Not unlike other traditions of omen and portent collecting, these texts were produced through highly trained scribal activity. In this sense they differ from personal narratives of individual, anomalous experiences, which typically do not show such refined redactional organization. The Chinese texts are an indication that accounts of anomalies, including those of the anomalous frightful, can be developed into a highly organized literary presentation. It is not a great leap to see how, as in the Six Dynasties or the T'ang Era, similar redacted collections could have been gathered among Hellenistic cults or royal dynasties, through their paradoxographers, historians, antiquarians, or temple chroniclers. It is but a small step to include an analysis of gospel narratives within such specimens.[77]

Studies of reported experiences of supernatural violence by Hufford and of wonderful anomalies by McClenon are useful for guiding interpretation of aspects of the anomalous frightful in texts like the Gospel of Mark. If the anomalous frightful is treated as a literary theme in a narrative like Mark, and particularly in the group of stories in Mark 4:35-6:56, then interpretation should proceed with an understanding that the anomalous frightful evokes rich experiences of indeterminate perception mixed with fear. At its best, it beckons to be *felt* as much as *explained*. Repulsion, disgust, confusion, or annoyance are as much the outcomes of the anomalous frightful as are any identifications of redactional trends in texts that report them.

With this in mind, care is needed to develop good descriptions of the impact of the anomalous frightful in terms relevant to the ancient evidence. It may be correct to say that the anomalous frightful is "uncanny." But ever since Freud's 1919 essay, "Das Unheimliche," the meaning of "uncanny" has taken on many of the hues of modernity. Freud argued that adult experiences of ghosts, magic, sorcery, monsters, demons, or spirits are in reality intrapsychic repetitions of anxiety from an infantile stage of primitive narcissism. Perhaps this theory aided Freud in his clinical practice. It certainly piqued the interest of later writers on religion. But I have not used an approach like this, based on clinical validation or based on theoretical congruence with psychoanalytic ideas, in my investigation of the anomalous frightful in the Gospel of Mark. An enormous amount of work remains yet to be done in order to uncover the meaning of Markan narratives in their own context, much less the meaning of psychological ideas today. Some of this uncovering is attempted here, within this book. Building a proper bridge between any such analytic work now and some psychological interpretation later is a large task that awaits another effort.[78]

But before taking cover under the pretense of "just uncovering" ancient evidence, I should admit that modern psychology has had immense influence on historiography. Intellectual and religious movements in Europe for nearly two centuries before Freud's essay include a long development of ideas about what specifically is uncanny. Theories of mind, theories of the supernatural, and theories of the unconscious grew and changed.[79] The ambiguity of human behavior was subjected to new explanations. The term "hallucination" changed from its classical description, meaning "wandering in mind, dreaming, talking idly," to a new description, meaning "mental pictures projected inside the mind like a magic lantern."[80] During this same period, philosophical theories about the associations of ideas and the proper weighing of probabilities flourished. These approaches led thinkers to tally past occurrences of events and to assess the probability of their reoccurrence. This had a powerful impact on theories of the supernatural, miracles, and proofs of the divine.[81] Interpretation of the uncanny through modern theories of hallucinating imaginations grew in prominence, and eventually there was born an intellectual preference for psychology, so endemic now in the hermeneutics of modernity. As a result of this heritage, a commentator on Mark today, while trying to understand how and why material in the Gospel of Mark might be representative of the anomalous frightful in its ancient context, will do well to avoid initial and critical confusion of modern theory with ancient evidence. Beyond this, we need to understand that there is no interpreter of Mark today who is not thoroughly under the influence of such European intellectual history. This can be taken in two ways. Interpreted as a liability, it means that we can never really know what Mark or anybody else in the ancient world was trying to say. Interpreted as an asset, it means that, as in our investigative exploits into anything, *both* our own understanding *and* our interpretation of Mark are subject to probabilities (likelihood and unlikelihood). The ways in which we think generally, and the ways in which we think about Mark specifically, are both together subject to scrutiny. I should propose that, in any given circumstance, it may be possible to acquire a more accurate understanding of the facts of Mark than of the facts of our own thinking. But that is a discussion for another time.

Notes

1. Aelius Aristides *Oration* 47.71, in *Aelius Aristides: The Complete Works*, trans. Charles Allison Behr (Leiden, The Netherlands: E. J. Brill, 1981). See Brunno Keil, *Aelii Aristides Smyrnaei* (Berlin: Wiedmann, 1958), 2:393. Aristides makes this comment in a context in which he had just described how Asclepius appeared to him. He "grasped" Asclepius three times.

2. *Martyrdom of the Holy Apostle Peter* 30(3). Text as numbered in *The Apocryphal New Testament: A Collection of Apocryphal Christian Literature in an English Translation* ed. and trans. J. K. Elliott (Oxford: Clarendon Press, 1993), 421. In this account Peter, upset with the competition from Simon, prays and requests that Simon fall down. Simon subsequently falls, breaking his leg in three places.

3. G. W. H. Lampe, *A Patristic Greek Lexicon* (Oxford: Clarendon Press, 1961), at the entry, παράδοξος.

4. Raymond Bloch, *Les Prodiges dans l'Antiquité (Grèce, Étrurie et Rome)*, Mythes et Religions (Paris: Presses Universitaires de France, 1963) and Harold Remus, *Pagan-Christian Conflict over Miracle in the Second Century*, Patristic Monograph Series 10 (Philadelphia: Philadelphia Patristic Foundation, 1983). Johannes Ludus (*De Ostentis* procemium) suggests that Jewish traditions define σημεῖα to be indicators of meterological phenomena, and define τέρατα to be monsters appearing unnaturally (ὡς παρὰ φύσιν φαινόμενα).

5. See Remus (*Pagan-Christian Conflict*, 48-50) on the debates. Bloch (*Les Prodiges dans l'Antiquité*, 16-18) demonstrates how fear and terror are linked to τέρατα (signs). Hesiod (*Theogony* 743) has a δεινὸν δὲ καὶ ἀθανάτοισι θεοῖσι τοῦτο τέρας (a terrifying prodigy, even for immortals).

6. See Auguste Bouché-Leclercq (*Histoire de la Divination dans l'Antiquité*, [Paris: E. Leroux, 1879-82], 4:74-100) on the history of divination in general. Chief Latin terms are *prodigium, portentum, ostentum, monstrum, miracula*. Bouché-Leclercq observed (4:81 n.1) that earlier theories of resolution are not dependent on divination but, rather, on specific aspects of divine power and its ability to protect. There are reflected later in the Greek θεοὶ ἀποτρόπαιοι (warding-off gods) and especially in the various epithets for these deities: τρόπαιοι (victory-bringing), ἀποτρόπαιοι (evil-averting), ἀλεξίκακοι (keeping-away-evil), λύσιοι (loosing = expiating-atoning-ransoming), φύξιοι (putting-to-flight), ἀποπομπαῖοι (carrying-away-evil), καθάρσιοι (cleansing). See Erica Reiner, "Apotropaia," in *Astral Magic in Babylonia*, Transactions of the American Philosophical Society 85, pt. 4 (Philadelphia: American Philosophical Society, 1995), 81-96. She refers to numerous omen texts and texts for undoing or loosening evil, observing that "while omen collections were serialized, that is, arranged in books or chapters with more or less canonical divisions and numberings, this does not seem to have been the case with the *namburbû* texts [expiating and loosing texts]" (p. 82). See also J. C. Greenfield and M. Sokoloff, "Astrological and Related Omen Texts in Jewish Palestinian Aramaic," *Journal of Near Eastern Studies* 48 (1989): 201-214 for information on later formulations of lunar portents/omens and their relationship to the much earlier Akkadian series *Enūma Anu Enlil* (an omen collection, including lunar, solar, stellar, meteorological phenomena), as well as information on the idea of "Favorable Days" as found in these sources. Information processing of omen and portent texts created an enormous scribal enterprise. Interpretive rules were developed; see the discussion in Stephen J. Lieberman, "A Mesopotamian Background for the So-Called *Aggadic* 'Measures' of Biblical Hermeneutics?," *Hebrew Union College Annual*

58 (1987): 157-225. Elsewhere the Etruscans developed a priesthood of the *haruspices*, who specialized in interpreting *exta, monstra (ostenta, portenta, prodigia)*, and *fulgura*. The priesthood later was imported into Rome. There is a long and diverse history of organized and well-funded hermeneutical enterprises set up to explain the strange and anomalous.

7. Livy 21.62.1; 24.10.6. A passage in 24.10.10 reports how *miracula* circulated (*vulgata erant*). Both sets of *prodigia* report acclamations of "Triumph!" Livy is quite critical, thinking such stories to be believed by *simplices ac religiosi homines* (simple and religious men). See P. G. Walsh, *Livy: His Historical Method: Aims and Methods* (Cambridge: Cambridge University Press, 1961), 62-63. The materials now extant reach as far back as the Consuls Lucius Scipio and Lucius Laelius (190 B.C.E.). Naphtali Lewis (*The Interpretation of Dreams and Portents*, Aspects of Antiquity [London: Samuel Stevens, 1976], 114-132) offers an English translation of a good portion of the work by Julius Obsequens. See Hubert Cancik, (Libri fatales: Römische Offenbarungsliteratur und Geschichtstheologie," in *Apocalypticism in the Mediterranean World and the Ancient Near East*, ed. David Hellholm [Tübingen, Germany: J. C. B. Mohr, 1983], 565-574) for a catalogue of such writings. See also Elizabeth Rawson (Theology and the Arts of Divination," in *Intellectual Life in the Late Roman Republic* [Baltimore: Johns Hopkins University Press, 1985], 298-316) for the general influence of these trends on Nigidius and, especially, Varro's *Antiquitates Rerum Divinarum*.

8. Klaus Berger, "Hellenistische-heidnische Prodigien und die Vorzeichen in der jüdischen und christlichen Apokalyptik," *ANRW* ii/23.2 (1988), 1428-1469.

9. These ritual processes foreshadow what would be developed later in Christian theology. See Léon Halkin, *La supplication d'action de grâces chez les Romains*, Bibliothèque de la Faculté de Philosophie et Lettres de l'Université de Liège, fasc. 128 (Paris: Société d'Édition Les Belles Lettres, 1953), 9-13.

10. Halkin, *Supplication d'action de grâces*, 124.

11. Klaus Bringmann, "The King as Benefactor: Some Remarks on the Ideal Kingship in the Age of Hellenism," in *Images and Ideologies: Self-Definition in the Hellenistic World*, ed. Anthony Bulloch, Erich S. Gruen, A. A. Long, and Andrew Stewart, Hellenistic Culture and Society 12 (Berkeley: University of California Press, 1993), 11. See also Gail Corrington (*The "Divine Man": His Origin and Function in Hellenistic Popular Religion*, American University Studies, series 7: Theology and Religion 17 [New York: Peter Lang, 1986], 71-72), who made observations worth citing at length: "In the inscriptions from the Greek East, all references to power (δύναμις) also reflect the formulaic language of the decrees of deified rulers (κατὰ τὴν δύναμιν αὐτοῦ, *SIG* [*Sylloge Inscriptionum Graecorum*] 568.10, 569.30, 826.C.10, 834.10), or their military prowess (e.g., *OGIS* [*Orientis Graeci Inscriptiones Selectae*] 669.9). The term in plural, δυνάμεις, refers exclusively to actions of rulers, and is seen primarily in reference to the Ptolemies (*OGIS* 90.12, 139.8) and the Seleucids (*OGIS* 154.2, 219, 248.17). Similarly, with the single exception of a reference to 'the divine Plato' (μετὰ τὸν θεῖον Πλάτωνα, *OGIS* 721.5), all use of θεῖος, both in *SIG* and

OGIS is restricted, except for infrequent reference to the gods, to the emperors (e.g., *SIG* 888.105, ὁ θεῖος Αὐτοκράτωρ; cf. *OGIS* 504.18, 520.9, 515.10), to attributes of the emperors (e.g., *OGIS 458.15,* κατὰ τὴν θείαν βουλήσιν), or to items of emperors as to gods (e.g., *OGIS* 721.5, τὰς θείας σύριγγας). The priest of Hadrian's own cult praises him as θειότατον Αὐτοκράτωρα and θαυμασιώτατον ἡμῶν ἄρχοντα (*OGIS* 504.18), while Flavius Claudius Julius is praised for his ἀρεταί (*OGIS* 520.1-2). A late and somewhat surprising inscription from Lycia (ca. 311 C.E., *OGIS* 569) addresses the four emperors, Galerius, Maximinius, Constantine, and Valerius Licinnus, as σωτῆρες and θεῖοι σεβήστοι because they had not expelled the Christians from Lycia." On the impact of Augustus, see Fergus Millar, *The Emperor in the Roman World (31 B.C. - A.D. 337)* (Ithaca, N.Y.: Cornell University Press, 1977), 422. Text of Priene version of the decree in Victor Ehrenberg and A. H. M. Jones, *Documents Illustrating the Reigns of Augustus and Tiberius*, 2d ed. (Oxford: Clarendon Press, 1976), 81, with description, ἡ τοῦ θειοτάτου Καίσαρος γενέθλιος ἡμέρα (birthday of most divine Caesar).

   12. Text in Ehrenberg and Jones, *Documents*, 83.

   13. In the time of Tiberius, representations of emperors wearing cuirasses begin to show iconography of Helios and Nikê as patrons of the Emperor, with both deities providing powerful benefaction to him. See Klaus Stemmer, *Untersuchungen zur Typologie, Chronologie und Ikonographie der Panzerstatuen*, Deutsches Archäologische Institut: Archäologische Forschungen, 4 (Berlin: G. Mann Verlag, 1978). In a decree on the operation of the imperial cult from 18 C.E., one contemporary Roman official is called κηδεμών, a term previously used to identify as benefactors tutelary heroes, protectors, or guardians; compare Ehrenberg and Jones, *Documents*, 88. The idea of family *tutelus* or *genius* was robust among Romans; see Harold Axtell, *The Deification of Abstract Ideas in Roman Literature and Inscriptions* (Chicago: University of Chicago Press, 1907), 33, 40. For building decoration, see Mario Torelli (*Typology and Structure of Roman Historical Reliefs*, Jerome Lectures, 14th series [Ann Arbor: University of Michigan Press, 1982], 63-88) on Livia, the *Ara Pietatis Augustae*, and Roman development of a dynasty (*gens Julia*). By the time of Claudius in 22 C.E., Livia/*Pietas* worship had been transferred to the capitol. The program included temple construction as an *expiation* for catastrophic or unusual events. Lightning or earthquake damages were expiated (Aius Locutius, Apollo Palatinus, Jupiter Fulgur, Semo Sancus, Tellus, Venus Verticordia). A fire averted or the end of a plague was so celebrated (Aesculapius, Apollo Medicus, Ara Incendii, Ceres, Febris, Tellus, Terminius). After the finding of a sacred object, the uncanniness of its loss and retrieval was celebrated (Honos). On all of this see John E. Stambaugh, "The Functions of the Roman Temple," *Aufstieg und Niedergang der Römischen Welt* ii/16.1 (1978): 557.

   14. Thomas Africa, "Worms and the Death of Kings: A Cautionary Note on Disease and History," *Classical Antiquity* 1 (1982): 1-17. The disease was phthiriasis. Memnon wrote an epitome of the writing of Nymphis, who reported that the impious Satyrus (346 B.C.E.) was punished by heaven: "He had a

cancerous growth between groin and scrotum, which spread inwards and became
more and more painful. There was a constant discharge from his flesh which
caused an insufferable stench, and neither his retinue nor physicians could stop
this unbearably putrid flow."

15. See *The Acts of the Pagan Martyrs: Acta Alexandrinorum*, ed. and trans.
Herbert A. Musurillo, (Oxford: Clarendon Press, 1954), 48. It was not unknown
for stone statues of gods to perspire. See Lucian (*De Dea Syria* 36) for an account
of the statue of Apollo perspiring whenever an oracle is imminent. For other
divine manifestations in inanimate objects, see H. S. Versnel, "What Did Ancient
Man See When He Saw a God? Some Reflections on Greco-Roman Epiphany,"
in *Effigies Dei: Essays on the History of Religions*, ed. Dirk Van der Plas, Studies
in the History of Religions (Supplements to *Numen*) 51 (Leiden, The Netherlands:
E. J. Brill, 1987), 46. He mentions (1) a story of Camillus, who captured the city
of Vei, asking the city goddess Iuno whether she was willing to follow him or not
to Rome; it was said the statue answered him in a low voice (Plutarch, *Cam.* 6);
(2) the statue of *Dea Syria* stared back at people, following them with her eyes;
(3) images and statues were considered vehicles of a divine *Parousia*, as reported
in Herodotus 8.6, about how some people fetched statues and images for divine
assistance.

16. Musurillo (*Acts of the Pagan Martyrs*, 177) notes that αἰφνίδον is a term
in narratives of this period for an unexpected, sudden, or anomalous turn of
events; it is "a late form, frequent in the novelists to mark sudden changes of
fortune, theophanies, and miracles. Cf. Chariton i.xiv.1; v.ix.1; Heliodorus v.28
(149.7); Longus ii.25.3; Achilles Tatius viii.17.5; the Herpyllus-fragment (P.
Dublin), ed. F. Zimmermann, *Griech. Romanpapyri*, p.8.18." The terms αἰφνίδον
[quickly], ταχύς [suddenly], and ἐξαπίνης [immediately]color a narrative with
tones of the strange and unusual, as they do in *P.Oxy.* 1381 (Praise to Imouthes).
In this text, the strange and unusual are expressed as δυνάμεις (miracles), ἀρεταί
(virtues), and ἐπιφάνειαι (epiphanies), the latter explicitly in some detail. Students
of this type of ancient phenomena will be familiar with these terms. See Vincenzo
Longo, *Aretalogie nel mondo greco, 1: Epigrafi e papiri*, Università di Genova
Facoltà di Lettere: Pubblicazioni dell'Istituto di Filogia Classica, 29 (Genova:
Istituto di Filologia Classica e Medioevale, 1969), 94; see also *The Oxyrhynchus
Papyri*, ed. Bernard P. Grenfell and Arthur S. Hunt (London: Egyptian Explora-
tion Fund, 1915), 9:221-234.

17. Felix Jacobi, *Die Fragmente der Griechichen Historiker* (Leiden, The
Netherlands: E. J. Brill, 1957), §570 F6, F8-11, F13. Lycus of Rhegium is dated
to the third century B.C.E. Ulrich Wilamowitz-Moellendorff (*Antigonos von
Karystos*, Philologische Untersuchungen, 4 [Berlin: Weidmannsche Buchhandlung, 1881]) sifted through numerous references to authors named Antigonus. He
suggested that this Antigonus, or another who did the same type of writing, was
a contemporary of the geographical and mythographical writer, Eratosthenes (275-
194 B.C.E.). Before Pliny other such authors are: Callimachus, Philostephanos of
Cyrene, Archelaos the Egyptian, Orpheus, Bolos of Mendes, Philo of Herakleia,
Myrsilos of Lesbos, Ephorus of Kyme, Theopompos of Chios, Antigonos of

Karytus, Polemon the Perieget, Nymphodoros of Syracuse, Ps-Aristotle, Apollonios, Agatharchides of Cnidos, Lysimachus of Alexandria, Isigonos of Nikeia, Damaskios, Agathosthenes, Varro and Cicero. See K. Ziegler, "Paradoxographoi," in *Pauly's Realencyclopädie* 18.3 (1949), cols. 1137-66. These writers were not uncritical. Agatharchides of Cnidos commented on the most likely legend of how the Erythraean Sea got its name, and in so doing suggested that there had always been many disagreements among tellers of legends like these legends (τὰ τῆς ἀντιλογίας εἰς μῦθος), including accounts like those about "the Centaur, Geryon, the Cyclops, Chryses, Circe, Calypso, the Minotaur, Scylla, the Chimera, Pegasus, the Laestrygonians, Cerberus, a sea creature named Glaucus, Atlas, Proteus, Nereus, the Nereids, the sons of Aloeus . . . further, according to Hesiod, first there was a golden, then a silver, then a bronze age . . . Odysseus' fellow sailors were changed from men to pigs and from pigs to human form . . . Tantalus . . . individuals descend[ing] into Hades by choice." See Karl Müller, *Geographi Graeci Minores* (Hildesheim, Germany: Georg Olms, 1965; orig. published 1853), 1:114.5. Translation in Stanley Burnstein, *Agatharchides of Cnidus: On the Erythraen Sea*, Hakluyt Society, Second Series 172 (London: Hakluyt Society, 1989), 46.

18. Michael Trapp, "Sense of Place in the Orations of Dio Chrysostom," in *Ethics and Rhetoric: Classical Essays for Donald Russell on His Seventy-Fifth Birthday*, ed. D. Innes, H. Hine, and C. Pelling (Oxford: Clarendon Press, 1995), 163-75. In Tacitus' account of a floating banquet on Lake Agrippa, given for Nero by Tigellinus, the unusual, affronting, and foreign (that is, "non-Roman) nature of the lake and its activities is highlighted. See Tony Woodman, "Nero's Alien Capital: Tacitus as Paradoxographer *(Annals* 15.36-7)," in *Author and Audience in Latin Literature* (Cambridge: Cambridge University Press, 1992), 173-188. For Plutarch see Luis A. García Moreno, "Paradoxography and Political Ideals in Plutarch's *Life of Sertorius*," in *Plutarch and the Historical Tradition*, ed. Philip A. Stadter (London: Routledge, 1992), 150. García wrote that "the entire story simply elaborated the *topos* of Sertorius as Ulysses, a prototype for the ruler of the Cynic-Stoic tradition, the one who would put his wisdom at the service of his governing efforts as well as of vanquishing his enemies."

19. John Ferguson, *Utopias of the Classical World* (Ithaca, N.Y.: Cornell University Press, 1975), 157.

20. Alexander Giannini, *Paradoxographorum Graecorum Reliquiae*, Classici Greci e Latini: Secione Texti e Commenti, 3 (Milano: La Nuova Italia, 1967), §85 (Ps-Aristotle), §220 (Phlegon of Tralles), §215 (Antigonus).

21. André-Jean Festugière, *Personal Religion Among the Greeks*, Sather Classical Lectures 26 (Berkeley: University of California Press, 1954), 87.

22. Antonius Diogenes *The Wonders Beyond Thule* 110a, trans. B. P. Reardon, *Collected Ancient Greek Novels* (Berkeley: University of California Press, 1989), 779.

23. He claimed he found it in a grave that dated from the time of Alexander the Great. See Bowersock, *Fiction as History*, 36. On the marvelous and uncanny discovery of ancient, holy, or magical texts in graves as a theme in ancient

literature, see William Brashear, "Magical Papyri: Magic in Bookform," in *Das Buch als magische und als Repräsentationsobjekt*, ed. Peter Ganz, Wolfenbütteler Mittelalter-Studien, Bd. 5 (Wiesbaden: Otto Harrassowitz, 1992), 26-27.

24. Walter Trimpi, *Muses of One Mind: The Literary Analysis of Experience and Its Continuity* (Princeton, N.J.: Princeton University Press, 1983), 73-79. I cite Trimpi cautiously, because his enormous control over the ancient material makes citing him for just a bit of his argument rather disingenuous. One cannot well fathom ancient rhetoric without reviewing this scholar's work.

25. Apuleius *Metamorphosis* 3.22, trans. W. Adlington, rev. S. Gaselee, *The Golden Ass, Being the Metamorphoses of Lucius Apuleius*, Loeb Classical Library (London: William Heinemann, 1935), 133. See also Luther H. Martin, (Artemidorus: Dream Theory in Late Antiquity," *Second Century* 8 [1991]: 97-108) on distinctions between perception ascertained while awake (καθ᾽ ὕπαρ) and ascertained while asleep (καθ᾽ ὄναρ).

26. Andrew Laird, "Fiction, Bewitchment and Story Worlds: The Implications of Claims to Truth in Apuleius," in *Lies and Fiction in the Ancient World*, ed. Christopher Gill and T. P. Wiseman (Austin: University of Texas Press, 1993), 172.

27. On ἀπορεῖς see Plato *Meno* 80a. On ψυχαγωγεῖ see Plato *Phaedrus* 271c; compare E. Asmis, "*Psychagogia* in Plato's *Phaedrus*," *Illinois Classical Studies* 11 (1985-1986): 153-72.

28. See Terence Cave (*Recognitions: A Study in Poetics* [Oxford: Clarendon Press, 1990], 46) on how recognition scenes for Aristotle are "a focus for reflections on the way fictions as such are constituted, the way in which they play with and on the reader, their distinctive marks *as* fictions—untruth, disguise, trickery, 'suspense', or deferment, the creation of effects of shock or amazement, and so on."

29. Dionysius of Halicarnassus, *Epistula ad Ammaeum* I: 8, trans. W. Rhys Roberts, *Dionysius of Halicarnassus: The Three Literary Letters* (Cambridge: Cambridge University Press, 1901), 66, l. 15.

30. Jean-Pierre Vernant, "A 'Beautiful Death' and the Disfigured Corpse in Homeric Epic," trans. Andrew Szegedy-Maszak, in *Mortals and Immortals: Collected Essays*, ed. Froma I. Zeitlin (Princeton, N.J.: Princeton University Press, 1991), 71. These views of wretched death persisted. One story has it that "earth-born" monsters whom Herakles slew died by the shore, anomalously half in the water and half out, being prey to both birds and fish simultaneously. See Apollonius Rhodius *Argonautica* 1.1009. Charles Segal (*The Theme of the Mutilation of the Corpse in the Iliad*, Mnemosyne Supplements 17 (Leiden, The Netherlands: E. J. Brill, 1971), 2) argues that in the Homeric thematic and formulaic development, the theme modulated from utter violence to divine justice through three stages in *Iliad* 16-22, *Iliad* 23, and *Iliad* 24 (from Hector's intention to mount Patroclus' head on a stake to Achilles' compassion).

31. On the Curtius Rufus text see Mary Boyce and Franz Grenet, *A History of Zoroastrianism* 3: *Zoroastrianism under Macedonian and Roman Rule*, Handbuch der Orientalistik, erste Anteilung: Der nahe und der mittlere Osten, Bd.

8: Religion, erster Abschnitt: Religionsgeschichte des alten Orients, Lief. 2, 2 (Leiden, The Netherlands: E. J. Brill, 1991), 5 (authors referred to P. Bernard, "Fouilles d'Aï Khanoum en 1976-1977," *Comptes rendus de l'Académie des Inscriptions et Belles-Lettres* 91 [1978]: 434-41). The account is from Arrian, *Anabasis* 4.7.4. Boyce and Grenet wrote, "the purpose of the order [to keep the birds away] (if Curtius' account is accurate) may simply have been to preserve the body longer as witness to the harsh punishment of a regicide; but perhaps . . . it had an even grimmer aim, namely to deprive Bessus of that swift end to bodily corruption which is prized by Zoroastrians, an added cruelty which would have increased the horror of his death for other would-be resisters among the Iranians. According to Arrian, however, after having him mutilated, Alexander sent Bessus to Ecbatana, to be 'put to death in the full gathering of Medes and Persians'." On the Onesicritus text about the Sogdians, see Boyce and Grenet, *History*, 6. *Palatine Anthology* 7.76 has lines telling how Philocritus died and is subsequently buried in Egypt. Unfortunately, after his proper burial with enough soil covering him, the Nile floods and uncovers his body so that, even here, although previously properly buried "under earth," he ends up exposed, "under the waves" like one dead at sea, left without earth burial and therefore ἄταφος (unburied). Those thought barbaric are typically described as doing strange things to members of their society, both at the end of life as well as at its beginning. Soranus *(Gynaecology* 2.12.59) tells how Germans and Scythians exposed newborn infants to cold-water baths in order to "firm" them or to kill them. Other traits thought barbaric are: washing the neonate with wine, washing the neonate with the urine of another "uncorrupted" child, or sprinkling the child with myrtle and oak gall. See G. E. R. Lloyd, *Science, Folklore and Ideology: Studies in the Life Sciences in Ancient Greece* (Cambridge: Cambridge University Press, 1983), 170.

32. The Platonic material on fear in the underworld is also apparent in the Derveni Papyrus col. VI, where some souls of the previously deceased are angry and have a high penalty (ποινή) to pay; see Sarah Iles Johnston, *Restless Dead: Encounters Between the Living and the Dead in Ancient Greece* (Berkeley: University of California Press, 1999), 137-38. For the hymn see *Descensus ad infernos* 28 in *Die griechischen Dichterfragmente der römischen Kaiserzeit*, ed. Ernst Heitsch, 2d ed. (Göttingen: Vandenhoeck & Ruprecht, 1963), §58.

33. J. A. Robinson and M. R. James, *The Gospel According to Peter, and the Revelation of Peter: Two Lectures on the Newly Recovered Fragments Together with the Greek Texts* (London: C. J. Clay, 1892), 91. For Ἐρινύες καὶ Ποιναὶ καὶ Φόβοι (Erinys and Avengers and Fears) see Albrecht Dieterich, *NEKYIA: Beiträge zur Erklärung der neuentdeckten Petrusapoakalypse* (Leipzig, Germany: B. G. Teubner, 1893), 58. Dieterich reported earlier on another piece of evidence in an inscription from an amulet that contains the unusual word, ΠΡΟΣΔΕΜΟΝΑΚΕΦΟΒΟΥΣ, which witnesses to how "Fears" (Φόβοι) are agencies of assault; see Dieterich, *Abraxas: Studien zur Religionsgeschichte des spätern Altertum*, Festschrift für Hermann Usener (Leipzig, Germany: Teubner, 1891), 88-89. Dieterich suggests a development of the idea, that Fears *as entities* developed from a variety of traditions including: (1) biblical (the "Fear of God"

becomes "God as Fear," and then finally "Fear is a God), (2) a linkage between φόβος and the Gorgon (Hippolytus IV,36), and (3) the idea of a Χωρίον of φόβος as found in Pausanias Περιήγησις 2,7. On specifically Greek relations of avenging entities to violently dead and ἀλάστωρ, προστρόπιος, and παλαμναῖος (avenging god, vengeance, and avenger of blood), see Johnston, *Restless Dead*, 142-48.

34. Hans Dieter Betz, "Fragments from a Catabasis Ritual in a Greek Magical Papyrus," *History of Religions* 19 (1979-1980): 287-95; discussion of the phrase πρὸς φόβον κολάσεως (for fear of chastisement) is on p. 289. On καταβάσεις (descents) and the frequent use of such accounts (often based on Odysseus's experience with the dead in *Odyssey* 11), see Josef Kroll, *Gott und Hölle: Der Mythos vom Descensuskampfe*, Studien der Bibliothek Warburg, Heft 20 (Leipzig, Germany: Bibliothek Warburg, 1932), 371-72.

35. On παράδοξα (marvels) during chthonic descents, see Lucian, *Icaromenippus* 1. From another tradition, see also *Apocalypse of Zephaniah* 6-8, in which Zephaniah encounters strange architectural wonders and strange beasts; compare Martha Himmelfarb, *Tours of Hell: An Apocalyptic Form in Jewish and Christian Literature* (Philadelphia: Fortress Press, 1983), 15-16. On *Oracle of Trophonius*, see Pausanias Περιήγησις 9.39.13, trans. W. H. S. Jone, in *Pausanius: Description of Greece*, Loeb Classical Library (Cambridge, Mass.: Harvard University Press, 1965), 4:355.

36. Daniel Sperber, "On Sealing the Abysses," in *Magic and Folklore in Rabbinic Literature*, Bar-Ilan Studies in Near Eastern Languages and Culture (Ramat-Gan, Israel: Bar-Ilan University Press, 1994), 47-54.

37. δαίμονες, 1.5; ἐγεῖραι, 1.11, 3.20; προφητής, 1.13; σπλαγχνίζεσθαι, 1.27; ὀψίας, 1.68; νύξ, 1.70; ἐλαύνειν, 1.98; γαλήνης, 1.106; ἄνεμος [βίαιος], 1.110; ἐκπλήσσεσθαι, 1.117; προσορμίζεσθαι, 1.122; ἀπιστία, 1.151, 3.64, 4.35; δύναμις, 1.155; ἄρρωστος, 1.158, 3.104; ἐξιστάναι, 2.22, 5.123; θαρρεῖν, 3.135, 5.125; μαθητής, 4.44; ἀγέλη, 5.44; ἰατρός, 4.177; διδόναι (as a technical term of benefaction), 5.140; συμπόσιον, 6.5.

38. *PGM* 4.265-66, in *Papyri Graecae Magicae: Die griechischen Zauberpapyri*, ed. Karl Preisendanz (Leipzig, Germany: Teubner, 1928); trans. E. N. O'Neill in *The Greek Magical Papyri in Translation, Including the Demotic Spells*, ed. Hans Dieter Betz (Chicago: University of Chicago Press, 1986), 43. See also Heitsch, *Die griechsichen Dichterfragmente*, §59.7, suggesting the variant <παμ>φοβερόν.

39. For *nocturnos pavores* and *umbrarum terrorem* see Sarah Iles Johnston, "Defining the Dreadful: Remarks on the Greek Child-Killing Demon," in *Ancient Magic and Ritual Power*, Religions in the Graeco-Roman World 129 (Leiden, The Netherlands: E. J. Brill, 1995), 385. For Hekate texts see *Hymnus in Hecatem* 6 in Heitsch, *Die griechische Dichterfragmente*, §54 = Hippolytus *Refutationes* 4.35.5) and *Orphic Hymns* 1.5 in Apostolos N. Athanassakis, *The Orphic Hymns: Text, Translation, and Notes*, Texts and Translations 12; Graeco-Roman Religions Series 4 (Missoula, Mont.: Scholars Press, 1977).

40. Lewis Richard Farnell, *The Cults of the Greek States* (Oxford: Clarendon Press, 1896), 2:515, citing *Corpus Inscriptionum Graecorum* 3857 K. See 2:556 for how the dreadful Hekate is illustrated on a marble Hekateion in her triple-form, in which we may perceive two threatening identities, that of Τύχη and Νέμεσις.

41. *Orphic Hymns* 11.7. So also Hera, who once cast (ἔμβαλεν) a most inexpressive fear (ἀλεγεινότατος φόβος) into the heart of Medea.

42. *Orphic Hymns* 28.10. Perhaps this is a reflection on earlier Hermes symbolism, of the god carrying a κηρύκειον (herald's wand). The implements of speech, language, and communication underlie the strength of the power of memory. A child of Hermes, Aithalides, is blessed with a truly Hermetic memory, or a perfect memory of everything that happened. As a herald, his pronouncements are unequivocable. See Apollonius Rhodius, *Argonautica* 1.640. Involvement in the arena of Hermes' divine influence, speech and language, is unavoidable, and therefore might ever be an adventure in danger. Pertaining to this power of language, Empedocles theorized about the part of the human mind that is attuned to language (the νοητητός), suggesting that it is to be considered a τρίτην τινὰ δύναμιν (a third power), or third in a division, next to love and strife. See Empedocles Περὶ φυσέως 100(110), ed. by M. R. Wright, *Empedocles: The Extant Fragments* (New Haven, Conn.: Yale University Press, 1981). As the artificer of magical language and magical books, Hermes wields a divine power through communication and invocation. He has power over language, to clarify or to obfuscate, to build up or to tear down; see David G. Martinez, *P. Michigan XVI: A Greek Love Charm from Egypt (P.Mich. 757)*, Michigan Papyri 16, American Studies in Papyrology, 30 (Atlanta: Scholars Press, 1991), 42. Greek philosophical cosmogony mixed with Egyptian awareness of the power of Thoth (that is, Hermes) into Hermeticism. This development points to an ancient suspicion about divine power latent in speech and thought. In Egypt, the scribal *objets d'écriture* themselves were celebrated in religious pomp, a celebration recognizing the proximity to divine power possible through them. On the inscription at the Edfou Temple of Horus (140-124 B.C.E.), and on Hermeticism and Greek philosophy in general, see Garth Fowden, *The Egyptian Hermes: A Historical Approach to the Late Pagan Mind* (Cambridge: Cambridge University Press, 1986); pertinent lines of the inscription on p. 57.

43. Albrecht Scriba, *Die Geschichte des Motivkomplexes Theophanie: Seine Elemente, Einbindung in Geschehensabläufe und Verwendungsweisen in altisraelitischer, frühjüdischer und frühchristlicher Literatur*, Forschungen zur Religion und Literatur des Alten und Neuen Testaments Bd. 167 (Göttingen: Vandenhoeck & Ruprecht, 1995), 14-79. Scriba's full list includes (1) Bad-Weather Phenomena (*Unwetterphänomene*); (2) Luminous Glory (*Lichtglanz*); (3) Fire (*Feuer*); (4) Heavenly Retinues (*Himmlisches Gefolge*); (5) God's Gaze and Face (*Gottes Blick und Angesicht*); (6) Reactions of Horror (*Schreckreaktionen*); (7) Lands and Mountains (*Erde und Berge*); (8) Chaos Struggle and the Sea (*Motive Vom Chaoskampf, Meer*); (9) People, Human Beings, Animals and Angels (*Völker, Menschen, Tiere und Engel*); (10) Heavenly Sphere and Stars/Constellations (*Himmel und Gestirne*). Gerd Theissen, *The Miracle Stories of the Early*

Christian Tradition, trans. Francis McDonagh, ed. John Riches (Philadelphia: Fortress Press, 1983), 95. Franz Annen, *Heil für die Heiden: Zur Bedeutung und Geschichte der Tradition vom besessenen Gerasener (Mk 5, 1-20 parr)*, Frankfurther Theologische Studien Bd. 20 (Frankfurt am Main, Germany: Josef Knecht, 1976), 134. Barry Blackburn, *Theios Anēr and the Markan Miracle Traditions: A Critique of the* Theios Aner *Concept as an Interpretative Background of the Miracle Traditions Used by Mark*, Wissenschaftliche Untersuchungen zum Neuen Testament, 2. Reihe, 40 (Tübingen, Germany: J. C. B. Mohr, 1991), 220-27. Blackburn cites a comment by Rudolf Bultmann, (*History of the Synoptic Tradition*, rev. ed. [New York: Harper and Row, 1968], 221), who also had characterized many of the troubles of the clients of a θεῖος ἀνήρ (divine man) as problems of "dreadful or dangerous character."

44. John Day, *God's Conflict with the Dragon and the Sea: Echoes of a Canaanite Myth in the Old Testament*, University of Cambridge Oriental Publications 35 (Cambridge: Cambridge University Press, 1985), 84-126. Day's full list includes *Dragon and Egypt* (Isa. 30:7; 51:9-11; Ps. 87:4; Ezek. 29:3-5; 32:2-8 [the *tannin* monster]); *Chaoskampfmythos and the Exodus from Egypt* (Ps. 77:17-21 [ET 16-20]; Isa. 51:9-11; Exod. 15:1-18); *Chaotic Sea and Assyria* (Isa. 8:5-8; 17:12-14); *Chaotic Sea and Babylon* (Hab. 3:5, 8-10, 15 [with reference to Resheph and allusion to Yahweh's seven shafts of lightning and parallels in Ugaritic Ba'al mythology]); *Dragon and Babylon* (Jer. 51:34); *Dragon and Uncertain Political Enemy* (Isa. 27:1; Ps. 44:19-20 [ET 18-19]); *Cosmic Waters as the Nations in General* (Ps. 18:5-18 [ET 4-17]; 46:3-6 [ET 2-3]; 144:5-4).

45. George MacRae, "Miracles in the *Antiquities* of Josephus," in *Miracles: Cambridge Studies in Their Philosophy and History*, ed. C. F. D. Moule (London: A. R. Mowbray, 1965), 134.

46. Van Henten, "Das jüdische Selbstverständnis in den ältesten Martyrien," 136. On the topic of divine assistance in war in general, see Wolfgang Speyer, "Die Hilfe und Epiphanie einer Gottheit, eines Heroen und eines Heiligen in der Schlact," in *Pietas: Festschrift für Bernard Kötting*, ed. Ernst Dassmann and K. Suso Frank, Jahrbuch für Antike und Christentum, Erganzungsband 8 (Münster, Germany: Aschendorff, 1980), 55-77, especially for stories about such epiphanies and tracing the stories through contexts with very little in common.

47. *PGM* 12.248; Heitsch, *Die griechischen Dichterfragmente* §59,1.

48. On divination through Ocean creatures, see Bouché-Leclercq, *Histoire de la Divination dans l'Antiquité*, 2:261-65, "Oracles animés par les divinités des eaux," and 2:361-64. The roaring of Poseidon is in *Orphic Hymns* 17.4. See Jan Bremmer ('Effigies Dei' in Ancient Greece: Poseidon," in *Effigies Dei: Essays on the History of Religions*, ed. Dirk Van der Plas, Studies in the History of Religions [Supplements to *Numen*] 51 [Leiden, The Netherlands: E. J. Brill, 1987], 35-41), who suggests that Homer "innovated by making Poseidon the ruler of the sea, since the Greeks had many, evidently older, gods of the sea, such as Phorcys, Proteus and Nereus" (p. 38). Divine powers do tend to wage war against each other. Herakles does not fare well when he becomes the target of Hera's revenge through Iris and Madness. See Euripides *Herakles* 815-21. On the other hand, he

is singularly the hero who well fights Poseidon and the gods of the underworld (Herakles at the Gates). See Kroll, *Gott und Hölle*, 373-74 on this and the links between Poseidon and Hades. Conflicts rage, often won by stealth. Divine powers in this realm assault one another. Christopher A. Faraone, (*Talismans and Trojan Horses: Guardian Statues in Ancient Greek Myth and Ritual* [New York: Oxford University Press, 1992], 75) reminds us that "binding is one of the most popular means with which the gods fight each other in Greek myth: Cronus bound Zeus (Hesiod *Op.* 173a); Zeus is threatened with the same fate at the hands of Poseidon, Apollo, and Hera (*Iliad* 1.399-401); and Hephaestus binds Ares and Aphrodite in bed (*Od.* 8.296-299) and even his own mother (Pindar frg. 283 [Snell]; Plato, *Republic* 378d)." For prayers for safety, see Aristides, *Oration* 46.11. Compare to Apollonius Rhodius (*Argonautica* 4.316) for a description of exotic foreigners who are considered primitive (Scythians and Thracians, Sigymi, Graucenii, Sindi). What is noteworthy about them is that when they see ships come from across the sea, they are afraid because the ships seem like θῆρας (beasts) coming from the πόντου μεγακήτεος (gigantic-monster-filled ocean). We are reminded that not only Poseidon assisted at sea, since one epithet has Apollo as Ἐμβάσιος, "Apollo Embarkation"; see Apollonius Rhodius, *Argonautica* 1:359. Not atypically, the ability to navigate at sea and steer a vessel was considered an endowment of divine wisdom.

    49. Similar themes of abundance, sustenance, love, and vital harmony appear also in εἰκόνα γραπτήν (image in text) described in Longus, *Daphnes and Chloe* proem. M. L. West, (*Early Greek Philosophy and the Orient* [Oxford: Clarendon Press, 1971], 49.) suggests a Babylonian influence on Greek theories of Ocean encircling the inhabited universe. In Cuneiform sources it is called "The Bitter River". An iconographic depiction of this idea is found in an eighth-century B.C.E. map from the Babylonian town of Sippar. The map, from city center to lands outside the "last boundary," shows a topographical cosmology. See comments in Gerdien Jonker, *The Topography of Remembrance: The Dead, Tradition and Collective Memory in Mesopotamia*, Studies in the History of Religion (*Numen* Book Series) (Leiden, The Netherlands: E. J. Brill, 1995), 44-47.

    50. Mark S. Smith, *The Ugaritic Baal Cycle, 1: Introduction with Text, Translation and Commentary of KTU 1.1-1.2*, Supplements to *Vetus Testamentum* 55 (Leiden, The Netherlands: E. J. Brill, 1994), 225-26.

    51. Tikva Frymer-Kensky, *In the Wake of the Goddesses: Women, Culture, and the Biblical Transformation of Pagan Myth* (New York: Free Press, 1992), 86.

    52. Mark S. Smith, *The Early History of God: Yahweh and the Other Deities in Ancient Israel* (New York: Harper & Row, 1990), 7.

    53. Erwin Rohde, *Psyche: The Cult of Souls and Belief in Immortality among the Greeks*, 7th ed., trans. W. B. Hillis, International Library of Psychology, Philosophy, and Scientific Method (New York: Harcourt, Brace, 1925), 257. Rohde's description is vivid and worth quoting at length: "It was thoroughly orgiastic in character. The festival was held on the mountain tops in the darkness of night amid the flickering and uncertain light of torches. The loud and troubled

sound of music was heard; the clash of bronze cymbals; the dull thunderous roar
of kettledrums; and through them all penetrated the "maddening unison" of the
deep-toned flute, whose soul Phrygian *aulêtai* had first walked to life. Excited by
this wild music, the chorus of worshippers dance with shrill crying and jubilation.
We hear nothing about singing: the violence of the dance left no breath for regular
songs. These dances were something very different from the measured movement
of the dance-step in which Homer's Greeks advanced and turned about in the
paean. It was in frantic, whirling, headlong eddies and dance-circles that these
inspired companies danced over the mountain slopes. They were mostly women
who whirled round in these circular dances till the point of exhaustion was
reached; they were strangely dressed; they wore *bassarai*, long flowing garments,
as it seems, stitched together out of fox-skins; over these were doeskins, and they
even had horns fixed to their heads. Their hair was allowed to float in the wind;
they carried snakes sacred to Sabazios in their hands and brandished daggers or
else thyrsos-wands, the spear-points of which were concealed in ivy-leaves. In this
fashion they raged wildly until every sense was wrought to their highest pitch of
excitement, and in the "sacred frenzy" they fell upon the beast selected as their
victim and tore their captured prey limb from limb. Then with their teeth they
seized the bleeding flesh and devoured it raw."

54. Diodorus Siculus 4.3.2; see also 5.49.5, which describes the saving
presence of the Μεγάλοι Θεοί. Occasions when they rescue people in danger are
called ἐπιφάνεια καὶ παράδοξος; compare Guilia Sfameni Gasparro, *Soteriology
and Mystic Aspects in the Cult of Cybele and Attis* (Leiden, The Netherlands: E.
J. Brill, 1985), 24. See also Demosthenes *Oration* 11, where the Greek Θεοὶ
Μεγίστοι are called σύμμαχοι and βοηθοί. On every third year, see *Orphic Hymns*
53.5; compare Rohde, *Psyche*, 270 n.28.

55. Dio Chrysostom *Orations* 12.33. See Walter Burkert, "The Extraordinary
Experience," in *Ancient Mystery Cults*, Carl Newell Jackson Lectures 1982
(Cambridge, Mass.: Harvard University Press, 1987), 90-114. Burkert mentions
that religious experience in the mysteries "is patterned by antithesis, by moving
between extremes of terror and happiness, darkness and light" (p.93), referring to
a citation from Aelius Aristides (*Orations* 22) that Eleusis is the "most frightening
and most resplendent of all that is divine for men." See also Johnston, (*Restless
Dead*, 131): "And yet, several of our sources speak of initiates meeting something
'frightening' or 'shocking' in the darkness, which most likely means in the
darkness of the night of their initiation." Terms were φρίκη and ἔκπληξις, and the
cause of these emotions is described typically as a ghostly agent of some type
(Johnston, *Restless Dead*, 132 n.14).

56. Serapis text in *Aretalogia Serapidis* 9-10, ed. Heitsch, *Die griechische
Dichterfragmente*, §50. Chaeremon text in Josephus, *Contra Apionem* 1.289;
compare Van der Horst, *Chaeremon*, 9. See also Arthur Darby Nock, "Notes on
Ruler-Cult i-iv," in *Essays on Religion and the Ancient World*, ed. Zeph Stewart
(Cambridge, Mass.: Harvard University Press, 1972), 150. This dedication was
found at Erythrai.

57. Lynn R. LiDonnici, (*The Epidaurian Miracle Inscriptions: Text, Translation and Commentary,*Texts and Translations 36: Graeco-Roman Series 11 [Atlanta: Scholars Press, 1995]) notes use of ἐγκατακοιμάομαι (and other words for incubation); use of ὄψις (vision); use of ἐνύπνιον (during sleep); phrases such as ἐδόκει ὁ θεὸς ἐπιστὰς (the god, appeared, standing by), and so on. See also Bouché-Leclercq, *Histoire de la Divination dans l'Antiquité*, 3:273-275 on ἰατρομάντις and the non-Asclepian healing oracles of Telephus (Scholia Aristophanes, *Nub.* 919), Leonymus and Phormion of Croton (Pausanias Περιήγησις 3.19.12), and Apollo Korydos (Pausanias Περιήγησις 4.34.6-7). Bouché-Leclercq suggests that "les dieux chthoniens sont les dieux médicins part excellence. C'est pour cela que Démeter, que Pluton, que Dionysos, que Pan, que Sérapis, que, d'une manière générale, les *heros descendus* dans songes et visions nocturnes, est restée, de tout tempts, la méthode particulièrement affectée à la divination médicale." He refers to Iamblichus, *Myster.* 3.3: διὰ τὴν τάξιν τῶν νύκτωρ ἐπιφανείων ἡ ἰατρική τέχνη συνέστη ἀπὸ τῶν ὀνειράτων (the healing technique was constituted from dreams by means of the succession of epiphanies at night).

58. For Ptolemy XII, see Nock, "Notes," 147. On the epithet Ἐπιφανής, Nock (Notes," 154) writes that these representations did not "normally describe a deity incarnate and regularly visible in the person of a king; it implies rather the making of sudden ἐπιφάνειαι, appearances in person or manifestations of power. A god or a divine king is Ἐπιφανής when he by his ἐπιφάνειαι produces some striking result. A king may show his superhuman powers in healing or again in controlling the weather, but his normal field is war." Nock suggests that the earliest use of such an epithet was found in a 166 B.C.E. inscription in Babylonia (referring to *OGIS* §253).

59. Dietrich Roloff (*Gottähnlichkeit, Vergöttlichung und Erhöhung zu seligen Leben: Untersuchungen zur Herkunft der platonischen Angleichung an Gott*, Untersuchungen zur antiken Literatur und Geschichte, Bd. 4 [Berlin: Walter de Gruyter, 1970]) reviews the pre-Alexandrian phenomena. The concept of the θεῖος ἀνήρ, huge in its breadth, is well summarized by Corrington (*The "Divine Man"*, 45): "the categorical term, or trajectory, θεῖος ἀνήρ arose and developed . . . in the Hellenistic world as a response to, and an understanding of, the concept of power (δύναμις), especially the controlling powers of the universe, and the relationship of human beings to power. Control over, or manipulation of, this power or powers, originally a divine attribute, described formally in a recitation of the deity's ἀρεταί or δυνάμεις, is increasingly assigned to those human beings who can show that they possess that same control and manipulation of power: the thaumaturge thus shows that he possesses an attribute of divinity—power—and thus is regarded as divine, a θεῖος ἀνήρ. The thaumaturge may even be regarded as an epiphany, or revelation, or the godhead. Those who also may exhibit this possession of power and hence are also regarded as a θεῖος ἀνήρ are philosophers (σοφοί), rulers who possess great earthly power, religious figures, and even magicians (μάγοι), who are seen by their opponents and rivals as charlatans (γοήται) and even as sorcerers." Recent monographs have focused further on the

θεῖος ἀνήρ. See Blackburn, *Theios Aner and the Markan Miracle Traditions*, as discussed by Werner Kahl, *New Testament Miracle Stories in Their Religious-Historical Setting: A Religionsgeschichtliche Comparison from a Structural Perspective*, Forschungen zur Religion und Literatur des Alten und Neuen Testaments, Bd. 163 (Göttingen: Vandenhoeck & Ruprecht, 1994). Kahl, somewhat unfairly, criticizes Blackburn for indulging in *Religionsgeschichte* in a manner that does not, according to Kahl, move the discussion past Bultmann, even given Blackburn's comprehensive citations to just about any ancient evidence that seemed "miraculous." Not moving past Bultmann may not be, necessarily, a bad thing. Kahl develops a very different approach, based on the formalist work of Propp, anthropological work of Dundes, and narratology of Bremond and Greimas. See now also Erkki Koskenniemi (*Apollonios von Tyana in der neutestamentlichen Exegese*, Wissenschaftliche Untersuchungen zum Neuen Testament, 2. Reihe, Bd. 61 [Tübingen, Germany: J. C. B. Mohr, 1994]), who reviews the state of comparison of the New Testament to the work of Flavius Philostratus about Apollonius of Tyana. Koskenniemi criticizes previous studies of the θεῖος ἀνήρ for their methodological flaws. He argues that scholars have failed to distinguish between traditions about Apollonius of Tyana deriving from the first century C.E. and those deriving from the third. He further challenges the rhetorician and courtier Flavius Philostratus as a reliable historical source for information about Apollonius of Tyana.

60. See Walter Burkert (*Greek Religion*, trans. John Raffan [Cambridge, Mass.: Harvard University Press, 1985], 189), who observes about Greek religion that "man can never be entirely sure of his gods. The man who has climbed too high is all the more threatened with destruction: this is the jealousy of the gods."

61. For the ancient Greek φθόνος as Νέμεσις, see Eric R. Dodds, *The Greeks and the Irrational*, Sather Classical Lectures 25 (Berkeley: University of California Press, 1951), 30. On a connection to Roman games, see Michael B. Hornum, *Nemesis, the Roman State, and the Games*, Religions in the Graeco-Roman World 117 (Leiden, The Netherlands: E. J. Brill, 1993), 27. Matters pertaining to the Evil Eye are reviewed in Katherine M. D. Dunbabin and M. W. Dickie, "*Invidia Rumpantur Pectora*: The Iconography of Phthonos/Invidia in Graeco-Roman Art," *Jahrbuch für Antike und Christentum* 26 (1983): 7-37. For more detail, see Matthew W. Dickie (The Fathers of the Church and the Evil Eye," in *Byzantine Magic*, ed. Henry Maguire [Cambridge, Mass.: Harvard University Press, 1995], 15), who clarifies that "stories about the evil eye seem to have been one of the staples of the branch of literature that from the Hellenistic Age on catered to the public's taste for wonders [and] paradoxography." Dickie refers to Pliny (*Historia naturalis* 7.16), who attributes to two Hellenistic paradoxographers, Isigonus and Nymphodorus, stories about people with the power to fascinate (p.16 n.19). Giannini (*Paradoxographorum Graecorum Reliquiae*, Isigonus F19) gave the text as *qui visu quoque effascinent, interimantque quos diutius intueantur, iratis praecipue oculis; quod eorum malum facilius sentire puberes. Notabilius esse quod pupillas binas in oculis singulis habeant* (there are people of the same kind among the Riballi and the Illyrians, who also bewitch

with a glance and who kill those they stare at for a longer time, especially with a look of anger, and that their evil eye is most felt by adults; and that what is remarkable is that they have two pupils in each eye; trans. from Rackham, Pliny, 2:517).

62. One Egyptian wisdom text, found in *Instruction of Ankhsheshonq* 5, makes this quite clear. See the translation by Miriam Lichtheim, *Ancient Egyptian Literature: A Book of Readings* (Berkeley: University of California Press, 1980), 3:163-164. Along these lines, the *Papyrus Insinger* 34.21 (Lichtheim, *Ancient Egyptian Literature*, 3:212) offers the line, "Men cannot avoid the god of retaliation when he decrees it for them."

63. Translation of the Latin fragments of the *Oracles of Hystaspes* found in John R. Hinnells, "The Zoroastrian Doctrine of Salvation in the Roman World: A Study of the Oracle of Hystaspes," in *Man and His Salvation: Studies in Memory of S. G. F. Brandon*, ed. Eric J. Sharp and John R. Hinnells (Manchester: Manchester University Press, 1973), 125-48. Also *Oracle of the Potter* I.8, with English translation in *The Hellenistic Age from the Battle of Ipsos to the Death of Kleopatra VII*, ed. and trans. Stanley M. Burnstein, Translated Documents of Greece and Rome 3 (Cambridge: Cambridge University Press, 1985), §106. For a critical edition of the Greek text, see L. Koenen, "Die Prophezeihungen des 'Töfers'," *Zeitschrift für Papyrologie und Epigraphik* 2 (1968):178-209.

64. Howard P. Lovecraft (*Supernatural Horror in Literature* [New York: Ben Abramson, 1945], 16) suggests that "the one test of the really weird is simply this—whether or not there be excited in the reader a profound sense of dread, and of contact with unknown sphere and powers; a subtle attitude of awed listening, as if for the beating of black wings or the scratching of outside shapes and entities on the known universe's utmost rim."

65. "Le rêve est une seconde vie. Je n'ai pu percert sans frémir ces portes d'ivoirie ou de corne qui nous séparent du monde invisible. Les premiers instants du sommeil sont l'image de la mort; un engourdissement nébuleux saisit notre pensée, et nous ne pouvons déterminer l'instant précis où le *moi*, sous une autre forme, continue l'œuvre de l'existence." Gérard de Nerval, *Aurélia, ou le rêve et la vie*, in *Œuvres*, ed. Albert Béguine and Jean Richter, Bibliothèque de la Pléiade (Paris: Galliard, 1974), 1:359.

66. For basic matters about sleep patterns, see J. Allan Hobson, *Sleep* (New York: Scientific American Library, 1989), 132. Nerval (*Aurélia*, 1:413) writes, "Je crus comprendre qu'il existait entre le monde externe et le monde interne un lien; que l'inattention ou le désordre d'esprit en faussaient seuls les rapports apparents,—et qu'ainsi s'expliquait la bizarrerie de certains tableaux, semblables à ces reflets grimaçants d'objets réels qui s'agitent sur l'eau troublée [I have believed it comprehensible that there was a place between the external world and the internal world; that it was that inattention or perturbation of mind forged only apparent relations,—and that, therefore, the bizarre nature of some depictions is explained, similar to those grimacing reflections of real objects effected by troubled water]." This kind of literary or philosophical observation about how the mind works is found later, floridly, in Alfred Jarry; see Roger Shattuck, *The*

Banquet Years: The Origins of the Avant-Garde in France 1885 to World War I:
Alfred Jarry, Henri Rousseau, Erik Satie, Guillaume Apollinaire, rev. ed (New
York: Random House, 1968), 201.

    67. "Ces nymphes, je les veux perpétuer. Si clair, leur incarnat léger, qu'il
voltige dans l'air, Assoupi de sommeils touffus . . . Aimai-je un rêve?" In
Stéphane Mallarmé, "L'après-midi d'un faune," trans. P. Terry and M. Shroder in
Selected Poetry and Prose, ed. Mary Ann Caws (New York: New Directions,
1982), 33. Edgar Allan Poe was a major influence on what became the Symbolist
Movement, a movement immediately sired by Mallarmé and Rimbaud. Lines from
his poem, "A Dream Within a Dream," eloquently craft the perspective that would
flourish; see *The Works of Edgar Allan Poe in Ten Volumes*, commemorative
edition (New York: Funk & Wagnalls, 1904), 1:102. See Pierre-Louis Mathieu,
The Symbolist Generation 1870-1910 (Geneva: Editons d'Art Albert Skira S.A.,
1990), 7-30.

    68. See Bowersock (*Fiction As History*, 77-98) for a review of Hellenistic
and Roman theories about dreams and their interpretation. The work of
Artemidorus—crucial here, because it is organized, innovative, and was well-
known—attempted rationally to restructure dream interpretation. One of his
innovations is to show little concern for traditional distinctions between dreams
taking place during the day or at night, as well as between ὄνειροι (dreams saying
something about the future) and ἐνύπνια (dreams saying something about the
dreamer's state of mind).

    69. On abstract sets, see Daniel Weinberger, Karen Berman, James Gold, and
Terry Goldberg, "Neural Mechanisms of Future-Oriented Process: *In Vivo*
Physiological Studies," in *The Development of Future-Oriented Processes*, ed. by
M. Haith, J. Benson, R. Roberts, and B. Pennington, (Chicago: University of
Chicago Press, 1994), 231. On the "Fantastic," see Tzvetan Todorov, *The
Fantastic: A Structural Approach to a Literary Genre*, trans. Richard Howard
(Ithaca, N.Y.: Cornell University Press, 1975), 25. The "Fantastic" has turned out
to be a kind of specialized niche in literary criticism, almost a cottage industry
made up of discovering how imaginative texts that we identify as "fantastic" may
be subversive as they present their own defamiliarizing poetic. George W. Young
(*Subversive Symmetry: Exploring the Fantastic in Mark 6:45-56*, Biblical
Interpretation Series 41 [Leiden, The Netherlands: E. J. Brill, 1999]) should be
mentioned here, because of his review of the topic before his exegesis of Mark
6:45-56. In this literary niche, it is fair to say that generally, fantastic narratives
mix up verisimilitude (the "real") with absolute non-verisimilitude (the "marvelous"), so that fantastic narratives become "deviant," playing on two irreconcilable
frames of reference at once. See Maurice Lévy, *Lovecraft: A Study in the
Fantastic*, trans. S. T. Joshi (Detroit: Wayne State University Press, 1988; French
edition, 1966), especially the chapter, "The Metamorphosis of Space," pp.45-53,
with the appropriate summary, "disorder is the very source of the Fantastic." For
the idea of cosmography, see Robert Ford Campany (*Strange Writing: Anomaly
Accounts in Early Medieval China*, SUNY Series in Chinese Philosophy and
Culture [Albany: State University of New York Press, 1996], 2), who wrote,

"'Cosmography' means, simply, a description of the world. For convenience, I will use it in a not unrelated but much more specific and technical sense to mean the creation, development, and persuasive use (by some particular agent or group of agents) of a discourse concerning anomalies for the purpose of promoting, refining, confirming, or challenging a belief system, worldview, or ideology."

70. Roy R. Male, *Enter, Mysterious Stranger: American Cloistral Fiction* (Norman: University of Oklahoma Press, 1979), 10.

71. E. R. Dodds, "Supernormal Phenomena in Classical Antiquity," in *The Ancient Concept of Progress and Other Essays on Greek Literature and Belief* (Oxford: Clarendon Press, 1973), 156-210.

72. David Hufford, *The Terror That Comes in the Night: An Experience-Centered Study of Supernatural Assault Traditions*, Publications of the American Folklore Society new series 7 (Philadelphia: University of Pennsylvania Press, 1982), 15.

73. Hufford, *Terror*, 14. Means of transmission suggested in the cultural source hypotheses range from oral transmission of tradition to ritual transmission of hallucination through substance ingestion.

74. Hufford, *Terror*, 51. Hufford collected data of similar encounters from areas that have no traditions in common. He writes: "The common existence of these experiences, the stability of their contents, and their independence from tradition are so surprising that no quantity of summarized data is sufficient to document them. Questions of interpretation must inevitably arise. Furthermore, the variables governing peoples' ability and willingness to respond positively to questions about the experience are complicated and require study, as are the interrelationships of the various features of the experience. For these reasons, actual accounts, most of them transcribed from tape recordings, constitute the primary data of this book."

75. James McClenon, *Wondrous Events: Foundations of Religious Belief* (Philadelphia: University of Pennsylvania Press, 1994).

76. Robert Ford Campany, *Strange Writing*, 237-72.

77. New Testament commentators argue that miracle stories are used similarly in Mark. That is, they argue that miracle stories were transmitted, written, gathered, and used by Mark on the basis of some abstraction or hypothesis. This would be Markan "historiography" or "paradoxography," usually furthering some christology or other, or perhaps rationalizing supernatural ideas such as the "divine man." These rationalizations are a unique frame by which the Markan community understood the unusual, strange, or supernatural. It has been suggested that then-popular concepts about the θεῖος ἀνήρ (divine man) are reinterpreted in Markan miracle stories by an attempt to categorize "das Wirken des irdischen Jesu" (the activity of the historical Jesus) as actually "eine Erscheinung Gottes auf Erden" (an appearance of God on earth). For this, see Ludger Schenke, *Die Wundererzählungen des Markusevangeliums*, Stuttgarter Biblische Beiträge (Stuttgart: Katholisches Bibelwerk, 1974), 393. On this type of approach in general, see Petr Pokorny, "Das Markusevangelium: Literarische und theologische Einleitung mit Forschungsbericht," *ANRW* ii/25.3 (1985), 2022.

These analyses construe theological ideas in the Markan narrative through examination of how elements of the miraculous are used. The whole Markan narrative creates a "historical framework" for the manifestation of an essentially ahistorical divine power (the ideal type, θεῖος ἀνήρ). The manifestations and the historical framework *together* create the meaning of the narrative. This analysis is similar to examinations of narratives composed by Tacitus and Plutarch about Nero and Sertorius, respectively. In this light, one could speak of Mark's theological meaning, as it derives from narratives about Jesus, as one could speak of Tacitus' meaning derived from stories about Nero or Plutarch's from accounts of Sertorius. In all three, themes of the strange and unusual inhabit narratives about known historical individuals.

78. Sigmund Freud ("The Uncanny," in *The Standard Edition of the Complete Psychological Works of Sigmund Freud*, ed. and trans. James Strachey [London: Hogarth Press, 1974], 17:241) wrote, "if psycho-analytic theory is correct in maintaining that every affect belonging to an emotional impulse, whatever its kind, is transformed, if it is repressed, into anxiety, then among instances of frightening things there must be one class in which the frightening element can be shown to be something repressed which *recurs.*" On the influence of Freudian ideas, see Lorne Dawson, "Otto and Freud on the Uncanny and Beyond," *Journal of the American Academy of Religion* 57 (1988): 283-311. I should note that psychological theory indeed can be used to create interesting, albeit precarious, interpretations about ancient historical evidence. See Leo Bersani and Ulysse Dutoit, *The Forms of Violence: Narrative in Assyrian Art and Modern Culture* (New York: Schocken Books, 1985), in which—in perhaps one of the few places in the published universe—we may find discussion about both the iconography of Ashurbanipal and the writings of the Marquis de Sade. See also René Girard (*La violence et le sacré*, Collection *Pluriel* [Paris: Éditions Grasset, 1972], who chooses to use Freud, although much of his development of a theory of envy might benefit from reference to writings of Melanie Klein. See also Julia Kristeva (*Powers of Horror: An Essay on Abjection* [New York: Columbia University Press, 1982], 118), who about Markan narratives of the feeding of multitudes suggests that "by surreptitiously mingling the theme of 'devouring' with that of 'satiating,' that narrative is a way of taming cannibalism. It invites a removal of guilt from the archaic relation to the first pre-object (abject) of need: the mother." These authors deal with themes similar to the theme of the anomalous frightful. *Pace* their brilliance, their general approach is not followed here. Their interpretations depend for the most part on modern formulations of psychological theory, and then on the systematic application of that theory to ancient texts. I prefer to assess ancient evidence about the anomalous frightful on its own terms. There may be, after all, less agreement between psychological theorists than between historians and critics of literary antiquity. On the risk of misconstruing both psychology and history and, therefore, making invalid modern psychological interpretations of ancient texts, see Martin, "Artemidorus: Dream Theory in Late Antiquity," 105-108.

79. Terry Castle, *The Female Thermometer: 18th-Century Culture and the Invention of the Uncanny* (New York: Oxford University Press, 1995).

80. Castle, *Female Thermometer*, 128. Daniel Defoe illustrates the shift underway, placing emphasis squarely on the capacities of what is identified as the imagination; see Daniel Defoe, *Roxana: The Fortunate Mistress*, ed. Jane Jack (London: Oxford University Press, 1981), 264: "but I grew sad, heavy, pensive, and melancholy; slept little, and ate little; dream'd continually of the most frightful and terrible things imaginable: Nothing but Apparitions of Devils and Monsters; falling into Gulphs, and off from steep and high Precipices, *and the like*; so that in Morning, when I shou'd rise, and be refresh'd with the Blessing of Rest, I was *Hag-ridden* with Frights, and terrible things, form'd merely in the Imagination." Terry Castle cites this text in "'Amy, Who Knew My Disease': A Psychosocial Pattern in Defoe's *Roxana*", in *Female Thermometer*, 55.

81. Gerd Gigerenzer, and others, *The Empire of Chance: How Probability Changed Science and Everyday Life*, Ideas in Context Series (Cambridge: Cambridge University Press, 1989), 1-36.

3

Not Having the Answer Is the Answer:
How to Read Mark, to See Why

Once we acknowledge that bewilderment and uncertainty are valid outcomes of reading the Gospel of Mark, then we do well to discover precisely what it is that seems bewildering or uncertain. I propose that it is possible to identify elements of Mark that either report the anomalous frightful or are intended to create in a reader the effects of the anomalous frightful. Elements in Mark that create and promote fear or uncertainty come to light when certain aspects are recognized. The manner in which stories begin and end is to be carefully noted. Apparently unfinished or interrupted story lines, strange turns of events, unexpected content, and uncanny acts are all to be identified and examined. Aside from the examination of internal traits of Mark, elements of the anomalous frightful may be most clearly identified by comparison to similar elements external to Mark, in other witnesses where use is made of like material and the anomalous frightful is also evident. Consisting of perplexing uncertainty mixed together with varying representations of fear, the anomalous frightful had a vibrant persistence in a variety of ancient contexts and literary presentations. Detecting it in the Gospel of Mark is actually not at all surprising, given these comparative facts. Reading in this way may assist with ongoing analysis of particular lexical elements and themes in the Gospel of Mark, and facilitate a better of understanding of the cultural context and a better literary interpretation. These two operations, analysis and interpretation, may be conceived as separate stages. While a proper identification of elements in a context is one thing, and tends to stem from a certain kind of work, a satisfying interpretation of them is quite often another. The anomalous frightful is uncovered through these types of operations, and when done so is seen both as a literary theme and as a type of human experience that, to one degree or another, may be triggered or rekindled in readers.

Performing these operations on stories in Mark can help to clarify two things. First, some of the specific content of Mark may be better understood as literature. Its signified objects, signifiers (symbols), evocations, and illustrations may be more clearly uncovered and described. Second, the reception and interpretation of Mark, even by its ancient audiences, may possibly be grasped more clearly. Readers are acting appropriately if, today in our own reception of Mark, we feel unsettled, ambivalent, or aghast. It is true that for the modern reader who stands at a considerable distance from the kinds of events, entities, or situations that Mark describes, such a response may not readily occur. But based on an investigation of the text in its ancient Mediterranean context, it is reasonable to conclude that ancient audiences also puzzled over Mark because they had similar responses. We can legitimately suppose that the author of Mark intends us not to feel satisfied with our reading, but instead would seek us to feel agitated, unsettled, and confused.

Most commentators do not report that their reading of the Gospel of Mark produces in them these results, or brings about in them an experience like the experience of dreaming. Even so, exposure to unusual happenings, interest piqued but not sated by narrative innuendos, mental pause over vague connections between puzzling evidence, and obfuscation of clear meaning are each experiences that dreamers and readers of Mark must negotiate. For both, attempts to discern a meaning often leave behind no consensus of interpretation. Judgment under conditions of uncertainty persists, therefore, as the formidable problem at hand. It is the problem encountered by every attempt at interpretation of Mark, as is illustrated well by the long history of variegated interpretations of this Gospel. It is the problem that a student of Mark learns to expect. But then a student might ask how this could be, and legitimately wonder if it may be possible that Mark is written to create just this type of systematic uncertainty.

How We Usually Read Mark

At first, the Gospel of Mark engages us as a set of facts. These facts are verbal, literary, and rhetorical, and they have religious, theological, and historical dimensions. The facts and their implications beckon for a rational decipherment of some type, and usually we attempt to comply.

Trained and untrained readers alike feel an urge to discern these facts. But their implications, diversely perceived by all, seem an encryption for some, a verisimilar narrative for others, or a myth for yet others. Although I cannot review even most of the literature on Mark within this space (nor should I, for fear of extinguishing my reader's good will) I do want to sort some of it out by placing it within these three domains. We should understand some of the general ways in which the Gospel of Mark has previously been conceptualized.

Encryption

Perception of Mark as an encrypted message that must be decoded has a long history, although we are more aware of it now in our postmodern context. Any allegorical reading acts as a decoding of an encryption, whether for moral or spiritual ends.[1] D. F. Strauss once attributed to Kant an interpretation of "the doctrines of the Bible and the church as symbols of the ideal," and suggested that De Wette "ascribed to the evangelical history, as to every history, and particularly to the history of religion, a symbolical, ideal character, in virtue of which it is the expression and image of the human mind and its various operations."[2] More recent decryption approaches have focused specifically on the text and theories about texts. One clear case is found in the work by Fernando Belo,[3] who presents an identification of structural oppositions in Mark (p.241), along with a narrative interpretation based on the work of Julia Kristeva and Roland Barthes.[4] From Kristeva comes the interpretation of texts as limited and limiting materializations of language ("matérialisme dialectique"). Texts are bodies, finite phenomena fabricated out of a flux of discourse or language. They should be subject primarily to something like geometry: a science of measuring or statistical weighing of their elements. They should not be subject to extratextual logic or rules of rhetoric.[5] As for Belo, structuralist oppositions within textual elements are fully outlined in his self-identified materialist ecclesiology of Mark.[6] In his narrative interpretation, Belo also borrows heavily from Roland Barthes. In the cited work by Barthes, a fictional narrative by Balzac is broken into many smaller units, each of which is numbered, assigned meaning and valence, and then read like a code. Barthes wrote that "in operational terms, the meanings I find [in reading] are established not by 'me' or by others, but by their systematic mark: there is no other proof of a reading than the quality and endurance of its systematics; in other words: than its functioning."[7] Belo identifies seventy-two narrative units in Mark through narrative markers, subsequently decoding them quite thoroughly.

George Aichele also adumbrates methods of textual de-encryption, viewing Belo's approach as fundamentally correct, although quirky and flawed. Aichele criticizes Belo as too traditional, meaning that he is too theologically oriented.[8] Aichele wants to demonstrate that our reading of a text like Mark may very well lead to uncertainty and anomalous conclusions. Actually, I think that Aichele demonstrates that our reading of most any text at all, except for perhaps the most mundane and least metaphorical, should lead us to this conclusion. Aichele hypothesizes a two-step operation ongoing in us during any event of reading: (1) when we read anything, we export onto it our own mental state or ideology, and (2) when we interpret our reading, we import back an interpretation that seems to reconfirm the meaning and value of our own exported mental state or ideology. Once we question our interpretation, we enter into an experience of defamiliarization and uncertainty. We experience the need to reread the text more carefully, to see what truly it might be offering us in its presentation. For Aichele this experience is proper. It is of higher value than our typical reading experience, which has little value because it occludes a text's real and usually strange nature. The argument is that our usual experience surreptitiously validates our own ideology in a solecistic way. This is said to be especially true of the reading of the Bible that goes on within Christian communities, which reading, Aichele generalizes, churns out bromides of tradition or theology in its somewhat unsurprising processes. Aichele suggests that "a postmodern theology of reading" should attempt "to understand the tensions between the resistance inherent in the physical aspects of a text and the ideological pressures brought to bear upon the text by its readers." For Aichele, "reading is a juggling of codes, trying to get all the meanings to work out right" (p.143). This means taking to heart those texts within Mark that comment on other parts of Mark (comments about the disciples, about the parables, or about narrative acts). These lines function as a metatextual commentary. Since these lines come bundled together with the whole Markan text, the whole taken together is best accepted as a "text reading itself," and in so doing passes off to us a certain kind of ambiguity. As is usual in this type of approach, when there is an interpretive emphasis on the linguistic tokens of texts and their inter-/intra-textuality, then there is also a tandem, interpretive emphasis on theories of fiction, narrative, and imagination (the "Fantastic"). So it is with Aichele. What seems a most plausible starting point in (subversive) acts of reading is to assume that a text does not represent any other matter than itself. Using these guidelines, it is implausible to read texts primarily in light of a hypothetical historical or cultural context proposed for and external to them. It is more plausible to read them primarily (if not only) in their own terms. These hermeneutical issues are perennial and can be found in many contemporary authors such as Erhardt Guttgemans, who argues for a linguistic and psychological approach to the texts of Scripture.[9]

I should also identify another method of deciphering an encryption. Redaction critics have long developed methods of decoding Mark, sometimes resulting in conclusions not unsimilar to those of structuralists or poststructuralists. William Wrede suggested that the mountain (τὸ ὄρος) that appears in Markan narrative settings is "an ideal mountain," one of Mark's ways to enhance his narrative with a vivid sense, and through this sense to lend literary support to the redaction of traditions about the secrecy of Jesus.[10] For another example, Johannes Schreiber concludes that the scene of the disciples rowing against the wind in Mark 6:48 is really a Markan symbol for both the disciples' misunderstanding and their disbelief, identifying the latter as a broad Markan redactional theme.[11] In regard to other material, Schreiber argues that all Hellenistic Divine Man (θεῖος ἀνήρ) elements are fully re-encoded by the Markan narrative elements of time, place, and plot. Presentation of these elements in a historical narrative fundamentally reinterprets them, as James M. Robinson has also suggested.[12] Elements of the θεῖος ἀνήρ and their placement into a historical (that is, verisimilar) narrative become encryptions of a new meaning. For Schreiber, this results partly from how the preaching of the cross in Mark consists fundamentally of eschatological ideas represented through a dramatically historical staging in time and place.[13] Eschatological ideas of God's final redemption and salvation are represented as a history, such as an event that takes place in Judea. Elsewhere on but a portion of a single verse, Schreiber squeezes out a redactional interpretation: what is most important about Mark 13:35 is the full fourfold division of night time hours signified here. He argues that this verse is a Hellenistic interpretation of events involving the Syro-Palestinian Jesus, and that the four-fold division of the night given here in Mark is specific to a Roman context. The "Lord of the House" (13:35), in code as it were, is read as an emphasis on the role of Jesus as Hellenistic Κύριος, and not as Jewish Messiah. Schrieber de-encrypts this, reading it as a Markan encryption of a Hellenistic interpretation of Jewish apocalyptic speech.[14] As noted in chapter 1, he also promotes the view that Mark's crucifixion narrative accrues "mythological language" around an initial, historical report about a paradoxical death. By decoding Mark's text, then, we might be able to discover early, apocalyptic interpretations of the crucifixion.[15]

Inevitably I do injustice to the massive literature of Markan redaction criticism by omitting so much of it from my snapshot here. I should suggest, however, that any redaction-critical interpretation that attempts to decode messages from Mark's text about its historical setting, its generating sodality, or its perspectives on cultural movements contemporary to it (that is, missionary endeavors, Gentile/Jewish conflict, Roman governing strategies) is based on an assumption that these data are encrypted in the sentences and paragraphs. Redaction criticism that argues, as Wrede did, that a proper interpretation of gospel texts begins with the detection in them of a historical progression of traditions, always works from the hypothesis that this information is in fact encoded in the text, awaiting anyone who might cleverly uncover it. Yet all must admit that there is no more certainty that a history of traditional elements can be accurately identified in Mark than there is in the claim that there is in Mark an accurate description of real events.

Verisimilar Narrative

To read Mark as a verisimilar narrative is to read Mark as a history, with an eye for detecting information that provides accurate depictions of important events. We should acknowledge that verisimilitude is crucial in a historical approach, and that verisimilitude is first and foremost a literary and rhetorical issue. We are reminded of this already in Aristotle: "We regard all knowledge as beautiful (καλός) and valuable (τίμιος), but one kind more so that another, either in virtue of its accuracy (κατ' ἀκρίβειαν), or because it relates to higher (βελτιόν) and more wonderful (θαυμασιώτερος) things."[16] Satisfaction about accuracy is important when determining the kinds of qualitites present in a narrative that seems to be an account of things past. Taylor went so far as to list narrative elements from Mark 1:1-6:56 that seem "lifelike" and therefore warrant an investigation into the veracity of the Gospel narrative that presents such accurate items. He argued that the least developed portions of Mark convey a more primitive tradition, and suggested that "in [Mark's] stories about Jesus and his miracle-stories the wealth of detail is given, not created. [Mark's] objectivity is a sign of the high historical value of the Gospel."[17] With a broader interest, this same sensitivity is also present in Wilfred Knox,[18] who interpreted Mark as one might interpret historians such as Flavius Josephus, Diodorus Siculus, or Nicolas of Damascus.

Knox made detailed observations about Mark's use of sources, confusion of these very sources, and accuracy of report, especially in relation to contemporary Mediterranean events and movements. He suggested that Mark's information about the Herodians fits a narrow period of time in Palestinian history.[19] Mark's use of πάλιν (again) in 3:9, 4:1, 8:1, and 10:32 is similar to the use of this term in historical narratives by Plutarch and Josephus.[20] The account of the death of John the Baptist in Mark may disagree with that in Josephus, but both authors on this matter struggled unsuccessfully with their sources.[21] Geographical confusion in Mark has its parallel in some narratives of Josephus, which demonstrates how easy it was for historical writers to make topographical errors.[22] These are all narrative problems that must be faced by the reader who searches for the verisimilitude of the Gospel of Mark.

Mark as verisimilar narrative became a question in the eighteenth and nineteenth centuries, when there was interest both in the history of earliest Christianity and in accurately ascertaining that history. This interest developed within discussions among comparativists of myth and religion, especially among Deists and rationalists. These discussions had roots in disputes between Protestant and Catholic scholars, and are illumined in the correspondence of Thomas Jefferson and John Adams.[23] Among the participants was Joseph Priestly, whose works on these matters include *History of the Corruptions of Christianity* (1782), *History of Early Opinions concerning Jesus Christ* (1786), and *Socrates and Jesus Compared* (1803). Priestly's work rests on a history of Unitarian and/or anti-Trinitarian dissent and scholarship, and therefore was an effort fueled by theological disputation. Earlier Gottfried Arnold developed the idea of a "fall" of the church after its earliest historical stages. C. F. Dupuis in 1795 published *Origine de tous les cultes,* presenting a theory about universal decline and decay in human religious thought, from its initial golden age in pure belief in a Universal God to its later ages of debased "mythologies and cults."[24] Almost a century later, with Edwin Hatch in 1888, comes a precedent for what we may now recognize as comparisons between Christianity and antiquity. This was focused on deliquescing early Christian use of the term μυστήριον (mystery) and suggesting that pagan Mystery Religions infiltrated primitive Christianity. In his 1880 Bampton Lectures, Hatch had already suspected pagan influence on the organization and government of the primitive church. He added his voice to a chorus of theories about how primitive Christianity progressed, in one way or another, into the different forms of its acculturated future.[25]

The search for primitive Christianity wasn't only spurred by rationalism, with its barely concealed disgust with the miraculous and its angst about Hellenic elements having perhaps polluted the primitive table of the Lord. Benz outlined how what he calls the "German Idealism" influenced European Romanticism. He quotes from Friedrich Christoph Oetinger (1702-82), a pietist, biblical theologian, and student of New Testament scholar Johannes Albrecht Bengel (1687-1752). "The spirit contains all within itself," Oetinger wrote,

> to a certain degree reason exalts the whole to the level of an abstract idea and at the time of the Golden Age one will find true to the highest degree what is, after so many false definitions, the true definition of knowledge, the true knowledge. The quintessence of divine things, the base of which is in the spirit and which then spreads into the reason. God buried it in the spirit. The seeker has with God's help to take it in to the reason. Reason must be in accord with the spirit, and the spirit by the same token must be in accord with God.[26]

Benz observes, reasonably, that this movement was influenced by Jacob Boehme, cabalistic tradition, and Reformed theologian Jean Coccejus (the latter known for the *Föderaltheologie* that was his life's work, to locate in scriptural notions of covenant and testament a most accurate representation of what is real and true). There was afoot here a theological effort to locate scriptural texts that seem to bear the highest amount of verisimilitude of what is fundamentally true. This effort led to ideas of universal history and, eventually, to grand theories of historical development.

Universal Spiritualists in America had their own ideas about the "Primitive History," or what they called the "ancient Spiritualism." Andrew Jackson Davis around 1870 agreed that the Bible came together through historical processes of canonization. Within the canonical texts, he sought to uncover the "real history of Jesus." In so doing, Davis displayed a Spiritualist sensibility about the gospel texts as he identified those that he suspected bear the highest verisimilitude to what would have been said or done by the real Jesus.[27] He demonstrated an awareness of critical theories of canonization that had been developed by another scholar, Johann Salomo Semler (1725-91), who emerged from Pietism and would eventually return to theosophy, alchemy, and freemasonry. Semler was an impeccably trained scholar, at first a teacher of Arabic and then a professor of Latin philology. He initiated a critical enterprise that approaches the Bible as a series of manuscript and theological traditions much in need of sorting out. In this enterprise, questions were raised about the reliability of documentary evidence to transmit verisimilar representation of the true nature of what scholars then hypothesized to be primitive Christianity. Some critical readers of Mark then undertook their work within the guidelines of a broader question about how historiography in general, if ever, might ascertain anything that is primitive, or *ursprünglich*. This primarily Protestant effort has sharpened awareness about methods for reading and critical assessment. Semler encouraged a "humanist" reading of the Bible, through *Hermeneutic* and *Kritik*, but distinguished that from discernment of the more primitive "Mind of Christ" in the text.[28] Christian Gottlob Wilke (1786-1854) hypothesized an oral *Urevangelium,* and suggested specifically that Mark is the *Urevangelist* whose work "was not a copy of an oral primitive gospel, but an artful composition." Wilke's efforts support a broader theory that there was, originally, a written, not oral, Gospel.[29] Franz Overbeck would later work diligently to distinguish hypothetical moments of *Ur- oder Entstehungsgeschichte* (primitive or formative history) in the *Geschichte jedes Organismus,* after having earlier concluded that between the New Testament *urchristliche* (primitive) and later *patristische* (institutional) literature there is a barrier.[30]

Throughout these theological and historiographical developments, verisimilitude plays an essential part. To each observer, something or other from the gospel traditions seems more original or more accurate, as observed within guidelines based on one rationale or another. All of these approaches accentuate the reception of the text as a verisimilar narrative, seeking to establish plausible and accurate statements about "what really happened," or perhaps, "what really *important* happened."

Myth

In applying the term "myth" to the Gospel of Mark and to the synoptic gospels, scholars mean different things. D. F. Strauss (*Life of Jesus,* §8, §102) argues that an approach to the gospel narratives as myth means they are to be interpreted as representations of a broad, pan-Mediterranean worldview. He felt confident that by his day, scriptural and pagan myths were correctly thought to stem from similar sources. Gospel narratives like the miraculous feedings are seen as ancient myths emerging in new stories. Later, Rudolf Bultmann uses the term "myth" to refer to at least two ideas. First, he compares stories about Jesus to "nature myths," such as the Babylonian myth about Marduk's battle with "the dragon of Chaos" and Greek and Roman myths about the births and destinies of kings. Second, he speaks of a "Christ myth," seen particularly manifested in the

Gospel of Mark. For Bultmann, the Christ-myth is optimally displayed in Pauline writings like Philippians 2:6-11. It is a myth that emerged in early Christian theology specifically in Hellenistic cities. In this myth, Christ is not the "historic Jesus" from Galilee and Judea, but the "Christ of faith and of the cult," an entity who takes on the generic trappings of a Hellenistic spiritual being. For Bultmann, Mark is the first occasion in which traditions about the historic Jesus merge with the Hellenistic Christ-myth.[31]

With a different content, Burton L. Mack uses the terminology of myth to explicate Mark. In his work, myth may be summarized as a set of materials overlaid on other materials in order to produce a new ideological effect. Mack argues that in Mark we witness the early development of "the fantasy of an order of things without precursor," or a "myth of the historical Jesus as the account of a divine origination." This myth includes contents of apocalyptic violence that had come to the fore in early Christian thinking, and it occludes traditions about Jesus as a simple, powerful, and challenging teacher. This latter, more primitive tradition about Jesus was usurped by a tradition that had ecclesiastical designs to control a representation of Jesus for its own ends. "Positioned as a banner of the Christian mission to the world, the Christ event [in Mark] marks the borders between those outside the fold as unenlightened and those inside as redeemed." Mack suggests that this myth is essentially racist and violent in its nature, and Mack promotes a pinched and somewhat maudlin view that Mark's theology is colonialistic and intolerant.[32]

Elizabeth Malbon's work on Markan elements of topographic, geopolitical, and architectural space is another identification of myth in Mark. Here Claude Lévi-Strauss provides an approach wherein myth "operates to mediate irreconcilable opposites by successively replacing them by opposites that do permit mediation." Mythic binary opposition is traced in Mark, starting from individual sentences that adumbrate topographic, geopolitical, and architectural phenomena. Larger literary sections are ascribed by how they represent a general shift from Galilee to Judea, or from the Desert to the Sea, or from Jewish Homelands to Foreign Homelands. Malbon suggests that, taken as a whole, these oppositions form a binary-oppositional mythic structure throughout Mark. This structure depicts a thematic movement away from the opposition between Chaos (Earth) and Order (Heaven) to a singular focal point in the Markan mythic narrative, the Way (ὁδός). Such narrative opposition is represented in Mark by use of a geopolitical opposition of Familiar *vs.* Strange, a topographical opposition of Promise *vs.* Threat, and an

architectural opposition of Profane *vs.* Sacred.[33] Malbon does not
hypothesize a binary, concentric, or chiastic *literary* structure in Mark that
corresponds to the binary *mythic* structure. Instead, from beginning to end
of Mark, there is a narrative movement that progresses from "Order *vs.*
Chaos" to "New Way." Malbon's analysis depends on the plentiful
topographic, geopolitical, and architectural indicators throughout Mark.[34]

Secrecy and Clumsiness in Mark

As such processes of trained reading have continued, interpretation that
results in confusion is typically avoided. Trained commentators can be
expected to provide a "technical reading"—erudite, accomplished,
refusing to admit defeat (that is, refusing to admit that it cannot make
enough sense of the text being read). The code is to be competently
exposed, the myth cleverly revealed, the history validated by the accuracy
of the text's verisimilitude. Technical reading aims to eliminate confusion
and to avoid an interpretation that instills uncertainty, bewilderment, or
confusion. A few interpreters have noted, however, that some uncertainty
and bewilderment in reading Mark are legitimate and even to be expected.
In their own way these interpreters have set precedents for what I seek to
do.

One outcome of uncertainty is found in analysis of Mark as a
clumsily written work. John Meagher constructs a concept of "clumsiness" in direct opposition to what he perceives as traditional tenets of
form and redaction criticism.[35] To him, the developers of these critical
methods are too satisfied with their implausible results.

First, Meagher describes the essentials that he thinks must be in
place in order for form criticism to make sense. The first essential is a
valid proposal about a set of specific and unchanging social situations, out
of which identifiable traditions emerged. These are hypothesized social
or religious environments of early religious communities that contribute
the conditions in which the tradition took form. Form criticism seeks to
develop an index by which to identify forms, and bases this index on
hypothesized social contexts. A specific type of social context contributes
the necessary if not material conditions for production of a specific type
of literary form or religious expression. In order for the index to be
reliable, the method's logic demands that there be a consistent identification of the hypothesized social contexts, otherwise the index as developed

in conjunction with these hypotheses achieves neither validity nor reliability. Meagher correlates a second essential with this first, suggesting how form criticism seeks to identify one type of form per one type of hypothesized social context. For Meagher, none of this has ever been accomplished well or with any accuracy whatsoever.

Second, Meagher determines that Mark is too inconsistent for redaction criticism to work well with it. He argues that Mark represents a genuinely oral style of production, and that the inconsistencies and "wrong-headedness" apparently present in it are the result of the author's mishandling of previous material. Meagher likens this mishandling to that of a storyteller who mixes up the punch line of a joke. In fact, he suggests that jokes are a general category of oral transmission, which category fits Mark best. Meagher discerns solecisms in Markan clumsiness, caused primarily by immature narrative skill. Very little if any of this narrative material can be used to ferret out details about earlier or later traditions, forms, or the redactor's fingerprints. A reading of Mark, then, will always, legitimately, produce bewilderment and puzzlement about its composition. Such a result can never be resolved technically. Instead, it needs to be tolerated and, to whatever extent possible, appreciated.

Meagher works methodically on the particular matter of incipience, suggesting that narrative confusion in Mark consists of four basic elements of "clumsiness"—examples of mistakes and problems that happen in any oral transmission. They are (1) informational improvidence, (2) inadvertent dislocation, (3) formal breakdown, and (4) massive misunderstanding.[36] Meagher argues that if these problems are ascertained appropriately, then a reader will be oriented properly, thereby able to make sense of the uncertain narrative phenomena in the Gospel of Mark. He suggests that "the Gospel of Mark shows evidence of a distorting clumsiness as besets the ordinary, if occasionally creatively talented, story-teller in every time and place."[37] This clumsy narrative in Mark is the primary cause of our interpretive bewilderment and uncertainty. If a commentator were to recognize this primary cause, then exegetical results would properly take it into account and include it in their conclusions. Subsequently, according to Meagher, commentators can avoid what he identifies as inappropriate results from form or redaction criticism. The story of the demonized man in a cemetery (Mark 5:1-20) can then make sense, not through a redactional unraveling of various narrative sources or traditions, but through appreciation of how the idiosyncratic emphases and the displacements of syntax within the story are mistakes made by an excited, if not somewhat befuddled, storyteller.

What is important about Meagher's work is his frank admission that reading the Gospel Mark might result in confusion and uncertainty. Confusion and uncertainty are not seen by Meagher as due *per se* to the specific types of things reported by Mark. The actual *content* of the narratives (the narrative "semantics") does not cause uncertainty here. Instead, confusion and uncertainty are created by the haphazard nature in the arrangement of the elements. In Meagher's analysis, these elements are primarily syntactical and compositional. He enables us to see that confusion and obfuscation in Mark may stem simply from the syntax of Mark's narrative.

Focusing on narrative meaning, semantics, and speech acts, Frank Kermode suggests that the Gospel of Mark creates obscurity simply because it is narrative. It is not so much that the gospel is a *Markan* narrative, as much as that it simply is *narrative*. He suggests that "we are so habituated to the myth of transparency that we continue . . . to ignore *what is written* in favor of *what is written about*."[38] While reading, we fantasize objects of reference, catapulting over narrative anomalies in order to confirm plausible meanings.

For Kermode what is held back in any narrative, anywhere, is similar to what is held back in parables. This a perspicuous insight, and also a matter that has been in literary discussion for centuries. The phenomena of riddle and parable are well attested in the ancient world. In his commentary on Proverbs, Origen discusses both παραβολή (parable) and αἴνιγμα (riddle) in order to differentiate them.[39] In doing so, he develops an early and quite sophisticated theory about narrative in Mark, especially narrative about discipleship. This was somewhat of a new development, since the two terms, παραβολή and αἴνιγμα, were not traditionally yoked together in ancient critical discussion. Ancient rhetorical use of παραβολή (or *similitude*) occurs primarily in matters of comparison, and the goal is to clarify, not to make obscure.[40] Nevertheless, stories or narrative presentations could seem like τὰ αἰνίγματα, as Origen points out, especially those stories told by Jesus in the Gospels. This kind of interpretive sensitivity, and its use as a literary conceit, is illustrated in the *Tabula of Cebes*. There, the narrator describes how his group puzzled over a πίναξ (tablet) found affixed to a shrine at a temple of Kronos. The pictorial scenes inscribed on it raise questions. A mysterious old man nearby tells them that listening to the explanation of the puzzling pictorial scenes is a dangerous experience, especially if one does not pay close attention. When asked how that could be, the old man replies, "Just this: if you pay attention (προσέξετε) and understand (συνήσετε) what is said, you will be wise and happy. If, on the other hand, you do not, you will become foolish (ἄφρονες), unhappy (κακοδαίμονες), sullen (πικροί), and stupid (ἀμαθεῖς), and you will fare badly in life."[41] Words, sentences, and stories might find no easy references. Even with clear grammar, ambiguous explanations or ambiguous utterances could plague relations with the divine. In one shining example of how murky things could be, one story has it that Jupiter grants a king's prayer, but in so responding "hides the truth in sayings dark and torturous, and alarms the man by an ambiguous utterance."[42] Given the precariousness of oral communication and the propensity for misunderstanding, sometimes silence was thought best.[43]

In reworking this theme of enigmatic riddle and its relation to the generic impact of any narrative, Kermode states that "we are programmed to prefer fulfillment to disappointment, the closed to the open" (p.64). Our reading of any narrative leads us typically to an illusion that the content of the narrative must be accessible to our simple judgment. We naturally default to an interpretive option that provides a closed and definitive conclusion for our reading. We shun uncertainty and incompleteness, and usually maintain no desire for riddles. Unless it is garbled, a narrative does not appear to us at first to hide anything. Kermode suggests that this phenomenon stems from our "habitual attitudes towards endings" (p.65). He argues that our desire for completed endings has a tendency to cause us to create ersatz endings through metaphors or synecdoches that are not actually present in the stories we are reading.[44]

In this view, uncertainty and dismay are not mistaken outcomes of reading the Gospel of Mark. As Kermode suggests, Mark's "story moves erratically, and not always forward; one thing follows another for no very evident reason. And a good deal of the story seems concerned with failure to understand the story."[45] Notably, there is a fair amount of close reading of the Gospel of Mark in Kermode, undergirding his observations. His chapter on the use of ἵνα (so that) in Mark 4:12 is crucial, explaining how in Mark the parables are meant to obscure. To this observation Kermode adds a philosophical understanding of fiction,[46] so that with both a close reading of Mark and literary theory, he confirms that interpretation of the Gospel of Mark may have a legitimate outcome of uncertainty, if not bewilderment. Indeed, an outcome of uncertainty and bewilderment is not an indication of failed critical method. Rather, it is simply the result of exposure to narrative and, Kermode stressses, exposure to the μυστήριον (mystery) that narrative always reveals while yet also hiding. The Gospel of Mark in particular provides such an experience.

As interpretive options, the work of Meagher and Kermode can be contrasted to Martin Dibelius, *Formgeschichte des Evangeliums*, where Dibelius uses Hellenistic and Jewish narrative analogies (*Paradigma, Novelle, Legende*) to clarify the meaning of synoptic narratives. He argued that the miracle stories in Mark are *Novelle,* stories about epiphanies. These stories report an "effacement of the boundary between God and the man sent by God."[47] That is to say, they report occasions in which what normally is veiled and occluded becomes revealed and clarified. This use of the category "epiphany" by Dibelius supports his basic theological hypothesis that these narratives represent a gracious and unambiguous depiction of divine power through Jesus. There is no anomaly in this depiction. The Gospel tradition reports encounters and epiphanies, and these represent clarity and immediacy. Epiphanies were complex types of manifestations that, in general, seemed "to be clear, unmistakable and distinct phenomena, concrete and sometimes even tangible."[48] For Dibelius, the *Novelle* are depictions of such tangible benefits as performed by Jesus. They are presentations about Christian hope, reported through *Heilungsberichte* about Jesus.[49] There is no indication in Dibelius that the outcome of reading the *Novelle* or *Heilungsberichte* is anything other than clear and certain conviction about salvation. Yet, in my view, unambiguous convictions about salvation or benefaction are indeed *not* the first result of reading the Gospel of Mark.

Meagher and Kermode, through emphases on syntax and semantics respectively, make room for indeterminacy. Usually readers of Mark prefer the opposite: a finished interpretation, a proper de-encryption, a clear theological statement, or a definitive explanation of the facts. It is important to complement such preferences with methods for reading Mark that allow for an outcome of uncertainty or even an awareness of the uncanny. A general conviction has developed over a time, that if words can be defined and narrative forms identified, then what the Gospel of Mark means may be ascertained. I seek to complement, if not to contradict, this long history of *quaestiones et solutiones*[50] interpretation of Mark.

Mark 4:35-6:56

So much for general approaches. In my specific approach to the Gospel of Mark, I focus especially on Mark. 4:35-6:56, which contains nine stories that represent the anomalous frightful in both of its primary aspects: unsettling uncertainty and fear. Exegetical details of how this is exactly so come later. These stories are (1) Jesus pacifies a dangerous sea (4:35-41); (2) Gerasene demoniac (5:1-20); (3) Sickness and death of a girl (5:21-24, 35-43); (4) Uterine pathology of a woman (5:25-34); (5) Rejection of Jesus at home city (6:1-6); (6) Sending of the Twelve (6:7-13, 30-31); (7) Antipas, John, and fear of retaliation because of violent death (6:14-29); (8) Five thousand men eat bread and fish (6:35-44); (9) Jesus a ghost on a dangerous sea (6:45-52). I choose these stories because I perceive them as a cycle. Not only is the anomalous frightful represented in this cycle, but the whole draws attention to itself as a unit within the Gospel. There are some specific observations that lead to this assessment.

Mark. 4:35-6:56, as a cycle, begins and ends with narratives that share common elements. The beginning story (4:35-41) and closing story (6:45-52) are the boating stories in Mark that clearly contain the aspect of danger and terror at sea. Both accounts are set in narrative time through the genitive participial construction, ὀψίας γενομένης [ἦν] ("it became late," 4:35; 6:47). Although these are not the only occasions of this genitive absolute in Mark (see 1:32; 14:17; 15:42), in this two cases the construction introduces events of danger and uncertainty in boats on the sea (θάλασσα). In both narratives the action happens at night; the second emphasizes its nighttime focus in the phrase τετάρτην φυλακὴν τῆς νυκτός (fourth watch of the night, 6:48). In both boating accounts an ἄνεμος (windstorm) rises (4:37, 39; 6:48, 51); these narratives in fact show the only use of the term ἄνεμος in Mark except for the phrase "four winds" in 13:27. When Jesus intervenes, the ἄνεμος in both narratives ceases (ἐκόπασεν; 4:39; 6:51). This unique verb, κοπάζω (cease), is found in Mark only in these two boating narratives. The combination of ἄνεμος and κοπάζω creates a correspondence between the two narratives; similar elements link the stories, articulating a unit of material, beginning and end.

The phrase εἰς τὸ πέραν (to the other side) occurs primarily in Mark only in the material between the two boating narratives (4:35; 5:1, 21; 6:45); the one exception is Mark 8:13 (following the feeding of the four thousand and a prelude to recalling the feeding of the five thousand; 8:1-10; 6:30-44). The specific phrase εἰς τὸ πλοῖον (into the boat) occurs within this material (4:37 [twice]; 5:18; 6:45, 47, 51), except for one occasion in Mark 8:10 (again, after the feeding of the four thousand). Its complementary phrase, ἐκ τοῦ πλοίου (out of the boat), occurs only in this material (5:2; 6:54).[51] These are directional markers that indicate the journeying unique to this cycle, and they contribute to this cycle a vocabulary of travel and direction.[52] The depictions of travel framed within the two boating narratives end definitely with the *hapax legomenon* of 6:53, προσωρμίσθησαν (they moored by anchor). This is not yet the end of travel in Mark, but it is a strong ending to the cycle of nautical embarkations and landings reported within and between 4:35-41 and 6:45-56. With this mooring, the cycle anchors its ending.

The term θάλασσα in the two boating stories is the location in which action takes place. The metaphorical and traditional meanings of this location, and the depths of these meanings, are most fully developed in Mark only in these two stories. Appearances of θάλασσα in other Markan passages are fairly assessed as brief narrative indications of location without any emphasis on the specific nature of that location (Mark 1:16, 2:13, 3:7, 4:1, 7:31). The narrative value of θάλασσα as geographical location in 4:1 is stressed by its use twice in the one verse. The θάλασσα in Mark 1:16 and 7:31 is locally identified as θάλασσα τῆς Γαλιλαίας. Mark 9:42 and 11:23, while not representing travel, do show θάλασσα to mean more than mere location. In these two verses, the θάλασσα is a place where things can be thoroughly buried or submerged. In 9:42, one who scandalizes would be better off sunk (cast away) in the θάλασσα. This touches upon the notion of θάλασσα as an abyss in which mortals are swallowed up. In 11:23, a person with faith can command a mountain to be submerged into the sea.

A third boating story is sometimes identified in Mark 8:13-21.[53] I distinguish this third story from the first two, since the elements of "danger at sea" and "nighttime anomalies" that are present in the two boating narratives of 4:35-41 and 6:45-56 are absent. Mark 8:13-21 is a boating narrative with different narrative elements and, indeed, with a different narrative intent. In this account, it is discovered that bread is scarce (καὶ ἐπελάθοντο λαβεῖν ἄρτους). The symbolic discussion of bread that follows in 8:15-21 is material far different from that in Mark 4:35-41 and 6:45-56. Instead of emphases on terror or danger at sea, we find here an anagogic discourse about ἄρτος (bread). The mention of the disciples' misunderstanding about bread in 6:52 seems to stand alone and is not developed as it is in chapter 8.

The symmetry between the two boating narratives draws attention to itself as a symmetry, and therefore to the material contained between the stories. Comparison to the manner in which Matthew and Luke use these materials is most enlightening, and one sees an organization of materials unique to Mark that creates a thematic consistency. In the synoptic parallels there is no hint of such a like symmetry, with beginning and

82 Chapter 3

ending having similar color and elements. In the materials that are synoptically parallel in Matthew, there are absolutely no suggestions of narrative symmetry. Matthew's use of this material is so different—in ellipses, in wording, and in organization—that its difference commands attention to what is unique to Mark. Compared to Matthew, material synoptically parallel in Luke shows more congruence with the Markan arrangement, but major compositional differences remain. Luke's account of Jesus in his πατρίς (fatherland) is very much longer, contains very different content, and is placed very far forward within the whole Jesus narrative (Luke 4). Luke omits the second boating narrative and gives only the briefest of accounts about John the Baptist's death (Luke's three verses [9:7-9] compared to Mark's sixteen [6:14-29]). What is noteworthy are the different orders found in the other synoptic gospels, as well as the differences in number of verses used for the various narrative vignettes; an able student can see these distinctions clearly in a Greek synopsis of the Gospels.

Within two Greek manuscript traditions of Mark, there is capitulation of paragraphs at the end of Mark 4:34 and the beginning of Mark 7:1.[54] This is an indication that identification of Mark 4:35-6:56 as a cycle may be further supported by the way the cycle is articulated from material before and after it. Mark 4:34 ends a lengthy and noticeably well-crafted section on parables and their interpretation,[55] a section with an emphasis on λόγος (word) (Mark 4:14, 15, 16, 17, 18, 19, 20, 33). Neither this term nor its ramifications occur in 4:35-6:56. It is likely that chapter 4 is preceded by yet another well-crafted composition.[56] These self-contained units alert a reader's attention to the sense of beginning fashioned by the first boating story. After the second boating story, the narrative moves on, as Mark 7:1 begins with a new set of actors (οἱ φαρισαῖοι καὶ τινες τῶν γραμματέων). The events reported here are very different from those of 4:35-6:56, with an entirely new focus introduced around the theme of παράδοσις (tradition) (Mark 7:3, 5, 8, 9, 13). There is here a very nice symmetry surrounding the cycle of 4:35-6:56, with one pole being λόγος (word) and the other παράδοσις (tradition). Observations by another commentator about Mark 7, that it consists of two major sections (7:1-13 and 7:14-23), also lend support to my argument that there is a compositional distinction between Mark 4:35-6:56 and what follows.[57] I believe I am further supported by distinctions in syntax. The parentheses that C. H. Turner identifies in Mark appear frequently only after 6:56, especially in Mark 7.[58]

Articulation from material fore and aft can be seen in other aspects.

Narrative use of Scripture, or stories about the interpretation of Scripture, cease from just before 4:35 (Mark 4:32 alludes to Psalm 103:12) until after 6:56 (Mark 7:6 cites Isaiah 29:13, Mark 7:10a cites Exodus 20:12 [Deuteronomy 5:16], and Mark 7:10b cites Exodus 21:16). The Markan term ὁδός (way) appears trivially in 6:8, gaining its more strategic, deliberate, and thematic use only later (in the phrase ἐν τῇ ὁδῷ [on the road] in 8:27, 9:33, and 10:52). The Markan verb ἀκολουθεῖν [to follow] appears only once in the cycle (6:1), again trivially, without the thematic emphasis that it has before and after the cycle. The narratives following 4:35-6:56 report healing miracles of Jesus that have a very different emphasis on cures of perceptual faculties (deafness in 7:31-37 and 9:14-29; dumbness in 7:31-37; cf. 9:14-29; blindness in 8:22-26 and 10:46-52).[59] These types of miracles are different in content from those in the cycle (two stories about the θάλασσα (ocean); a platoon of demons; a child's death and woman's hemorrhaging). The Greek of 4:35-6:56 does not employ what Pryke identifies as redundant participles, in which Mark indulges elsewhere.[60] The nine narratives in this cycle contain no rhetorical chreiai like those identified elsewhere in Mark by such investigators as James R. Butts, Vernon K. Robbins, and Burton L. Mack.[61]

The term θεός (god) does not appear at all in the boating-narrative cycle, except on two occasions. The first is the benaming of Jesus, by demonic acclamation, "the son of θεός the highest." The second is in the same verse, a binding adjuration against Jesus, done in the name of θεός (Mark 5:7). Consonant with the general absence of this term is the absence of the term βασιλεία (kingdom). In the cycle, there is no reference at all to the βασιλεία τοῦ θεοῦ (kingdom of God), something frequently mentioned in the rest of Mark both before and after.[62] The designation ὁ υἱὸς τοῦ ἀνθρώπου (son of man) also is missing.[63] The term σημεῖον (sign) occurs not at all in the cycle, and its absence is perhaps most important from the point of view of the kinds of events reported in the nine narratives. Appearing to be displays in an arena of divine power, the events are never identified as "signs" of anything in particular. Elsewhere in Mark, similar displays are indeed so described (8:11-12; 13:4, 22). Mark's abundant use of πάλιν (again), in the manner discussed by David Peabody as a "chief redactional element," is evident in this cycle in 5:21, but there quite disputed.[64] The *absence* of this redactional feature calls attention to the distinct style of 4:35-6:56.[65]

In Mark the principal encounter with demonic forces (δαίμονες) occurs in this cycle (5:1-20), including use of the verb δαιμονίζεσθαι (to

demonize), used only once previously in a brief, summary statement
(Mark 1:32). The largest Marcan narrative in which Jesus does not appear
occurs here (6:14-29), an account at some length of John the Baptist and
Antipas. Use of the terms εὐκαιρεῖν (to have opportunity; 6:31) and
εὔκαιρος (opportunity; 6:21) uniquely tie together narratives about
Antipas and the feeding of the five thousand. The later feeding of the four
thousand (Mark 8:1-9) is not framed into its context with a key term
linking it to another story. In Mark 4:35-6:56 are found the only examples
in Mark of time-keeping at night that use the substantive νύξ (night) (διὰ
παντὸς νυκτός [through the night] in 5:5 and τετάρτην φυλακὴν τῆς
νυκτός [fourth watch of the night] in 6:48), indicating an emphasis on
night. Here, the travels of Jesus and the disciples are emphasized as taking
place in a κύκλῳ (circle, 6:6, 36). The places in the circle (πόλεις and
κώμας [cities and towns]) are described in the plural forms only in this
material (6:6, 33, 36, 53, 56), with the one exception being the occurrence
of κώμας in 8:27. Finally—and significantly—Mark uses the substantive
φόβος (fear) only in this cycle (4:41).

Certainly Uncertain, Clearly Confused

By examining this cycle for its concerted representations of the anomalous frightful, I am not attempting especially to decode it, nor to explain
it as a true picture, nor to read it as a myth. I am promoting a much
narrower goal. The information contained in these narratives, when
received with appropriate sensitivity after having been attuned to its
cultural and historical context, legitimately leads to bewilderment and
uncertainty, both of which are valid outcomes of reading. This is not so
because the Markan stories are incipient, and this is not so because, *qua*
narratives, the Markan stories occlude and engender ambiguity. This is so
because some people, places, and things, when written about in certain
kinds of ways, are strange and anomalous. I think this to be a semantic
problem and not a syntactic problem. Even if the Markan narrative is not
scintillating Greek prose, it still performs well in getting across what is
necessary to represent the anomalous frightful. I shall argue that the
narrative materials in Mark 4:35-6:56 are so semantically robust that they
easily entangle the properly sensitized reader in the dimensions of
anomaly, fear, indeterminacy, perplexity, uncanniness, uncertainty,
ghastliness, gloom, hopelessness, revenge, terror, impurity, and violence.

The cycle is verily put together so that these dimensions rain down upon the reader. It is worthwhile to get drenched by them.

Certainly, it would be unfortunate for a reader, after such an entanglement and sousing, to take away from this only a trivial, formulaic idea about tradition or a fatuous deliquescence of a hypothetical moment in history, when one thing or another may or may not have happened according to someone's opinion. I believe that both of these conclusions desiccate that which is really being brought to the fore in Mark, and I believe that those who tend to settle for these conclusions probably have another think coming. In the cycle of Mark 4:35-6:56, so many signals are sent about the anomalous frightful that we must respond to them or we shall risk not getting the message. If this text cannot engage our imagination about the anomalous frightful, when that is exactly what it seems to want to do, then anything else we have to say about it will be pallid. If we cannot find the sense of the words and vignettes in Mark, then we will not likely be able to put much breath into a plausible meaning for them.

Notes

1. Beryl Smalley ("The Spiritual Exposition," in *The Study of the Bible in the Middle Ages* [South Bend, Ind.: University of Notre Dame Press, 1964], 242-63) translates from the opening of the *Historia Scholastica*: "Holy Scripture is God's dining room, where the guests are made soberly drunk. . . . History is the foundation . . . allegory the wall . . . tropology the roof" (Migne *Patrologia Latina* 198.1053).

2. David Friedrich Strauss, *The Life of Jesus Critically Examined*, trans. George Eliot (Philadelphia: Fortress Press, 1972 [1835]), 774-75.

3. Fernando Belo, *A Materialist Reading of the Gospel of Mark*, trans. Matthew J. O'Connell (Maryknoll, N.Y.: Orbis Books, 1981).

4. Julia Kristeva, Σημειωτική: *Recherches pour une sémanalyse* (Paris: Éditions du Seuil, 1969) and Roland Barthes, *S/Z*, trans. Richard Miller (New York: Hill and Wang, 1974).

5. According to Kristeva, Σημειωτική, 21, "cette science se construit comme une critique du sens, de ses éléments et ses lois-comme une *sémanalyse*."

6. Belo, *Materialist Reading*, 241. Oppositions include use-value/exchange-value; poor/rich; loaves/bodies; God/money; gift/debt; masters/servants; adults/children; closed-circle/exodus; crowd/disciples; scribes/disciples.

7. Barthes, *S/Z*, 11. These methods have analogues in the "Chicago School," and from that school R. S. Crane ("Introduction," in *Critics and Criticism: Ancient and Modern* [Chicago: University of Chicago Press, 1952], 13) writes,

"These are, stated generally, the problems that face us whenever we reflect on the undeniable fact that what a poet does *distinctly as a poet* is not to express himself or his age or to resolve psychological or moral difficulties or to communicate a vision of the world or to provide entertainment or to use words in such-and-such ways, and so on—though all these may be involved in what he does—but rather, by means of his art, to build materials of language and experience into wholes of various kinds to which, as we experience them, we tend to attribute final rather than merely instrumental value." A more complete exposition of an Aristotelian approach is found in Richard McKeon's essay, "Rhetoric and Poetic in the Philosophy of Aristotle," originally published in 1962 and now included in *Selected Writings of Richard McKeon* 1: *Philosophy, Science, and Culture*, ed. by Z. K. McKeon and W. Swenson (Chicago: University of Chicago Press, 1998), 137-64. I should note that, in the end, there may not be much difference between analysis that searches for "functioning" of an encryption and analysis that searches for "final causes" of a ποιητική (poetic art).

8. George Aichele (*Jesus Framed* [London: Routledge, 1996], 136-40) reviews Belo.

9. On ancient arguments about how poetry (and by extension, any language) makes sense, see Philip De Lacy, "Stoic Views of Poetry," *American Journal of Philology* 69 (1948): 241-71; Claude Imbert, "Stoic Logic and Alexandrian Poetics," in *Doubt and Dogmatism*, ed. J. Barnes (Oxford: Clarendon Press, 1980), pp.182-216; and James Porter, "Content and Form in Philodemus: The History of Evasion," in *Philodemus and Poetry: Poetic Theory and Practice in Lucretius, Philodemus, and Horace*, ed. Dirk Obink (New York: Oxford University Press, 1995), 97-147. Ancient discussions are precursors to contemporary discussions, and revolve around the terms λέξις, φαντασία, and διανόημα (word form, images conjured up by word, word meaning). They entertain such ideas as whether poetry makes sense primarily because of the sound of the words, because of the word arrangement, or because of the moral and philosophical inferences construed through the words. See especially Christopher Shields, "The Truth Evaluability of Stoic *Phantasiai*: *Adversus Mathematicos* VII 242-46," *Journal of the History of Philosophy* 31 (July 1993): 325-47. See Erhardt Güttgemanns, *Candid Questions Concerning Gospel Form Criticism: A Methodological Sketch of the Fundamental Problematics of Form and Redaction Criticism*, trans. William G. Doty, Pittsburgh Theological Monograph Series 26 (Pittsburgh: Pickwick Press, 1979 [1970]). Güttgemanns suggests (p. 245) that "we never encounter 'presentations' directly in texts, but only in each case by means of the medium of a linguistic phenomenon, in the gestalt of the words shaped by the linguistic structure (*langue*) of the genres." A more complete theory is worked out later in his *Fragmenta semiotico-hermeneutica: Eine Texthermeneutik für den Umgang mit der Hl. Schrift*, Forum Theologicae Linguisticae: Interdisziplinäre Schriftenreihe für Theologie und Linguistik, Bd. 9 (Bonn: Linguistica Biblica, 1983), especially chapter 7. Here Güttgemanns ultimately recommends turning to Jacques Lacan for development of the sense of a "third world" of *Bedeutung* and *Sinn*, a world existing between the *Welt der Körper* and

Welt des Sprechens. I am not so convinced as Güttgemanns that a turn to psychoanalytic theory will help our interpretive situation.

10. William Wrede, *The Messianic Secret*, trans. J. Grieg (Cambridge: James Clarke, 1971[1901]), 136.

11. Johannes Schreiber, *Theologie des Vertrauens: Eine redaktionsgeschichtliche Untersuchung der Markusevangeliums* (Hamburg: Furche-Verlag H. Rennebach, 1967), 97.

12. Schreiber, *Theologie des Vertrauens*, 89. See James M. Robinson (*The Problem of History in Mark*, Studies in Biblical Theology 21 [London: SCM Press, 1957], 34), who suggests that "the struggles between demoniacs and the Son of God are sufficiently historical in tone to serve as a bridge between the passages with predominantly cosmic language and the narratives where the language remains more completely within immanent categories of human debate and conflict."

13. Schreiber, *Theologie des Vertrauens*, 89.

14. Schreiber, *Theologie des Vertrauens*, 93.

15. Schreiber, *Theologie des Vertrauens*, 170, 244.

16. Aristotle *On the Soul* 1.1, trans. W. S. Hett, Loeb Classical Library (London, 1964).

17. Vincent Taylor, *The Gospel According to St. Mark: The Greek Text with Introduction, Notes, and Indexes* (London: Macmillan, 1957), 135-39.

18. Wilfred Knox, *The Sources of the Synoptic Gospels* 1: *St. Mark*, ed. Henry Chadwick. (Cambridge: Cambridge University Press, 1953).

19. Knox (*Sources of the Synoptic Gospels* 1:10) wrote, "There was never any serious question of using the Herodian dynasty to solve the problem of Palestine after the death of Herod Agrippa in A.D. 44. In practice 'Herodians', i.e. a body of Jewish opinion which seriously regarded the rule of the Herodian dynasty as the best solution of the Jewish problem, can hardly have been a factor in Jewish life after the time of Herod Agrippa, when it still seemed possible that the Roman government might reconstitute the kingdom of the Herod the Great. We are thus dealing with a tradition, which dates from the period between the deposition of Archelaus by Augustus in A.D. 6 and the death of Agrippa in A.D. 44, and reflects a period of history which had ceased to mean anything to the Church by the time when Matthew and Luke were compiled."

20. Knox (*Sources of the Synoptic Gospels* 1:19) wrote, "[see] Plutarch, *Alexander* 32 (684A) and 33 (685A), where Parmenio's second appeal for help at Gaugamla (πάλιν) is due to the fact that here Plutarch or his source has conflated Callisthenes' account with another and made nonsense of the whole affair (cf. Tarn, *Alexander the Great* ii,182f.) So in Josephus *Antiquities* xiv, 34 and 37 we read of Pompey's advance from Damascus into Palestine in 63 B.C. and Aristobulus' gift of a golden vine (from Strabo). At 37 ambassadors come 'again' (πάλιν), Antipater on behalf of Hyrcanus, Nicodemus on behalf of Aristobulus. But this is simply Nicolas of Damascus' account of the same incident disguised by πάλιν."

21. Knox, (*Sources of the Synoptic Gospels* 1:50) wrote, "The death of the baptist is presumably a piece of popular rumour, which may or may not be reliable but is not part of the Gospel tradition proper, in the sense that it does not come from the disciples; nor does it even profess to come from the disciples of John. It may or may not have reached Mark in a written or fixed oral form. The doubts cast on its reliability seem to rest on rather uncertain reasoning. It is objected that the story is inconsistent with the version of Josephus. This is true enough, but Josephus at this point is at his most unreliable, and his account of the Baptist's teaching is ludicrous: 'He commanded them to practise virtue and to behave with justice to one another and with piety towards God and so to come together in baptism. For so their baptism would be acceptable to God, if they made use of it not to secure pardon for their sins, but for the purification of the body if the soul had first been cleansed by righteousness' (*Ani.* xviii,117)."

22. Knox (*Sources of the Synoptic Gospels* 1:45) wrote geographical notices on Mark 6:32-47: "for a similar kind of [geographical] mistake, cf. Josephus, *BJ* iii.29ff, where Agrippa joins Vespasian on his march against the Jews at Antioch, although his forces are already engaged in coping with raids from Galilee (*Vita* 398); it appears, however, from *Vita* 407 that he really joined him on his march from Antioch to Tyre. But in *BJ* Josephus omits the section of his source which deals with the march from Antioch to Tyre and so takes Agrippa north to Antioch."

23. Jonathan Z. Smith, *Divine Drudgery: On the Comparisons of Early Christianities and the Religions of Late Antiquity* (Chicago: University of Chicago Press, 1990), 1-35. An index of the descriptions used by Joseph Priestly to articulate his view about how primitive Christianity was usurped by heathen forces appears on pages 9-11.

24. Smith, *Divine Drudgery*, 29-30.

25. See Graydon F. Snyder, *Inculturation of the Jesus Tradition: The Impact of Jesus on Jewish and Roman Cultures* (Harrisburg, Pa.: Trinity Press International, 1999), 57-87 for the history now made elegantly accessible. From the Tübingen School to the Jesus Seminar, hunches and guesses have riddled the work of attempting to establish what evidence might either itself be chronologically earliest, or what evidence testifies to earliest phenomena and occurrences.

26. Ernst Benz, *The Mystical Sources of German Romantic Philosophy*, trans. Blair R. Reynolds and Eunice M. Paul, Pittsburgh Theological Monographs new series 6 (Allison Park, Pa.: Pickwick Publications, 1983), 40; quoting Oetinger *Sammtl. Schriften* 6:141. Oetinger was a true biblical scholar whose publications include the *Biblische Wörterbuch*.

27. Ann Taves, *Fits, Trances, and Visions: Experiencing Religion and Explaining Experience from Wesley to James* (Princeton, N.J.: Princeton University Press, 1999), 181-86.

28. See Stefan Alkier, *Urchristentum: Zur Geschichte und Theologie einer exegetischen Disziplin*, Beiträge zur historischen Theologie 83 (Tübingen, Germany: J. C. B. Mohr, 1993), 26, 33. The broad discussion in Alkier ranges over Vico, Voltaire, Hume, Gibbon, and Reimarus, and lands squarely on Lessing

and Kant. See also Arnaldo Momigliano, "New Paths of Classicism in the Nineteenth Century," in *Studies on Modern Scholarship*, ed. by Glenn Bowersock and T. J. Cornell (Berkeley: University of California Press, 1994 [1982]), 223-85, especially for discussion about Uesner's work on Christian hagiography and sacred calendars (and pagan influences thought to stand behind them), and for discussion about Julius Wellhausen, Eduard Schwartz, and Ulrich Wilamowitz and their theories about the more primitive (that is, "truer") human religion and culture. This often turns out to have been an imagined ancient scenario quite congruent with the scholars' personal political beliefs and their place in their own society.

29. See Christian Gottlob Wilke, *Der Urevangelist oder exegetisch kritische Untersuchung über das Verwandtschaftsverhältniss der drei ersten Evangelien* (Dresden: Gerhard Fleischer, 1838); "Ist nicht die Kopie eines mündlichen Urevangeliums, sondern es ist künstliche Komposition," as cited in Güttgemanns, *fragmenta semiotico-hermeneutica*, 224. See also criticism contemporary with these positions in *A History and Critique of the Origin of the Marcan Hypothesis 1835-1866: A Contemporary Report Rediscovered: A Translation with Introduction and Notes of* Geschiedenis en Critiek der Marchushypothese *(History and Critique of the Marcan Hypothesis) by Hajo Uden Meijboom, 1866*, ed. and trans. John Kiwiet, New Gospel Studies 8 (Macon, Ga.: Mercer University Press, 1993), 20.

30. For the historiography, see Franz Overbeck, *Christentum und Kultur: Gedanken und Anmerkungen zur modernen Theologie* (Basel, Switzerland: Benno Schwabe, 1919; repr. Darmstadt: Wissenschaftliche Buchgesellschaft, 1968), 21. On the New Testament, see Franz Overbeck, *Über die Anfänge der patristischen Literatur* (Basel, Switzerland: Benno Schwabe, n.d.), 24 (originally published in *Historischen Zeitschrift* 48 [1882]: 417-72).

31. Rudolf Bultmann, *History of the Synoptic Tradition*, 2d rev. ed., trans. John Marsh (Oxford: Basil Blackwell, 1963), 253, 293, 306, 370.

32. Burton L. Mack, *A Myth of Innocence: Mark and Christian Origins* (Philadelphia: Fortress Press, 1988), 9, 24, 367.

33. Elizabeth Struthers Malbon, *Narrative Space and Mythic Meaning in Mark* (San Francisco: Harper & Row, 1986), 2-3, 155.

34. Whether these, taken together, reflect a "mythic" structure or simply a florid use of indicators, which provide setting, time, motivation, or circumstances of the activities of Jesus, is quite debatable. Malbon's own sensitivity to the metaphorical possibilities of geography is reminiscent of the same sensitivities readily seen in the ancient mosaic map of the church in Madaba. See Michael Avi-Yonah, *The Madaba Mosaic Map, With Introduction and Commentary*. (Jerusalem: Israel Exploration Society, 1956) and Herbert Donner and Heinz Cüppers, *Die Mosaikkarte von Madeba, 1: Tafelband*, Abhandlungen des Deutschen Palästinavereins (Wiesbaden: Otto Harrassowitz, 1977). In that mosaic, many place names (some still extant at that time and some already extinct) and place shapes are exhibited in a symmetrical, mythic pattern around Jerusalem, all in clear mythic opposition to Egypt. For geography that is meant to display

particular themes and theological notions in Scripture, see Amos Frisch, "Jerusalem and Its Parallels: Five Cities with Jerusalem in the Bible," *Abr-Nahrain* 32 (1994): 80-95. In a mosaic from Gerasa from roughly the same period (sixth century C.E.), similar traits are present. See Carl Hermann Kraeling, *Gerasa: City of the Decapolis: An Account Embodying the Record of a Joint Excavation Conducted by Yale University and the British School of Archaeology in Jerusalem (1928-1930), and Yale University and the American Schools of Oriental Research (1930-1931, 1933-1934)* (New Haven, Conn.: American Schools of Oriental Research, 1938), 341-45. In this case, the traits are orientation, landscape styles, and the depictions of walled cities. Each city is symbolically represented in a manner already developed on the Column of Trajan, 133 C.E.. It is debatable as to whether it is the author of Mark who is such a "mythic cartographer" (the Gospel-writer as the "mythic cartographer") or Malbon (the exegete as she who paints the "mythic landscape").

35. John C. Meagher, *Clumsy Construction in Mark's Gospel: A Critique of Form- and Redaktionsgeschichte*, Toronto Studies in Theology 3 (New York: Edwin Mellen Press, 1979).

36. Meagher, *Clumsy Construction in Mark's Gospel*, 7-11. Meagher explains four categories of faulty narrative: (1) *Informational improvidence.* Stories need a context in order to make clear their thrust. Context is vital for any use of double-meanings, irony, or humor. Meagher suggests that a "failure to provide [context] may change the character, effect, and even intelligibility of the tale" (p.7), a failure that Meagher calls "Informational improvidence." (2) *Inadvertent dislocation* occurs when storytelling attempts to provide a necessary background for the story context, but provides it wrongly. "Many elements of many stories are highly adjustable, and the story will work equally well if something in the same category is substituted for the item originally used. . . . But what seems superficially like a satisfactorily near equivalent to the original will not always do" (p.8). (3) *Formal breakdown.* In stories, punch lines may lose their effectiveness if "uncertain or careless or inattentive memory reproduces them with even the slightest change" (p.9). (4) *Massive misunderstanding* derives "not from omission or mismanagement of information, nor from distortion of indispensable formal structures (large or small), but from a global failure of the teller to grasp the main import of the tale" (p.11).

37. Meagher, *Clumsy Construction in Mark's Gospel*, 29.

38. Frank Kermode, *The Genesis of Secrecy: On the Interpretation of Narrative*, Charles Eliot Norton Lectures 1977-1978 (Cambridge, Mass.: Harvard University Press, 1979), 118-19.

39. Origen *Commentarius in Proverbia Salomonis* 1:6, ed. C. H. E. Lommatzsch, *Origenis Opera Omnia* (Berlin: Haude et Spener, 1841), 13:219-34. A parable is a story about something that had come about. Yet it is not just a story; it is a narrative "of power," because of its rhetorical expressiveness (μὴ γενομένου μὲν κατὰ τὸ ῥητὸν, δυναμένου δὲ γενέσθαι, τροπικῶς δηλωτικὸς πραγμάτων ἐκ μεταλήψεως τῶν ἐν τῇ παραβολῇ λελεγμένων [a figurative verbal illustration of events, communicated by things spoken in parables, happens not just because of

what is stated, but because of the *power* of what is stated]). When speaking "outside the house" to the crowds, Jesus speaks αἰνίγματα (riddles), "because the crowds and the ones outside are not much different from the waves of the sea and the blowing salt spray itself." Trying to distinguish between obscure representations was an ancient intellectual task. Clement of Alexandria (*Stromata* 5.4. 20/3-5.4.21/3) reports that Egyptian hieroglyphic writing could be read as συμβολική (symbolical), and in three ways: κατὰ μίμησιν (mimetically), ὥσπερ τροπικῶς (metaphorically), or κατά τινας αἰνιγμούς (as a type of riddle). Pieter Willem Van der Horst (*Chaeremon: Egyptian Priest and Stoic Philosopher: The Fragments Collected and Translated with Explanatory Notes*, Études prélimiaires aux religions orientales dans l'empire romain. 101 [Leiden, The Netherlands: E. J. Brill, 1984], 69 n.1) is prepared to guess that this information stems from the book *Hieroglyphica* written by Chaeremon, and so perhaps may be indicative of a well-developed philosophical, critical theory about strange and obscure letters or texts.

40. Marsh H. McCall Jr., *Ancient Rhetorical Theories of Simile and Comparison*, Loeb Classical Monographs (Cambridge, Mass.: Harvard University Press, 1969). The discussions about παραβολή (parable) and related figures of speech persist over wide areas of the Hellenistic, Roman, and Byzantine worlds.

41. *Tabula of Cebes* 3, trans. and ed. John T. Fitzgerald and L. Michael White, *The Tabula of Cebes*, Texts and Translations 24: Graeco-Roman Religion Series 7 (Chico, Calif.: Scholars Press, 1983).

42. *Verum ambage remota abdidit et dubio terruit ore virum*, from Ovid, *Fasti* 3.337-338, trans. James G. Frazer, *Ovid's Fasti*, Loeb Classical Library (Cambridge, Mass.: Harvard University Press, 1951), 145.

43. Luther H. Martin ("Secrecy in Hellenistic Religious Communities," in *Secrecy and Concealment: Studies in the History of Mediterranean and Near Eastern Religions*, ed. Hans G. Kippenberg and Guy S. Stroumsa, Studies in the History of Religions [*Numen* Book Series] 75 [Leiden, The Netheralnds: E. J. Brill, 1995], 112) writes about a Hellenic "culture of mystery," with an emphasis on keeping the mystery secret by not speaking about it, along with which comes a notion of pedagogic silence (σιωπή); compare Epictetus 2.14.1 (style of teaching involved a "falling into silence"); Philo, *De vita contemplative* 76 (Therapeutae were silent as they received instruction); Lucian *Vitarum auctio* 3: Pythagoreans on learning in silence (Pythagoras' five-year period of silence for novitiates). According to Martin, "the Hellenistic culture of silence was taken up by early Christians into their own pedagogical practices as well. 'Be quiet [*hēsuchios*],' catechumens are instructed in the *Didache*, 'ever fearing the words you have heard' (Didache 3.8 with parallel in Barnabas 19:4). And, in the admonition of Ignatius, 'It is better to be silent [*soōpan*] than to talk' (Ign. *Eph.* 15:1), for it is in the *hēsuchia theou* that *mystēria* are wrought (Ign. *Eph.* 19:1; see also Hipp. *Ref.* 1 proem)."

44. Kermode, *Genesis of Secrecy*, 64, 65.

45. Kermode, *Genesis of Secrecy*, 69.

46. Kermode, *Genesis of Secrecy*, 160 n.23 referring to John Searle, "The Logical Status of Fictional Discourse," in *Expression and Meaning* (Cambridge: Cambridge University Press, 1979), 58-75. I should also recommend René Wellek and Austin Warren, "The Mode of Existence of a Literary Work of Art," in *Theory of Literature*, new rev. ed. (San Diego: Harcourt, 1975), 142-57. The *objet d'art* exists only within an interpretive collusion of an observer with the material remains (written, acoustic, plastic) of the piece. These objects have no beginnings and no ends.

47. Martin Dibelius, *Die Formgeschichte des Evangeliums*, 6th ed. (rev. 3d ed.), ed. Günther Bornkamm (Tübingen, Germany: J. C. B. Mohr, 1971), 130, 93.

48. H. S. Versnel, "What Did Ancient Man See When He Saw a God? Some Reflections on Greco-Roman Epiphany," in *Effigies Dei: Essays on the History of Religions*, ed. Dirk Van der Plas, Studies in the History of Religions (Supplements to *Numen*) 51 (Leiden, The Netherlands: E. J. Brill, 1987), 47.

49. Dibelius, *Formgeschichte*, 96.

50. Compare this to a curious parallel from the *Ad Herrenium* 16.23 on the trope *ratiocinatio*. Through it we "ask ourselves the reason for statements made, and seek the meaning for each successive affirmation." Eusebius' *Quaestionum evangelicarum libro* is one of the earliest examples of this kind of commentary, showing philological and theological acumen put to work in problem solving. The text of Eusebius is found in *Patrologia Graeca* 22 and stems from a variety of manuscripts and catenae traditions, which one hopes are not as dubious as at first glance they seem.

51. This observation is also supported by another reader using method quite different from mine. In Paul L. Danove (*The End of Mark's Story: A Methodological Study*, Biblical Interpretation Series 3 [Leiden, The Netherlands: E. J. Brill], 249-50) the theme πλοῖον is matched with the place referent εἰς τὸ πέραν only in these two accounts, Mark 4:35-41 and 6:45-52. I take this observation to show these two narratives are uniquely paired. It should be noted that Danove also illuminates the two feeding stories in Mark. In the first feeding story Danove identifies the themes as (1) φάγω (eat), (2) πέντε ἄρτοι (five loaves), (3) δύο ἰχθύες (two fish), and identifies the place referent as εἰς ἔρημον τόπον (into a wilderness area). For the second feeding he identifies the themes as (1) φάγω (eat) and χορτάζω (sate), and concludes there is no place referent. That is, the first feeding story, which occurs within the cycle I've identified, presents itself *emphatically* with a specific geographic/place referent, the specificity of which is instrumental to me in order to show how this cycle develops the anomalous frightful.

52. Roy D. Kotansky ("Jesus and Heracles in Cádiz [τὰ Γάδειρα]: Death, Myth, and Monsters at the 'Straits of Gibraltar' [Mark 4:35-5:43]" in *The Bible and Culture: Ancient and Modern Perspectives*, ed. Adela Yarbro Collins, SBL Symposium Series [Atlanta, Ga.: Scholars Press, 1998], 173) suggests that τὸ πέραν signifies the "known boundaries of the cosmos" and refers to the explication of this idea in James S. Romm, *The Edges of the Earth in Ancient Thought* (Princeton, N.J.: Princeton University Press, 1992), 9-44. The phrase τὸ πέραν

is taken as a reference to Lands Beyond ᾿Ωκεανός, bringing to mind myths of Helios setting "beyond it" (compare *Odyssey* 10.19, with Helios sailing around the outer River of Ocean, or "beyond it"). Odysseus (*Odyssey* 24) sails beyond Ocean, into the Land of the Dead, past meadows, where dwell phantoms. Kotanksy develops an argument that εἰς τὸν πέραν originally in the pre-Markan sources means "to the other side" in these very terms, about a fabulous geography of western journeys to fantastical lands across the frontier of the θάλασσα (τὸ πέραν). The geographical traditions for describing the world and its boundaries, of course, changed over time. They are likely already traditional in Homer and Theognis. See Richard Sacks, *The Traditional Phrase in Homer: Two Studies in Form, Meaning and Interpretation*, Columbia Studies in the Classical Tradition, 14 (Leiden, The Netherlands: E. J. Brill, 1987), 33-43 for phrase ἐπ᾿ ἀπείρονα πόντον (over a boundless sea) and ἐπ᾿ ἀπείρονα γαῖαν (over a boundless land). The cycle of narrative materials that I have identified does indeed contain a vocabulary of travel that is substantially different from vocabulary found in the rest of Mark.

53. Eduard Meyer, *Ursprung und Anfänge des Christentums* 1: *Die Evangelien*, 5th ed. (Stuttgart: J. G. Cotta'sche Buchhandlung Nachfolger, 1962), 130; Adela Yarbro Collins, "Mysteries in the Gospel of Mark," in *Mighty Minorities? Minorities in Early Christianity—Positions and Strategies: Essays in Honour of Jacob Jervell on His 70th Birthday*, ed. by D. Hellholm; H. Moxnes; T. Seim (Oslo: Scandinavian University Press, 1995), 15 ("the third boat scene in chapter eight"); Robert M. Fowler, *Loaves and Fishes: The Function of the Feeding Stories in the Gospel of Mark*, SBL Dissertation Series 54 (Chico, Calif.: Scholars Press, 1981), 57-67.

54. See Henry Barclay Swete (*The Gospel According to St. Mark: The Greek Text with Introduction, Notes and Indices* [London: Macmillan, 1898], xlvi) in reference to Codex Alexandrinus and Codex Vaticanus.

55. Gert Lüderitz ("Rhetorik, Poetik, und Kompositionstechnik im das Markusevangelium," in *Markus-Philologie: Historische, literargeschichtliche und stilistische Untersuchungen zum zweiten Evangelium*, ed. H. Cancik, 165-203, Wissenschaftliche Untersuchungen zum Neue Testament, Bd. 33 [Tübingen, Germany: J. C. B. Mohr, 1984], 185) comparing opening and closing clauses of a ring composition: Mark 4:2 (καὶ ἐδίδασκεν αὐτοὺς ἐν παραβολαῖς πολλά [and he taught them by means of numerous parables]) corresponds to the closing verse Mark 4:33 (καὶ τοιαύταις παραβολαῖς πολλαῖς ἐλάλει αὐτοῖς τὸν λόγον [with many paralbes like these he spoke the word to them]). In general for the sense of form here, see Philip Sellew, "Oral and Written Sources in Mark 4:1-34," *New Testament Studies* 36 (1990): 234-67. The conclusion to the discourse on parables is emphasized when the final verse (Mark 4:34) is expanded in the *Ps.-Clementine Homilies* into a more definitive end, with an explanation to boot: Διὸ καὶ τοῖς αὐτοῦ μαθηταῖς κατ᾿ ἰδίαν ἐπέλυε τῶν οὐρανῶν βασιλείας τὰ μυστήρια (and therefore, to his disciples privately he unlocked the mysteries of the kingdom of heaven). See *Ps.-Clementine Homilies* 19.20. Text from §16,37b in *Antilogomena: Die Reste der ausserkanonischen Evangelien und urchristlichen Überlieferung*, ed. Erwin Preuschen, 2d rev. ed. (Gieszen, Germany: Alfred Töpelmann, 1905).

56. B. M. F. van Iersel, "Concentric Structures in Mark 1:14-3:35(4:1)," *Biblical Interpretation* 3 (1995): 75-97.

57. René Kiefer, "Traditions juives selon Mc 7,1-23," in *Texts and Contexts: Biblical Texts in Their Textual and Situational Contexts: Essays in Honor of Lars Hartman*, ed. T. Fornberg and D. Hellholm (Oslo: Scandinavian University Press, 1995), 675-88. Knox (*Sources* 1:52) offers similar observations about hypothetical sources for Mark 7:1-23, feeling compelled to distinguish Mark 7 *compositionally* from the narrative material in Mark 4:35-6:56 further, and claiming a uniquely distinct source behind 7:31-37 that he labels "The Book of Localized Miracles."

58. J. K. Elliott, *The Language and Style of the Gospel of Mark: An Edition of C. H. Turner's "Notes on Marcan Usage" Together with Other Comparable Studies*, Supplements to Novum Testamentum 71 (Leiden, The Netheralnds: E. J. Brill, 1993), §4. Identified in Mark 7:2, 3, 4, 18, 19, 35, 36a. Parentheses, described by Quintilian *Institutio Oratoria* 9.3.23 with the terms *interposition* and *interclusion*, are explanatory and used to clarify a narrative that is obscure because of strange customs reported by it. This term "parenthesis" is, however, used with fluidity in Markan commentary. Marie-Joseph Lagrange (*Evangile selon Saint Marc*, Etudes bibliques [Paris: Victor Lecoffre, 1911], lxxvii-lxxviii) identifies as parenthetical clauses what others call "γάρ explanatory."

59. Blackburn, *Theios Anēr and the Marcan Miracle Traditions*, 184-99.

60. E. J. Pryke (*Redactional Style in the Marcan Gospel: A Study of Syntax and Vocabulary as Guides to Redaction in Mark*, Society for New Testament Studies, Monograph Series 33 [Cambridge: Cambridge University Press, 1978], 99) finds examples in Mark 1:35; 2:14; 3:33; 7:24, 25; 8:13, 28; 9:5; 10:1, 24, 51; 11:14; 12:12, 26, 35, 42; 14:40, 45, 48; 15:2, 12; 16:1.

61. James R. Butts ("The Chreia in the Synoptic Gospels," *Biblical Theology Bulletin* 16 [1986]: 132-38) identifies χρείαι (pregnant maxim illustrated with an anecdote) in Mark 2:16-17b, 18-19; 4:10-11; 7:24b-30; 8:11-12; 9:38-39; 10:13-14; 11:15-17; 12:13-17, 38-31; 13:1-2; 15:39; see also his "The Voyage of Discipleship: Narrative, Chreia, and Call Story," in *Early Jewish and Christian Exegesis: Studies in Memory of William Hugo Brownlee*, ed. Craig A. Evans and William F. Stinespring (Atlanta: Scholars Press, 1987), 199-219. Vernon K. Robbins ("Progymnastic Rhetorical Composition and Pre-gospel Traditions: A New Approach," in *The Synoptic Gospels: Source Criticism and the New Literary Criticism*, ed. Camille Focant, Bibliotheca Ephemeridum Theologicarum Lovaniensium 110 [Leuven, Belgium: University Press, 1993], 111-47) argues for two extended χρεία in Mark chapters four and fourteen. Burton L. Mack (*Anecdotes and Arguments: The Chreia in Antiquity and Early Christianity*, Occasional Papers of the Institute for Antiquity and Christianity 10 [Claremont, Calif.: Institute for Antiquity and Christianity, 1987] focuses on "Pronouncement Stories" and reviews Mark 2:15-28, 7:1-23, 12:13-17.

62. Mark 1:15; 4:11, 26, 30; 9:1, 47; 10:14, 15, 23, 24, 25; 12:34; 14:25; 15:43.

63. Elsewhere in Mark 2:10, 28; 8:31, 38; 9:9, 12, 31; 10:33, 45; 13:26; 14:21, 41, 62.

64. David Barrett Peabody, *Mark as Composer*, New Gospel Studies 1 (Macon, Ga.: Mercer University Press, 1987), 128. The difficulty is either in the variation in the manuscripts, with both presence or absence of πάλιν (again), or in where the word is placed in the sentence, before the phrase εἰς τὸ πλοῖον (into the boat) or before the verb συνήχθη (congregated). The πάλιν is absent in Θ and other Caesarean witnesses. See Bruce M. Metzger, *A Textual Commentary on the Greek New Testament* (London: United Bible Societies, 1975), 85. Other Markan uses of πάλιν are in 2:1, 13; 3:1, 20; 4:1; 7:14, 31; 8:1, 13, 25; 10:1, 10, 24, 32; 11:3, 27.

65. Peabody (*Mark as Composer*, 21) develops certain criteria to identify the elements of Mark's redaction: "There are three criteria for increasing the probability that any given redactional feature within the gospel comes from the hand of the author. These criteria are (1) the compositional function of the redactional feature (2) the distribution of the redactional feature within the gospel and (3) the interlacing of redactional features within the same immediate literary context (usually the same verse)." The Criterion of Interlacing in particular is demonstrated through examination of the compositional use of πάλιν (again). According to Peabody, "The isolation of the hand of the author of Mark requires a process of interlacing that begins with a redactional feature in Mark which is almost certainly from the hand of the author. There does seem to be one such feature of Mark's text, namely πάλιν used retrospectively uniting two or more separated pericopes. It may be repeated here that this understanding of πάλιν does not make the study begin with a single vocabulary item in contrast to the expressed intention of the study to concentrate on literary features composed of two or more elements . . . this literary feature includes at least two elements: (1) the vocabulary item πάλιν and (2) its usage in a retrospective manner (the uses of πάλιν at Mark 11:3 and 15:13 do not qualify for this description) to unite two or more separated pericopes . . . the similarity in language between a πάλιν passage and its 'previous referent' [note: Peabody located nine uses of πάλιν that were narrative anaphora] . . . could be added as a third element describing this literary feature of Mark's text." See *Mark as Composer*, 26. Peabody's elaborate investigation of a single adverb throughout Markan narrative does indeed emphasize, from the view of this study, the conspicuous absence of πάλιν from 4:35-6:56. Peabody also identifies a substantial redactional feature Mark, which he describes as "καὶ προσκαλεσάμενος τὸν ὄχλον (and summoning the crowd) plus third person singular past tense of λέγω (speak) plus αὐτοῖς (to them)." Used to begin a sentence, this common Markan feature occurs only twice in the Gospel of Mark after 6:56 (7:14, 8:34). This stylistic feature draws together material in Mark 7 and Mark 8, grouping and distinguishing it from previous material; see *Mark as Composer*, 25.

4

Mark 4:35-41:
Jesus Stills a Dangerous Sea

Our cycle begins with action at sea, set at night (ὀψίας γενομένης [having become late], 4:35). Nighttime critically describes the narrative situation, indicating anomalous if not nefarious doings. Darkness is the condition of the Chaos, before the creation wrought by God (Genesis 1:1), and is called "Night" (Genesis 1:5) as it takes its place in scriptural cosmogonies ("You made the Darkness, and it is Night," Psalm 104:20). For the Creator, night is always as if it were day (Psalm 139:11-12; Isaiah 59:10). Jeremiah proclaims the Creator's covenants and promises with day and night, that the cosmic principles and ordinances of heaven will be kept (Jeremiah 33:25). *Genesis Rabbah* 6:9 shows the development of these ideas into ideas of personal piety and moral standing: "And to rule over the day and the night (Genesis 1:18). These are the righteous, who rule over what was created to give light during the day and over what was created to give light during the night. Of this power, Joshua 10:13 says, "And the sun stood still and the moon stayed."[1] Night, representative of Chaos, is the time of the miraculous parting of the waters for the Israelites and the subsequent violent, mass drowning of Pharaoh's army (Exodus 14:19-29). Sudden destruction comes during the time of night (Psalm 91:5; Isaiah 15:1-2; Jeremiah 6:5). Job 27:20 has a description of such a cataclysm: "Terrors overtake them like a flood, in the night a whirlwind carries them off. The east wind lifts them up and they are gone; it sweeps them out of their place" (NRSV). With alliteration, terror and night are here linked (*balāhôt* and *laylāh*). Similar images appear elsewhere in Job 34:30 ("In a moment they die; at midnight the people are shaken and pass away, and the mighty are taken away by no human hand") and Job 34:25 ("Thus, knowing their works, he overturns them in the night, and they are crushed"). In Micah 3:6 a portentously dreadful last night is predicted, a

97

time of no vision, no revelation, and a time during which the day would
become as black ("the sun shall go down on the prophets"). In Isaiah
34:14, night is personified as Lilith, the night-hag killer of newborn
babies.[2] Lilith was a female demon haunting Edom. A figure like her
appears later in the *Testament of Solomon* 13, there named Obyzouth, a
night hag with wildly disheveled hair. She was described as monstrous,
in appearance like a Gorgon and similar to a Gello or a Lamia. Seventh-
century C.E. Aramaic exorcism texts were addressed against her as her
traditions grew in their circulation after antiquity.[3] Night, throughout
Scripture and on into medieval traditions, is a setting and metaphor for
anomalies, dangers, terror, and destruction. These are connotations
evoked by the Markan nighttime narrative, an episode of the Dark.

   Homeric metaphors of darkness (σκότος or νυκτὶ ἐοικώς) bear early
witness to Greek traditions of Night as anomalous and frightful, the time
when strange and uncanny events take place.[4] In Hesiod, Νύξ is born from
Χάος (Chaos), and gives birth to Θάνατος, Μοίραι, Νέμεσις, and Ἔρις
(Death, Fates, Nemesis, and Strife). Νύξ indicates danger, bringing
proximity to divine power through terrible and powerful cosmic forces.[5]
This kind of tradition was widespread, and its influence is evident in a
sculpted scene described by Pausanias: "There was a woman carrying a
white boy asleep in her right arm, and a black boy in her left who seems
to be asleep, facing in different directions; the inscription proves, but you
could guess without any inscription, that the children are Death and Sleep,
and Night is the nurse of both of them." The phrase "facing different
directions" may mean "completely twisted around," symbolizing an
apotropaic foot-twisting to ward off Sleep, Death, and nefarious Children
of Night.[6] Elements of Night, ever dangerous, are elements from which
one needs protection.

   Greek cosmological writers also wrote of Night. For Eudemus of
Rhodes, Night is that out of which a first principle (ἀρχή) is created.
Epimenides believed that Night and ʼΑέρ are those things out of which all
things are created. Museaus held that Night and Τάρταρος are also those
things out of which the whole is created.[7] A fragment of Parmenides
juxtaposes νύξ ἀδαής (dark night) to its opposite, φλογὸς αἰθέριον πῦρ
(ethereal flame of fire). These are the two origins of types of thought, the
latter light and gentle, the former heavy and dense. Fragments of
Empedocles indicate that the genesis of living forms was their emergence
out of the Night (that is, heavier material), when a type of fiery material
ascended.[8] The Orphic Hymn Νυκτός acclaims Night the Γενέτειρα
(mother) of all humans, stating Νὺξ γένεσις πάντων (Night is the origin

of everything). With her is dreaming and reveling as she circles forever in pursuit of παίκτειρα ἠεροφοίτοις (*aer*-traversing dancing creatures). Νὺξ answers prayers and night-glistening fears (φόβους νυχαυγεῖς) flee, since she overpowers their lesser Darknesses (*Orphic Hymn* 4).

Orphic cosmology also used complex metaphors of Night. In the *Hieronymi et Hellanici Theogonia,* Adrasteia (Nemesis) is likened to ' Ανάγκη (Necessity), being ἀσώματος (without body) and "extending her influence in the whole world," without fixed physical attributes yet fixing to everything its boundaries. Adrasteia is construed a τρίτη ἀρχὴ (third principle). In a Ἱερὸς Λόγος (Sacred Discourse) reported by Hermias, this Adrasteia is a divine power, specifically exercising control over things which dwell ἐν τῷ νυκτί (in the night). In another Ἱερὸς Λόγος reported by Proclus, the χρησμοί of Νὺξ (oracles of Night) undergird everything come into being. Again as reported by Proclus, the goddess Νύξ is a basic principle poised with the Orphic goddess Φάνης, a symmetry articulating a Night/Day opposition in balance.[9] These Orphic principles did not remain abstract cosmogonic theories only. In the last sentence of the Orphic *Golden Verses,* the cosmology is applied very personally to the individual: "Then, if you leave the body behind and go to the free αἰθήρ (aether), you will be immortal, an undying god, no longer mortal."[10] In this theoretical system, escaping the body is due to attainment of ethereal and enlightened existence. Night in this cosmological background is always that which is opposite the free and ethereal life, is the heavy, non-ethereal, undeveloped origin of everything that comes to be ordered, developed, and true.

So it is that Night, as a literary theme, metaphor, or narrative setting for events, is a rich source of imagery and connotation for what is dangerous, incipient, risky, anomalous, and uncertain. Night symbolizes a necessity upon the divine to make distinctions, create, separate the formed from the unformed, or stabilize chaos. This aspect of Night was pressed into service broadly. Special events took place at night, especially initiations and all-night festivals, the latter well-represented from Athens to Jerusalem.[11] Various creatures of the Night were well-known. They include the Egyptian god Harpocrates, Lilith, the dream-disturbing "PRK-demon," and nightmare demons like the ' Εφίαλτες and the *Fauni Facarii* (or their instigator, Pan). They were all part of the anomalous frightful of Night.[12]

Not only does the narrative emphasis on nighttime activity in Mark 4:35- 41 bring forth the anomalous, so too does the setting. Although the actual term θάλασσα (ocean) does not occur in Mark 4:35-41 until 4:39, it is the critical theme around which the actions and ideas of the narrative revolve. There has been some question about the exact connotation of θάλασσα here, as to whether θάλασσα carries grand traditional themes of the sea, especially like those found in Scripture, or whether it is simply a geographical designation for the watery locale of this story. In a synoptically parallel text Luke uses λίμνη (lake) instead (Luke 8:22-25). The fuller designation, Λίμνη Γεννησαρέτε (Lake Gennesaret), appears in Luke 5:2. It so happens that in Psalms 106:35, 113:8 the LXX translates 'gm (troubled pool) with λίμνη. Both passages are about God's miraculous conversion of dry rock into drinkable water, and therefore perhaps give λίμνη a richer meaning. But the great themes of ym (sea) in Scripture are not translated into Greek with λίμνη, even though in Greek literature λίμνη could refer to the ocean in general (*Iliad* 24.79, *Odyssey* 3.1; Aeschylus *Supplices* 529). Luke's usage agrees with the geopolitical designations of Josephus in *War* 3.516, a passage that contains the designation, Γεννησὰρ χώρα (Gennesaret area). Freyne comments about this, that "the more usual name for this expanse of water [Sea of Galilee] was 'the lake of Gennesar(itis)' or 'the lake of Tiberias'. Of the gospel writers Luke is the only one to reflect this more general and accurate description consistently."[13] The designation λίμνη was typically mundane, a term used by administrators, bureaucrats, geographers, or businessmen to describe geopolitical areas. A notable exception to this is its use in very different texts when referring to an eschatological pool of fire and brimstone (see Revelations 19:20; 20:10, 14, 15; 21:8; *Apocalypse of Peter* 8).[14] In Daniel 7:2-3, a passage full of apocalyptic symbolism, the Aramaic term used is *ym '*, the full phrase in this verse then translated in LXX by the phrase τὴν θάλασσαν τὴν μεγάλην (the great ocean). It seems that θάλασσα/*ym* is the preferred biblical terminology for grand themes of the sea.[15]

Like νύξ, the term θάλασσα has significance in diverse traditions, a fact gleaned from the work of Richard Kratz, John Day, and others like them.[16] Narratives of events on the θάλασσα easily evoke traditional imageries. Matthew 8:24, parallel to Mark, adds a detail about a σεισμὸς μέγας (great earthquake). For Matthew, the earthquake initiates the catastrophe,[17] a cosmic crisis that shakes *both land and sea*. This is an elaboration of one aspect of the symbolism of θάλασσα: dangerous anomaly and uncertain emptiness. In Mark, the activity of Jesus and the disciples in a boat, at night and on the θάλασσα, compounds connotations about the sea's dangers and anomalies.

Traditional ideas about chaos include forced overthrow and brute shaking. Kratz pointed to Psalm 89 for *ym* as chaos,[18] especially verses 9-10: "You rule the raging of the sea; when its waves rise, you still them. You crushed Rahab like a carcass; you scattered your enemies with your mighty arm" (NRSV). Rahab is a monster, through poetic parallelism here likened to the sea. The poetry evokes themes of both safety and danger. A Hebrew psalm from Qumran (4Q381) combines these themes into a single piece about Rahab and personal safety.[19] Traditions about Leviathan and Behemoth, both monsters related to the sea, fared in similar ways during the second century C.E. Both would be eaten at a messianic banquet (2 Bar 29:4), meaning they would be fully incorporated, their destructive power destroyed. The sea, and anomalies and terror related to it, was ever a vibrant source for describing danger and its abatement. Job 26:12-13 develops this theme with a unique emphasis on wisdom: "By his power he stilled the Sea; by his understanding he struck down Rahab. By his wind the heavens were made fair; his hand pierced the fleeing serpent" (NRSV). Rahab was "cut to pieces" by Yahweh at the Exodus, when the "waters of the great deep" were dried up (Isaiah 51:10). The deep of the sea is also the abode of the monster, Leviathan (Job 3:8, 40:25-41:26). In Isaiah 27:1, the future destruction of Leviathan, a fleeing and twisting serpent, is promised, "on that day." In Psalm 74:12-17 Leviathan receives a crushed head by a blow from God, when the sea is divided at the Exodus. In an Ugaritic poem, Leviathan is described as seven-headed and, in the Ugaritic scenario, subjected to crushing by El. The tradition of divine conflict with Leviathan is also found much later in an Aramaic incantation bowl, "The Spell of the Monster Leviathan."[20] A monster in the sea is an essential element in the Book of Jonah, where a "great fish" (*gdôl dg*) swallows up Jonah (1:17). The LXX translates this as κήτει μεγάλῳ (by a great sea monster), bringing with it a whole constellation of images stemming from Greek traditions about sea monsters.[21] The θάλασσα, whether in containing monsters or being a monster itself, is a violent, devouring enemy. It well represents the experience of the anomalous frightful. Survival through such danger is a robust, widespread theme.

The sea, or in general the "waters," is often depicted as at God's command, especially subject to God's *g`r* (rebuke). For this, Day points to Psalm 104:6b-7: "the waters stood above the mountains, at your rebuke they flee; at the sound of your thunder they take flight" (NRSV). Chaos, when combined with "waters," is not only a monster, or an oppositional creature that needs be conquered, but also an entity with the identity *t°hôm*, the Deep, a menace that must be overpowered. Psalm 104:1-30 is to be compared to Genesis 1:1-31; both show God's overpowering creative force. The image of Yahweh as a Rider on the Clouds (Psalm 104:3) may stem from Canaanite tradition. In this material, the essential focus is divine power at the creation of the world or in later divine conflicts. The list of Scripture texts that contain or develop the theme of God's fight against the sea demonstrates how impressive was this tradition to biblical writers.[22]

Focusing on a different set of metaphors, Kratz indicated six passages that liken the sea to the place of the dead, recommending a comparison to "Waters of Death" in the *Gilgamesh Epic*. Reviewing this and similar material, Nicholas J. Tromp uncovered vivid imagery for death expressed in water terminology: *tᵉhôm* (deep), *ym* (sea), *myîm rbbîm* (many waters), and *msbrîm* (breakers). Matthias Krieg's observations also support this field of metaphors linking death with water, suggesting that these metaphors are a primary component of Scripture's imagery for death. For water and death, Krieg cites Psalms 18:12-13 and 69:38-41, and Jonah 2:5-7,12-14. For the Deep and death, Krieg cites Job 3:6-11, Psalms 7:14-16 and 88:15-18, 29-32, and Isaiah 38:10-20 (see appendix C, "Waters of Death"). This field of metaphors illustrates the rich symbolism in Scripture that represents the terrible uncertainty of mortal fate.

Greek traditions about Poseidon, a storm god and earth shaker, coincide with these Near Eastern depictions of the sea as monstrous. Hellenistic astrological theories hypothesized that events occurring in conjunction with the domains of Poseidon would be monstrous and uncanny, consistent with the spread of Poseideon's reputation as a violent and stormy divine power.[23] At Palmyra in the first century C.E. he was identified and honored as the powerful "El-Creator-of-the-Earth," who unlike the Ugaritic El, maintained an abode specifically in the midst of the sea. His attributes were less those of the creator of the world than its masterful possessor.[24] Again, at Palmyra in 32 C.E., the sanctuary of Bêl received a new *cella*. Excavations of the sanctuary from this level reveal iconography from the new room, described by Hans J. W. Drijvers:

> One of the four reliefs that decorated the two crossbeams south of the entrance-porch of the *cella* shows a fight between a snake-tailed female monster and a god in a chariot with another god on a horse, who are attacking her. Six deities in a row are watching the fight. They are difficult to identify, but Herakles, the Arab god Arsu, Atargatis, Ichthys and Shadrafa seem to be present. The whole panel is hard to interpret, but it seems clear that it pictures a fight against a chaos monster, such as that of Zeus against Typhon, and of Babylonian Bêl against Tiamat

as related in the Babylonian Creation Epic.[25]

The consecration of the room took place on the sixth of Nisan, at the fixed New Year Festival from the old Babylonian sacred calendar, a calendar adopted at the Palmyra sacred site. Texts preserved from this site at Palmyra tell how the Babylonian Creation Epic used to be recited. A chief feature of the epic was the sea—that is, the defeat of the watery chaos monster. Evidence for Bêl (and Nebo) throughout Syria during this period provides an *interpretatio babyloniaca* for these ancient deities, demonstrating how watery chaos had prevailed in its traditional cosmological role.[26]

Syncretism of traditions about θάλασσα and its overpowering was widespread. Berossus, a Syrian court mythographer for Antiochus I Soter, wrote several ἱστορίας περὶ τοῦ οὐρανοῦ καὶ θαλάσσης καὶ πρωτογονίας καὶ βασιλέων καὶ τῶν κατ᾽ αὐτοὺς πράξεων (histories about heaven, the sea, the initial cosmic events, and kings and their deeds).[27] He recorded a creation story about a divine woman named Θαλάτθ who had been installed as ruler over living creatures, which creatures the story describes as strangely unusual (θαυμαστά). Berossus mentions that Greeks would translate her name as Θάλασσα. He tells the story of how Bêl, likened to Zeus elsewhere, split Θαλάτθ (or Θάλασσα) in two, creating two spheres: one heavenly, the other earthly. Berossus also reports a tradition about a cosmic catastrophe of flooding water, still yet another depiction of deadly waters.[28] Lucian witnesses to this same chaotic aspect of water when he reports a legend about Deucalion from the Syrian Hierapolis, concerning how a flood had destroyed the first, unruly, violent race of humans. In Lucian's day an annual festival celebrated the abatement of those deadly waters. Strangely, the festival was annually inaugurated by a water miracle that used to involve a floating head blown miraculously onto shore after floating from Egypt.[29] These are all traditional treatments of the sea, maintaining an emphasis on divine conflict and power. Hellenistic traditions maintained the sea as a ferment of chaotic forces.

Hope in the saving beneficence of the Dioscuri, or some other divine power, is well attested by those navigating chaotic waters. Barry Blackburn listed several ancient testimonies about seas and waters that were safely calmed by beneficent figures, including humans with divine power.[30] Thankful sailors have left inscriptional evidence (see especially the sequence of epigrams in *Palatine Anthology* 6.263-296). One researcher described a large group of votive offerings made by such seamen: "When they had survived a shipwreck or the threat of a shipwreck, they dedicated their clothes or their hair to the gods of the sea. Their apparel, or a not too indispensable part of their body, was given in exchange for their physical safety."³¹ Surviving a storm by calling on the Dioscuri (or some other saving benevolence) became proverbial.³² Themes of safety or destruction through exposure to the θάλασσα never lost their vigor. The terms σώζειν (to save) and ἀπολλύειν (to destroy) illustrate the basic choices when facing danger at sea, as those in the boat with Jesus so indicated by their question to Jesus: οὐ μέλει σοι ὅτι ἀπολλύμεθα (is it of no concern to you that we are being destroyed?).³³ The same was said of the voyage from life to death. Cumont observed, with numerous detailed observations, the role and intervention of the Dioscuri in a cosmological conception of the two hemispheres, the one below and the one above. A sarcophagus relief from the tomb of P. Aelius Sabinus in Rome shows one of the divine twins, armed with a sword, leading the way through Ocean, which is depicted as lying down on a couch. Inscriptions on the relief are of antiphonal responses, all pertaining to funereal honors and hope for a good outcome in life after death. One voice says, Θάρσει, Εὐγένει (Be bold, noble person!) and the other, Οὐδεὶς ἀθάνατος (Nobody is immortal).³⁴ This scene combines the specific idea of escape from calamity at sea, and a likely Pythagorean idea about the Dioscuri beng ἡ συμφωνία τῶν ἀπάντων (the harmony of all things).³⁵ It is an example of "being saved" through the ultimate danger, death, illustrated through salvation at sea.

Mark 4:35-41 emphasizes danger: καὶ γίνεται λαῖλαψ μεγάλη ἀνέμου καὶ τὰ κύματα ἐπέβαλλεν εἰς τὸ πλοῖον ὥστε ἤδη γεμίζεσθαι τὸ πλοῖον (and a tremendous hurricane occurred, and the waves crashed into the boat so that the boat was swamped) (4:37). The θάλασσα gulps one up whole.³⁶ The Λαῖλαψ (Storm), a most dangerous event on the sea, in Ovid (*Metamorphoses* 7.771) is the metaphorical name given one of the hunting dogs of Cephalus. The beast was unnaturally fast, sudden, and devastating when loosed from its leash, snapping and chasing, running this way and that.³⁷ The term λαῖλαψ is in hendiadys with πυθολέτα in *PGM* 6.33, an acclamation of Phoibos Apollo as the "hurricane and dragon-slayer" (Λαῖλαψ καὶ Πυθολέτα), a magical text similar to another text from Porphyry with a syncretism of Apollo and Horus: "Sun, Horus, Osiris, Apollo son of Zeus, Divider of the hours (ὡρῶν) and seasons (καιρῶν), of the winds (ἀνέμων) and the thunderstorms (ὄμβρων)."³⁸ Storms and storm winds here are addressed as part of a mix of divinities.³⁹ Divine power over storms in both Mark and the magical text is evident, and divine command-and-control over seasonal and meteorological phenomena is a primary theme in both texts. In analysis of the magical text, Christine Harrauer referred to a curse tablet published by Wünsch: ὁρκίζω σε, τὸν θεὸν τῶν ἀνέμων καὶ πνευματῶν Λαιλαμ ("I adjure you, Lailam, god of the winds and of the spirits"). In *PGM* 4.182 λαιλαπετέ was addressed in a magical formula as a divine power who controls the sea, controls the thunder, and breaks rocks.[40]

The uses of Λαῖλαψ in the LXX are few, but also related to the imagery of storms: dreadful, sudden, and full of divine wrath. In Job 27:20 Job says of the wicked: "Terrors overtake them like a flood; in the night a whirlwind [λαῖλαψ] carries them off" (NRSV). A similar image appears in Job 21:18 and in a prophetic oracle against the nations (Jeremiah 25:32).[41] The hurricane is depicted as frightful and unusual, a metaphor for an inexplicable and sudden bad turn of events. It is in such a depiction of the anomalous frightful that God speaks to Job in Job 38:1. Corresponding to this, Sirach 48:9,12 depicts Elijah taken up to heaven in a terrifying λαῖλαψ.

These references to θάλασσα-related storm dangers evoke themes of catastrophe. Here Mark's account is full of the anomalous frightful as it depicts Night, Sea, and Storm. In the story, Jesus is asleep in the stern. Awakened by his agitated fellow travelers, he decisively ends the immediate danger of the Storm and the Sea. As Mark has it, καὶ διεγερθεὶς ἐπετίμησεν τῷ ἀνέμῳ καὶ εἶπεν τῇ θαλάσσῃ, σιώπα, πεφίμωσο, καὶ ἐκόπασεν ἄνεμος καὶ ἐγένετο γαλήνη μεγάλη ("and he awoke and commanded the wind and said to the sea, `Be silent! Be muzzled!' and the wind ceased and a great calm occurred"; 4:39). With these commands, the danger on the Sea abates as Jesus confronts the θάλασσα and its dangerous anomalies, preserving those in the boat through this nighttime episode of near-death experience. An apparently good result; one might think that the story would make a happy ending of it. After all, many boats were traveling with the boat that ferried Jesus, and the sense of the story is that the many felt safe with this one, seeking to be in his retinue, much like the way in which many sailed with Apollonius of Tyana because it was safe with that θεῖος ἀνήρ (divine man) whenever boating conditions were dangerous (Philostratus, *Apollonius* 4.13). One would expect this savior to be complimented for his benefaction, perhaps with an offering, a hymn of thanksgiving, or some type of votive recompense.

But a problem remains. As with other examples of one divine power overcoming another, the humans caught in between are subject to uncertainty and fear. When one power conquers another, what makes that new conquering power any safer than the previous one? On what will the

benefaction of the new victor depend, and will the new power be a jealous
power? Jesus does save those in the boat, demonstrating a divine power
over the water that, as a theme, was longstanding.[42] Once this rescue is
accomplished, and the humans are saved from the uncanny Ocean, then
the critical moment of acclamation and demonstration of proper fealty to
the new conquering power arrives. Such expected human responses were
keys for continued benefaction. An example of such acclamation and
demonstration of faith under these circumstances is found in Psalm
107:28-32:

> Then they cried to the Lord in their trouble, and he brought them out
> from their distress; he made the storm be still, and the waves of the sea
> were hushed. Then they were glad because they had quiet, and he
> brought them to their desired haven. Let them thank the Lord for his
> steadfast love, for his wonderful works to humankind. Let them extol
> him in the congregation of the people, and praise him in the assembly
> of the elders (NRSV).

The standard custom was to offer thanksgiving after deliverance, but that
is curiously absent here. Instead, what here follows in Mark is a mix of
instruction by Jesus and puzzling questions about the perception and
attitudes of the disciples. The mix of teaching and taunt that occurs in
these verses raises a question about the nature of the benevolence of
Jesus.[43] As Mark 4:40-41 describes it, once calm is accomplished, Jesus
asks those in the boat with him, τί δειλοί ἐστε; οὔπω ἔχετε πίστιν; ("Why
are you cowardly? Do you not yet trust?"). A focus on the frightful is
articulated through this question, but in a way that does not highlight the
much needed relief from ocean danger that the disciples had just
experienced. Instead, an interrogation of the disciples ensues, and the
interrogation implies a threat to the disciples.

The theme of the anomalous frightful is vibrant here, not only
because powerful control over dangerous anomalies is reported, but also
because an uncertainty about the intentions of Jesus emerges. We may
compare this to two previous paradigmatic boating narratives that involve
storms, danger, and a main character sleeping on board: *Odyssey* 13.70ff
and Jonah 1:4-7. Günter Kettenbach tried to make something of this
comparison, tying the two accounts together as a background for Mark's
narrative. He suggested in particular that, taking after Odysseus, Jesus
appears wise, unencumbered: ἄνδρα φερουσα θεοῖς ἐναλίγκιά μήδε
ἔχοντα (a man wise as the gods are wise). Kettenbach understood this
theme to be a Markan image of the new king (Jesus), who would reign in

his new kingdom (the Kingdom of God). Specifically, the image includes not only the divine control of the Sea and Storm but also the peaceful authority exhibited while sleeping in the stern of the boat.[44] In this interpretation, the beneficial authority and royal power of Jesus is highlighted. I agree that a conflict of divine power is illustrated in this story. Such conflicts were often reported to have made human onlookers afraid, and so it is implied here in the questions put to the disciples, those very men who responded to the terrible storm by waking Jesus, and then still feared. Fear of this type is not an unusual theme. But in Mark, one party to the divine conflict turns to the human witnesses and demands an explanation of their behavior, behavior that under such conditions is completely normal. The story suggests that these disciples are uncomfortable with their proximity to Jesus, the stronger divine power. In spite of the clear benefit of safety, as narrated in the account, uncertainty emerges to overshadow that theme. What sort of power is this, if it is this strongly beneficent yet also critical of the human responses?

The vocabulary used in the interrogation of the disciples is rich in symbolism. The term δειλός (fearful) is used eleven times in the LXX, with two good examples: Deuteronomy 20:8 (Τίς ὁ ἄνθρωπος ὁ φοβούμενος καὶ δειλός τῇ καρδίᾳ; [Who is the person who is fearing and fearful in heart?]) and Sirach 2:12 (Οὐαὶ καρδίαις δειλαῖς καὶ χερσὶν παρειμέναις [Woe to fearful hearts and weakened hands]). Its cognate, δειλία (cowardice), is used ten times, with two other good examples: Psalm 54:5 (ἡ καρδία μου ἐταράχθη ἐν ἐμοί, καὶ δειλία θανάτου ἐπέπεσεν ἐπ᾽ ἐμε [My heart is terrified within me, and fear of death has fallen upon me]) and Sirach 4:17 (φόβον καὶ δειλίαν ἐπάξει ἐπ᾽ αὐτόν [fear and cowardice will come upon him]). The verb δειλᾶν is used seventeen times, with similar meanings. Notably, in Deuteronomy and Joshua it is linked with the verb φοβέω several times (Deuteronomy 1:21; 31:6,8; Joshua 1:9; 8:1; 10:25) in this manner: μὴ φοβεῖσθε μηδὲ δειλιάσητε (Do not fear nor be afraid).

While there is a robust use in the LXX of words with the stem δειλ-, the terms were also under considerable discussion in Hellenistic religious and philosophical circles. Theophrastus in his Χαρακτῆρες sketches three types relevant to the vocabulary and themes of this Markan passage: cowardice (Δειλίας), mistrust (Ἀπιστία), and "fervent religiousness" (Δεισιδαιμονία). He defined δειλίας as ὕπειξίς τις ψυχῆς ἔμφοβος (shrinking of the soul through fear).[45] A very pertinent example of this type is well illustrated through danger-at-sea stories (Χαρακτῆρες 25.3-9).

The Coward is one who on a voyage . . . if a high sea gets up, will ask it there is any one on board who has not been initiated (τις μὴ μεμύη-ται). He will put up his head and ask the steersman if he is half-way, and what he thinks of "the face of the heavens" (τὰ τοῦ θεοῦ, literally: "the things of god"), remarking to the person sitting next him that a certain dream makes him feel uneasy (ὅτι φοβεῖται ἀπὸ ἐνυπνίου τινός); and he will take off his tunic and give it to his slave (i.e., get ready to jump overboard); or he will beg them to put him ashore.

The picture is comic through exaggeration. Cowardice stems from excessive sensitivity and anxiety about misfortune and danger. The companion character to this, Δεισιδαιμονία, has similar traits, though focused especially on human-divine relations. Aptly, its description is δειλία πρὸς τὸ δαιμόνιον (cowardice in the face of the daimonic) (Χαρακτῆρες 16.1). The main feature of this character is a compulsive trait: any accident or a strange, one-time event calls for cultic purification, oracular response, or expiation. The third character, Ἀπιστία, is that of obsessive mistrust. Its description is ὑπόληψις τις ἀδικίας κατὰ πάντων (a presumption of dishonesty in everyone) (Χαρακτῆρες 18.1). An individual like this carries his own money, not allowing servants to carry it. At every mile he sits down to recount it, just to make sure it's still all there. The critical aspect here is not just lack of trust during strange and unusual situations, but chronic mistrust in situations where one normally would trust.

Discussions on these topics continued through and beyond the time of the Gospel of Mark. Plutarch (Περὶ Δεισιδαιμονίας) broadens one part of the philosophical debate, linking πάθος (affect) and φόβος (fear), and suggesting how the first causes the second. These two emotions are interrelated to the extent that δεισιδαιμονία means something like an excessive sensitivity toward and expectation of divine influence in everyday affairs. Plutarch argued that this dynamic stems from emotional fear of the gods.[46] Seneca also criticized this particular kind of fear, especially as it is related to the Roman, abstract deification of fear as represented in the deities *Pavor* (Terror, Panic) and *Pallor* (Paleness, Fear).[47] His criticism is extensive, and it was known well enough to be quoted in Tertullian (*Apology* 7). The idea of fear developed through these reflections became a self-standing study in itself, the focus for a variety of reflections about human behaviors and beliefs.

Peter John Koets outlined these developments, expanding on what numerous Hellenistic writers thought about the topic of δεισιδαιμονία, a religious experience to which both negative and positive qualities were attributed. They discussed the negative qualities of δεισιδαιμονία in relation to ἀθεότης (atheism). This aspect takes its place in wider-ranging philosophical treatments of lack of belief in the gods, wrong belief in the gods, and the ways humans tend to believe in divine power. Some disputed whether theological convictions help people to overcome fear or, instead, induce more fear in them.[48]

The rhetorical questions of Jesus to those in the boat with him borrow from all of this vocabulary and are to be taken in two ways: as an invitation to trust in Jesus, and as criticism of the completely normal responses of the disciples. Jesus recognizes their fear and demands to know why they are afraid. The response of his fellow-travellers highlights the problem: καὶ ἐφοβήθησαν φόβον μέγαν . . . τίς ἄρα οὗτός ἐστιν ὅτι καὶ ὁ ἄνεμος καὶ ἡ θάλασσα ὑπακούει αὐτῷ (they feared greatly . . . who therefore is this that the wind and the sea obey him?). The uncertainty stirred up in this response is present because these disciples do not know who the very powerful Jesus is. Their response, which admits that Jesus does have beneficial power and that this power has preserved them through danger, is mixed with their uncertainty as to whether or not it is safe to be near him. These are representations of two main facets of the anomalous frightful: perplexing uncertainty over what happened and what might happen next, and fear of what could have been and of what Jesus might be. Overcoming the powers of ἄνεμος and θάλασσα is one thing, as it was a much needed salvation in a time of crisis. But to be so saved and then questioned, in the manner that Jesus subsequently questions, and that by the very same power who extends the critical benefaction at the moment of imminent death, creates a narrative conundrum. We read that Jesus in the boat has mighty power, and he intends to save. But afterward those in the boat with him are not shown to have grasped what his beneficent intentions truly might be. There is no acclaim for Jesus as a savior. Instead, the narrative report shows the disciples afraid and Jesus with little if any sympathy for this normal and expected human response to the anomalous frightful. Those in the boat are in fact saved from drowning in the stormy violence, and clearly the narrative implies that being alive is better than being dead. Yet the narrative provides no resolution of the uncertainty evoked by their proximity to such a saving, divine power as Jesus. After they are questioned by Jesus, and have no answer for him, the story simply moves on. There is no instruction and no reflection.

The narrative outcomes of the whole beg that the reader remain uncertain. Is this a simple sea voyage with a potentially catastrophic

sinking? Is this Jesus keeping his disciples safe, albeit with a curious
questioning at the end? The cosmic elements of Night, Sea, and Storm
baptize the reader into a world of metaphor and symbol that had great
weight as well as widespread occurrence. What is to be made of this,
since all the these elements are present in a deliberately abbreviated and
fast-paced account? Does this indicate something about Jesus? If Jesus
were thoroughly capable of saving them, why would those in the boat
with him not feel more secure but, apparently, less secure after the event?
What kind of divine power does Jesus exercise, if in the end he voices
criticism of those with him and does not comfort them? Every element of
story (character, setting, and plot) sensitizes the reader to the strangeness
that comes with the anomalous frightful, as do the elements of the
narrative plot. The resolution of the narrative seems simple: Jesus and
those with him move on from this scene. But what really happens here?
Though drowning is prevented, the mysterious further meaning to the
events is not fully expressed, yet the reader suspects that it should be
there. This is the narrative cycle's first display of the anomalous frightful:
events that are frightening on a cosmological scale remain unresolved.

Notes

1. *The Book of Legends (Sefer Ha-Aggadah): Legends from the Talmud and
Midrash*, ed. Hayim Nahman Bialik and Yehoshua Hana Ravnitzky, trans. William
G. Braude (New York: Schocken Books, 1992), 550 §136.

2. Also *Pahad lyla* ("terror of the night") in Psalm 91, like the Mesopotamian
lú.líl.lá ("wind-man"); see *Dictionary of Deities and Demons in the Bible*, ed.
Karel van der Toorn, Bob Becking, and Pieter Van der Horst (Leiden, The
Netherlands: E. J. Brill, 1995), s.v. "Terror of the Night," by M. Malul.

3. Emil Schürer, *The History of the Jewish People in the Age of Jesus Christ*,
rev. ed., ed. Geza Vermes, Fergus Millar, and Martin Goodman (Edinburgh: T &
T Clark, 1986), 3:353-354. B. Shab 151b instructs not to sleep alone in a house,
due to a risk of being snatched away by Lilith. Lilith was linked to others who
were similarly unpredictable and destroying agents; see 4Q510 1 4-5: "And I, the
Instructor, proclaim the majesty of his beauty to frighten and ter[rify] all the spirits
of the destroying angels and the spirits of the bastards, the demons, Lilith, the
howlers, and [the yelpers]"; compare Bilhah Nitzan, *Qumran Prayer and
Religious Poetry*, trans. Jonathan Chipman, Studies on the Texts of the Desert of
Judah 12 (Leiden, The Netherlands: E. J. Brill, 1994), 237. All these attacking
creatures are metaphorical adaptations of child-stealing images. They strike
suddenly. Here, their broader purpose is "to lead astray the spirit of understanding

and to appall their hearts and their souls in the age of the dominion of wickedness"; compare Nitzan, *Qumran Prayer and Religious Poetry*, 245. On the history of the tradition, see J. Trachtenberg, *Jewish Magic and Superstition: A Study in Folk Religion* (New York: Athenaeum, 1979), 36-37. Translation of seventh-century C.E. Aramaic exorcism text in Dennis Duling, "The Testament of Solomon," in *The Old Testament Pseudepigrapha*, ed. James Charlesworth (Garden City, N.Y.: Doubleday, 1983), 1:697 n.5: "bound is the bewitching Lilith who haunts the house of Zakoy, with a belt of iron on her pate; bound is the bewitching Lilith with a peg of iron in her mouth; bound is the bewitching Lilith who haunts the house of Zakoy with a chain or iron on her neck; bound is the bewitching Lilith with fetters of iron on her hands; bound is the bewitching Lilith with stocks of stone on her feet." On these types of incantations see *Curse Tablets and Binding Spells from the Ancient World*, ed. and trans. John Gager (New York: Oxford University Press, 1992), 230, especially his own example §123.

4. G. E. R. Lloyd (*Polarity and Analogy: Two Types of Argumentation in Early Greek Thought* [Cambridge: Cambridge University Press, 1966; repr., London: Bristol Classical Press, 1992], 42-43) comments, "The comparison 'like night' (νυκτὶ ἐοικώς) conveys the terror which a god or hero causes (*Iliad* i 47, cf. 12 464), and Night herself, one of whose names is the euphemism εὐφρόνη and one of whose epithets is 'deadly', ὀλοή (Hesiod *Theogony* 224), is a personage of whom Zeus himself stands in awe (*Iliad* 14 258ff)." In *Odyssey* 10.28, during a storm (λαῖλαψ), night (νύξ) "rushed down from heaven." "Night rushing down" appears to be formulaic, occurring also in *Odyssey* 12.314; compare Plutarch (*Timoleon* 249F) with a scene of battle between Greeks and Carthaginians, when "darkness hovering the hills and mountain summits *came down* to the field of battle," reporting that this was a λαῖλαψ.

5. Hesiod, *Theogony* 211-225 (trans. Hugh G. Evelyn-White, *Hesiod, The Homeric Hymns, and Homerica*, Loeb Classical Library [London: Heinemann, 1914], 95): "And Night bare hateful Doom and black Fate, and Death, and she bare Sleep and the tribe of Dreams. And again the goddess murky Night, though she lay with none, bare Blame and painful Woe, and the Hesperides who guard the rich, golden apples and the trees bearing fruit beyond glorious Ocean. Also she bare the Destinies and ruthless avenging Fates, Clotho and Lachesis and Atropos, who give men at their birth both evil and good to have, and they pursue the transgressions of men and of gods: and these goddesses never cease from their dread anger until they punish the sinner with a sore penalty. Also deadly Night bare Nemesis (Indignation) to afflict mortal men, and after her, Deceit and Friendship and hateful Age and hard-hearted Strife."

6. Pausanias, Περιήγησις 5.18.1 (trans. Peter Levi, *Pausanias: Guide to Greece*, rev. ed. (London: Penguin, 1981), 251; compare Robert Garland, *The Greek Way of Death* (Ithaca, N.Y.: Cornell University Press, 1985), 59. On the apotropaic nature of the scene, see Christopher A. Faraone, *Talismans and Trojan Horses: Guardian Statues in Ancient Greek Myth and Ritual* (New York: Oxford University Press, 1992), 133 (Appendix III).

7. Eudemus, reported in Damascius, *De principiis* 124; Epimenides, reported in Philodemus, *De pietate* 47a; Musaeus, reported in Philodemus, *De pietate* 137,5; texts in G. S. Kirk and J. E. Raven, *The Presocratic Philosophers* (Cambridge: Cambridge University Press, 1962), 21.

8. On the Parmenides text see Kirk and Raven (*Pre-Socratic Philosophers*, 278 [§353]), where it is identified as Fragment 8. The fullness of the cosmological opposition is articulated in four examples: (1) light *vs.* dark, (2) fire *vs.* earth, (3) dense *vs.* rare, (4) sameness *vs.* difference. For Empedocles, see *Empedocles, the Extant Fragments*, ed. M. R. Wright (New Haven, Conn.: Yale University Press, 1981), §53. That text states that "πῦρ brought up (ἀνάγω) the shoots of Night-dwelling (ἐννυχίους) men and women." The editor illuminates this sentence by comparing it to literary themes of "bringing up the dead" as found in Sophocles and elsewhere. The specific cosmological theory is that living beings emerge out of Night as if they emerge out of Chaos and shadowy Death. Again, here night is related to chaos, death, and their anomalies. Plato (*Phaedon* 81c) reports that Socrates endorsed a theory that the corporeal, heavy (βαρύ), perceivable part of humans is opposite that part known as ψυχή. It is this latter, lighter part that descends into chthonic locales (Hades) after death.

9. Texts found in *Orphicorum Fragmenta*, ed. Otto Kern (1922; repr., Dublin: Weidmann, 1972). See F54 for the *Hieronymi et Hellanici Theogonial*, F105 for the Ἱερὸς Λόγος reported by Hermias, F162 for the Ἱερὸς Λόγος reported by Proclus, and F103 for Proclus on Νύξ and Φάνης,.

10. *Golden Verses* 70-71 (trans. Johan C. Thom, *The Pythagorean* Golden Verses: *With an Introduction and Commentary*, Religions in the Graeco-Roman World 123 (Leiden, The Netherlands: E. J. Brill, 1995), 99.

11. Walter Burkert (*Ancient Mystery Cults* [Cambridge, Mass.: Harvard University Press, 1987], 97-99) comments on the initiation scene in Apuleius (*Metamorphoses* 11.23.6-8) held at night. Hippolytus (*Refutatio Omnium Haeresium* 5.8) describes the ancient rites at Eleusis: νυκτὸς ἐν Ἐλευσῖνι ὑπὸ πολλῷ πυρὶ τελῶν τὰ μεγάλα καὶ ἄρρητα μυστήρια βοᾷ καὶ κέκραγε λέγων, ἱερόν, βριμόν, τουτέστιν ἰσχυρὰ ἰσχυρόν (at night in Eleusis, by much torch light, [the hierophant], celebrating the great and unutterable mysteries, with a shout cried, Holy One! Terrible One! Strongest of Strong!). Demosthenes (*De Corona* 259) describes Sabazian rites, mentioning τὴν μέν νύκτα νεβρίζων καὶ κρατηρίζων ("at night dressing in fawnskins and becoming immensely intoxicated"). Relevant also is a text that Morton Smith discovered but never, exactly, produced, a letter to Theodore attributed to Clement of Alexandria, in which it is said that mysterious activities occurred between the disciples and Jesus during a specifically nighttime ritual: καὶ ἔμεινε σὺν αὐτῷ τὴν νύκτα ἐκείνην, ἐδίδασκε γὰρ αὐτὸν ὁ Ἰησοῦς τὸ μυστήριον τῆς βασιλείας τοῦ θεοῦ (and he remained with him for that night, for Jesus taught him the mystery of the kingdom of God); see Morton Smith, *Clement of Alexandria and the Secret Gospel of Mark* (Cambridge, Mass.: Harvard University Press, 1973), 452. On all-night festivals, see Walter Burkert (*Greek Religion*, trans. John Raffan [Cambridge, Mass.: Harvard University Press, 1985], 232), who writes about the παννυχίς; but better

information on all-night festivals and especially *Sukkot* is in Jeffrey L. Rubenstein, *The History of Sukkot in the Second Temple and Rabbinic Periods*, Brown Judaic Studies 302 (Atlanta: Scholars Press, 1995), 125-28, with extensive literary citations. Mishnah *Sukkah* 4 refers to stories about Sukkoth festival's all-night dancing and burning of torches in the Jerusalem Temple. Compare also to other all-night festivals, νυκτελία. Such festivals also find testimony in *P.Oxy.* 525.10 for Isis and *Greek Anthology* 9.524.14 for Dionysus. See also Epiphanius (*Panarion Haeresis* 51.22.3) for discussion of Epiphany Festival and the Παννυχίς, especially with comparison of a Christian view of "time fulfillment" and the myth of Kore giving birth to Aion; 5-6 January was the celebration date for both festivals. See Günther Zuntz, Αἰών *in der Literature der Kaiserzeit*, Wiener Studien, Beiheft 17; Arbeiten zur Antiken Religionsgeschichte 2 (Wien: Österreichische Akademie der Wissenschaften, 1992), 12-14.

12. Christine Harrauer (*Meliouchos: Studien zur Entwicklung religiöser Vorstellungen in griechischen synkretistischen Zaubertexten*, Wiener Studien, Beiheft 11: Arbeiten zur Antiken Religionsgeschichte 1 [Wien: Verlag der Österreichische Akademie der Wissenschaften, 1987], 77) discusses Harpocrates in Ptolemaic times, who has qualities of a creature of night since he is νυκτερόφοι-τος (night-roaming). In magical texts we may find a syncretism between Harpocrates and Meliouchos. For Qumran text 4Q560, see Robert H. Eisenman and Michael Wise, *The Dead Sea Scrolls Uncovered: The First Complete Translation and Interpretation of 50 Key Documents Withheld for Over 35 Years* (Shaftesbury, Dorset: Element, 1992), §47. They translate the key lines: "I [adjure you] . . . [and forbidden to disturb by night in dreams or by day] in sleep, the male PRK-demon and the female PRK-demon, those who breach (?) . . ." The term "PRK" is difficult, but perhaps has something to do with grabbing, snatching, or assaulting. See also an Aramaic gold amulet for protection against a *mhblh* [destroyer-demon] that is described in the amulet text as "strange, difficult, and frightening;" Roy Kotansky, "Two Inscribed Jewish Aramaic Amulets from Syria," *Israel Exploration Journal* (1992): 270. On nightmares, see Wilhelm Heinrich Roscher, "Ephialtes: A Pathological-Mythological Treatise on the Nightmare in Classical Antiquity," trans. A. V. O'Brien, in *Pan and the Nightmare: Two Essays*, Dunquin Series 4 (Zürich: Spring Publications, 1974; orig. German publ. in 1900).

13. Sean Freyne, *Galilee, Jesus and the Gospels: Literary Approaches and Historical Investigations* (Philadelphia: Fortress Press, 1988), 41 n.15.

14. For the mundane use, see Ruth Vale, "Literary Sources in Archaeological Description: The Case of Galilee, Galilees and Galileans," *Journal for the Study of Judaism* 18 (1987): 209-226. For the apocalyptic use, see the "pool" of punishment in front of the divine throne in Revelation 20:14,15, just as the θάλασσα is in front of divine thrones in Daniel 7:2-9. Materials in front of God's throne vary, ranging from Ocean to "pavement . . . as clear as heaven" (Exod. 24:10); see Paul H. Seely, "The Firmament and the Water Above, Part 1: The Meaning of *raqia* in Gen. 1:6-8," *Westminster Theological Journal* 53 (1991): 227-40. The heavens are solid, like molten glass (Job 37:18), and they do not sag;

the king sits in a vaulted *cancelli*; there is a Coptic charm (Seely refers to Angelicus Kropp, *Ausgewählte koptische Zaubertexte* [Bruxelles: Édition de la Fondation égyptologique reine Élisabeth, 1930], 3:63-78) that speaks of "Thraki" in regard to the earth, stretched out over the abyss, a possible transliteration of Hebrew *trqîm*, probably from Greek θωράκειον (parapet); see Daniel Sperber, "Some Rabbinic Themes in Magical Papyri," *Journal for the Study of Judaism* 16 (1989): 93-103. In these sources, heaven is designed like a temple or throne room. No scene like these is found in the Markan narrative. Conversely, the Rainer Fragment of the *Apocalypse of Peter* offers the image of a βάπτισμα ἐν σωτηρίᾳ, given to the elect who call on the Lord from within the ᾿Αχερούσίας Λίμνη (Acherusian Sea). This text indicates a thematic link between Eleusinian mysteries and later apocalyptic visions, as noted already by Eduard Norden ("Die Petrus-Apokalypse und ihre antiken Vorbilder," in *Kleine Schriften zum klassischen Altertum* [Berlin: Walter de Gruyter, 1966], 218-33) and further elaborated by Erik Peterson ("Die ‚Taufe' im Acherusischen See," in *Frühkirche, Judentum und Gnosis: Studien und Untersuchungen* [Darmstadt: Wissenschaftliche Buchgesell-schaft, 1982; orig. publ. in 1955], 310-32).

15. In relatively isolated cases, we find a blending of Semitic terms for "Sea" and "Lake." From the synagogue excavations at Dura Europas, an Aramaic inscription on a pictorial depiction of the parting of the sea at the Exodus emerges, labeling the Exodus Sea *'m'* (pond, lake) instead of *ym'* (sea); see Carl Hermann Kraeling, *The Synagogue*, The Excavations at Dura-Europas: Final Report 8, pt. 1 (New Haven, Conn.: Yale University Press, 1956), 269-70.

16. Reinhard Kratz, *Rettungswunder: Motiv-, traditions- und formkritische Aufarbeitung einer biblischen Gattung*, Europäische Hochschuleschriften 123 (Frankfurt am Main: Peter Lang, 1979) and John Day, *God's Conflict with the Dragon and the Sea: Echoes of a Canaanite Myth in the Old Testament*, University of Cambridge Oriental Publications 35 (Cambridge: Cambridge University Press, 1985).

17. The Gospel of Matthew seems fond of σεισμοί (Matt. 24:7, 27:54, 28:2); in the New Testament only Acts of the Apostles reports more earthquakes than Matthew. Earthquakes are veritable initiators of epiphanies, encounters, or divine conflicts. Lucian (*Philopseudes* 22) tells a story about the Gorgon, whose monstrous appearance once was initiated by a σεισμός and a βοῆς οἷον ἐκ βροντῆς (a noise as of thunder). In astrological prognostications, σεισμοί and ἠχαί ἐκ τοῦ οὐρανοῦ (tumultuous noises from heaven) are signs of ominous events to come; see *Catalogus codicum astrologorum graecarum*, ed. Franz Cumont and Franz Boll (Brussels, 1898) for "Codex Parisini," 181, F 441, entitled Σεληνοδρό-μιον, σεισμολόγιον, βροντολόγιον.

18. Kratz, *Rettungswunder*, 28. On God's shaking of the universe, see Brevard Childs ("The Enemy from the North and the Chaos Tradition," *Journal of Biblical Literature* 78 [1959]: 187-98), especially on the key term *r'š* (shake) in a variety of scriptural traditions about the violent overthrow of God's (that is, Israel's) enemies. This tradition persists into magical traditions, as found in lines from the *Sepher Ha-Razim*: "I adjure you by the One whose voice shakes the earth

and moves mountains in His anger . . . and shakes the pillars of the world with his glance"; see Michael A. Morgan, *Sepher Ha-Razim: The Book of Mysteries*, Texts and Translations 25: Pseudepigrapha Series 11 (Chico, Calif.: Scholars Press, 1983), 69. Nitzan (*Qumran Prayer and Religious Poetry*, 254) well compares these lines to 4Q511 37 3-5: "[Their fo]undations shall shake and the earth shall tremble [. . . All their depths sh]all shake and a[ll that is upon it] shall be terrified and pani[cked]."

19. Eileen M. Schuller, *Non-Canonical Psalms from Qumran*, Harvard Semitic Studies 28 (Atlanta: Scholars Press, 1986), 96-97. Her translation and annotations show a compositional amalgam of Psalms 86 and 89, the first with lines about safety and the latter with lines about God's cosmic power.

20. Schürer, *History of the Jewish People*, 3.1:354. On the Ugaritic El, see H. L. Ginsberg, "Ugaritic Myths, Epics, and Legends," in *Ancient Near Eastern Texts Relating to the Old Testament*, ed. James B. Pritchard, 3d ed. (Princeton, N.J.: Princeton University Press, 1969), 137.

21. John Boardman, "'Very Like a Whale': Classical Sea Monsters," in *Monsters and Demons in the Ancient and Medieval Worlds: Papers Presented in Honor of Edith Porada*, Franklin Jasper Walls Lectures 10, ed. Ann E. Farkas, Prudence Harper, and Evelyn Harrison (Mainz am Rhine: Verlag Philipp von Zabern, 1987), 73-84. Philostratus the Younger (*Imagines* 5 ['Ηράκλης ἐν σπαργάνοις]) describes a picture of mortally wounded serpents: "But the serpents, already exhausted, are stretching out their coils upon the ground and drooping their heads towards the babe's hands, showing withal a glimpse of their teeth; these are jagged and poisonous, and their crests sag to one side as death approaches, their eyes have no vision in them, their scales are no longer resplendent with golden and purple colors, nor do they gleam with the various movements of their bodies, but are pale and, where they were once blood-red, are livid" (in *Philostratus the Elder and the Younger* Imagines *and Callistratus* Descriptions, trans. Arthur Fairbanks; Loeb Classical Library (Cambridge, Mass.: Harvard University Press, 1979), 307. In the various traditions these monsters are lethal. By the time of the paintings in the Catacomb of Saints Marcellinus and Peter and in the Catacomb of Callixtus, Jonah's "big fish" is depicted as a serpentine figure with something like a dog's head (large teeth, snapping at Jonah). On the Catacomb of Saints Marcellinus and Peter, see Fabrizio Mancinelli, *Catacombs and Basilicas: The Early Christians in Rome* (Rome: Scala, 1981), 41. On the Catacomb of Callixtus see Pierre du Bourguet, *Early Christian Painting*, trans. Simon Watson Taylor, Compass History of Art 3 (New York: Viking Press, 1965), pl. 3. See also W. Wischmeyer, "Zur Entstehung und Bedeutung des Jonasbildung," in *Actes du Xe Congres International d'Archeologie Chretienne, Thessalonique 28 Septembe - 4 Octobre 1980, 2: Communications*, Studi di Antichità Cristiana 37 (Roma: Pontificio Istituto di Archeologia Cristiana, 1984), 708-719 for history of the continuity of sea monster themes and imagery. For yet another tradition about subduing a serpent, see the Ptolemiac inscription, ἡρώων θεός μέγας μέγας, on a stele from the fifteenth year of Ptolemy XIII (67 B.C.E.). The image accompanying the words is that of Ptolemy riding on

a horse, holding out his right hand to subdue a serpent. This image is discussed in Paul Perdrizet, *Negotium Perambulans in Tenerbris: Études de démonologie gréco-orientale*, Publications de la Faculté des Lettres de l'Université de Strasbourg, fasc. 6 (Strasbourg: Faculté des Lettres de l'Université de Strasbourg, 1922), 9. The Hebrew text of Jonah 1:7 has a line in parallel with it, about the "great fish" (*gdôl dg*), since just before it reports about how the sailors "feared the great [*gdôl*] Lord." The LXX translates this phrase with the same construction that appears in Mark 4:41, ἐφοβήθησαν φόβον μέγαν. With this phrase in Mark, those in the boat with Jesus are shown specifically terrified by the *calm* and, consequently, afraid of Jesus' saving power. In Jonah, it was the *storm* (the terrible sea with its monsters) that created terror for the sailors.

22. See Day (*God's Conflict with the Dragon*, 51) for a parallel construction of Psalm 104 and Genesis 1. See also Kratz (*Rettungswunder*, 41-44) on similar Scripture in Psalms 24:1-2; 95:4-6; 96:11-13; 98:7-9; 135:6-7; 146:6; Sirach 43:23-26. Day (*God's Conflict,* 31) discusses the Canaanite Rider tradition as articulated in Ugaritic term, *rkb `rpt*, and (pp. 84) offers a list of conflict themes: *Dragon and Egypt*: Psalm 87:4; Isaiah 30:7; 51:9-11; Ezekiel 29:3-5; 32:2-8 (the tannin monster, more than a crocodile); *Chaoskampfmythos* and the Exodus from Egypt: Exodus 15:1-1; Psalm 77:17-21; Isaiah 51:9-11; *Chaotic Sea and Assyria*: Isaiah 8:5-8; 17:12-14; *Chaotic Sea and Babylon*: Habakkuk 3:5, 8-10, 15 (reference to Resheph and allusion to Yahweh's seven shafts of lightning have parallels in the Ba`al traditions); *Dragon and Babylon*: Jeremiah 51:34; *Dragon and Uncertain Political Enemy*: Psalm 44:19-20; Isaiah 27:1; *Bashan*: Psalm 68:23 (Bashan is not a name for the chaos monster but the place of that name, probably denoting Mt. Hermon as the mount of the gods); *Beast of the Reeds probably not a sea monster*: Psalm 68:39; *Cosmic Waters as the Nations in general*: Psalm 18:5-18; 46:3-6; 144:5-4.

23. On the astrological theories, see Auguste Bouché-Leclercq, *Histoire de la Divination dans l'Antiquitè,* (Paris: E. Leroux, 1879-82), 2:361. As a matter of record, Poseidon made his way to Berytus, where honors for him ensued. Native Berytians carried this Poseidon to Delos for similar honors, along with their hero, Herakles-Melqart; see Javier Teixidor, *The Pagan God: Popular Religion in the Greco-Roman Near East* (Princeton, N.J.: Princeton University Press, 1977), 42-46. Athenians of the fourth century B.C.E., as another group of out-of-towners, also had a cult for Poseidon on Delos; see Franciszek Sokolowski, *Lois sacrées des cités grecques, supplement,* École Française d'Athènes: Travaux et Mémoirs des Anciens Membres Étrangers de l'École et de Divers Savants 11 (Paris: De Boccard, 1962), §10B.

24. On these facets of Poseidon see "The Cult of Poseidon" in Teixidor, *Pagan God*, 42-46, with complete references for Aramaic, Phoenician, and Cilician inscriptions.

25. Hans J. W. Drijvers, "After Life and Funerary Symbolism in Palmyrene Religion," in *La Soteriologia dei culti orientali nell'Impero Romano: Atti del Collòquio Internazionale, Roma 24-28 Settembre 1979*, ed. by Ugo Bianchi and M. Vermaseren, Études préliminaires aux religions orientales dans l'Empire

Romain 92 (Leiden, The Netherlands: E. J. Brill, 1982), 716.

26. See Hans J. W. Drijvers (*Cults and Beliefs at Edessa*, Études préliminaires aux religions orientales dans l'Empire Romain 62 [Leiden, The Netherlands: E. J. Brill, 1980], 53), writing that "we have therefore ample evidence for the spread of Bel and Nebo in the Syrian area, where Northern Syria in particular seems most to favour these gods. In fact we do not deal with the Babylonian cults as such, but we may assume that at least the name Bel replaced the name of a local Ba'al due to a strong influence of the ancient city and culture of Babylon. Most Bels actually are an *interpretatio babyloniaca* of a local deity. Whether the same is the case with Nebo is dubious." The history of syncretism is lengthy and not confined only to Syrian areas. Drijvers points out (p.54) that older Aramaic inscriptions imply that Bel and Nebo found strong adherents in Aramaic-speaking parts of the Near East and of Egypt. An ostracon of the six or fifth centuriesB.C.E. from Elephantine lists four main deities of the Babylonia pantheon: "to my brother Haggaiyour brother Yarhw. The well-being of my brother (may) Bel and Nebo, Šamaš and Nergal." There once was a Nebo temple in Elephantine (mentioned in letters found at Hermopolis). Drivjers observes (p.54) that an Aramaic funerary inscription from fifth century B.C.E. found at Daskyleion in northwest Anatolia invokes Bel and Nebo to protect a tomb. He writes (p.56) that "other Aramaic inscriptions from Persian times, which were found at Arebsun in Cappadocia, also mention the name of Bel. From the entire content of these inscriptions, however, it becomes clear that they do not deal with the cult of the Babylonian god Bel, but offer an example of the assimilation of Ahura-Mazda to the Semitic deity."

27. Felix Jacobi, *Die Fragmente der griechischen Historiker* (Leiden, The Netherlands: E. J. Brill, 1957), §680 F1.1. This is reported by Syncellus.

28. On Bêl's splitting of Θαλάτθ, see Drijvers, *Cults and Beliefs at Edessa*, 60. The Hellenistic mythographer Abydenos preserves our text, describing how the ancient Babylonians believed that all things had their ἀρχή from the θάλασσα. Abydenos reports about the ancient myths, that Bêl killed (or, "made to cease" [παῦσαι]) the θάλασσα, and that from it Bêl distributed to each people-group (ἐκάστωι) a geographical place (χώρα); see Jacobi, *Fragmente der Griechischen Historiker*, §685 F1(b). Apollonius Rhodius (*Argonautica* 1.492) has Orpheus singing about the origins of the world: that the earth, heaven, and sea were once mingled together in one form, only to be separated later by a battle. On the Great Flood, see Jacobi, *Fragmente der griechischen Historiker*, §680 F 4. Josephus (*Contra Apionem* 1.128) reports that Berossus, an antiquarian mythographer and precedent for Josephus himself, wrote περὶ τοῦ γενομένου κατακλυσμοῦ καὶ τῆς . . . φθορᾶς τῶν ἀνθρώπων καθάπερ Μωσῆς ("about the cataclysmic event that happened and about the corruption . . . of [that generation of] men, as had Moses"); see Jacobi, *Fragmente der griechischen Historiker*, §680 T3.

29. Lucian, *De Dea Syria* 7-13. A celebration of the abatement of cosmic flood waters also occurs earlier, on the last day of the Athenian festival called Anthesteria, on that day called χύτροι (pots); see Jan N. Bremmer, *The Early Greek Concept of the Soul* (Princeton, N.J.: Princeton University Press, 1993 [1987]), 120-21. For parallels to the story about the floating head of Orpheus that

periodically drifts to Lesbos, see Walter Burkert, *Homo Necans: The Anthropology of Ancient Greek Sacrificial Ritual and Myth*, trans. Peter Bing (Berkeley: University of California Press, 1983), 202.

30. Barry Blackburn, *Theios Aner and the Markan Miracle Traditions: A Critique of the Theios Aner Concept as an Interpretative Background of the Miracle Traditions*, Wissenschaftliche Untersuchungen zum Neuen Testament 40 (Tübingen, Germany: J. C. B. Mohr, 1991), 193-95. Blackburn's extensive notes include Poseidon, the Dioscuri, Sarapis, Oceanus, Isis, Athena, Medea, the Persian Magi, Epimenides, Empedocles, Apollonius of Tyana, Julius Caesar, and various Hellenistic kings. See also Kratz (*Rettungswunder*, 95-106) on Magi and Apollonius of Tyana.

31. F. T. van Straten ("Gifts for the Gods," in *Faith, Hope and Worship: Aspects of Religious Mentality in the Ancient World*, ed. H. S. Versnel, Studies in Greek and Roman Religion 2 [Leiden, The Netherlands: E. J. Brill, 1981], 97) refers to *Palatine Anthology* 6.164 and 6.245. He continues: "A number of terracotta *pínakes* and stone votive reliefs offered by rescued sailors have also survived. Our first example is a relief from Piraeus (fourth-third centuries B.C.E.). On the right we have the view of a boat in which a small figure of the skipper is standing. His right hand is raised in worship before his *sotêres*, the two Dioscuri. They have galloped through the air to his assistance, and now, in the calm after the storm, one of the Dioscuri has dismounted in order to receive the thanks of their protege. A later relief (first century C.E.) comes from Tomis on the Black Sea with the inscription: 'This has been dedicated by Dioskourides, the son of Ariston, in redemption of his vow to Heros Manimszos.' In the upper part of the relief we see the hero on horseback by an altar on which a sacrifice is being offered to him. Below, a ship is depicted in shallow relief with the skipper and his boy in the centre imploring the help of the hero with raised hands." See Apollonius of Rhodes (*Argonautica* 1:248) on the women lifting their hands to the αἰθήρ on behalf of the sailors, invoking safety from the ἀθάνατοι; same imagery also in 4:593, when the sons of the Tyndareus do the same. See also Emily Vermeule (*Aspects of Death in Early Greek Art and Poetry*, Sather Classical Lectures 46 [Berkeley: University of California Press, 1979], 187), who writes that "the gullet of the salt is less kind than the hollows of the earth to the dead, who are more lost in it. More Greek cenotaphs replace the bodies of drowned men than of soldiers lost on the battlefield, and early epigrams stress the substitution of the stone, the *sema*, for the man. 'This is the *sema* of Arniadas; grinning Ares ruined him as he fought by the ships . . .'; 'this is the *sema* of Deimias whom the shameless *pontos* lost'; Neos of Sikinos got a *mnema*, but 'the sea veiled me, myself.' Tombstones carved with wrecked ships begin later, in late classical to Roman times, but stress the same loneliness as the epigrams do: the dead man by his ship on an empty shore, or the ship going on alone. A man lost at sea might be less likely to join his family in the underworld, unless the incomplete burial could be strengthened by ceremony and a stone image, a partly magical function."

32. See Apollonius of Rhodes (*Argonautica* 4.588-89) for Castor and Polydeuces praying on behalf of the sailors for safe journey through the Ausonian Sea. For the proverbial thought, see Epictetus (*Discourses* 2.18.27-29): "The man who exercises himself against such external impressions is the true athlete in training. Hold, unhappy man; be not swept along with your impressions! Great is the struggle, divine the task; the prize is a kingdom, freedom, serenity, peace. Remember God; call upon Him to help you and stand by your side, just as voyagers, in a storm, call upon the Dioscuri. For what storm is greater than that stirred up by powerful impressions which unseat the reason? As for the storm itself, what else is it but an external impression? To prove this, just take away the fear of death, and then bring on as much thunder and lightning as you please, and you will realize how great is the calm, how fair the weather, in your governing principle" (trans. W. A. Oldfather, *The Discourses as Reported by Arrian, the Manual, and Fragments*, Loeb Classical Library [London: William Heinemann, 1926]). The divine twins in particular are archaic. O. Gruppe (*Griechische Mythologie und Religionsgeschichte*, Handbuch der klassischen Altertums-Wissenschaft in systematischer Darstellung 5 [München: C. H. Beck'sche Verlagsbuchhandlung, 1906], 725) suggests that the Greek Ζεὺς πατήρ is similar, in respect to being father of divine twins, to the Vedic *Dyaus*, father of the Açvins: *Divó nápata* or *Divás putrâsas*. Lewis Richard Farnell (*Greek Hero Cults and Ideas of Immortality*, Gifford Lectures 1920 [Oxford: Clarendon Press, 1921; repr. 1970], 175-80) criticizes the theory of direct influence from Vedic myth.

33. Mark 4:38. See Roy D. Kotansky ("Jesus and Heracles in Cádiz [τὰ Γάδειρα]: Death, Myth, and Monsters at the 'Straits of Gibraltar' [Mark 4:35-5:43]" in *The Bible and Culture: Ancient and Modern Perspectives*, ed. Adela Yarbro Collins, SBL Symposium Series [Atlanta : Scholars Press, 1998], 169, 185): "The whole context of the sea, in fact, betokens the mythical 'waters of death'." See LXX Jonah 1:6b, ὅπως διασώσῃ ὁ θεὸς ἡμᾶς καὶ μὴ ἀπολώμεθα. On the terms in use as metaphors, see *Anthologia Graeca* 5.11: Εἰ τοὺς ἐν πελάγει σῴζεις, Κύπρι, κἀμὲ τὸν ἐν γᾷ, ναυαγόν, φιλίη, σῶσον ἀπολλύμενον (Cypris, you save them in the open sea, would that you save me now, dear friend; I'm shipwrecked on the land; Save that which is being destroyed!). Mark's use of ἀπολλύειν (destory) follows this lexical usage. For σώζω (save) in context of safety at sea in other Greek verse, see *Anthologia Graeca* 6.164, 166, 349; 7.269; 9.9. In the same verse contexts for ἀπολλυμένην see 7.272. Shipwreck themes in Greek and Latin literature are partially indexed by W. Kroll, "Schiffahrt," in *Pauly's Realencyclopädie*, zweite Reihe (1921), cols. 412-14. The same use of σώζω and its compounds are found in the shipwreck story in Acts 27:20, 31, 43; 28:1. Also to be mentioned here is use of these terms in Mark 8:35: ὃς γὰρ ἐὰν θέλῃ τὴν ψυχὴν οὗ σῶσαι ἀπολέσει αὐτήν, a phrase repeated elsewhere and in synoptically parallel materials. See also James 4:12, ὁ δυναμενος σῶσαι καὶ ἀπολέσαι; 1 Corinthians 1:18, τοῖς μὲν ἀπολλμένοις μωρία ἐστίν τοῖς δὲ σῳζομένοις ἡμῖν δύναμις θεοῦ ἐστιν; compare Mark 3:4, ψυχὴ σῶσαι ἢ ἀποκτεῖναι.

34. Franz Cumont (*Recherches sur le symbolisme funéraire des Romains,* Haut-Commissariat de l'État Français en Syrie et au Liban, Service des Antiquités: Bibliothèque archéologique et historique 35 [Paris: Paul Geuthner, 1942; repr., New York: Arno Press, 1975], 36, 76, 83) suggests that the notion that a sojourn of the deceased occupies one of the two hemispheres stems from the astronomer-priests. It is inseparable from a cosmology that represents the starry sky as a solid sphere, surrounding the earth and in a like manner spherical, being unmovable at the center of the universe.

35. Thom (*Pythagorean* Golden Verses, 111), referring to Iamblichus, *Life of Pythagoras* 155.

36. See Diskin Clay ("Sailing to Lampsacus: Diogenes of Oenoanda, New Fragment 7," *Greek, Roman, and Byzantine Studies* 14 [1972]: 49-59) for a vivid account of the near-death experience of Epicurus at sea. Clay translates (p.50): "of the rocks, from which it did not yet wash him in [to dry land], but the sea gulped him down and belched him back up again (ἀναροφῆσαι ἡ θάλασσα καὶ ῥῆξαι πάλιν). It was then that he was lacerated (συντρίβω), as you would expect, and he swallowed down (κάψεν) a great mouthful [of salt water]; he was badly skinned (ξαίνω) when he crashed upon the sea-eaten rocks (ἀλιβρῶσι λίθοις). But gradually he succeeded in swimming (διένηχε) through to open water (εἰς ὕδωρ), and just then he was borne along on the waves (κυμάτων) to the festival drum [?] and, flayed almost to an inch, he barely escaped (ἐσώθη μόγις) with his life. Now he spent the next day in this state upon a high promontory and the following night and the next day until nightfall (τὸ ἐξῆς διῆγε τὴν ἡμέρα οὕτως καὶ τὴν ἐπιοῦσαν νυκτὰ πάλιν ἡμέραν ἕως ἑσπέρας), exhausted by hunger and his injuries. . .We now understand that events which lay beyond our control (τὸ αὐτόματον) are benefits despite appearances—the very doctrine he commends to you as reasonable. For your herald (κῆρυξ) who brought you to safety (διέσωσεν ὑμᾶς) has died; for afterwards chance. . . ." Clay compares this to the account of Odysseus being washed up on the island of Scherie (*Odyssey* 5.367-463), a text that includes report of a strong wind (ἄνεμος), two days and two nights on the waves (ἔνθα δύω νύκτας δύο τ᾽ ἤματα κύματι πηγῷ), a great wave (κῦμα), Odysseus swimming (νῆκε), and having skinned stripped off from his hands upon the rocks (πρὸς πέτρησι). This account of Odysseus reports that, after the hero is desperately bandied about on the water, at dawn on the third day the winds cease and a calm prevails (ἄνεμος μὲν ἐπαύσατο ἠδὲ γαλήνη ἔπλετο νηνεμίη). My observation is that it is not uncommon to find themes of wind, cliffs, wave, and mountainous coast linked together. See *Odyssey* 3.286-290: "but when he in his turn, as he passed over the wind-dark sea in the hollow ships, reached in swift course the steep height (ὄρος) of Malea, then Zeus, whose voice is borne afar, planned for him a hateful path and poured upon him the blasts of shrill winds (ἄνεμος), and the waves (κῦμα) were swollen to huge size, like mountains"; *Odyssey* 5.400-405: "But when he was as far away as a man's voice carries when he shouts, and heard the boom of the sea upon the reefs—for the great wave thundered against the dry land, belching upon it in terrible fashion, and all things were wrapped in the foam of the sea; for there were neither harbors where ships

might ride, nor roadsteads, but projecting headlands, and reefs, and cliffs" (trans. A. Murray, *Homer: The Odyssey*, Loeb Classical Library [Cambridge, Mass.: Harvard University Press, 1995]).

37. *Paulys Real-Encyclopädie der Classischen Altertumswissenschaft*, ed. Georg Wissowa and Wilhelm Kroll (Stuttgart: J. B. Metzler, 1905-), vol. 5 s.v. "Λαῖλαψ".

38. For *PGM* 6.33 see E. O'Neil in Betz, *Greek Magical Papyri*, 111. For the Porphyry text see Harrauer, *Meliouchos*, 75.

39. See Kotansky ("Jesus and Herakles") on raging μεγάλη λαῖλαψ in Homer, *Odyssey* 12.408. The Homeric context also includes the quieting of the Storm and then the appearance of a whirlpool. Apollonius Rhodius (*Argonautica* 1.1203) tells of the κατάιξ (hurricane) that rampages suddenly, at the time of year when Orion sets.

40. Christine Harrauer (*Meliouchos*, 75) refers to Richard. Wünsch, *Antike Fluchtaflen*, 2d ed. (Bonn: A. Marcus and E. Weber, 1912), §4.5. On *PGM* 4.182 see Harrauer (p.76 n.76), suggesting a complicated scenario of how Λαιλαμ in the curse tablet might be related to Λαῖλαψ in the magical texts. She suggests "that Λαῖλαψ was nothing other than the Graecization of `l m` or even more accurately, *l-`l m* . . . what in the magical texts appeared as ειλαμ / ιλαμ / ευλαμ, etc., [until] Λαιλαμ; from here to the interpretation [of these terms] as Λαῖλαψ was but a short step." Λαιλαμ appears in *PGM* 4.1984, one part of a four-name epithet of Helios: Λαιλαμ / Ἰάω / ζουχε / πιποη. 2 Enoch [J] 70.4-6 speaks of disobedient people of God who, in particular, will relate to storms and waves as divine powers in and of themselves: ". . . the time of the destruction of all the earth, and of every human being and of everything that lives on the earth, is drawing near. For in his days there will be a very great breakdown on the earth, for each one has begun to envy his neighbor, and people against people have destroyed boundaries, and the nation wages war. And all the earth is filled with vileness and blood and every kind of evil. (And) even more than that, they have abandoned their Lord, and will do obeisance to unreal gods, and to the vault above the sky, and to what moves above the earth, and *to the waves of the sea*" (trans. F. I. Anderson in *The Old Testament Pseudepigrapha*, 1: *Apocalyptic Literature and Testaments* ed. James E. Charlesworth [Garden City, N.Y.: Doubleday, 1983], 200). *Anthologia Graeci* 6.349 has an invocation addressed to Nereids, Poseidon, and Waves (Κύματα).

41. Jeremiah 25:32, "Thus says the Lord of hosts: See, disaster is spreading from nation to nation, and a great tempest is stirring from the farthest parts of the earth" (NRSV). See also Wisdom 5:23, "A mighty wind will rise against them, and like a tempest it will winnow them away. Lawlessness will lay waste the whole earth, and evil-doing will overturn the thrones of rulers" (NRSV).

42. See N. Wyatt (*Myths of Power: A Study of Royal Myth and Ideology in Ugaritic and Biblical Tradition*, Ugaritisch-Biblische Literatur 13 [Münster: Ugarit-Verlag, 1996], 128) for a quite ancient version of victory over the Water as found in a twenty-fourth century B.C.E. text from the period of Akkad, which he translates: "O father! you whose task is to be the barrier against the waves of

the Sea, furious warrior, attack! O Tispak! O father! you whose task is to be the barrier against the waves of the Sea, God, king of the gods."

43. Wendy Cotter ("The Markan Sea Stories: Their History, Formation, and Function in the Literary Context of Greco-Roman Antiquity" [Ph.D. diss., University of St. Michael's College, 1991], 406) concludes that, based on comparisons to the symbolism of emperors, here "Jesus becomes a type of Lord of the Earth. In his miracle he literally commands the elements to be silent. Translated to the sociopolitical realm of life, this action means that Jesus has the power to take charge of the forces that cause war, discord, and social upheaval. According to the way the storm symbolism is used for Augustus, Jesus' power over the storm means that he has command over the very events that Τύχη/*Fortuna* can muster at will. Jesus is presented as the Lord who will bring peace and stability to all those who turn to him."

44. Günter Kettenbach, *Einführung in die Schiffahrtsmetaphorik der Bibel*, Europäische Hochschuleschriften 512 (Frankfurt am Main: Peter Lang, 1994), 289. The chapter of importance is "Jesus Christus im Heck." One can understand the desire to use this material to analyze Mark. Odysseus came on the boat, spreading out a rug and a linen sheet on the stern (πρύμνα) of the boat, on which to fall asleep. He slept soundly, "as if dead (θανάτῳ ἐοικώς)." Kettenbach's observations about how the sleeping Jesus is symbolic of his divine and royal status parallels observations made by Bernard F. Batto ("The Sleeping God: An Ancient Near Eastern Motif of Divine Sovereignty," *Biblica* 68 [1987]: 153-76), who suggests that "patently, Mark was drawing upon the long biblical tradition of the creator's battle with the chaos monster, though the latter is reinterpreted more specifically as the diabolic kingdom of Satan and his cohorts. Just as the Israelites had called upon Yahweh to awaken and save them in their tribulation, so Jesus' beleaguered disciples wake Jesus for help against the sea which threatened to engulf them. Accordingly, the image of the sleeping Jesus is modeled after that of the sleeping divine king. His sleeping indicates not powerlessness but the possession of absolute authority" (p.175). Kettenbach's claims about the meaning of Odyseus' sleep (p.311) seem to run somewhat far afield, since Homer clearly shows that the lovely and peaceful sleep of Odysseus is that of a man who now, finally, is able to sleep in peace, at last having opportunity to forget all the troubles and suffering he has endured (*Odyssey* 13.92). These are not themes of a divine hero with so much command over nature that he can peacefully sleep; they instead are themes of an overworked, overwhelmed, and suffering Odysseus: *Od.* 5.223, ἤδη γὰρ μάλα πολλὰ πάθον καὶ πολλὰ μόγησα (I have already suffered much and toiled much); 19.118, μάλα δ᾽ εἰμὶ πολύστονος (I am a man of many sorrows); 5.339 and 20.34 for the descriptor κάμμορος (ill-fated).

45. Theophrastus, Χαρακτῆρες 25.1, in *The Characters of Theophrastus: An English Translation from a Revised Text with Introduction and Notes*, ed. R. C. Jebb and J. E. Sandys (London: Macmillan, 1909), 134-35.

46. Morton Smith, "De Superstitione (Moralia 164E-171F)," in *Plutarch's Theological Writings and Early Christian Literature*, ed. Hans Dieter Betz, Studia ad Corpus Hellenisticum Novi Testamenti 3 (Leiden, The Netherlands: E. J. Brill,

1975), 1-35. Plutarch said that πάθος is an ἀπάτη (tricky deception). As a result, δέος (dread) is had when thinking about θεούς (gods). See *De Superstitione* 165B2.

47. Fragmentary texts from a work by Seneca against superstition are found in Saint Augustine, *De civitas dei* 6.10. See Harold Lucius Axtell, *The Deification of Abstract Ideas in Roman Literature and Inscriptions* (Chicago: University of Chicago Press, 1907), 79.

48. Peter John Koets (Δεισιδαιμονία: *A Contribution to the Knowledge of the Religious Terminology in Greek* [Purmerend, The Netherlands: J. Muuss, 1952]) finds several uses of the term: (1) *Used in a favorable sense*: (a) to fear the gods, (b) to be awe-struck, (c) to be conscience-smitten (Diodorus Siculus 27.4), (d) to regard an event as a divine intervention (Diodorus Siculus 36.13), and (e) to feel uneasy because of a prediction (Diodorus Siculus 19.108.2). (2) *Used in an unfavorable sense*: (a) to be full of nervous, superstitious fear, (b) to be excessively scrupulous, and (c) to fear "demons" (Clement of Alexandria *Protrepticos* 10.108.1). (3) *Further negatives about this religious experience:* (a) fear (terror) of the divine powers (Theophrastus Χαρακτῆρες 16; Stobaeus *Eclogues* II 92 W = δεισιδαιμονία δὲ φόβος θεῶν ἢ δαιμόνες, as collected in Jacob von Arnim, *Stoicorum Veterum Fragmenta* [Stuttgart: Teubner, 1903], §408), (b) exaggerated piety or excessive religious zeal, (c) the regarding of natural phenomena as bad omens, (d) religion (belief in divine providence; in judgment after death), (e) taboo, (f) veneration of unworthy objects, (g) certain ways of observing of Jewish law (Josephus *Antiquities* 12.259), (h) Christianity (by pagans), (i) paganism (by Christians), and (j) sinful human sacrifice (by Christian apologists). On the general arguments then made about the ways in which humans rely on the divine, see P. A. Meijer ("Philosophers, Intellectuals and Religion in Hellas," in *Faith, Hope and Worship: Aspects of Religious Mentality in the Ancient World*, ed. H. S. Versnel, Studies in Greek and Roman Religion 2 [Leiden, The Netherlands: E. J. Brill, 1981], 216-63), who notes that in Stobaeus (*Eclogues* II.147.18) the triad ἀθεότης-εὐσέβεια-δεισιδαιμονία appears, the same three concepts already found together in Theophrastus Περὶ εὐσέβειας.

5

Mark 5:1-20:
A Demoniac Legion

In its capitulation, the Codex Alexandrinus refers to this account as Περὶ τῶν λεγεῶνος (*Concerning the Legion*),[1] revealing one ancient interpretation that the focus of this story is the "Legion." The specific narrative geography of this account (εἰς τὴν χώραν τῶν Γερασηνῶν [into the Chora of te Gerasenes], 5:1) is problematic because of textual variants in the lines that provide the information.[2] The variants Gerasa and Gadara refer to two prominent Hellenistic cities in the Decapolis, neither of which was near a θάλασσα (ocean) in which a "herd of pigs" might drown. One well-known Bible atlas identifies the variant Gergesa as a town located on the east shore of the Sea of Galilee, therefore near the θάλασσα by way of a steep incline.[3] But this variant is not well attested in the manuscript traditions, and locating it in cartography seems unwarranted. The specific geopolitical entity introduced in this account is actually called τὴν χώραν τῶν Γερασηνῶν, a technical designation for an incorporated area linked to a πόλις. This πόλις with its surrounding fields (εἰς τὴν πόλιν καὶ εἰς τοὺς ἀγρούς [into the city and into the fields]) is indicated in 5:14, and the geographical and political designation Δεκάπολις (Decapolis)is given in 5:20 for the area into which the exorcised man goes at the end of the story. These geographical designations emphasize thoroughly hellenized areas.

A χώρα properly consisted of countryside and villages in socio-economic relationship to a city.[4] Archaeological finds in Galilee have shown a dynamic interrelationship between πόλις (city) and χώρα (surrounding land), and perhaps Mark correctly depicts the historical significance of these realities in Galilee.[5] Under foreign political and military control, chief cities might not have been granted the more independent status of πόλις but instead made the capitals of toparchies. Such were the conditions in which Herod Antipas found himself, as indicated in the story about his court in Mark 6:21 (τοὶς μεγιστᾶσιν αὐτοῦ καὶ τοὶς χιλιάρχοῖς καὶ τοὶς πρώτοις τῆς Γαλιλαίας [for his courtiers, chiliarchs, and leaders of Galilee]).[6] The territory of Antipas had been divided into two parts, each with its chief cities and areas that were in Galilee proper and in areas across the Jordan.[7] A sense of the significance of geopolitical realities is indeed evident in Mark, but there is little apparent interest in exact locations or roads between locations.

Mark combines two important ideas, that of the Hellenistic πόλις and that of the chaotic and powerful θάλασσα. The πόλις with its surrounding area, fields, citizens, and resident aliens on the one hand, and the sea with its enormous and cosmic destructive power on the other, are the essential locations in which the action takes place. Already introduced to the sea, we know it has a rich meaning. Mark introduces us to the other reality, the Hellenistic πόλις, through its backyard, the cemetery.

Fustel de Coulanges began his exposition on the ancient city with a discussion of family dead and their burial near kin.[8] To have the dead near, in order to provide continuity between the living and the dead, demanded a place. Ancient Mesopotamian cultures developed imagery and depictions of their dead corresponding to the organization of the entire cosmos, the depictions depending heavily on representations of place. The individual's role and status in the city, the placement of individuals and individual families in written genealogies, and the resting of the bones of significant individuals in specific places all reinforced social patterns that developed within these ancient cities. In particular, the spirit of the individual departed (*etemmu*) "was closely connected with (and in fact dependent on) the presence of the bones in the grave for its care."[9] Collecting the bones of the prominent dead and moving them from a temporary resting place to a permanent burial was a widespread practice. Joseph makes his brothers promise to carry his bones out of Egypt "when God comes to you" (Genesis 50:24). Simon sends for the bones of his brother Jonathan, and buried them in Modein, "the town of his ancestors" (1 Maccabees 13:25). The bones of Hippodameia reportedly were carried to Olympia from Argolis. Bones of important individuals, often benefactors of one kind or another, required proper and, often, special burial.[10] These tombs were places to be protected. The remains of the dead were not to be altered or disturbed, and many inveighed against doing so, threatening curses on disturbers.[11]

Archaic Greek burials and mourning rites were oriented to family and place.[12] This was common, and the Roman *Parentalia* (13-21 February) speaks volumes about such family and place orientation, as also does the role of the expiator in the Roman *Lemuria* (9, 11, 13 May). In the latter, the father of a family is to go through his house, using a prescribed ritual, and drive out the shades of dead relatives.[13] Roman cities themselves were organized around unique celebrations of *Mundus* (ritual pit) and *Terminus* (god of boundary-markers). The latter involved sacrifices of materials similar to the materials used in sacrifices for the dead.[14] Such ideas flourished elsewhere. Cults of the dead in ancient Judah very much depended on an established place.[15] In general, cities everywhere were complex places of geographical organization and meaning. They were made up of the living and the dead.

In Mark 5:1-20, Jesus has little to do with any part of the general civic life of a πόλις other than involvement with the locally well-known yet strange occurrences in the cemetery of a particular πόλις. These occurrences do not involve identified citizens or members of identified families, or for that matter any famous foreigners, heroes, or enemies. Rather the actions involve an anonymous ἄνθρωπος who, as a victim, is plagued with a violent "daimōnization" while he inhabits the tombs and graves of other people. The setting of the cemetery brings clearly into focus the theme of a place for the dead, including any ghosts of the dead believed possibly present there. The violent activity reported in connection with the anonymous individual in the setting of a cemetery raises the question specifically about what kind of *daimōnic* activity is reported here, in this type of place. The set of narrative elements found in Mark 5:1-20 includes the πόλις (with implications of its social sense of place and its organization), the cemetery, the dead, binding with chains, adjurations, *daimōns* (spirits of the dead), θάλασσα, mass drowning, violence, and confrontation. A representation of the anomalous frightful emerges from these, especially in the manner in which they are presented, wherein the cemetery is not a place of rest but of unrest, and wherein spiritual entities have been creating irrepressible violence for uncertain and fearful ends. Nothing is said in this narrative about the particular orientation of the cemetery or its specific location in regard to the πόλις. Instead, just the opposite is communicated. The anonymous ἄνθρωπος is out of place, wherever this true place is meant to be; his house and origin are elsewhere (in 5:19, ὕπαγε εἰς τὸν οἶκόν σου πρὸς τοὺς σούς ["go to your house and to your people"]). Likewise, the unclean spirits are ambiguously placed. Although apparently they prefer the cemetery, either the tombs or the θάλασσα are domiciles acceptable to them, the latter being an abode of mysterious depth and chaotic destruction.

The phrase ἐν πνεύματι ἀκαθάρτῳ (by an unclean spirit; 5:2) is, in general, a phrase favored by Mark for this story. In Matthean and Lukan parallels to this account, it appears only in Luke 8:29. As a phrase favored by Mark, it brings its own ambiguity, and for at least two reasons. The first point of ambiguity in the phrase ἐν πνεύματι ἀκαθάρτῳ is how actions of an individual could be due to an independent agent operating external to the individual's will. In Mark, the preposition ἐν is used four times in phrases containing the word πνεῦμα: ἐν πνεύματι ἀκαθάρτῳ in 1:23 and 5:2 and ἐν [τῷ] πνεύματι [τῷ] ἁγίῳ in 1:8 and 12:36. In all cases, the πνεῦμα, whether holy or unclean, is a force from outside the person, compelling to act or to speak.[16] This creates a fundamental uncertainty. What is a human who is driven so? How could such a person act without volition? In matters of daimōnization, there is ever a gray area between holding and being held, possessing and being possessed. In 5:8 Mark reports that Jesus has already said, ἔξελθε τὸ πνεῦμα τὸ ἀκάθαρτον ἐκ τοῦ ἀνθρώπου (unclean spirit, come out of the human), yet who is the addressee of this statement? Two things are addressed at once, the man and the unclean spirits, thereby causing uncertainty. In the cases of unclean spirits, Jesus here relates to the human being who is being compelled while at the same time talking to the compelling power. To this is attached yet another uncertainty, that created by the grammatical shift in this story between the presentation of a *singular* unclean spirit and a *plurality* of entities with the one name, Λεγιών (5:10). The query about the entity's name in 5:9 helps create the confusion, for the question of identity is asked in the singular (τί ὄνομα σοι) but the answer returned is in both singular and plural (λεγιών ὄνομά μοι, ὅτι πολλοί ἐσμεν). Asking such a question suggests an exorcistic theory about how control over the right *single* name might facilitate divine expungement of a *single* entity. There is only one man; he gives no more than one name, but it implies a plurality.[17] What kind of entity is many but with one name? With whom is Jesus dealing?

A second point of ambiguity stems from the terminology. The ἄνθρωπος is later in the narrative called τὸν δαιμονιζομένον (the demonized man; 5:15). Variant readings of 5:12 add to the verb form παρεκάλεσαν (they exhorted) the subjects δαιμόνες (demons) or τὰ δαιμόνια (the demons). Perhaps this was an attempt to integrate the singular-plural grammatical difficulty through the plural Matthean δαιμόνες or Lukan δαιμόνια. Even so, what is the relationship between πνεῦμα ἀκάθαρτον and τὸν δαιμονιζομένον? Franz Annen suggested that in Mark, as in much literature of this time, there was no distinction between the two.[18] In Mark 7:25-26 and 3:22, 30 the terms πνεῦμα ἀκαθάρτον and δαιμόνιον appear linked together as synonyms. Elsewhere in Mark, they are not so linked, although the possibility persists that they are synonymous throughout, even when not used in close proximity to each other. In *PGM* 4.3080 πνεῦμα and δαιμόνιον are paired with καί,[19] but the usage is lexically different from the usage in Mark in that the adjective ἀκαθάρτον is missing. *PGM* 15.16 offers the phrase τὰ πνεύματα τῶν δαιμόνιων (the spirits of the daimōnes). Minucius Felix opined that ancient poets had thought *daemones* to be *spiritus*.[20] In *PGM* 4.1238 we find a Coptic "unclean daimōn." In astrological materials it is said that φόβος (fear) occurs after an exposure to a πνεῦμα ἀκαθάρτον (unclean spirit). With a similar emphasis on the intrusive and disrupting quality of such entities, but with different terminology, Chrysippus endorsed the influence of φαύλας δαίμονας (foul demons), a belief also attributed to Empedocles, Plato, Xenocrates, and Democritus.[21] *Orphic Hymn* 1.31-33 (Πρὸς Μουσαῖον), refers to δαίμονας οὐρανίους τε καὶ ἠερίους καὶ ἐνύδρους καὶ χθονίους καὶ ὑποχθονίους ἠδ᾽ ἐμπυριφοίτους (heavenly, aetherial, watery, chthonic, sub-chthonic and fiery-laden daimōns). The *Testament of Solomon* refers to πνεύματα with the adjectives ἀέρια (aerial), ἐπίγεια (earth-bound) and καταχθόνια (chthonic).[22] An Aramaic amulet contains the line "the evil spirit and the shadow spirit and the demons."[23] Terminology clearly is quite fluid throughout traditions about these entities and their earthly effects. Vettius Valens (*Anthologiarum Libri* 1.1) says that under the sign of Κρόνος certain types of violent deaths (τοὺς δὲ θανάτους βιαίους ἐν ὕδατι [violent deaths by water]) are to be expected, and that these deaths are attended by παθῶν δαιμονισμοῦ (emotions of "daimōnality"), which are linked to ἀκαθαρσία. This example from Vettius presents elements like those of Mark 5:1-20, specifically in regard to daimonic entities, highly emotional events, the violent drowning of living beings, and uncleanness.

In the Markan account, the actual vocabulary is not δαιμόνιον but τὸν δαιμονιζόμενον. In the summary of Mark 1:32-34, the participle δαιμονιζόμενον in 1:32 is matched in 1:34 with the substantive δαιμόνιον. But this does not occur in 5:1-20. Instead, the participle is emphasized, being used in 5:15, 16, and 18. This form is found in *PGM* 4.3009 (Πρὸς δαιμονιζομένους), *PGM* 13.242 (ἐὰν δαιμονιζομένῳ εἴπῃς), Lucian *Philopseudes* 16 (τοὺς δαιμονιζομένους), and Josephus *Antiquities* 8.47 (τοῦ δαιμονιζομένου). It seems a reasonably well-known designation for one thought to be troubled by or under the influence of a δαίμων or δαιμόνιον.[24] In contrast, the participle δαιμονιζόμενος does not occur in the LXX. Neither is the phrase πνεῦμα ἀκαθάρτον common in the LXX, although the appearance once in Zechariah 13:2 in the articular form, τὸ πνεῦμα τὸ ἀκαθάρτον, is a notable similarity. Outside of scripture, the *Testament of Benjamin* 5.2 promises that "if one does good then the unclean spirits will flee from you (τὰ ἀκάθαρτα πνεῦμα φεύξεται ἀφ᾽ ὑμῶν)." Participial terminology in these matters seems to have been common to the traditions of magic, but not to Scripture.

Use of the term *rwh* in the Dead Sea Scrolls, even in texts where critics agree that it refers to demons, is likewise complex and multifaceted.[25] In these texts, the phrase "unclean spirit" is not predominant. Elsewhere, in apocalyptic texts such as 1 Enoch, usage of terminology for "evil spirit" is abundant.[26] A conjunction of these ideas is found in Josephus *War* 7.185, which reports that a certain plant (called Baaras) had exorcistic qualities against a certain kind of δαιμόνιον: τὰ γὰρ καλούμενα δαιμόνια, ταῦτα δὲ πονηρῶν ἐστιν ἀνθρώπων πνεύματα τοῖς ζῶσιν εἰσδυόμενα καὶ κτείνοντα (for those entities called daimons, these are spirits of evil people, entering the living and killing them). In this case, what is emphasized is the *evil disposition* of humans,[27] that such a disposition develops out of evil inclinations, and sometimes is transferred to other humans in highly intrusive ways. Elsewhere, a Jewish inscription from Rome of the second century C.E. records a father's lament about the early death of his daughter who had been "snatched away" by a πονηρὲ δαίμων (evil daimōn).[28] These texts touch on the far-reaching topic of cosmic dualism, that is, on good and evil divine powers, and on good and evil human dispositions. A developed theory of cosmic dualism is not primary in Mark 5:1-20, meaning that the events of this narrative should not be taken as apocalyptic events of an idealized battle between Good and Evil. Instead, they are to be taken as events of daimonic violence and its subsequent exorcism within a more local context of conflict between divine powers. Granted that the Legion meets Jesus with the acclamation, Ἰσους υἱὲ τοῦ ὑψίστος (Jesus son of the highest). The epithet ὑψίστος (highest) was common enough, in both Jewish and non-Jewish traditions, and perhaps was equivalent to the Latin *exsuperantissimus*.[29] Even so, two equally matched cosmic powers ready to do battle are not depicted here.

The terminology for unclean spirits, demons, or specific spirits in the Gospel of Mark appears not to be diagnostically precise. The reader is left with the impression of divine conflict, yet without exact details about the nature of the opposing entities. The most detail that is ever given in Mark concerns a type of spirit called, in 9:17, πνεῦμα ἄλαλον. A lengthy case history of symptoms follows, supporting this label, yet the entity is generically summarized by Jesus ambiguously as τοῦτο τὸ γένος (9:29).

Mark 5:1-20   131

In 5:1-20 there is another lengthy description of symptoms and behavior. Two word groups are used to refer to the same phenomenon (πνεῦμα ἀκαθάρτον and τὸν δαιμονιζομένον). In addition, a plurality within the entity is identified as Λεγιών. No clear diagnostic categories are given, and the picture here remains unclear.

The effect of these spiritual entities is evident in the history of events in this cemetery. An ἄνθρωπος had his home among the tombs (ὃς τὴν κατοίκησιν εἶχεν ἐν τοῖς μνήμασιν). His was a torturous existence.

> καὶ οὐδὲ ἁλύσει οὐκέτι οὐδεὶς ἐδύνατο αὐτὸν δῆσαι διὰ τὸ αὐτὸν πολλάκις πέδαις καὶ ἁλύσεσιν δεδέσθαι καὶ διεσπάσθαι ὑπ᾽ αὐτοῦ τὰς ἁλύσεις καὶ τὰς πέδας συντετρῖφθαι καὶ οὐδεὶς ἴσχυεν αὐτὸν δαμάσαι, καὶ διὰ παντὸς νυκτὸς καὶ ἡμέρας ἐν τοῖς μνήμασιν καὶ ἐν τοῖς ὄρεσιν ἦν κράζων καὶ κατακόπτων ἑαυτὸν λίθοις (and nobody anymore was able to bind him with chains, because frequently he was given chains and shackles and the chains were torn apart by him and the shackles were shattered, and nobody had the power to subdue him. And all day and all night he was among the tombs and hills, screaming and mutilating himself with stones) (5:3-5).

The binding of the man indicates a previous series of violent episodes, and the phrase οὐδεὶς ἴσχυεν αὐτὸν δαμάσαι shows a violent power struggle that had been taking place. The encounter between Jesus with the human/entity is far more pacific than the previous reported activities. I should note that chained hands or feet not uncommonly occur in scenarios of the anomalous frightful, where uncertainty centers on fearful outcomes of strangely irrepressible power. This is so also of military overpowering, including the kind that some apocalyptic scenarios depict (Pliny *Epistles* 7.7; see appendix D, "Chains and Haunted Houses"). In this narrative the cemetery is a site of a history of unresolved trouble and continuing disorder. No resolution for this disorder had yet been made, not even through previous attempts to bind the violent man and stop the unclean disorganization.

Let us take care to notice here another cluster of elements of the anomalous frightful: demons, bindings, opposition, and unclean creatures. The cemetery setting here represents proximity to impurity, but not necessarily impurity as expressed in rabbinic literature.[30] What is happening here is more than contamination by contact with tombs. Instead, there is depicted an active agent of ongoing impurity.[31] From a later and different context we may find a clue to understand the basic elements. In his collection of curses and binding spells, John Gager

includes one from the fifth century C.E. in upper Egypt: "Rouse yourselves, you *daimones* who lie here [at the tomb] and seek out Euphemia,
to whom Dorothea gave birth, for Theon, to whom Proechia gave birth.
Let her not be able to sleep for the entire night, but lead her until she
comes to his feet."[32] The concept of δαίμονες (demons) at or near the
grave, being themselves the disembodied presences of the deceased, was
common, and the use of δαίμων to describe a dead person was a matter of
course in Hellenistic grave inscriptions.[33] The same meaning for δαίμων
prevailed elsewhere. The Derveni Papyrus col. VI has δαιμόνες ἐμποδὼν
(hindering demons) equated with ψυχαί (souls) of the dead. Johan C.
Thom discusses the occurrence of the phrase καταχθόνιοι δαίμονες
(underground demons) in the *Golden Verses*, plausibly concluding that
these were spirits or souls of the dead.[34] The epithet καταχθόνιος
(underground) was common for various deities who were intimately
related to death, the grave, the journey after death, or the underworld.
These θεοὶ καταχθόνιοι could have been Pluto, Demeter, Persephone, and
the Furies, as well as others from a variety of religions, such as the
Anatolian Μὴν Καταχθόνιος (The Underground Mên).[35]

Linked specifically to the idea of the dead as δαίμονες is the question
of the violence that these dead had suffered. Their demise through
violence was considered unjust. Consequently, there were strong desires
to know who is avenged and who not, within a long-cultivated sensitivity
for *ius talionis*. This was widespread throughout all ancient Mediterranean areas. Unjust death, which was linked to violent death (βιαιοθάνατος) and inopportune death (ἄωρος), commonly was thought to cause the
dead to become ἀλάστορες (avenging entities).[36] We need to know that
revenge and recompense were constant, stemming from murder and
violent death. Under Athenian law, an important moment of legal
proceedings was the institution of a δίκη φόνου, a right of blood-revenge.
It was a crucial step in the resolution of crimes of homicide, being a type
of sanctioned revenge meant to cleanse the impurity of homicide.[37] In
Scripture, rights of asylum were sought for protection against avenging
family members. Adonijah, fearing Solomon, grabbed hold of the horns
of the altar (1 Kings 1:50-51). Scripture also offers themes of bloodguilt
and subsequent reparation. There is the *g'l hdm* (avenger of blood) in
Numbers 35 as well as *dmîm* (excessive blood-shed = bloodguiltiness),
something that attaches itself to Saul's house because of the deaths of the
Gibeonites (2 Samuel 21:1). In the latter case, *dmîm* is an impurity
cleansed by a retaliatory murder of third-generation kin, along with
impaling of their cadavers "on the mountain before the Lord." In an

attempt to control the desire for blood vengeance, Mishna *Sanhedrin* 3.4 stipulates that a murder victim's family not be witnesses at trial. The instruction is an attempt to separate from a court proceeding the ancient and ever-present drive of family revenge. Conversely, a Jewish inscription from the first century B.C.E. at Rheneia focuses on divine and not human vengeance, calling for τὸν θεὸν τὸν ὕψιστον to visit justice upon unknown parties who had poisoned and murdered τὴν ταλαίπωρον ἄωρον Ἡράκλεαν (the miserable untimely-dead Heraklea). Their criminal act is legally described as ἐχχέαντας αὐτῆς τὸ αἷμα ἀδίκως (those having poured out her blameless blood unjustly).[38] A similar problem is described by Pausanias (Περιήγησις 3.17.7-8), who reports that another Pausanias, the military commander at Plataea, could not win sympathy as a suppliant to the Spartan Athena since he had not been not able to wash off the impurity of his murders (φόνου δὲ ἄγος ἐκνίψασθαι μὴ δυνηθέντα).[39]

Josephus (*War* 1.521) tells how Alexander plotted against Herod, in order to avenge the δαίμονες of the deceased Hyrcanus and Mariamme, who were thought unjustly dead. In *War* 1.599 Josephus reported that the δαίμονες of the deceased Alexander and Aristobulus had been wandering about and subsequently, by their daimōnic long arm of retaliation, causing traitors to be brought to justice. Based on this particular context, Gerd Theissen suggested that spirits of the dead are depicted in Mark 5:1-20 also.[40] Though brief, his observations point in the right direction.

Unlike pollution stemming from birth and death in general, the μίασμα (defilement) of murder included a demonic element.[41] The *Tetralogies* of Antiphon contain numerous testimonies to this. The dead who became ἀλάστορες were "polluted, sacrilegious, and dangerous," and there grew a link between the victim of homicide and angry spirits. In order to purify a city it was necessary to put an end to their revenge, and such purification rituals for the crime of murder were ancient.[42] Furthermore, purifications were of concern for more than just cases of civilian homicides. On the military side, the proper disposal of enemy soldiers made for correctly accomplished purification. Pausanias commented on stories about Marathon, and about how the Athenians had buried the Persian soldiers adequately so that impurity would not result because of a lack of earth covering the corpses (Περιήγησις 1.32.3). It was reported that sometimes at night one might hear there the sounds of the ancient battle. If one were deliberately to listen for these sounds, and in fact hear them, then the anger of those "daimonic spirits" would fall on him. In general though, the warriors of Athens at Marathon were thought to be heroic, as were warriors elsewhere. Such an idealization tended to remove

problems of revenge for killing of the enemy.[43] Those who claimed
victorious heroes as their own, based on blood relation or on political
allegiance, did not necessarily fear those who had been violently killed.
Indeed the opponents of those killed violently considered their enemies
to be justly dead.

Diodorus reports how Philip II, king of Macedon, threw into the Gulf
of Pagasai the bodies of 6,000 dead enemy soldiers along with 3,000
prisoners of war, an extraordinary act of revenge on his part meant to
expiate what he perceived as their impiety (Diodorus Siculus 16.35.6).
Pausanias (Περιήγησις 2.34.7) tells how Minos had captured Nisaia and
Megara due to the treachery of Skylla, daughter of Nisos. Subsequently,
for her punishment Minos had her thrown into the sea, a punishment and
a purification.[44] Her body was washed up on shore, exposed, then torn to
pieces and eaten by birds. Herodotus (*History* 3.30) recounts that
Cambyses, seeking expiatory retaliation, ordered Prexaspes to kill
Cambyses' brother, Smerdis. One story is that Prexaspes drowned him in
the sea. The notion of the ocean as a fit place in which to sink guilt and
catastrophe was quite flexible in its application. Even statues, if they fell
on and killed someone, might be thrown into the sea, as Pausanias
reported about the statue of Theagenes (Περιήγησις 6.11.6). That an
ocean was necessary in order to resolve catastrophic guilt indicates that
the guilt was thought especially strong and beyond the usual kinds. The
need to sink and obliterate it in the ocean shows how this kind of guilt
was anomalously frightful, or full of perplexing uncertainty, odd fear, and
miasma.

Sinking and drowning like this falls into the category of καταποντισμός, a destructive act that was a desperate attempt to abide by θέμις.[45]
Καταποντισμός was a punishment typically reserved for crimes of high
impiety or murder. A Homeric precedent for the act and the attitudes
behind it is found in *Iliad* 21.121-29, where it is reported that Achilles
killed Lycaon, hurled him into the Scamander River, and wished for him
the same end as that of the unburied.[46] Another example is part of the
tradition of Ino-Leukothea, when she and her son were hurled down a
steep cliff into the sea because of her infanticides (*Odyssey* 5.333-335).
An Anatolian-Phoenician tradition of Atargatis and Ichthys parallels this,
as reported by Zanthus of Lydia. Because of her impiety, on her capture
by Moxos, Queen Atargatis was drowned together with her son, Ichthys,
in the lake of Ascalon, where they were eaten by fish.[47] In LXX Exodus
15:4, καταποντίζειν is the main verb describing the destruction of
Pharaoh's best militiamen and their chief officers in the waters of the sea.

With these extraordinary rituals of expiation in mind, let us return to the setting of an ancient city specifically. In these cities, the dead and the living created a social matrix by the establishment of a place for each and by the establishment of a relationship between the two. Erwin Rohde noted generally that many people thought of the dead, according to a phrase of Plato's, as "χθόνιοι hovering suspended over their graves," which served as the site of their cult.[48] Such a belief testifies remarkably about the relevance of the place of the dead to the geography of the living. It happened, too, that some early Christians used similar terminology for their dead as they performed rituals in close proximity to them. Elsewhere, Latin terminology for the spirits of the departed was widespread, often with meanings similar to the Greek δαίμονες. This terminological distribution and influence had a far-reaching impact. In their terminology, Jewish inscriptions from Rome and Monteverde most likely borrowed the Latin epithet, *Dis Manibus*.[49]

Experience of the dead as δαίμονες is an example of the anomalous frightful, because in such experience the belief that the dead have passed out of earthly affairs became uncertain. The effect they had on the living was a fearful one, unless they could be controlled by magical or ritual techniques. A more precise term for a daimōn of the deceased was νεκυδαίμων (dead man's ghost). An inscription from Carthage uses this appellation for a daimōnic entity, toward which magical adjurations are directed. Generally, the νεκυδαίμονες adjured against are related to πολυάνδριοι κε βιαιοθάνατοι κε ἄωροι κε ἄποροι τάφης (spirits of the dead in cemeteries, ones dead by violent means, ones dead at a highly inopportune time, and unburied). Magical texts are filled with spells and adjurations based on the power of these particular daimōnic entities. Once νεκυδαίμονες were under control, magical operations using them include "sending" them to perform a further magical operation on someone else (verbs used: πέμπειν, ἀναπέμπειν, ἐκπέμπειν). Ancient Egyptian texts display a similar invocation of the deceased, especially for matters dealing with violence and war. Although David G. Martinez observed that "the more specific νεκυδαίμων [was] late and apparently confined to magic,"[50] the thematic set of daimōns, violence, revenge, and expiation to which this specific terminology points is not at all late.

Mark 5:1-20 does not use the specific term νεκυδαίμων, but there are thematic elements of the unsettled dead, the influence of these dead on the living, the implication that violence created vengeful spirits of the dead, and the idea that violence accompanied the impact of these dead later on the living. Like a νεκυδαίμων, the spiritual entity victimizing the ἄνθρωπος is "sent" (πέμπω). Confrontation and control are central themes, just as in other situations where control over the spirits of the (violently) dead is emphasized. This narrative emphasis on a πνεῦμα ἀκαθάρτον and on daimōnization (the participle δαιμονιζομένον used in Mark 5:15, 16, 18) belongs to the general context of spirits, demons, angels, or other similar entities. The location of the daimōnization specifically in the cemetery points to the narrower context of βιαιοθανα-σία (violently killed), ἀλάστορες (engeful dead), δαίμονες of the dead, and the anomalous frightful that surrounds experiences and interpretations in these matters.

Plunging of animals down a steep cliff appears as a καταποντισμός, an elimination of impurity and implementation of revenge.[51] In this story, ideas about purity, impurity, and violence all come together. We find Jesus and those with him placed in the center of a cluster of violent fears. In this narrative, the anomalous frightful is present in themes of fear and uncertain conclusions to strange and violent events. It is represented with special clarity in the name Λεγιών (Legion). This reference to Roman military power is worth clarifying in order to grasp the sense of the violence and the retaliatory power brought into focus here by this story.[52]

According to some traditions, Alexander the Great established Gerasa. A folk etymology derived the city name from his placement of his γέροντες (mercenaries) there.[53] Perhaps the city of Gerasa, at least for the writer of Mark, had such a reputation as an establishment for military powers. Activity of Roman legions in the wider area included military engagements, establishment of outposts, and a variety of troop movements and increasing encroachments. Military presence grew from four to seven legions during the reign of Augustus on the eastern front with Parthia.[54] Details of such changes were probably not known to Mark, who likely also did not know much about exact inner workings of the Roman military. As in the cases of other confronting and spiritual entities in Mark, exact designations and detailed analyses are not the means by which the character of the Legion is drawn into the narrative. Some general aspects about legions, however, probably were known, two of which fit well with the themes of this Markan account. These aspects may assist us to appreciate what the Λεγιών brings to this story.

First, legions specifically, and Roman military institutions generally, were tightly organized into units, "pluralities" acting as single entities. Initially, this incorporation was formed by the individual's oath to the emperor on entering service in the military. The *sacramentum* (oath) was weighty. Breaking it was *nefas* (abominable).[55] Soldiers were gathered into units, each of which had its own *genius* (individuating spirit). The *genius* of the legion could easily be celebrated and memorialized anywhere.[56] It borrowed from Greek tradition about Orion, son of Mars, to find a divine patron in this heroic image of virtue, hunting, and soldiering.[57] This organization of sworn, tightly organized military troops would come in the centuries after Mark to include in its worship Jupiter Dolichenus, originally a local Ba`al from Doliche (Tell Dülük) in Commagene, a god of thunder. This deity was depicted as embracing the heavens, providing safety, success, and triumph.[58] Like this god of thunder, legions were military units meant to enforce through overwhelming power, using their power to seek revenge and retaliation when necessary. A large, moving incorporation, the legions honored their *genii.* Though made up of many, they exercised power as one and attributed to their corporate nature a single spiritual force (*genius*). The image of the legion as a tenacious corporate entity that seeks to resist confronting powers, and to maintain itself as a unit while so resisting, is an image of the legion that appears in Mark. The tenacity of the legion to work together in its powerful opposition is implied in Mark as the ἄνθρωπος/Λεγιών rushes forward to Jesus and then demands that, as a whole, it be sent, military style, into the χοίροι.[59]

Second, legions hated to be defeated. They intended to conquer and enforce Roman power, and found no honor in defeat. For military legions, loss of the standard (*signa*), or the eagle of the legion, was an embarrassment and a trigger for massive retaliation against its conquering enemies whenever the opportunity presented itself.[60] Augustus chose a festival date for the celebration of the capture of Alexandria to coincide exactly with the anniversary date for the dedication of the temple of Mars Ultor. His choice was a political statement, among other things meant to portray him as the conquerer of the Orient. Mars the Avenger triumphed in this publicity, and Augustus benefited from the propaganda of superior Roman retaliatory power.[61] After three legions were destroyed during the campaign of General Varus in Germany in 9 C.E., campaigns were mounted to avenge deaths and regain. In 16 C.E. the avenging deity Mars Ultor was honored after the victory of Germanicus over the Cherusci, his victory perceived as a retaliation for the previous defeat of the legionary forces of Varus as well as a reclaiming of the *aculiae* lost by Varus.[62] By 41 C.E., the last standard lost in the defeat of Varus was reacquired and placed in Rome. In 54 C.E., after the first Armenian victory, a statue of Nero was erected in the temple of Mars Ultor. The legion *XII Fulminata*, at the beginning of Jewish revolt in 66 C.E., was transferred to Cappadocia because it lost its *signa* to Jewish rebels.[63] Later in 70 C.E., after the victory over the Judeans, an image of Mars Ultor appeared on coins of Vespasian. I should think it evident that legionary retaliation and revenge were tokens of Roman awareness of divine benefaction in their favor, most specifically of the avenging benefactor Mars.

Mars Ultor, important both to the legions and in general to Roman military policy, deserves closer attention, because in his benefaction of Roman military organization he represents a divine power (Mars) specific to revenge and retaliation (Ultor). Whenever a divine power is assigned the role of benefactor of violence and retaliation, then the theme of the anomalous frightful is close at hand. Conflict is elevated to divine dimensions and is envisioned as an implementation of all-powerful fear in the attempt to eradicate any uncertainty about its power to control.

One of the ways in which Mars Ultor was part of the life of legions is demonstrated by a sacred calendar from a Roman military garrison. This calendar, the *Feriale Duranum* discovered at Dura Europas, comes from the archive of the *cohors XX Palmyrenorum,* stationed there between 200 and 250 C.E.. Of note are the conjunction of two dates: 9-11 May and 12 May. The second date was a day dedicated to Mars Ultor. The days immediately preceding were days dedicated to the dead, or those on behalf of whom vengeance and retaliation were most often initiated. On 9-11 May the Rose Festival (*Rosalia*) was celebrated in the legion,[64] when roses were to be strewn upon the standards. This specific legionary date coincided with the civilian *Lemuria* at Rome, as reported by Ovid (*Fasti* 5.430-39). The *Lemuria* were sacred days dedicated to the dead and to the expunging of any traces of their *lemures* (ghosts). R. O. Fink, A. S. Hoey, and W. F. Snyder commented that

> the *Rosaliae Signorum* is the military form of a festival taken over from civil life, and it was attached to the *signa* primarily because this was a natural way to make it an integral part of the army's religion. The most frequently attested *rosalia* are those celebrated at graves in the spring of the year for the propitiation and cheering of the dead.

Soldiers revered fallen comrades in this way, honoring them in order to vouchsafe their blessed afterlife. As an example of this, an inscription from Gerasa from the second or third century C.E., honors a fallen soldier: "*D(is) M(anibus), C(aio) Iul(io) Zenophilo, mil(iti) Leg(ionis) III Cyr(enaicae).*"[65] In general, afterlife for soldiers, and their comrades' views of that afterlife, are not frequently mentioned by many sources.

Some reported that soldiers who died in battle became part of the host of the violently dead, while others did not.[66] The propitious scheduling of the *Rosalia Signorum* connected the Roman legion to Roman life by way of the festival for the dead. This scheduling is a direct, liturgical tie of the Λεγιών (legion) to the uncertain and fearful world of the violent dead, daimōns, and to the power to avenge with death, all of which represent the anomalous frightful in Mark 5:1-20.

Rituals dedicated to the dead and celebrated on 9-11 May show a way that Legions honored and celebrated their dead. The violence of death, and the condition of the dead in the afterlife, are themes directly relevant to Mark 5:1-20, which depicts the daimōnized ἄνθρωπος/Λεγιών who lives in the cemetery, creates havoc, and who seems to have been a living anomaly of violent behavior that was irrepressible. The conflict of divine powers in this cemetery can be read as a contest about which power will have final authority over another, including vengeance and the ability to determine the final destiny of the vanquished (εἰς τοὺς χοίρους or ἔξω τῆς χώρας).

Vanquishing an enemy through superior power is directly related to the 12 May date of the *Feriale Duranum*, when circus races honored Mars Pater Ultor.[67] Significantly, this mightiest god of vengeance was celebrated the day after the festival for commemorating the dead. Such was the liturgy of a cohort of a Λεγιών. The editors of the *Feriale Duranum* suggested that "the games mentioned are not to be understood as *ludi castrenses* to be performed at Dura, but without doubt as the games held in the Circus Maximus at Rome, called *circenses* instead of *ludi* to emphasize their importance over 'average' games" (p.127). Arenas for games were situated in conjunction with military bases.[68] Although it is not made explicit in the *Feriale Duranum*, Roman games, especially in the capitol, often had for a symbolic focus the goddess Nemesis. The games and the competition they enshrined were convenient for the celebration of political and military power over adversaries.[69] Powerful vengeance and ability to retaliate were interpreted at the games as matters of Fate and Destiny. Conquering might was interpreted as a divine benefaction of assurance of victory in conflict. In the second century, iconography for Nemesis at arenas came to include the Griffin depicted on a wheel of fate. The notion of the wheel of fate indicates themes of providential favor through divine conflict. So it was in the first century C.E. and well before. In urban games, where prisoners of war, criminals, or enemies of the state were tormented and executed, Nemesis symbolically represented the security of the empire. This security rested on the

power to avenge and to vanquish enemies.[70] In foreign policy, this power
was based on the legions and their ability to act on behalf of Rome.

All of this is the kind of material that enriches the symbolic meaning
of the ἄνθρωπος who sallies forth from the cemetery to encounter Jesus
while he is under control of a plurality of violent daimōns identified as
Λεγιών. This story hinges on themes about the power of soldiers, armies,
their massive campaigns, the institution of military violence,[71] and the
anomaly they effect on those they conquer. The scene in Mark brings
forward many aspects of the uncertain dead: their untimely or violent end,
their likely post-death existence, their lack of place, the fear they cause
the living, and the violence they engender. We find Jesus walking into the
middle of this scene of the intensely anomalous frightful, in a story whose
setting and characters are extremes: πόλις and μνημεῖον, ἄνθρωπος and
πνεῦμα ἀκαθάρτον, βασανίζω and σωφρονέω, λεγιών and θάλασσα. With
minimal actions and statements by Jesus, the anomalous frightful is
contained, negotiated, and dispatched. Like his power over the cosmic
elements of Sea, Storm, and Wind, victory in these other areas of divine
struggle and conflict comes almost too easily. No explanations are given.
Yet the citizens of this area seem to understand what all this means, and
that the cost to them (in loss of livestock) is too high. Hearing the account
of events, and seeing the ἄνθρωπος who was once tormented now
καθήμενον ἱματισμένον καὶ σωφροῦντα (sitting, clothed and in his right
mind), they respond: καὶ ἤρξοντο παρακαλεῖν αὐτὸν ἀπελθεῖν ἀπὸ τῶν
ὁρίων αὐτῶν (and they pleaded with him to leave their area [5:17]).
Bringing an end to a scene of the anomalous frightful in this way was not
considered acceptable. Too much of the anomalous frightful had been
present for so little effort expended to remove it. On seeing what uncanny
events have taken place, the crowd wants Jesus to leave, and these people
show no conviction that it is a good thing that he has come. The salvation
that he brings seems uncertain, unstable, and questionable.

In a fairly simple story, many elements of the anomalous frightful are
presented, from the haunted cemetery of a πόλις to the violence and
vengeance of a unified, opposing might (a λεγιών) that is irresistible,
creates havoc with the living, and is a divine power of such magnitude
and pollution that it needs sinking in the θάλασσα. Jesus comes into
contact with all of these elements, and his exposure to such a depth of
impure disorganization is extensive. The narrative gathers together the
many elements of such disorganization, showing Jesus to have thorough
contact with each: the unclean spirit, violence in a cemetery, ghosts, an
opposing entity dedicated to complete destruction, and finally the

obliteration of animals so that impurity is removed. Jesus survives his encounter with impure violence inexplicably, since no reason is offered here to explain why or how he does survive. There are no rituals of cleansing, rituals for calling upon protecting powers, nor any other action as expected in such situations. Those with him in his simple, apparently unprotected state, also survive. From the realm of the restless dead to the realm of organized military opposition, all are exposed to archaic and primitive terrors but all make it through alive. Mark neither acclaims nor explains these events.

Is it clear what kind of benefaction and salvation Jesus bestows, once this story comes to an end? The question raised explicitly in the first narrative, after the ocean storm, comes again to the fore here: τίς ἄρα οὗτός ἐστιν. What kind of entity is Jesus that the anomalous frightful simply falls to pieces around him? Why is he not polluted, caught up in retaliation and revenge, and also subjected to these very powers once he is so exposed to them? Why is more not made of his "victory" over these things than is reported in this account? What is such power if, instead of receipt of acclamation by the one who wields it and then the investiture of this man with the role and status of a new ruler, the man who has this power instead simply moves on to another location? The reader is led to dream through all of these questions, seeing clearly the details embedded in this story, but finding no hints as to what they mean.

Notes

1. Henry Barclay Swete, *The Gospel According to St. Mark: The Greek Text with Introduction, Notes and Indices* (London: Macmillan, 1898), xlviii.

2. Γερασηνῶν in *Alef*, B C D; Γαδαρηνῶν in A C; Γεργυστηνῶν in W; Γεργεσηνῶν in *Alef²*, L Δ. Bruce M. Metzger (*A Textual Commentary on the Greek New Testament* [New York: American Bible Society, 1994], 84) writes that "of the several variant readings, a majority of the Committee preferred Γερασηνῶν on the basis of (a) superior external evidence (early representatives of both the Alexandrian and Western types of text), and (b) the probability that Γαδαρηνῶν is a scribal assimilation to the prevailing text of Matthew (8:28), and the Γεργεσηνῶν is a correction, perhaps originally proposed by Origen. The reading of W (Γεργυστηνῶν) reflects a scribal idiosyncrasy."

3. Yohanan Aharoni and Michael Avi-Yonah, *The Macmillan Bible Atlas*, rev. ed. (New York: Macmillan, 1977), map 231.

4. A. H. M. Jones, *The Greek City from Alexander to Justinian* (Oxford: Clarendon Press. 1940), 96-98. Hellenistic dynastic families, subsequent Roman control, and ongoing local politics made these cities socially and politically complex.

5. Seán Freyne, "Jesus and the Urban Culture of Galilee," in *Texts and Contexts: Biblical Texts in Their Textual and Situational Contexts: Essays in Honor of Lars Hartman*, ed. T. Fornberg and D. Hellholm (Oslo: Scandinavian University Press, 1995), 605. See also Eric Meyers, "Galilean Regionalism: A Reappraisal," in *Approaches to Ancient Judaism, 5: Studies in Judaism and Its Graeco-Roman Context*, ed. William Scott Green, Brown Judaic Studies 32 (Atlanta: Scholars Press, 1985), 115-31. Freyne (p.601) suggests that the author of Mark was well aware of general "local geographical significance" if not even the details, as evident by statements like "the *borders* of Tyre," "the *territory* of the Gerasenes," or "the *villages* of Caesarea Philippi" (5:1; 7:24; 8:27). Another option for interpretation is to see in Mark only a loose use of terms such as χώρα, much as used by an earlier Greek writer like Hellanikos of Lesbos, contemporary to Herodotus, who used χώρα to describe an entire "*land* of the Chaldeans." See Felix Jacoby, *Fragmente der Griechischen Historiker* (Leiden, The Netherlands: E. J. Brill, 1957), §687 F1.

6. Freyne ("Jesus and the Urban Culture of Galilee," 608) writes that "the bequests of land that went with the foundation of Tiberias were at somebody's expense, yet when it and Taricheae were transferred to the kingdom of Agrippa II by Nero, significantly these places are not said to have a χώρα but rather they are given σὺν ταῖς τοπαρχίαις, that is, they were toparchic capitals rather than πόλεις in any strict sense (Josephus *War* 2,225; *Antiquities* 20,159). Equally Josephus assumes that Sepphoris had villages associated with it which could have provided it with sufficient resources to resist Rome, had it so wished (Josephus *Vita* 346). In neither case can there be any question of a city territory in the strict sense, and hence these references must point to a situation of wealthy citizens owning land in the countryside around, but residing in the city itself, as in the case of Crispus, the prefect under Agrippa I, who resided in Tiberias and was part of the elite of the city, but who was absent at his estates across the Jordan when Josephus arrived in Galilee in 66 C.E. (Josephus *Vita* 33ff.)." See also A. N. Sherwin-White, "The Galilean Narrative and the Graeco-Roman World," in *Roman Society and Roman Law in the New Testament* (Oxford: Oxford University Press, 1963; repr., Grand Rapids, Mich.: Baker Book House, 1978), 127. The term μεγιστᾶνες appears in the LXX and Tacitus, in the latter a designation for the barons of Armenia (as a local polity under foreign control) who resisted Roman authority. In Mark, it most likely refers to an inner circle of friends of Antipas. The χιλίαρχος is a Greek term for the Roman *tribunus militum*; see Hugh J. Mason, *Greek Terms for Roman Institutions: A Lexicon and Analysis*, American Studies in Papyrology 13 (Toronto: Hakkert, 1974), 99. The χιλίαρχοι here could well be heads of the police-army of the local dynast, Herod Antipas.

7. See Seán Freyne (*Galilee from Alexander the Great to Hadrian, 323 B.C.E. to 135 C.E.: A Study in Second Temple Judaism*, University of Notre Dame Center for the Study of Judaism and Christianity Series 5 [South Bend, Ind.: University of Notre Dame Press, 1980], 70), who notes that during Antipas' reign (he was deposed by Claudius), Galilee came under no great external threats or pressure. Antipas' territory was divided into two parts, Galilee and Peraea, each separated by the territory of Scythopolis, Pella and Gadara, with Gerasa and Philadelphia bordering immediately on the east of Paraea. The city Gadara became the capital of Peraea. This Gadara is not to be confused with Gadara of the Decapolis, which included Hippos, Gadara, Scythopolis, Pella, Gerasa, Philadelphia, and Arbila. See Hans Bietenhard ("Die syrische Decapolis von Pompeius bis Traian," *Aufstieg und Niedergang der römische Welt* ii/8 [1978]: 220-51 on the varying lists of cities in the Decapolis found in Pliny *Natural History* 5.16.74 and Claudius Ptolemaeus 5.7.14-17. See also David E. Aune ("Jesus and the Romans in Galilee: Jews and Gentile in the Decapolis" in *Ancient and Modern Perspectives on the Bible and Culture: Essays in Honor of Hans Dieter Betz*, ed. Adela Yarbro Collins, Homage Series 22 [Atlanta: Scholars Press, 1998], 245 n.61), who suggests that not much can be made of the Semitic term *gdr* in geography, as the term was "used as the name of many ancient Semitic towns, and there is often a great deal of confusion in the identification of these towns." Among his examples we find (1) "Gadara" was among five administrative districts in Josephus (*Antiquities* 14.91; an error for "Gazara"?); (2) "Gaza," southernmost of five principle Phoenician cities, was widely known by that name in antiquity; see Diodorus 19.59.2; Strabo 19.59.2; 19.80.5; Arian *Anabasis* 2.26-27; (3) "Gazara" was not infrequently mistakenly called "Gadara." See Strabo 16.2.29 and 16.2.45, Josephus, *Antiquities* 12.308; (4) "Gezer" was sometimes called "Gazara"; see 1 Maccabees 4:15, 9:52; Josephus, *Antiquities* 13.261; Josephus, *Bellum* 1.50; it was also mistakenly called "Gadara" in Josephus, *Antiquities* 14.91; (5) "Gadara" was also the name of a city in the Decapolis (Josephus, *Bellum* 1.86,155,170); (6) "Gadara" was also the name of a city in the Perea, earlier known as "Gilead" (Josephus, *Bellum* 4.413). Aune reaffirms that Mark "appears to have retained toponyms which he found in the traditions he used, even though he was apparently not personally familiar with the geography of Galilee" (p.246).

8. Numa Denis Fustel de Coulanges, *The Ancient City: A Study on the Religion, Laws, and Institutions of Greece and Rome* (1864; New York: Doubleday, 1956; repr., Baltimore: Johns Hopkins University Press, 1980), 7-17. See Arnaldo D. Momigliano ("The Ancient City of Fustel de Coulanges," in *Studies on Modern Scholarship*, ed. Glen W. Bowersock and T. J. Cornell [Berkeley: University of California Press, 1994], 170-72) on the broader goals of Fustel de Coulanges, who intended to outline Aryan history and a foundational link in it between ancient religion, especially with regard to its practices of memorial of the family dead, and the development of institutions of private property.

9. Gerdien Jonker (*The Topography of Remembrance: The Dead, Tradition, and Collective Memory in Mesopotamia* [Leiden, The Netherlands: E. J. Brill, 1995], 192) refers to tablets in the omen series *Šumma ālu*, "Whenever a City (Stands on a Hill)" (p.197). This series of omen texts discusses the geographical placement of cities and, especially, the location of burial grounds in them, along with a topography of "footprints of the demons, the dead, and the spirits of the dead." The month of *Abu* (August) apparently was the season for intentional transactions between the living and the dead, in conjunction with Dumuzi and autumnal fertility rites; see J. A. Scurlock, "Magical Uses of Ancient Mesopotamian Festival of the Dead," in *Ancient Magic and Ritual Power*, ed. Marvin Meyer and Paul Mirecki, Religions in the Graeco-Roman World 129 (Leiden, The Netherlands: E. J. Brill, 1995), 96.

10. For the bones of Hippodameia see Pausanias (Περιήγησις 6.20.7): "They say Hippodameia went away to Midea in the Argolid, because Pelops was very angry with her over Chrysippos' death. But they also say that they brought back Hippodameia's bones to Olympia, by the command of an oracle" (trans. Peter Levi, *Pausanias Guide to Greece* [Harmondsworth: Penguin, 1971], 2:344). For brief overview of bones of the special dead, see Robert Garland, "Heroes," in *Greek Way of Death* (London: Duckworth, 1985), 88-93. In scriptural traditions, the remains of kings are buried with their fathers (2 Samuel 2:32, and others). Later rabbinic legal opinions hold that, although funerary utensils might be transferred between families, the tombs themselves are not to be moved and are to remain in their unique place (*Śĕmahot* 14.2); see *The Tractate "Mourning" (Śĕmahot): Regulations Relating to Death, Burial, and Mourning*, ed. and trans. Dov Zlotnick, Yale Judaica Series 17 (New Haven, Conn.: Yale University Press, 1966), 85: "All funeral urns that are inherited may be moved from place to place and transferred from family to family. A tomb may be neither moved from place to place nor transferred from family to family." Speculation about the desire of the patriarchs to be buried in the Land of Israel resulted in the opinion of Rabbi Hananiah, that in general the one who had died outside the Land, and had been buried outside, had two agonies: the agony of dying and the agony of having been buried outside the Land; see *Genesis Rabba* 96.5 in *The Book of Legends: Sefer ha-aggadah: Legends from the Talmud and Midrash*, ed. Hayim Nahman Bialik and Yehoshua Hana Ravnitzky; trans. William G. Braude (New York: Schocken Books, 1992), §41.

11. See Richard Lattimore (*Themes in Greek and Roman Epitaphs* [Urbana: University of Illinois Press, 1962], 106-125) for Greek and Latin inscriptions that either ask for the tomb to be respected and protected or threaten various curses on offenders who disturb the tomb. A local example from the area of Mark's geography is in a text identified as the Διάταγμα Καίσαρος, ostensibly an imperial edict prohibiting movement of the remains of the deceased or change of place of the burial site; see Victor Ehrenberg and A. H. M. Jones, *Documents Illustrating the Reigns of Augustus and Tiberius*, 2d ed. (Oxford: Clarendon Press, 1976), §322. Moshe Schwabe and Baruch Lifshitz (*Beth She'arim, 2: The Greek Inscriptions* [New Brunswick, N.J.: Rutgers University Press, 1974], 223) argue

that "at Beth She`arim very few inscriptions dealt with the protection of the grave, and in one of them the transgressor is not even threatened with a fine, as was usual in Asia Minor among Jews." This is identified by the editors as a unique feature of the rock-tombs in the hills around Scythopolis, perhaps making this graveyard locale different from other Hellenistic cemeteries. Pieter W. van der Horst (*Ancient Jewish Epitaphs: An Introductory Survey of a Millennium of Jewish Funerary Epigraphy [300 B.C.E. - 700 C.E.]*, Contributions to Biblical Exegesis and Theology 2 [Kampen: Kok Pharos Publishing House, 1991], 54-60) confirms this observation, noting that Jewish tomb inscriptions containing threats and curses are found in the ancient area of Asia Minor. It should be remembered that Scythopolis represents a material culture different from the more northwesterly parts of Galilee. L. Y. Rahmani (*A Catalogue of Jewish Ossuaries in the Collections of the State of Israel* [Jerusalem: Israel Antiquities Authority, 1994]) notes protective formulae on ossuaries, both in Hebrew and Greek terminology. These are to be found in his specimens: §70, Inscription B (*dwstm abwnh wl' lmptm* ["Dostas, our father, and not to be opened"]); § 142 with a Greek inscription which translates: "of Rufus; whoever/moves it/breaks his vow" (τὸν ὅρκον αὐτοῦ); §259 with a protecting formula in Greek ('Ορκίζω/μηδένα ἀ/ραι Τερτιάν ["I adjure you, nobody move Tertia"]); §559 with a formula imprecating blindness to whomever might move the bones of a Maryame, wife of Mathia (. . . πάταξε αὐτοῦ ουρουν ["smite him," ουρουν]). On the latter, the author suggests that ουρουν is a transliteration of the Hebrew `wrwn ([with] blindness), used here instead of an LXX Greek term for blindness. The actual term ουρουν shows that the Hebrew letter `ayin is left out (p.197).

12. Emily Vermeule, *Aspects of Death in Early Greek Art and Poetry*, Sather Classical Lectures 46 (Berkeley: University of Califronia Press, 1979), 11. Arthur Darby Nock ("Cremation and Burial in the Roman Empire," in *Essays on Religion in the Ancient World*, ed. Zeph Stewart (Cambridge, Mass.: Harvard University Press, 1972), 286) comments: "Through the history of man's conduct in face of the mystery of death . . . the dead man's remains, whether buried or burned or exposed, are actually localized in a particular spot. Hence that spot retains its importance, even when it is dogmatically held that the essential element in the man whom we loved is elsewhere."

13. On the *Parentalia* see Ovid (*Fasti* 2.533): *est honor et tumulis; animas placate paternas parvaque in extinctas munera ferte pyras* (honor is also paid to the tombs; appease the souls of your father and offer small gifts to the extinguished pyres). On the *Lemuria* see Ovid, *Fasti* 5.430-439. The exact command spoken to the shades is in line 443: *Manes exite paterni* ([my] paternal ghosts, leave now). See J. M. C. Toynbee, *Death and Burial in the Roman World* (Ithaca, N.Y.: Cornell University Press, 1971), 64.

14. Joseph Rykwert, *The Idea of a Town: The Anthropology of Urban Form in Rome, Italy and the Ancient World* (Cambridge, Mass.: MIT Press, 1988), 117-26.

15. Elizabeth Bloch-Smith (*Judahite Burial Practices and Beliefs about the Dead*, Journal for the Study of the Old Testament Supplement Series 123; JSOT/ASOR Monograph Series 7 [Sheffield: University of Sheffield Press, 1992], 119-20 [Isaiah 57]) describes rock-cut tombs and mortuary practices of a cult of the dead. She dates this text to the late sixth century B.C.E., since it describes Jerusalem bench tombs developed only at that time. Scholars disagree about who ran the cult, whether it was royal, or belonged to the whole community. Whoever ran it, ritual for the dead appears to have been a normative and usual religious practice ("feeding and consulting the dead were common practices" [p.120]). Bloch-Smith argues that Isaiah attempts to prove his prophetic credentials over against this cult. The necromantic use of the dead, who for such use needed to be geographically proximate, involved compelling them to perform certain tasks or services for the living. See translation of this passage by T. Lewis, *Cults of the Dead in Ancient Israel and Ugarit*, Harvard Semitic Monographs 39 (Atlanta: Scholars Press, 1989), 156. Specialists in necromancy were available at these sites, with a professional apparatus and a technical vocabulary. Usually in Scripture they are condemned (Isaiah 8:19); see Ann Jeffers, *Magic and Divination in Ancient Palestine and Syria*, Studies in the History and Culture of the Ancient Near East 8 (Leiden, The Netherlands: E. J. Brill, 1996), 167-202. Necromancy stands along with astrology, hemerology (prognostication using day book records), heptascopy (examination of liver entrails), hydromancy, and rhabdomancy (divination by throwing sticks or arrows). See also Brian Schmidt, "The 'Witch' of En-Dor, 1 Samuel 28, and Ancient Near Eastern Necromancy," in *Ancient Magic and Ritual Power*, 111-29.

16. See John Doudna (*The Greek of the Gospel of Mark*, Journal of Biblical Literature Monograph Series 12 [Philadelphia: Society of Biblical Literature and Exegesis, 1961], 24-25) on the instrumental dative. Usage in Mark 6:32 is consistent with Attic and Hellenistic papyri. Doudna writes, "There would seem to be an extension of the local use in 1:23 and 5:2: ἄνθρωπος ἐν πνεύματι ἀκαθάρτῳ. Blass-Debrunner, after discussing a usage that is classical, refers to this as 'less classical' (§219.4). Compare the reading of 3:30: πνεῦμα ἀκάθαρτν ἔχει and Romans 8:9 where the expressions ἔχει πνεῦμα and ἐστὲ . . . ἐν πνεύματι are parallel grammatically but the local significance is somewhat to the fore where ἐν is used. Nothing here conflicts with the practice of the papyri: the local sense of ἐν is extended to mean, when used with the dative of the person, 'in the power of . . .' 'in the possession of . . .' [reference made to Mayser, *Grammatik der griechischen Papyri aus der Ptolemäerzeit, 2v* II.ii, 295. 41]. The manner in which the spirit in Mark 1:23 and 5:2 overrules the action of the deranged person and the fact that in both instances *it* rather than the *man* converses with Jesus supports this understanding of ἐν."

17. This meaning of the plurality is not that suggested by Otto Bauernfeind, (*Die Worte der Dämonen im Markusevangelium*, Beiträge zur Wissenschaft vom Alten und Neuen Testament, dritte Folge, Heft 8 [Stuttgart: Verlag W. Kohlhammer, 1927], 26-27), who refers to *PGM* 4.3039, Lucian *Philopseudes* 16, and other texts that contain information on or reports about exorcisms of many

different entities (sometimes hundreds) simultaneously or seriatim. These witnesses clearly testify to actual plural objects for expungement. The grammar of these texts easily accounts for this, unlike the situation in Mark, where a shift occurs between singular and plural that is often noted with alarm by careful commentators.

18. Franz Annen, *Heil für die Heiden: Zur Bedeutung und Geschichte der Tradition vom besessenen Gerasener (Mk 5,1-20 parr)*, Frankfurther Theologische Studien 20 (Frankfurt am Main: Josef Knecht, 1976), 159-62.

19. *PGM* 4.3080: καὶ ὑποταγήσεται σοι πᾶν πνεῦμα καὶ δαιμόνιον. This is possibly a hendiadys and, therefore, expressive of a single, complex idea (it could be translated something like "every daimonic spirit"); see S. Eitrem, *Some Notes on the Demonology in the New Testament*, Symbolae Osloenses 12 (Oslo: A. W. Brügger, 1950), 1.

20. Minucius Felix *Octavius* 26.9. See Joseph Bidez and Franz Cumont, *Les Mages hellénisées: Zorastre, Osanès et Hystaspe d'après la tradition grecque* (Paris: Société d'Éditions Les Belles Lettres, 1938), 2:289.

21. The material in *PGM* 4 tells how to drive out δαίμονας, but says nothing about πνεύματα. Δαίμονας are not always bad; they sometimes are ἀγνούς (holy), as in *Orphic Hymns* 7.2 (Hymn to the Stars). On the astrological material see *Catalogus codicum astrologorum graecarum*, ed. Franz Cumont and Franz Boll (Brussels, 1898), "Codex Athenienses," 181 line 5. This latter astrological use of πνεῦμα ἀκαθάρτον is difficult to interpret. It is in a context describing the woes that befall one born during February while under the sign of Ichthys. On Chrysippus and others, see Plutarch *De oraculorum defectu* 17 (fragment in Hans Friedrich August von Arnim, *Stoicorum Veterum Fragmenta* [Leipzig: B. G. Teubner, 1903-1924], 2§1104).

22. Theodor Hopfner, *Griechische-ägyptischer Offenbarungszauber, 2 Bd.*, Studien zur Palaeographie und Papyruskunde, 21, 23 (Amsterdam: Verlag Adolf M. Hakkert, 1921), 1§182. See also *PGM* 12.326 for similar mix of substantives and adjectives.

23. Joseph Naveh and Shaul Shaked, *Amulets and Magic Bowls: Aramaic Incantations of Late Antiquity* (Jerusalem: Magnes Press, 1985), 71 (amulet #7).

24. Adolf Deissmann (*Light from the Ancient East*, 4th ed., trans. Lionel R. M. Strachan [London: Hodder & Stoughton, 1922], 256 n.1) comments on *PGM* 4.3007 that the meaning of δαιμονίζομαι parallels the meaning of σελνιάζω (under the influence of the moon).

25. Arthur Everett Sekki (*The Meaning of ruah at Qumran*, SBL Dissertation Series 110 [Atlanta: Scholars Press, 1989]) suggests that Hebrew *rwh 'mt* never refers to spirits of the dead in Qumran texts. He comments that "although *ruach* in the plural can refer to men in the sense of 'dispositions,' it never refers to men's spirits as disembodied souls nor is it ever used as a metaphor to mean 'persons'" (p.160).

26. See *1 Enoch 15.8*: [the Lord, the Great Glory, said to me . . .] "But now the giants who are born from the (union of) the spirits and the flesh shall be called *evil spirits* upon the earth, because their dwelling shall be upon the earth and

inside the earth. *Evil spirits* have come out of their bodies. Because from the day that they were created from the holy ones they became Watchers; their first origin is the spiritual foundation. They will become evil upon the earth and shall be called *evil spirits*. The dwelling of the spiritual beings of heaven is heaven; but the dwelling of the *spirits of the earth*, which are born upon the earth, is in the earth." Also in 2 Enoch [A] 4:1-21, the contents of the seven heavens are listed. The description of the second heaven includes, "And they showed me prisoners under guard, in measureless judgment. And there I saw the condemned angels . . . they [the angels] are *evil rebels* against the Lord, who did not listen to the voice of the Lord, but they consulted their own will" (trans. F. I. Anderson in *The Old Testament Pseudepigrapha*).

27. *'Abot de-Rabbi Natan* 16 states, "Rabbi Joshua says: A grudging eye, evil impulse, and hatred of mankind put a man out of the world," a saying that is explained: "Evil Impulse? What is that? It is said: 'By thirteen years is the evil impulse older than the good impulse. In the mother's womb the evil impulse begins to develop and is born in a person. If he profanes the Sabbath, it does not prevent him; if he commit murder, it does not prevent him; if he goes off to another heinous transgression, it does not prevent him. Thirteen years later the good impulse is born.'" Also *'Abot de-Rabbi Natan* 37 mentions one of seven types of Pharisee as he who "masters his evil impulse" (trans. Judah Goldin, *The Fathers According to Rabbi Nathan*, Yale Judaica Series 10 [New Haven, Conn.: Yale University Press, 1955; repr., New York: Schocken Books, 1974]). A similar set of ideas appears in *Sentences of the Syriac Menander* Epitome 30-31: "An evil heart causes griefs and sighing; jealousy is the cause of evil and strife" (trans. Tjitze Baarda in *Old Testament Pseudepigrapha*, 2:591-92. On the dualism in the Qumran docment *Treatise of the Two Spirits* see Emil Schürer, *The History of the Jewish People in the Age of Jesus Christ*, ed. Geza Vermes, Fergus Millar, and Martin Goodman, rev. ed. (Edinburgh: T & T Clark, 1986), 3:172 n.83.

28. William Horbury and David Noy, *Jewish Inscriptions of Graeco-Roman Egypt, With an Index of the Jewish Inscriptions of Egypt and Cyrenaica* (Cambridge: Cambridge University Press, 1992), §141. On being "snatched away" in an untimely fashion, see Menander Rhetor (Περὶ ἐπιταφίου [Περὶ ἐπιδεικτικῶν II.11] 420.1) suggesting funereal comments for a young person who has died: "But, it seems, Fate (δαίμων) mocked them all. The child was entrusted to foster parents; they had the greatest hopes of him. But alas, alas (οἴμοι τῶν κακῶν)! Now he has been snatched away (ἀναρπάζω)" (trans. D. A. Russell and N. G. Wilson, *Menander Rhetor* [Oxford: Clarendon Press, 1981], 175).

29. A. D. Nock, C. H. Roberts, and T. C. Skeat, "The Guild of Zeus Hypsistos," in Nock, *Essays*, 1:422-26.

30. Otto Böcher (*Dämonenfurcht und Dämonenabwehr: Ein Beitrag zur Vorgeschichte der christlichen Taufe*, Beiträge zur Wissenschaft vom Alten und Neuen Testament, fünfte Folge, Heft 10 [Stuttgart: Verlag W. Kohlhammer, 1970], 119) refers to the notion that "spirits of impurity" haunt graves. This idea is expressed in bSanhedrin 65b and bNidda 17a. Rudolf Pesch (*Der Besessene von Gerasa: Entstehung und Überlieferung einer Wundergeschichte*, Stuttgarter

Bibelstudien 56 [Stuttgart: KBW Verlag, 1972], 23) refers to the same texts and to a talmudic notion that possessed people are noted by four things: (1) traveling abroad at night; (2) spending the night in cemeteries; (3) tearing up their clothes; (4) destroying whatever was given to them. See jTerumoth 40b. This description at first appears quite close to the narrative in Gospel of Mark, but a broader analysis should be made of the full talmudic traditions in question, as found in bHag 3b-4a, jGittin 38b, and jTerumoth 2a. The broader discussion is really about the four signs of a *šwth* (madman), not about demon or spirit possession in particular. See Menahem Luz, "A Description of the Greek Cynic in the Jerusalem Talmud," *Journal for the Study of Judaism* 20 (1986): 49-60. This tradition about the madman refers to the reputation and images of Greek Cynicism, and is not a statement primarily about beliefs or theories of demons or spirits.

31. Such as is discussed in Mishna *Oholoth* with its extensive terminology for contact with a corpse and types of uncleanness from such contact. Robert Parker (*Miasma: Pollution and Purification in Early Greek Religion* [Oxford: Clarendon Press, 1983], 32-73) reviews other widespread theories in which pollution is created by proximity to or contact with a corpse. Corpses, like neonates, seemed like objects existing between two worlds. "The corpse, in particular, was anomalous both socially (no longer in human society, not yet among the dead) and physically (all the outward marks of a living person, but lifeless)" (p.62).

32. *Curse Tablets and Binding Spells from the Ancient World*, ed. and trans. John Gager (New York: Oxford University Press, 1992), 103 (§30). Gager comments that many parallels with other texts indicate that almost every line of this spell is copied from recipes in reference works much like those in the *PGM*. That is, there was a long tradition of development and use of such spells. Overall, the spell consists of elements of five separate invocations of the spirits and deities, and of most interest, a series of threats and promises directed to the *spirits of the dead people in the cemetery*. See also in *Curse Tablets* §109 (p.205), identified as "Mesopotamian" but with exact original location unknown, which has an invocation to "the spirit who resides in the cemetery." Similarly *Curse Tablets* §110 (p.207) from Alexandria (third century C.E.), which Gager translated: "I call upon you, mistress ruler of all mankind, all-dreadful one, bursting out of the earth, who also gathers up the limbs of MELIOUCHOS and MELIOUCHOS himself, Ereschigal . . . Hekate, true Hekate . . . Hermes of the underworld . . . and Persephone . . . *and daimones who are in this place*. Restrain from me, Ionikos, the strength and the power of Annianos, so that you seize him and hand him over to the ones untimely dead, so that you melt away his body, his sinews, his limbs."

33. Otto Gruppe (*Griechische Mythologie und Religionsgeschichte*, Handbuch der klassischen Altertums-Wissenschaft in systematischer Darstellung 5 [München: C. H. Beck'sche Verlagsbuchhandlung, 1906], 759) suggests that those who were killed in a unjust manner, otherwise known as the accursed dead (ἀραιοί [cursed] and προστρόπαιοι [the ones seeking vengeance for crimes done against them]), "in der Nähe des Grabes unbeschränkt war (were unrestricted in proximity to the grave)." Erwin Rohde (*Psyche: The Cult of Souls and Belief in*

Immortality among the Greeks, 7th ed., trans. W. B. Hillis [New York: Harcourt, Brace, 1925], 176) writes that "at Athens even in the fourth and fifth centuries the belief still survived in undiminished vigor that the soul of one violently done to death, until the wrong done to him was avenged upon the doer of it, would wander about finding no rest, full of rage at the violent act, and wrathful, too, against the relatives who should have avenged him, if they did not fulfil their duty. He himself would become an 'avenging spirit'; and the force of his anger might be felt throughout whole generations." See Rohde (*Psyche*, 210 n.148) for a brilliant description of the background of avenging spirits. On the dead as δαίμονας see Walter Burkert, *Greek Religion*, trans. John Raffan (Cambridge, Mass.: Harvard University Press, 1985), 181. On this term used for the deceased, see *Paulys Real-Encyclopädie der Classischen Altertumswissenschaft*, ed. Georg Wissowa and Wilhelm Kroll (Stuttgart: J. B. Metzler, 1905), s.v. "Daimon," by Waser. Col. 2011 offers references to early appearances of this terminology in Aeschylus and Euripides as well as discussion of the term ἀνθρωποδαίμων much later in Procopius. Discussion there also about designation τοὺς τοῦ μακαρίτου δαίμονας (daimōns of the dead) in Lucian *De Luctu* 24 and the designation δαίμονες μητρῷοι καὶ πατρῷοι (mother- and father-daimōns) in Lucian (*De Morte peregrini* 36), suggesting an equation here to the Latin *manes*. References to familial δαίμονας are found in a "sorcery inscription" from Cyprus: [Δεμονες] οι κατα γην κε δεμονες οι [τινες εστε] κε πατερες κε μητερες, text already published by L. Macdonald, "Inscriptions Relating to Sorcery in Cyprus," *Proceedings of Society of Biblical Archaeology* 13 (1890-1891): 174. See also Iiro Kajanto (*A Study of the Greek Epitaphs of Rome*, Acta Institui Romani Finlandiae, II:3 [Helsinki: Helsingfors, 1963], 9-12) for *manes* and θεοῖς καταχθονίοις and δαίμοσιν, all equivalent designations on tomb inscriptions.

34. On the Derveni Papyrus, see comments in Sarah Iles Johnston (*Restless Dead: Encounters Between the Living and the Dead in Ancient Greece* [Berkeley: University of California Press, 1999], 134), relating these souls of the dead to the hobgoblin agent known as Ἔμπουσα. *Golden Verses* (trans. Johan C. Thom, *The Pythagorean Golden Verses: With an Introduction and Commentary*, Religions in the Graeco-Roman World 123 (Leiden, The Netherlands: E. J. Brill, 1995), referring to line 3: τοὺς τε καταχθίνιους σέβε δαίμονας ἔννομα ῥέζων (and [pay reverence to] the spirits of the dead by performing the prescribed rites). Thom notes that the phrase καταχθίνιους δαίμονας (or variants) has three possible interpretations: (a) gods of the underworld, that is deities like Hades, Persephone, Demeter, Hekate, and the Erinyes; (b) spirits of the underworld, unspecified beings occupying a position between gods and humankind, to whom the task of watching over and punishing humans is often relegated; or (c) souls of the dead. Choosing the third, he points to other examples: *Anthologia Graeca* 7.333; Gold Leaf A1-3 in Gunther Zuntz (*Persephone: Three Essays on Religion and Thought in Magna Graecia* [Oxford: Oxford University Press, 1977], 277-393 [Kern, *Orphicorum Fragmenta*, F32c-e]), in particular the phrase δαίμονες ἄλλοι. The notion of "queen of the dead" as present in the Leaves is found also in *Orphic Hymn* 29.6 (Hymn to Persephone), in particular the phrase ὑποχθονίων βασίλεια.

Lattimore (*Themes*, 96 n.70) lists more than 300 examples of the phrase καταχθίνιους δαίμονας (or variants) in Greek inscriptions.
  35. Eugene N. Lane, *Corpus Monumentorum Religionis Dei Menis*
(MNRDM), Études préliminaires aux religions orientales dans l'Empire Romain
109 (Leiden, The Netherlands: E. J. Brill), 3:53, 76-77.
  36. Gruppe, *Griechische Mythologie*, 761. *Paulys Real-Encyclopädie* (s.v.
"Nekydaimon" by Karl Preisendanz [col. 2246]) refers to stories of the *manes* or
δαίμονες of the murdered dead appearing to the living: Suetonius (*Nero* 34; the
passage is to be read as extreme irony, but does speak of Persian magi whom Nero
[jokingly] employed to fend off from him the angry ghost of Agrippina) and
Suetonius (*Otho* 7; haunted by a terrible nightmare of Galba's ghost). Other
examples in D. Felton (*Haunted Greece and Rome* [Austin: University of Texas
Press, 1999], 8-9): Livy 3.58.11, the ghost of the slain Verginia roams from house
to house and never rests until all people involved in her death are brought to
justice; *Aeneid* 1.353-7, the murdered Sychaeus appears to Dido in her sleep, to
say that her brother Pygmalion is the one who killed him, and he warns her to flee;
Apuleius. *Metamorposes* 9.29, a jilted wife arranges for a ghost to kill her
husband; Apuleius. *Metamorphoses* 9.31, the ghost of a murdered husband
appears to his daughter in her sleep, revealing his wife's complicity in his murder.
On the widespread appearance of these themes, see Theodor Hopfner (*Griechisch-
ägyptischer Offenbarungszauber*, 1:§§343-46), who cites Horace (*Odes* 5.92) with
a good indication of the type of experience it was thought to be when an avenging
daimōn came to visit: *nocturnus occurram furor*. On the Latin use of *furor* linked
with the Greek avenging deities 'Ερινύες, see Dorothy May Paschall, *The
Vocabulary of Mental Aberration in Roman Comedy and Petronius* (Chicago:
University of Chicago Press, 1939; repr. as Language Dissertations 27 in
Supplement to Language: Journal of the Linguistic Society of America 15
[January-March 1939]; repr., New York: Krauss Reprint, 1966), 42 n.27. This
University of Chicago dissertation is an extensive study of Latin and Greek
vocabulary for anger, superstition, vengeance, possession, rage, grief, violence,
and fanaticism. On patterns of revenge-seeking in magical operations seeking
justice for homicide, see H. S. Versnel ("Beyond Cursing: The Appeal to Justice
in Judicial Prayers," in *Magika Hiera: Ancient Greek Magic and Religion*, ed.
Christopher A. Faraone and Dirk Obbink [New York: Oxford University Press,
1991], 70), who reports on certain prayer-types in *defixiones*: "Thematically,
however, all these texts have in common the fact that they beg the gods for
retaliation, revenge, and justice and that they usually concern themselves with
cases of abnormal and therefore suspicious death. Often the deceased is
envisioned as an ἄωρος or βιαιοθάνατος, that is, someone who has died 'before
his time' or in a violent and unnatural manner. As is typical in traditional, pre-
modern societies, the inexplicable death (by lingering illness) is frequently
attributed to the evil practices of enemies, who are suspected of using poison or
magic spells. These revenge prayers aim at forcing the usually unknown
perpetrator to atone for his or her crime."

152 Chapter 5

37. Ian Kidd, "The Case of Homicide in Plato's *Euthyphro*," in *'Owls to Athens': Essays on Classical Subjects Presented to Sir Kenneth Dover*, ed. E. M. Craik (Oxford: Clarendon Press, 1990), 214. The right of δίκη φόνου was usually permitted to a blood relative at least a cousin, or to the master of a slave.

38. Deissmann, *Light*, 413-24.

39. Menander Rhetor (Περὶ προσφωνητικοῦ [Περὶ ἐπιδεικτικῶν II.10] 417.25) as illustration mentions that a sword can be dedicated as gift, "not to Ares or to Terror [Δειμός] or Fear [Φόβος], but to Justice and Themis, *a gift pure of bloodshed* [καθαρὸν φόνων]"; trans. Russell and Wilson, *Menander Rhetor*, 169).

40. Gerd Theissen (*The Miracle Stories of the Early Christian Tradition*, trans. Francis McDonagh; ed. John Riches [Philadelphia: Fortress Press, 1983], p.89 n.21) notes that the spirits of the dead, which for various reasons did not find rest but, instead, continued to exist as demons, could prove particularly vindictive. He argues that spirits of the dead are implied in Mark 5:1-13, and that in this story the spirits had been staying near graves. He suggests that perhaps the implication is that it had once been known that the spirits had scores to settle with the Gerasenes. Theissen's suggestions, though incipient, are to be taken as catalytic to my approach. His reference to Hans Dieter Betz (*Lukian von Samosata und das Neue Testament: Religionsgeschichtliche und paränetische Parallelen: Ein Beitrag zum Corpus Hellenisticum Novi Testamenti*, Texte und Untersuchungen 76 [Berlin: Akademie-Verlag, 1961], 153), on the struggle between exorcist/magician and demon, is indeed relevant to the specific statements of Jesus to the entity (use of specific name; use of adjurations—here, entity against Jesus and then simple, directive words of Jesus to entity). Yet most of the violence implied by this scene happens before the arrival of Jesus, and such violence is not an aspect of the expungement. It is the description of the previous life in the cemetery and the people's response to that life.

41. Parker, *Miasma*, 107. See also J.-P. Vernant ("Le pur et l'impur," in *Mythe et Société en Grèce ancienne* [Paris: Éditions la Découverte, 1982], 126), who wrote that there was no simple and univocal idea of contamination. A material element was involved, yet also an invisible element. Impurity is at the same time objective and subjective, a reality external and internal to humans.

42. Parker (*Miasma*, 108) explains the development. Demons, the corpse of the victim, the anger of the victim at the unjust murder, and the impurity of the murder are all phenomena that blend together. Parker notes that "παλαμναῖος is applied to the killer, the demons that attack him, and the (demonic) pollution that radiates from him; words like μιάστωρ [crime-stained wretch who pollutes others], ἀλάστωρ [avenging spirit], and ἀλιτήριος [offending agent], work in similar ways." See also Arthur Adkins ("Pollution," in *Merit and Responsibility: A Study in Greek Values* [Chicago: University of Chicago Press, 1960], 89): "pollution was felt to be dangerous." Pollution is not simply a moral issue. Within this ancient Greek context, homicide and violent death are the chief domain for theories about pollution and its cleansing. These feelings are not in any way exclusively Greek. On cleansing rituals see Johnston, "Purging the Polis," in *Restless Dead*, 250-87, and Rohde, *Psyche*, 180. Rohde summarizes some of these

practices: "The details of purification and expiation—the former serving the interests of the state and its religious needs, the latter intended as a final appeasement of the injured powers of the unseen world—were closely united in practice and are often confused in the accounts which have come down to us. A hard and fast distinction between them cannot be drawn. So much at all events is clear; the expiatory rites indispensable when murder had been committed had the closest possible similarity with the ritual of sacrifice to the gods of the underworld. And, in fact, the deities invoked at such rites of expiation—Zeus Meilichios, Zeus Apotropaios, and the rest-belong to the underworld circle of gods." Apollonius Rhodius (*Argonautica* 4.470-80) depicts Jason's treacherous murder (δολοκατασία) of Apsyrtus in the vestibule of a temple to Artemis. In order to purify himself from the φόνος, Jason cuts off "extremities" (ἐξάργματα) from the body of his victim (nose, ears, etc.), strings them together, and then drapes them under the armpits of his victim's corpse. Three times he licks the blood of Apsyrtus, and three times he spits it out to the ground. All this is done to atone (ἱλάομαι) for the treachery and impurity of the murder. See Parker (*Miasma*, Appendix 7) for a list of figures in Greek myth who submitted to purification for murders they committed.

43. Jan N. Bremmer, *The Early Greek Concept of the Soul* (Princeton, N.J.: Princeton University Press, 1993 [1987]), 105.

44. On the purifying power thought available only in salty ocean water, see Gruppe, *Griechische Mythologie*, 889 n.1. It was said that this power also worked when the water is channeled and made available for various cultic uses.

45. *Dictionnaire des Antiquités d'après les Textes et les Monuments*, ed. Charles Daremberg and E. Saglio (Paris: Librarie Hachette, 1877; repr., Graz: Akademische Druck und Verlagsanstatt, 1962), s.v. "Katapontismos" by Gustav Glotz.

46. On refusal of burial (becoming ἄταφος) as a horrendous fate, see Bremmer, *Early Greek Concept of the Soul*, 90-92.

47. Jacoby, *Fragmente der Griechischen Historiker*, §765 F 17. See also Walter Burkert, *Homo Necans: The Anthropology of Ancient Greek Sacrificial Ritual and Myth*, trans. Peter Bing (Berkeley: University of California Press, 1983), 204. For identification of the goddess Atargatis with the goddess Derketo of Ascalon, both as representations stemming from 'Asherah, see Walter A. Maier III, *'Ašerah: Extrabiblical Evidence*, Harvard Semitic Monographs 37 (Atlanta: Scholars Press, 1986), 118-21.

48. Rohde, *Psyche*, 170. The passage is Plato *Phaedo* 81C-D. The exact wording for the phrase to which Rohde refers is ψυχή . . . περὶ τὰ μνημάτά τε καὶ τοὺς τάφους κυλινδουμένη. In this passage, other prominent terminology occurs in regard to the dead and to seeing them. Note especially the term ὤφθη in reference to the appearances of φαντάσματα and εἴδωλα.

49. On Christian use see Graydon F. Snyder (*Ante Pacem: Archaeological Evidence of Church Life before Constantine* [Macon, Ga.: Mercer University Press, 1985], 83): "the liturgy of the cemetery centered on the agape meal as adapted through the social matrix of the Roman world. In the ancient world the

grave of a special person housed the δαίμων of the deceased. That δαίμων had
certain powers and could be consulted." Commenting on pictorial scenes of the
resurrection of Lazarus, Snyder (p. 61) writes, "In the social matrix the people
believed the dead remained in the houses or places prepared for them. They ate
with the dead, talked to them, asked for their assistance. In the case of special
dead, they revered and honored the daemon of the dead present in the *aedicula* or
heroon." For Latin developments in terminology see *Paulys Real-Encyclopädie
der Classischen Altertumswissenschaft*, s.v. "Manes," by Marbach. See especially
col.1060, where the observation is made that from Greek inscriptions we learn that
the *Manes* signified in collective meaning most likely θεοὶ καταχθόνιοι, but in
individual meaning, δαιμόνες. For Jewish evidence see David Noy, *Jewish
Inscriptions of Western Europe* 2: *The City of Rome* (Cambridge: Cambridge
University Press, 1995), 489-95. Van der Horst (*Ancient Jewish Epitaphs*, 43)
notes that the Greek phrase καταχθίνιους δαίμονας is often an imitation of the
Latin *Dis Manibus*, suggesting that in Jewish and Christian usage it came to lose
its "original meaning."

50. See Carthage evidence in Augustus Audollent, *Defixionum Tabellae*
(Paris: Albert Fontemoing, 1904; repr., Fankfurt/Main: Minerva, 1967), §242. For
an example of the usual focus on violent dead, see L. Macdonald, "Inscriptions,"
174 lines 30-31. Numerous references in *Paulys Real-Encyclopädie* (s.v.
"Nekydaimon," by K. Preisendanz) show the frequency of this constellation of
terms in relation to the dead, especially in matters of harnessing the power of the
daimōn of the deceased. For spells and adjurations based on the power of
νεκυδαίμονες see *PGM* 4.361, 368, 397, 2031, 2061 5.334; 7.1006; 12.493; 16
(whole text); 19a.15; 51 (whole text). On the aspect of "sending" see Preisendanz,
s.v. "νεκυδαίμων," 2252. The verb πέμπειν (imperative form, πέμψον) appears in
Mark 5:12, as the Λεγίων asks to be sent into the herd of swine. For ancient
Egyptian evidence see J. F. Borghouts, *Ancient Egyptian Magical Texts*, Nisaba:
Religious Texts Translation Series 9 (Leiden, The Netherlands: E. J. Brill, 1978),
§10. One text comes from the beginning of an instruction for scaring away an
enemy: "Oh you who calculates his spell, prominent in the East, to wit any male
dead (*mt*), any female dead, any male enemy, any female enemy, any male
opponent, any female opponent, any male spirit, any female spirit, any intruder,
to wit any passer-by, to wit any trembler—in my neighborhood (or) as something
seen from afar (or) as a movement of any limb—to wit those living ones, followers
of Horus, who are under the supervision of Osiris who, though having grown old,
do not die: let the name of this magic be known to me which comes for NN born
of NN!" Compare observations on νεκυδαίμονες made by David G. Martinez in
P. Michigan XVI: A Greek Love Charm from Egypt (P.Mich. 757), Michigan
Papyri 16; American Studies in Papyrology 30 (Atlanta: Scholars Press, 1991), 46.

51. Such a plunging into the sea, if not linked as a punishment for a horrible
crime, is at least an event connected with terror, anomaly, or divine conflict. A
legend about how the Erythraean Sea got its name includes an account of the horse
herds of Erythras (a Persian, son of Myozaeus), which while grazing and feeding
(φορβάδων ἀγέλη) are attacked by lions, terrified, rush to the sea, and leap in (τῷ

δέει ... ἐπὶ τὴν θάλατταν ἠλαύνοντο). This is reported in Agatharchides; see Karl Müller, *Geographi Graeci Minores* (Hildesheim, Germany: Georg Olms, 1965; orig. published 1853), 1:113.6. Roy D. Kotansky ("Jesus and Heracles in Cádiz [τὰ Γάδειρα]: Death, Myth, and Monsters at the 'Straits of Gibraltar' [Mark 4:35-5:43]" in *The Bible and Culture: Ancient and Modern Perspectives*, ed. Adela Yarbro Collins, SBL Symposium Series [Atlanta: Scholars Press, 1998], 210) also mentions material in the tradition about the conflict between Herakles and Geryon; the latter's cattle subsequently are "driven" across the sea.

52. Annen (*Heil für die Heiden*, 20-21) offers discouraging commentary on an idea of Joachim Jeremais (*Jesu Verheißung für die Völker* [Stuttgart, 1956], 26-27), that behind the Greek word Λεγιών is an Aramaic word for soldiers, *legyôn '*. Jeremais tried to explain the confusion between singular and plural inflections of the verbs in the 5:1-20 account. But with or without such an analysis of Aramaic material behind Mark's Greek, the narrative emphasis in Mark 5:1-20 remains focused specifically on the institution of the Roman legion.

53. The literary sources for this are late and their veracity debated. On the one hand, their late date leads W. W. Tarn (*Alexander the Great* [Cambridge: Cambridge University Press, 1948], 2:233) to view the story about this establishment as unreliable myth. On the other hand, Schürer and his editors (*History of the Jewish People*, 2:150) conclude, on the basis of a coin and an inscription, that it is historically reliable that Alexander at least founded this city.

54. See Benjamin Isaac ("The Roman Army in Jerusalem and Vicinity," in *Studien zu den Militärgrenzen Roms* III: 13:. Internationaler Limeskongreß, Aaelen 1983, Forschungen und Berichte zur vor- und frühgeschichte in Baden-Württemberg [Stuttgart: Konrad Theiss Verlag, 1986], 635-40) for difficulties in assessing the military situation, especially of the *legio X Fretensis*. See also A. N. Sherwin-White, *Roman Foreign Policy in the East: 168 B.C. to A.D. 1* (Norman: University of Oklahoma Press, 1983), 338-39.

55. John Hegeland ("Roman Army Religion," *Aufstieg und Niedergang der römische Welt* ii/16.2 [1978]: 1478-79) comments on this oath: "Under the empire the recitation of the oath became a liturgical feature of army life. It was certainly recited upon enlistment, on the third of every January, and on the anniversary of the emperor's accession to power. It was once thought that the first of January was the date for the yearly recitation of the oath, but since the publication of the *Feriale Duranum*, the third has become the commonly accepted date. An entry in the *Feriale* shows *vota*, 'vows,' being taken on the third and in a military document vows naturally point to the *sacramentum*. The third of January was a festival day which included as well the burial of the preceding year's altar overlooking the parade ground and the dedication of a new altar for the current year. Coins commemorated this day. The oath-swearing scene is depicted on coins of the late first and early second century A.D., on which the *Imperator*, in a toga, is shown clasping hands over an altar, with an officer in military uniform, while in the background appears a soldier carrying a standard and another armed with a spear and a shield." Such depictions of a *dexterarum iunctio* indicate power, benefaction, and trustworthiness (πίστις or *fides*). They are found in a variety of

classical, Hellenistic, and Roman sources; see Arnaldo Momigliano, "Religion in Athens, Rome and Jerusalem in the First Century B.C.," in *Approaches to Ancient Judaism, 5: Studies in Judaism and Its Graeco-Roman Context*, ed. William Scott Green, Brown Judaic Studies 32 (Atlanta: Scholars Press, 1985), 4-5. Hittite soldiers also entered service by swearing an oath. In one Hittite case, the threat of breaking the oath is that the male soldier will turn into a woman; see Richard Beal, "Hittite Military Ritals," in *Ancient Magic and Ritual Power*, 64.

56. On the *genius* see Michael P. Speidel and Alexandra Dimitrova-Milčeva, ("The Cult of the Genii in the Roman Army and a New Military Deity," *Aufstieg und Niedergang der römische Welt* ii/16.2 [1978]: 1544) on *exercitus, legio, ala* (squadron), auxiliary cohort, *numerus* (rank), *vexillatio* (detachment), praetorian cohorts (urban cohorts), *cohortes vigilum*, and *equites singulares Augusti*. Speidel and Dimitrova-Milčeva (p.1546) write that "next in popularity after the *Genius centuriae* comes the *Genius legionis* . . . the *Genus legionis* could be worshipped anywhere, not just in the regimental sanctuary. Accordingly, dedications are found inside and outside the ancient camps: in the chapels of the *scholae* of the centurions or *mensores*, in the baths, on duty stations, in colonies where veterans had settled, and elsewhere, which again proves that the cult was spontaneous, not prescribed."

57. Michael Speidel, *Mithras-Orion: Greek Hero and Roman Army God*, Études préliminaires aus religions orientales dans l'Empire romain, 81 (Leiden, The Netherlands: E. J. Brill, 1980), 38.

58. John E. Stambaugh ("The Functions of the Roman Temple," *Aufstieg und Niedergang der Römischen Welt* ii/16.1 [1978]: 594) notes that by the first century C.E., on the slope of the Janiculum in Rome, there was a temple to this Syrian Ba`al, known there as Jupiter Heliopolitanus. In this temple structure is a complex of rooms that seems to have housed the celebration of mysteries, "open only to initiates; these would in some way involve the seven eggs and statue of a god buried in a triangular pit." Later, during the late second and early third centuries at Rome, temples were dedicated to the Syrian god of Commagene, known to Romans as Jupiter Dolichenus. Two temples were on the Esquiline and one on the Aventine. See Mary Boyce and Franz Grenet (*A History of Zoroastrianism* 3: *Zoroastrianism under Macedonian and Roman Rule*, Handbuch der Orientalistik, erste Anteilung: Der nahe und der mittlere Osten, Bd. 8: Religion, erster Abschnitt: Religionsgeschichte des alten Orients, Lief. 2, 2 [Leiden, The Netherlands: E. J. Brill, 1991], 3150, who note that at Commagene, "one of the chief divinities was the Storm-god, Tarhuis, who was worshiped throughout the Hittite world. His veneration in Kummuh is known from free-standing limestone stelae . . . Tarhuis' chief sanctuary was on a hilltop by Doliche (modern Dülük), a little town in the south of Commagene near the Syrian border. He was known accordingly to Hellenes as Zeus Dolichenos, to Romans as Juptier Dolichenus; and under the latter name he came to be worshiped far and wide throughout the Roman empire, his temples being sometimes found near or even beside those of Mithras." Michael P. Speidel (*The Religion of Iuppiter Dolichenus in the Roman Army*, Études préliminaires aux religions orientales dans l'Empire Romain 63

[Leiden, The Netherlands: E. J. Brill, 1978], 1) writes, "since the night of times, the storm god had been standing on a bull, grasping double axes and thunderbolt, wearing the 'Phyrgian' cap and a sword, thus uniting upon himself the symbols of power, both of nature and of society. In the Hellenistic age he had donned the royal cuirass. Now, like other Syrian Baals, he acquired the name of Rome's supreme god, *Iuppiter optimus maximus*. What oracles he gave, what pacts he concluded, and what changes he decreed in ritual and doctrine remains unknown—but already in Hadrian's reign Iuppiter Optimus Maximus Dolichenus, the god 'from where the iron grows,' appears as the lord of a major religion of the Roman Empire."

59. The image of an organized company of soldiers assaulting enemies in single-minded attack is not necessarily unique to a Roman legion. Heinz-Wolfgang Kuhn (*Altere Sammlungen im Markusevangelium*, Studien zur Umwelt des Neuen Testaments 8 [Göttingen: Vandenhoeck & Ruprecht, 1971], 192) detects these themes of organization, conflict, and attack and explains them as due to scriptural traditions about the Exodus. Kuhn finds possible word play between a Hebrew word used to describe Egyptian armies in Exodus 18:11 and Nehemiah 9:10 (*zwd* ["to be arrogant"]) and a Hebrew word for demon (*šwd* ["devastation"]). There are severe lexical difficulties with his explanation (that is, the specific form of *zwd* that Kuhn compared to *šwd* [*zdîm* to *šdîm*] did not appear in the scriptural texts), but Kuhn's desire to find a relevant symbolic background for the type of assault depicted in Mark 5:1-20 is exemplary. Mark's use of Λεγιών turns our attention to Roman legions specifically for a proper comparative source for the meaning of the organized and corporate opposition presented in Mark 5:1-20. The rush of the ἄνθρωπος/Λεγιών at Jesus is actually reported twice in the narrative (5:2 and 5:6). Annen (*Heil für die Heiden*, 10) considers this duplication to be one of the standard textual difficulties of this story. The ἄνθρωπος/Λεγιών chooses to go εἰς τοὺς χοίρους (5:12, 13), as over against going ἔξω τῆς χώρας (5:10). These two options have a remarkable similarity in sound between them. A reader may legitimately wonder if a link between these two seemingly unrelated choices ("into the swine" or "out of the area") is forged primarily through alliteration.

60. Hegeland ("Roman Army Religion," 1475-76) comments that "a recovered standard usually never marched again with a legion. They were returned home to be forever enshrined in the temple of Mars Ultor, or "Mars the Avenger." In 20 B.C.E. Augustus built a small shrine to house the standards lost to the Parthians by Crassus and Anthony. This shrine also housed trophies from various wars [built on the Capitol]." Hegeland refers to Suetonius, *Divus Augustus* 21.2-3, 29.1.

61. Stambaugh ("The functions of Roman temple," 555) suggests that it "served as a reminder of the avenging punishment inflicted by Augustus on the assassins of Julius Caesar."

62. See R. O. Fink, A. S. Hoey, and W. F. Snyder ("The *Feriale Duranum*," *Yale Classical Studies* 7 [1940]: 122-23) for this and basic historical facts that follow.

63. Suetonius, *Vespasian* 4, and Josephus, *War* 2.18.9, 2.19.9; see Hegeland, "Roman Army Religion."

64. Fink, Hoey, Snyder, "The *Feriale Duranum*," 115. Text for this date (line 8) is, *vi yi[du]s maias ob rosalias sin[o]rum suppl[icatio]*. In this ceremony military standards are brought out and set up near an altar in the courtyard of the *praetorium;* they are then decorated with crowns of roses (*rosae solutae*); there follows a ceremony of *supplicatio.*

65. *Gerasa, City of the Decapolis*, ed. Carl Hermann Kraeling (New Haven, Conn.: American Schools of Oriental Research, 1938), Inscriptions §211.

66. On dead soldiers as part of the violently dead, see Virgil (*Aeneid* 6.404) on the presence of "high-hearted heroes" in a crowd of the dead who plead with Charon for a passage across the river. Included in this crowd are other members of the unfortunate dead: boys, girls, and young men dead while their fathers are still living. See also *Aeneid* 6.368-371, where Death, Sleep, War, the [work of] Furies, and mad Strife are listed together, the context indicating that they all are highly unfortunate events. On honored dead soldiers thought not to have wretched postmortem destinies, see Garland (*Greek Way of Death*, 77), who writes that "at no period in Greek history are those who die defending their country counted among the *aôroi*, doubtless so as not to discourage the virtues of patriotism and self-sacrifice." See especially Garland's section on "The War Dead" (89-93). Other traditions on the Greek war dead are to be seen in Pausanias (Περιήγησις 1.32.3), where the ghosts of the warriors of Athens at Marathon are troubling the living. On funerals honoring of the war dead, see summation comments in Menander Rhetor Περὶ ἐπιταφιοῦ (Περὶ ἐπιδεικτικῶν II.11) 418.15, who mentions that "Thucydides, however, writing a funeral speech for those who fell at Rheitoi at the beginning of the Peloponnesian War, did not simply pronounce an encomium on the men, but made the point that they were capable of meeting death" (trans. Russell and Wilson, *Menander Rhetor*, 171). There is no indication in this public propaganda that one's own war dead are considered part of the untimely dead.

67. Fink, Hoey, Snyder, "The *Feriale Duranum*," 120 line 9: *iiii idus maias ob circenses ma[rtiales] marti pa[tri ult]ori ta[u]rum.*

68. Thomas Wiedemann, *Emperors and Gladiators* (London: Routledge, 1992), 45.

69. Michael B. Hornum, *Nemesis, the Roman State, and the Games*, Religions in the Graeco-Roman World 117 (Leiden, The Netherlands: E. J. Brill, 1993), 89. For this dedicatory focus on the goddess Nemesis within the games, but outside of the peculiarly Roman capitol context, see Louis Robert, *Les gladiateurs dans l'orient grec*, Bibliotheque de l'École des hautes études, IVᵉ section: Sciences historiques et philologiques 278 (1940; repr., Amsterdam: A. A. Hakkert, 1971), 51. Wiedemann (*Emperors and Gladiators*, 165) writes that "a gladiator was a man who might lack any positive quality except the skill to fight to the death. But that *virtus* was so important in defining who was a Roman that its public display might lead to the gladiator's being accepted back into the community of Romans."

70. A source for the symbolism of power and might is to be found in the history of Roman Legions in Palestine. During battles between Herod the Great and Antigonus (Josephus, *Antiquities* 14:452-53; *War* 1:330), Herod's brother, Joseph, was killed in a battle with Antigonus. At the time Herod was in Samosata, seeking more Roman aid. Partisans of Antigonus, called "Galileans," then rebelled against supporters of Herod ("the nobles of the country"). They threw into Lake (λιμνή) Gennesaret these supporters of Herod, an act of καταποντισμός (sinking in the ocean). Herod returned with military reinforcements and marched against them through Galilee. Up to two Roman legions under the command of Anthony eventually gathered to fight against them. These superior forces, bent on revenge, hemmed in these "Galileans" and shut them into an unnamed fortress. Opponents fled by night when they saw the size of the army lined up against them. See Freyne, *Galilee from Alexander the Great to Hadrian*, 66. During the period 70-120 C.E. (or perhaps a bit later), the Tenth Legion was stationed in Judea together with a number of auxiliary units. Auxiliary units were usually attached to a legion, thereby adding almost as many soldiers as were in the legion. It is possible that there were fewer forces than usual in Judea at this time, numbering perhaps 10,000 soldiers. From 120 C.E. to the beginning of the fourth century there were two legions in Palestine, the *Legio V Fertensis* and *Legio VI Ferrata*. To these were attached auxiliary units composed of about 25,000 soldiers. See in general for all these details Zeev Safrai, "The Roman Army in the Galilee," in *The Galilee in Late Antiquity*, ed. L. Levine (New York: Jewish Theological Seminary of America, 1992), 104-105.

71. See the brief review of Roman siege works in Palestine, from the first century B.C.E. to the revolt in 66-73 C.E., in Adam Zertal, "The Roman Siege-System at Khirbet al-Hamam (Narbata)," in *The Roman and Byzantine Near East: Some Recent Archaeological Research*, Journal of Roman Archaeology, Supplementary Series 14 (Ann Arbor, Mich.: Cushing-Malloy, 1995), 90-91. On the extensive history of military operations and fortress building in Galilee and in the Transjordan from the period from the Hasmoneans to that of Idumean Herod, see Israel Shatzman, *The Armies of the Hasmonaeans and Herod: From Hellenistic to Roman Frameworks*, Texte und Studien zum Antiken Judentum 25 (Tübingen, Germany: J. C. B. Mohr, 1991), 83-94. Interpretation of Λεγιών (Legion) in Mark as a symbolic reference to actual Roman military institutions is suggested by Ched Myers, *Binding the Strongman: A Political Reading of Mark's Story of Jesus* (Maryknoll, N.Y.: Orbis Books, 1988), 191. A reference by Mark in this manner is denied in *Theological Dictionary of the New Testament* (ed. Gerhard Kittel, trans. Geoffrey W. Bromiley [Grand Rapids, Mich.: William B. Eerdmans, 1967], s.v. "Λεγιών") by Herbert Preisker, who writes that "in the NT the word Λεγιών is not used for the military world, as elsewhere. It is used to denote transcendent forces. It thus shows us where the Church militant has to fight its war, namely, where the struggle is between the kingdom of God and demonic powers." Λεγιών in Matthew 26:23 is used in reference to "twelve legions of angels," and appears to be similar to an apocalyptic idea in 1 Enoch 1:9 that "ten thousand times a thousand" Holy Ones will execute judgment. This usage, in

reference to armies of God, is that from which Preisker drew his conclusions. But it seems most practical to search for the symbolism of this term in Mark 5:1-20 by starting from its literal reference to a Roman military institution and then moving out from there. See Mason (*Greek Terms for Roman Institutions*, 163), who notes that "λεγιών is that standard form in documents for *legio*."

6

Mark 5:21-43:
Uterine Affliction
and the Death of a Maiden

Two stories are combined here: the untimely death of a girl and the woman with a flow of blood. Frank Kermode observed the intercalation of these two stories, calling them "twinned."[1] Karel Hanhart noted the many links between them: (1) both females are called θυγάτηρ (daughter) (5:23, 34, 35); (2) both are "healed" (σωθῇ [5:23], σωθήσομαι [5:26], and σέσωκέν [5:34]); (3) the hemorrhaging woman and Jairus both come to Jesus in proximity to a crowd (5:22, 27); (4) πίστις (faith) is presented as the condition for being healed (5:34, 36); (5) the efficacy of Jesus' touch is emphasized (5:23, 28); (6) Jairus and the hemorrhaging woman "fall before" Jesus (πίπτει [5:22] and προσέπεσεν [5:33]); (7) Jesus speaks to both females with a command (ὕπαγε [5:34] and ἔγειρε [5:41]); (8) the disciples are witnesses to both healings (5:31, 40).[2] The account about the hemorrhaging female is artfully woven into the midst of the maiden's story in a flurry of participles (5:25-27: καὶ γυνὴ οὖσα . . . καὶ πολλὰ παθοῦσα . . . καὶ δαπανήσασα . . . καὶ ὠφεληθεῖσα . . . ἐλθοῦσα . . . ἀκούσασα) ["and there was a woman . . . and having suffered much . . . and having paid out many fees . . . and being in debt . . . coming . . . hearing"]).[3] These two stories form a unit that should be respected in interpretation.

J. Duncan M. Derrett, through the lenses of rabbinic literature, viewed the two daughters as a collective figure. "She" is representative of the Daughters of Jerusalem.[4] There is a certain appeal in this interpretation, whether or not rabbinic literature is relevant. Due to the composition of these two accounts, one within the other, we must make something out of both stories at once. But neither to aggadic[5] nor halakhic texts must we turn in order to understand these stories and the reflection they offer on one another. The hemorrhaging female, who has suffered a uterine μάστιξ (whip, scourge) of a twelve-year flow of blood, is representative of a pollution (μίασμα) that is uniquely related to women's biology and health, in this case represented pointedly as an assault. This is that type of pollution which creates danger for those exposed to it.[6] This type of μίασμα indicates especially uncanny dangers when men or women are not able to find safe passage from one fundamental condition to another (childhood to adulthood, satisfying and fulfilled life to death). Consequently, the bleeding is not only a specific attribute of this woman but also emblematic of a wider sensibility about women and the roles they played in ancient society. These roles enacted cultural expectations about the transition of girls/unmarried women (παρθένοι) to wives/mothers. These cultural expectations are found in ancient views about women, especially in evidence of their typical social roles and in evidence of contemporary theories about their nature.[7] Most of these expectations focus in particular on roles in family and procreation. In Mark, the woman's unstoppable flow of blood is symbolic of these wider expectations about women in general. Consequently, this story is not primarily about ritual impurity caused by a bodily discharge. When the bleeding woman is juxtaposed with the girl who is dead before opportunity to bear children, a composite female figure or character indeed emerges. "She" is a reference first to the role and status of women in general, a reference drawn out in two very particular aspects of unfortunate outcomes in these role expectations: illness and early death. These two outcomes are anomalously frightful since they are severe interruptions and terribly "bad luck," seeming to be a lack of opportune divine benefaction and therefore full of perplexing uncertainty and fear. Special attention and protection in regard to these kinds of outcomes included the development of theories of μίασμα concerning women, rituals of purification, and rituals of protection. The latter, usually *apotropaic* in nature, were used to promote both women's health and the health of their children. So it is that, with regard to a composite figure developed in these two stories, observations by Leila Leah Bronner[8] about scriptural and rabbinic themes of daughterhood are of more service than those of Derrett, because she specifically includes a brief discussion about Pseudo Philo (*Liber Antiquitatum Biblicarum* 40), a reworking of the lament of Jephthah's daughter. This lament serves as a parallel to Mark because it is about the ἄωρος θάνατος (untimely death) of a maiden, exactly the situation found with the daughter of Jairus.

Mark 5:21-43 163

When Jairus approaches Jesus, he comes as a community leader to a man reputed to be willing to use his power to help others. If Jesus were to respond, then his healing intervention might prove miraculously fruitful. Jairus' leadership means that in his community he is a man of esteem, of benefaction, and perhaps of a long family line of leadership. He falls before the feet of Jesus (πίπτει πρὸς τοὺς πόδας αὐτοῦ), accomplishing a προσκύνησις (bowing down)[9] and forming the setting for subsequent events. Jesus has power. The request for a benefaction of that power in the present dire crisis is made with humble caution. Generally, all requests for such benefits submerged humans into the uncertainty of the anomalous frightful. Catastrophic situations like this might or might not be resolved by opportune begging. Need of a benefaction meant one had to rely on an unpredictable outside agency believed probably able to resolve an uncertain and frightening situation.

The problem is the imminent death of his maiden daughter, who is twelve years old and is later addressed by Jesus as κοράσιον (little girl, maiden; 5:41). Two things are interlocked here. First, she is dying before achieving her next level of personhood as a married or otherwise autonomous woman.[10] In the Mishnah this status is discussed in a tractate on menstruation, where it is explained that this status is achieved at menarche. The picture in Mark is of a maiden dying before her menarche and therefore untimely dying, before her change in legal status. Second, Jairus is facing the ἄωρος (untimely) death of his child. Tragic in itself as the loss of a beloved, this kind of death also meant that the girl was about to trade her future wedding bed for a bed among the dead, a specific theme of loss that was present throughout antiquity. The ἄωρος (untimely) death of a child was thought terrifically bad fortune and, as such, an intrusion of the anomalous frightful. It was a perplexing disruption of family and personal life.

The story about the bleeding woman focuses on a different aspect of a woman's life. Menstrual blood was considered vitally important and, subsequently, powerful and polluting.[11] Pollution stemming from women in this sense was classified and labeled. One example is found in Mishnah *Niddah*.[12] Other examples are found in various sacred laws in which, although blood is not always specifically mentioned, regulations control the presence of a woman. The thought in these sources is that women bring a unique ability to pollute, simply by their presence, or by contact with them, or even by their earlier, private sexual expression with men (who then subsequently bore the woman's power to pollute). Examples are the laws for Mên Tyrannus or the Cyrene Cathartic Laws.[13] These prohibitions reinforce the general idea that since women had a unique ability to procreate they therefore also had a unique ability to pollute. A narrow focus on menstrual blood is a vivid representation of the vital and unpredictable aspect of women's role in human existence: children passing from nonbeing into life. Menstrual blood symbolizes the processes of birth (conception, pregnancy, delivery). Robert Parker's judgment is worth repeating, that "menstruation is viewed as a pollution by innumerable societies, and particularly because it commonly acts as a symbol on which men's attitude of suspicion and hostility towards women can focus . . . purity from menstrual contamination only appears as a condition for entering a temple in late sacred laws of non-Greek cults."[14] Conception and birth are essential stages of human life, in which much can go wrong. Proximity to these moments, or to the bodies that create these moments, held an impure quality likened to proximity to violence and death, a link also implied in the Mên Tyrannus inscription, which has the prohibitions, ἀπὸ . . . χοιρέων καὶ γυναικός.ἀπὸ νεκροῦ . . . ἀπὸ φθορᾶς (from garlic germander and from swine and from women . . . from a corpse . . . from corruption).

Contact with either the elements of birth or death created a problem of impurity.[15] Why? Because birth and death are the two focal points of human experience over which the least control can be exercised, and in which the anomalous frightful can emerge. As Parker suggests, "the pollutions of birth and death relate to the disorientation actually or conventionally produced by the great crises in human existence . . . birth and death intrude on human life at their own pleasure. They are an irresistible 'irruption of the biological into social life.' Although they are natural events, they are also violations of order" (p.63). What kind of violations would these have been? For one, the dead were sadly absent. They needed a place to rest and the living needed a tie to that place, lest those who had died might somehow be too much removed from those who survived them. In particular, those who had died by violence posed a problem for this continuity, creating a disrupting pollution consisting of unavenged violence and blood guilt. Violation of order (a violation otherwise known as "impurity" or "pollution") was usually thought to be somebody's fault. It was not easily resolved. In a similar way, birth was both a mystery and a precarious situation. It represents the generation of more humans and, subsequently, is a most vulnerable moment of the human condition. As a general rule, the more vital, unavoidable, necessary, important, and intrusive the human activity, the more likely it was to be assigned purity rituals, traditional etiologic legends, or protective magical operations.[16]

The death of children created a crisis situation of tremendous violation of order, a pollution that perhaps in some cases could never be fully resolved. According to some witnesses, the spirits of deceased children were not at rest. Such after-death wandering indicates that the disruption caused by their early death is a kind of violence not easily resolved or purified. In one magical papyrus, adjurations during the performance of magical operations are made to such dead μελλαξί τε καὶ παρθένοις (boys and maidens). In another text they are specifically labelled ἄωροι (untimely dead), implying the unresolved nature of their untimely demise.[17] In *PGM* 4.342 the same phrase is used in the broader context of invocations to Kore, Persephone, Ereschigal, Adonis, Chthonic Hermes, Thoth who hold the keys to Hades, and to θεοῖς καταχθονίοις, ἀώροις τε καὶ ἀώραις, μελλαξί τε καὶ παρθένοις (to katachthonic gods, to male and female untimely dead, to boys and girls). Erwin Rohde produced extensive references to the ἄωροι, showing that the term is related to ἄγαμοι (unmarried) and ἄτεκνος or ἄπαιδες (childless).[18] Each of these designations implies the short-circuiting of an expected tenure of life, exactly the situation of the daughter of Jairus. Tertullian (*De Anima* 56.3) writes, *aiunt et immatura morte praeventas eo usque vagari istic, donec reliquatio compleatur aetatum* (they also say that those souls which are taken away by a premature death wander about hither and thither until they have completed the residue of the years which they would have lived through).[19] Franz Cumont examined this belief and thought that the idea of the ἄωροι derived directly from ancient astrological theory about types and durations of lives. Ptolemy (*Tetrabiblios* 4.9) argues that an unfortunate fate, especially in cases of βιαίος θάνατος (sudden or violent death) as opposed to more usual ἴδιος θάνατος (appropriate death), is to be explained by various terrorizing conjunctions of planets and stars. These conjunctions conspire to disrupt human life. This idea of a rhythmic circle of life and death is well developed in the *Circle of Petosiris*. Theories of prognostication and interpretation of *prodigia* parallel these beliefs. Systems of periodic weeks, years, or times in general were linked with observation of both natural and strange phenomena. Whatever the explanation of ill-fated dead, it is an uncanny and strange thing to have encounters with them, either as ghosts or as images in dreams and appearances.[20]

Another way that the fate of these unhappy dead is depicted is through lamentation, such as in Ps.-Philo *Liber Antiquitatum Biblicarum* 40, the lament of Jephthah's daughter. The pertinent part of the text is found in 40:5.

> Hear, you mountains, my lamentation . . .
> . . . But I have not made good on my marriage chamber,
> and I have not retrieved my wedding garlands.
> For I have not been clothed in splendor while sitting in my woman's
>   chamber,
> And I have not used sweet-smelling ointment,
> And my soul has not rejoiced in the oil of anointing that has been
>   prepared for m.
> O Mother, in vain you have borne your only daughter,
>   because Sheol has become my bridal chamber,
>   and on earth there is only my woman's chamber.[21]

Margaret Alexiou and Peter Dronke outline the traditional Greek precedents for such a lament, found in drama, poems from the Palatine Anthology, funerary inscriptions, dream books, and erotic literature.[22] In Sophocles (*Antigone* 814-16) Antigone laments her untimely parting: "I have not shared in the wedding song, nor has any bridal hymn yet been sung for me: it is Acheron I'll wed." Lines from Euripides (*Iphigenia in Aulis* 460-61) emphasize a similar sadness: "And as for the wretched maiden—why do I call her that? Hades, it seems, will be her bridegroom soon." These themes are found in book 7 of the *Palatine Anthology*. Of several examples, two are worth noting: "Without having seen the marriage bed, I, Gorgippos, descend to the bridal chamber of blonde Persephone" (Simonides) and "You are envious, Hades. And you yourself, Hymenaeus, transformed the harmonious wedding-chant into the sound of wailing threnodies" (Errina).[23] A Cyrene funerary inscription from the second century C.E. is also noteworthy.

> Fortune allotted you only a short time, Capito, between life and death,
>   between the tomb and the marriage-chamber;
> A single night, cruel and deceitful, a night without flutes,
> A night without wedding-songs or marriage-feast for you.
> Alas for your ashes, short-lived creature—they fell alike
>   on wedding-robes,
> On wedding garlands not steeped in unguents, and on your books.
> Alas, wedding-song that is loud with lamentations, alas, torches,
> That light the way to your last, empty bed.[24]

The material from Artemidorus (*Oneirocriticon* 2.49) includes a theory about marriage and death. They are both considered τέλη (fulfillments). Either fulfillment, marriage or death, could be cheated. In novels, the theme is observed in Achilles Tatius 1.3, where lines of importance are, "Your bridal chamber is the grave; your wedlock is with death; the dirge your bridal song; these wailings your marriages songs."[25] The persistence of these themes is indurate. Brevity of duration and untimely death are lamented. They are terrible anomalies in the expected life cycle.

Lamentation is not the only response to an ἄωρος θάνατος (untimely death). The unhappy dead who died too early, though lamentable, are also depicted as noisy, annoying, and dangerous to the living. In one persistent tradition, they form the train of howling creatures who follow Hekate or Proserpina (in a Roman version, a syncretism toward Demeter).[26] In order to prevent a situation of dire μίασμα (defilement), banquets were held for Hekate, to avert any evil phantoms of the ἄωροι θάνατοι (untimely dead) that she might bring to a house in her role as mistress of spirits. Fish offerings were made to her in Rome, and fish symbolism is linked to her in iconography about death and dying. On a late Capitoline statue, Hekate is called Μεισοπόνηρος (Evil Crescent Moon). Purifications (ὀξυθύμια) of a house in the name of Hekate are meant to ward off ghosts, sending them out to the crossroads.[27] Some sources link Hekate with μορμόνας, which Hesychius defined as πλάνητας δαίμονας (wandering daimōns). These were fearful supernatural entities who stole or killed infants, like Γελλώ who παρθένος ἀώρως ἐτελεύτησε (died untimely, a virgin).[28] These are creatures of the anomalous frightful, supernatural enemies who epitomize the possible dangers attendant on women's lives. In these examples of the anomalous frightful there are linked themes of virginity, death of children, assault on children, and creatures of unclean activities.

Images of horrifying assaults due to ἄωρος θάνατος (untimely death) borne by these supernatural fearful entities are potent, and they persisted in antiquity through a variety of forms and syncretism. As with rules about women's pollution that link critical moments of human existence to women's lives and bodies, Hekate's role as a fierce danger to men and women also had wide distribution. A variety of religious syncretisms went into making this distribution, including associations of divine characters in magical texts of invocation. Such characters are Harpocrates and Meliouchos, ᾽Ορθία or ᾽Ορθωσία, βαυβω, Coptic *noure*, Ερεσχιγαλ, and οὐροβόρος (see appendix E, "Divinities Affecting Women"). The relationship of Hekate to the Moon developed over time, showing rich chthonic roots and contexts that are broader than magic. A black-figure vase pictures her standing over against Cora, holding torches; between them chthonian Hermes rides on a goat.[29] In her combinations with the Moon, Selene/Hekate is a dangerous entity. She is often prayerfully invoked, and in Seneca (*Medea* 750-751) she is so addressed, "And now, invoked by my magical enchantments, come, O Star of the Night, in your most sinister form, even the Menace with Three Faces."[30] Other Latin invocations are pictured metaphorically in Ovid (*Metamorphoses* 14.404-405), "Circe invokes the Night, the goddess of Night, Erebus, Chaos, and she addresses her prayers to Hekate in long, roaring howls," and *Metamorphoses* 7.192-195, "O Night! loyal friend of Mysteries and you who, with Luna, come after the fires/passions of day, stars of Gold, and You, Hekate in Three Heads, who comes at my call." The traditions about the menacing and devastating Hekate were persistent, continually reconfigured, and reported throughout a variety of sources. The devastation she brings is horrible, untimely, and polluted.

In spite of this dangerous side, Hekate also has a beneficent aspect, as a *protectrix* especially of children and mothers. The goddess of terrible events proved a benefactor, especially so for the vulnerable population of women and children, or exactly those types of people who dominate the narrative in Mark 5:21-43. When she exclaims "O, Phosphorescent Hekate has sent me a kindly ghost (φάσματα)," Menelaus responds to Helen in Euripides (*Helena* 596) with a question: "Do you not see me, a νυκτίφαντον (night appearance), Safe-Keeper of the door to the house?" These lines show the ancient fright attendant with nocturnal apparitions (not only a dreadful fright but also a fear of μίασμα [defilement]), only here translated into potential benefaction and salvation. She is called Hekate Kourotrophos in Hesiod, *Theogony* 450-52. When Hekate is combined with Artemis, then she is a Προθυρία (Door Protectrix), or protector of the home and hearth. She is also identified with Genetyliis, the goddess of one's birth hour and the protectrix of child birth.[31] Although these details about benefaction are not specifically mentioned in the story about the bleeding woman or about the daughter of Jairus, these two stories, taken together, point to the very experiences that Hekate as Genetyliis addressed. Hekate is shown as having control over Τυχή and Νέμισις in a marble Hekateion, protecting women, children, and the time of childbirth.[32] These positive attributes of Hekate are best understood in the context of the anomalous frightful that follows along with her. Apotropaic ritual done in relation to her, including use of elements of her domain in a logic of *similis similibus*, call on the very things that it wants to ward off.

A binding spell from Pseudo Orpheus (*Lithika Kerygmata* 20.14-18) focuses on μιάσματα (pollutions) and καταδέσμοι (curses).[33] This is an example of how uncleanness is seen as a type of misfortune, an experience of disorder that makes one uneasy since an unfortunate outcome might be at hand. Binding spells often call upon the untimely dead to effect a specific magical operation. The ἄωροι, often so called upon, represent a set of unfortunate and intrusively bad outcomes that includes unmarried virgins and childless women. Often, there is a link between ἄωροι (untimely dead) and βιαιοθάνατοι (violently dead).[34] The interruption of life through sudden or violent death is similar to the interruption of the beginning of life through physical or supernatural attacks on mothers and children. Menstrual blood symbolizes such a spectrum of attacks, dangers, and impurities, a spectrum inherent to women's experience.

Some Hellenistic philosophical and medical investigators, observing menses, thought that women have more blood than men. Rising and falling levels of blood, including the periodic menses, were explained as derivatives of lunar phases.[35] Traditions about the moon, its implication in women's blood, periodic menses, fertility, and conception are other indications of the strong sense that divine or cosmic powers are involved with all critical aspects of feminine biological experience. Because of the anomalous frightful related to fertility and to the risks of childbearing, women's bodies were thought to be in need of special protection. This was so especially in the domains of gynecological health, pregnancy, the birth of health babies, and infant care (see appendix F, "Gynecological Health"). Special protection was sought in a variety of ways. Jairus represents one way, as does the hemorrhaging woman: seeking favor from a source of divine power. Jean-Jacques Aubert's study of magical intervention in these affairs offers evidence for binding spells and anti-binding spells meant to open or close the womb. Other spells were meant to treat menorrhagia.[36]

It is not said in Mark that any of these beliefs or fears are or are not held by Jairus or anyone else. But the events that are reported are all very much a part of this symbolic world of women's health, especially as symbolized by women's blood. In any direction one turns, this symbolic world is repeatedly acknowledged, addressed, ritualized, and conceptualized, and it is representative of the anomalous frightful. In this case, the experience of receipt of favor or receipt of no favor balanced upon the fulcrum of potential gain *vs.* terrible loss. To such a vulnerable situation, especially when word has come that the daughter had untimely died, Jesus responds simply, μὴ φοβοῦ μόνον πίστευε ("do not fear, but only have faith; 5:36). Although there is much to fear, it is never made clear in this report in what there is much to believe. Is Jesus described here as the object of Jairus' trust? In the story Jairus approaches Jesus in that light. But given the anguish of these terrible events, Jesus says very little at all about them. On entering the house of Jairus with his chosen three (Peter, James, John the brother of James), Jesus encounters a full-scale lamentation scene, which is an entirely usual, expected, and traditional response to events. His query about the household lamentation and his comment τὸ παιδίον οὐκ ἀπέθανεν ἀλλὰ καθεύδει (the child has not died but is sleeping) seem negligible, as if he doesn't perceive the reality of what is happening. He dismisses the whole affair and sends out the mourners. With a few words he "wakes up" the girl. The language of "rising" in these lines is impressive, but quick (ἔγειρε . . . καὶ εὐθὺς ἀνέστη ["rise up! . . . and immediately she rose up"]).[37] Given the dismal nature and all the expectations surrounding the terrible meaning of these events, rising up out of them here seems remarkably easy, almost too easy.

Here is yet another encounter of Jesus with a well-developed domain of danger, bad outcomes, and human terror. Even his own activities cause bewilderment (καὶ ἐξέστησαν ἐκστάσει μεγάλῃ [they were overcome with amazement]; 5:42), much like the anomalous frightful always causes. It is the non-wonder-working audience that falls into ecstasy instead of the wonder-worker himself,[38] another facet that leaves the reader wondering about the meaning of these odd events and pondering what type of miracle worker Jesus is. The anomalous frightful of the ἄωρος θάνατος is here superseded, but by someone who is not explained, who simply moves on afterwards, who seems not to get involved in the least with specific and depressing elements of the loss, and who begins by saying that there is not a loss in the first place. From a point of view of behavior expected of heroic saviors, Jesus makes no claim on the family or on the girl, in a strange way demanding absolutely no *quid pro quo* for the benefactions rendered.[39] The girl is returned back to her father and a specific instruction is given to make none of these events known publicly (5:43, μηδεὶς γνοῖ τοῦτο). The reader is left again to wonder how it is that such a terrible fate is now so easily undone by a man who neither demonstrates an equally dreadful response nor appears to ask for anything except secrecy from those who benefit.

The middle story of the whole narrative, about the woman who has been for twelve years ἐν ῥύσει αἵματι (with a flow of blood), is the narrower symbolic focus of women's health that bears themes of untimely and uncanny loss. Its narrower focus intensifies the meaning of women's themes. Some have suggested that the description of this woman's μάστιξ (torture) by the phrase ἐν ῥύσει αἵματι (by a flow of blood) is influenced by terminology from Leviticus 15, where the term ῥύσις(flow) refers to a variety of bodily discharges. The specific phrase ᾖ ῥέουσα αἵματι is in Leviticus 15:19, and ῥέῃ ῥύσις αἵματος in Leviticus. 15:25. The terminology in Mark, if affected by the Leviticus 15 phrases, is remarkably free of the pleonasm that the LXX Leviticus Greek exhibits. Alternatively, Vettius Valens (*Anthologiarum Libri* 7.5) speaks of a αἵματος πολλὴν ῥύσιν (large flow of blood) under certain astrological conditions. Hippocrates Αφορισμοί 3.27 mentions ἐκ ῥινῶν αἵματος ῥύσεις (flows of blood out of areas of the skin).[40] Mark's text may fairly be compared to these two samples. The description of the woman's problem in Mark 5:29 as πηγὴ τοῦ αἷμα αὐτῆς (gushing source of her blood) is, on the other hand, very much closer to LXX Leviticus, as Marla J. Selvidge well notes.[41] The phrase τῆς πηγῆς τοῦ αἵματος αὐτῆς is in Leviticus 12:7, and the fuller πηγὴν αὐτῆς . . . τὴν ῥύσιν τοῦ αἵματος αὐτῆς in Leviticus. 20:18. The use of πηγή in Mark 5:29 may show that terminology from Levitical traditions found its way into Mark. However, the more general phrase τὴν ῥύσιν τοῦ αἵματος (or variants) is used elsewhere outside of the Greek Leviticus. It is possible that πηγή as used here is good Greek, creating an emphasis on the quality of the hemorrhaging, the main attribute the story assigns this woman. As such, we need identify no specific intention here to use themes from the Book of Leviticus. This is so especially when we remember that the story background is not Levitical purity, but a history of botched medical intervention and the subsequent personal and financial crisis of the woman. Rather than a focus on ritual purity, we find here a depiction of the anomalous frightful linked to women's health and, specifically, to blood that symbolizes that health. The hemorrhaging focuses this account on μίασμα. Such pollution is not to be understood as "ritual uncleanness" only, but as that kind of status assigned to people when vital aspects of human life seem interrupted or dislodged in or by them.[42] Blood was linked to fertility, danger, childbearing, and to the anomalous frightful in each of these situations. The account of long hemorrhaging makes the woman emblematic of the most important things going the most wrong.

Yet being in this most intense of conditions, the woman's encounter with Jesus is strangely the most passive. A mere touch ensues, and then Jesus guesses that something has happened. There are in fact no words exchanged between them until after the healing happens.[43] The woman becomes afraid of Jesus, again an indication of the fear and uncertainty relevant to the anomalous frightful: benefaction once given may later be taken away. Her προσκύνησις (bowing) to Jesus illustrates this fact, as she submits to him in hope of mercy. The benediction of Jesus to her (ὕπαγε εἰς εἰρήνη [go in peace]) and exhortation to be healed (ἴσθι ὑγιὴς ἀπὸ τῆς μάστιγός σου ["be healed from your torment"]) leave the reader wondering, how it is that so much is accomplished with apparently so little deliberate device. What is the explanation for this? None is given. Events simply move forward in this narrative. Is something important left out here? Had these characters dreamed up that terror that they thought they felt? Do they simply wake up from their nightmare? Is not the anomalous frightful either of sudden, untimely death or of hygenic dilemmas a monumental terror, in need of a monumental intervention? These considerations seem to make no difference in this story, even though they are represented in it. When Jesus encounters these worst-case, pernicious scenarios, the troubles seem to evaporate from around him, like so much mist dissipating. When Jesus encounters them, they simply crumble, and without much apparent labor on his part. The resolution of such terror by so little is a relief, but it is extremely awkward and uncanny. When a terrorizing and dangerous enemy is vanquished, what are people to do with its new conqueror?

Notes

1. Frank Kermode (*The Genesis of Secrecy: On the Interpretation of Narrative*, Charles Eliot Norton Lectures 1977-78 [Cambridge, Mass.: Harvard University Press, 1979], 131-35) suggests what my analysis shows with more detail, that "the woman, in the present instance, is ritually unclean so long as her hemorrhage continues; but she is at once, by an exercise of power, *dunamis*, relieved of this disability. The girl, dead or supposed dead, is also unclean, or supposed unclean; she is restored by an exercise of power which is, in antithetical contrast, explicit and willed. Between the opposites clean and unclean there are inserted—intercalated—figures of sexual or magical force. We can safely say that these stories do not have the same meanings we should have found in them had they been told *seriatim* (p.133)." The specific aspect of "ritual uncleanness" that Kermode detects in this story is actually not explicit in the text, but is Kermode's interpretation, presumably based on a reading of this story in light of ancient Jewish theories about bodily discharges.

2. Karel Hanhart, *The Open Tomb: A New Approach* Collegeville, Minn.: Liturgical Press, 1995), 131. As Marla J. Selvidge (*Women, Cult, and Miracle Recital: A Redactional Critical Investigation on Mark 5:24-34* [Lewisburg, Pa.:

Bucknell University Press, 1990], 81) observes, "There is ample evidence to suggest that there are definite similarities between the two miracle stories. Both women are called *daughters* (Mark 5:23, 34); both report the number twelve (Mark 5:25, 42). Both deal with the healing of females (Mark 5:23, 26). Both women had what seemed to be incurable diseases (Mark 5:23, 26). Both Jairus and the woman approach Jesus from out of the crowd (Mark 5:22, 27). Both healings had as their object salvation (Mark 5:23, 28). Both miracles involved faith (Mark 5:34, 36). Both believed in the efficacy of Jesus' touch (Mark 5:23, 28)."

3. James Hope Moulton and Nigel Turner (*Grammar of the New Testament in Greek* 4: *Style* [Edinburgh: T. & T. Clark, 1976], §10, "Word Order") observe that this is a primary example of "Mark's mannered style."

4. J. Duncan M. Derrett (*The Making of Mark: The Scriptural Bases of the Earliest Gospel* 1: *From Jesus' Baptism to Peter's Recognition of Jesus as the Messiah* [Shipston-on-Stour, Warwickshire, England: P. Drinkwater, 1985], 107) comments: "The two females collectively constitute Daughters of Jerusalem and this is the first time this biblical character has come within our range, a character proper to the two important books, *Lamentations* and *Canticles*. We must take the composite Daughter of Jerusalem seriously: she is really one person, for the woman shares characteristics with the girl, and vice versa. The joy at the end of the passage speaks of salvation come to the house of Israel. . . . Here Jesus very nearly concludes a betrothal with the girl for 5:40, which is highly ironical."

5. The turn to aggadic literature, should it be done, must be done carefully. The relation of this literature, with its methods of interpretation, to other Hellenistic literatures, with their interpretive methods and textual problem-solving, is not easy to establish. See Adam Kamesar ("The Narrative Aggada as Seen from the Graeco-Latin Perspective," *Journal for Jewish Studies* 45 [1994]: 52-70) for comparison of examples of aggadic literature to ζητήματα καὶ λύσεις (inquiries and resolutions), μῦθος (story-line), and σχῆμα σιωπήσεως (veiled meaning).

6. My approach follows observations by Robert Parker, "Birth and Death," in *Miasma: Pollution and Purification in Early Greek Religion* (Oxford: Clarendon Press, 1983), 32-73. Parker's observations stem in part from those of Mary Douglas, that "a society may use a supposed physical impurity as an unconscious symbol upon which it focuses fears or concerns of a much broader social character" (p.56) and that "pollution is in general a property of the betwixt and between: that which falls between or violates the categories into which a given society divides external reality" (p.61). See S. Eitrem (*Some Notes on the Demonology in the New Testament*, Symbolae Osloenses 12 [Oslo: A. W. Brügger, 1950], 28-29) for the relationship of the term μάστιξ to πληγή. The metaphor of the "whip" implies that this assaultive illness is viewed as a malevolent agency that intruded into the life of its victim.

7. See Sarah B. Pomeroy ("Women's Identity and the Family in the Classical *Polis*," in *Women in Antiquity: New Assessments*, ed. Richard Hawley and Barbara Levick [London: Routledge, 1995], 111-21), especially on the role of women in ancient funerals and as daughters and wives (for the latter, when various liabilities

or immunities are legally established). On preference for sons instead of daughters in classical Athens, see Sarah B. Pomeroy, *Goddesses, Whores, Wives, and Slaves: Women in Classical Antiquity* (New York: Schocken Books, 1975), 69. See Tal Ilan (*Jewish Women in Greco-Roman Palestine: An Inquiry into Image and Status*, Texte und Studien zum antiken Judentum 44 [Tübingen, Germany: J.C.B. Mohr, 1995], 46) on a somewhat friendlier ancient view of daughters. Ilan writes that "every source views the birth of a daughter as a disappointment. Yet at the same time, we hear of no practical instruction or theory recommending steps to reduce the number of daughters in a family." Ilan refers to Ben Sira 22:3 ("It is a disgrace to be the father of an undisciplined son, and the birth of a daughter is a loss"), Genesis Rabba 45.2 ("Anyone who does not have a son is as if dead"), Genesis Rabba 65.12 (sex of an unborn child is one of the seven secrets concealed from "man," along with the day of his death and the date when the Wicked Kingdom will be overturned), b.Nidd. 70b-71a (to assure the birth of a son, the man should conduct himself modestly at the time of sexual intercourse), b.B.B. 10b (to assure the birth of a son, the man should generously give to the poor), t.Qidd. 5,17 (Abraham was blessed in that he did not have daughters), and Jubilees 3:8-9 (on why the period of purification is longer for birth of daughter, in reference to Lev.12:1-5; cf. t.Nidd. 4:7 and b.Nidd. 30b). On differences in views about roles and status of Jewish women between rabbinic and diaspora evidence, see Ross Shepard Kraemer, *Her Share of the Blessings: Women's Religions Among Pagans, Jews, and Christians in the Greco-Roman World* (New York: Oxford University Press, 1992), 93-137. On theories of the natural or elemental make up of women (hot or cold, dry or wet), see Anne Carson, "Putting Her in Her Place: Woman, Dirt, and Desire," in *Before Sexuality: The Construction of Erotic Experience in the Ancient Greek World*, ed. David M. Halperin, John L. Winker, and Froma I. Zeitlin, 83-113 (Princeton, N.J.: Princeton University Press, 1990). On theories of women's role in procreation, see G. E. R. Lloyd, "The Female Sex: Medical Treatment and Biological Theories in the Fifth and Fourth Centuries B.C.," in *Science, Folklore and Ideology: Studies in the Life Sciences in Ancient Greece* (Cambridge: Cambridge University Press, 1983).

8. Leila Leah Bronner, "'The King's Daughter Is All Glorious Within': The Estate of Daughterhood," in *From Eve to Esther: Rabbinic Reconstructions of Biblical Women* (Louisville, Ky.: Westminster John Knox Press, 1994), 111-41.

9. Elpis Mitropoulou, *Kneeling Worshippers in Greek and Oriental Literature and Art*, PYLI Editions (Athens: Glauchi, 1975). The capacity of the symbolism of these acts to express a variety of emotions is quite impressive: p.16, despair (πτῆξαι ταπεινὴν προσπεσεῖν τ᾿ ἐμὸν γόνυ [to cower, to humble oneself, to kneel in submission]; Euripides *Andromache* 165); p. 17, submission (ἱκέτης προσπίπτω [a suppliant, I do submit]; Xenophon *Cyropaedia* 4.6.2). The diversity of Near Eastern examples of these actions is impressive (compare pp.59-70 for 72 examples). In iconography, the kneeling supplicant figure is on one or two knees with hands clasped. Greeks encountered the Persian προσκύνησις (bowing); see W. W. Tarn, *Alexander the Great* (Cambridge: Cambridge University Press, 1948], 2:360. On Jairus' leadership status I note that the synagogue inscription of

Theodotus in Jerusalem, presented in Adolf Deissmann (*Light from the Ancient East*, 4th ed., trans. Lionel R. M. Strachan [London: Hodder & Stoughton, 1922], 440) shows the honoring of a family of such leaders (compare Jean-Baptiste Frey, *Corpus Inscriptionum Iudaicarum* [Rome: Pontificio Istituto di Archeologia Cristiana, 1936; repr., New York: KTAV, 1975], 2: §1404). For discussion of the ἀρχισυνάγωγος (synagogue leader) in Judaism see Frey, *Corpus Inscriptionum Iudaicarum* 1: xcvii-xcix; it is well-established in inscriptional evidence for Jewish leaders; see also David Noy (*Jewish Inscriptions of Western Europe* 1: *Italy [Excluding the City of Rome], Spain and Gaul* [Cambridge: Cambridge University Press, 1993], §14) for a Latin *archisynagogos* in Ostia (first-second centuries C.E.). The term ἀρχισυνάγωγος was also used in non-Jewish cults; see *The Vocabulary of the Greek New Testament Illustrated from the Papyri and Other Non-Literary Sources*, ed. James Hope Moulton and George Milligan (Grand Rapids, Mich.: William B. Eerdmans, 1982), s.v. ἀρχισυνάγωγος; and *Theological Dictionary of the New Testament*, ed. Gerhard Friedrich Kittel, trans. Geoffrey W. Bromiley (Grand Rapids, Mich.: William B. Eerdmans, 1971), s.v. ἀρχισυνάγωγος, by Wolfgang Schrage, 7:844-47.

10. Mishnah *Niddah* 5.6 accepts as valid betrothal vows if the girl is at least twelve years and one day old; see Judith Romney Wegner, *Chattel or Person? The Status of Women in the Mishnah* (New York: Oxford University Press, 1988), 38-39. See also Ilan (*Jewish Women*, 64) for a summary of other evidence about marriage age: *Lamenations Rabba* 1.2 (compare *yQidd* 1.7, 61a): boys married at the age of 12; *Abot* 5.21: males marrying at age 18; *bQidd* 29b: If male is twenty without marrying, the Holy One would become angry; *bYeb* 12b: from eleven years and one day to twelve years and one day = "a minor." Frey (*Corpus Inscriptionum Iudicarum* 1:cxvi-cxvii) reviews Jewish inscriptional material with summation of names and ages; compare Pieter W. van der Horst (*Ancient Jewish Epitaphs: An Introductory Survey of a Millennium of Jewish Funerary Epigraphy [300 B.C.E. - 700 C.E.]*, Contributions to Biblical Exegesis and Theology 2 [Kampen, The Netheralnds: Kok Pharos Publishing House, 1991], 103-104): "We do not have many inscriptions recording the age at which women were married, but the few who record it mention ages varying from 12 to 18 years. Fifteen was probably an average age for a girl to marry." On the importune "snatching away" of the young, see Richard Lattimore, *Themes in Greek and Roman Epitaphs* (Urbana: University of Illinois Press, 1962), 150-51. Pomeroy (*Goddesses, Whores, Wives, and Slaves,* 68) finds in classical Athens the average age of menarche and of a woman's marriage at fourteen. Aline Rousselle (*Porneia: On Desire and the Body in Antiquity*, trans. Felicia Pheasant [Oxford: Basil Blackwell, 1988], 33) notes the Roman custom of calling a twelve-year-old married girl *uxor* [(fully) married woman]. Soranus (*Gynaecology* 24) writes, "Menstruation which is about to occur for the first time must be inferred . . . above all from the growth of breasts which, broadly, takes place around the fourteenth year"; see Mary Lefkowtiz and M. Flint, *Women's Life in Greece and Rome: A Sourcebook in Translation* (Baltimore: Johns Hopkins University Press, 1982), 219. See Sarah Iles Johnston, "Hecate and the Dying Maiden," in *Restless Dead:*

Encounters Between the Living and the Dead in Ancient Greece (Berkeley: University of California Press, 1999), 203-249.

11. See Jean-Jacques Aubert ("Threatened Wombs: Aspects of Ancient Uterine Magic," *Greek, Roman and Byzantine Studies* 30 [1988]: 430-32) for details on magical practices in which menstrual blood plays an important part. Pliny (*Natural History* 28.78) indicates general assumptions about how contact with this blood was considered unhealthy, for both plants and animals. Aubert refers to Democritus of Abdera (*On Antipathies;* fifth century B.C.E.) and to statements by Metrodorus of Scepsis (first century B.C.E.) for similar ideas. Uterine magic is pervasive across cultures, as one might expect, given the desire for healthy children; see Hans Dieter Betz, "Jewish Magic in the Greek Magical Papyri (*PGM* VII.260-271)," in *Envisioning Magic: A Princeton Seminar and Symposium*, ed. Peter Schäfer and Hans G. Kippenberg, Studies in the History of Religions (*Numen* Book Series) 75 (Leiden, The Netherlands: E. J. Brill, 1997), 46-63.

12. See *Niddah* 1.6-7 (in *The Mishnah: Translated from the Hebrew with Introductory and Brief Explanatory Notes*, trans. Herbert Danby [Oxford: Oxford University Press, 1933]: "And of what did they speak when they said, 'It is enough for her [that she be deemed unclean only from] her time [of suffering a flow]'? Of a first flow; but if it was a second flow, she conveys uncleanness during the twenty-four hours that have gone before. Yet if she suffered the first flow by reason of constraint, then, even for the second flow, it is enough for her [that she be deemed unclean only from] her time [of suffering a flow]. Although they have said, 'It is enough for her [that she be deemed unclean] only from her time [of suffering a flow],' she must needs make examination, unless she is a menstruant [and making count of her prescribed seven days of uncleanness], or is abiding in the blood of her purifying [after giving birth], or has connection and uses the test-rags (unless she is abiding in the blood of her purifying), or is a virgin whose blood is clean."

13. See the Mên Tyrannus material in Wilhelm Dittenberger, *Sylloge Inscriptionum Graecarum* (Hildesheim, Germany: G. Olms, 1960), §1042. Important lines are: καὶ [μηθένα] ἀκάθαρτον προσάγειν, καθαριζέστω δὲ ἀπὸ σκόρδων καὶ χοιρέων καὶ γυναικός, λουσαμένους δὲ κατακέφαλα αὐθημερὸν εἰσπορεύεσθαι, καὶ ἐκ τῶν γυναικέων διὰ ἑπτὰ ἡμερῶν λουσαμένην κατακέφαλα αὐθημερὸν εἰσπορεύεσθαι, καὶ ἀπὸ νεκροῦ διὰ ἡμερῶν δέκα καὶ ἀπὸ φθορᾶς ἡμερῶν τετταράκοντα (And nothing unclean must be presented, but cleanse from garlic germander and from swine and from women, yet wash from head to foot on the same day as going in. And wash from head to foot, on the very day of going in, after having been with a woman in the previous seven days. And wash from head to foot, on the very day of going in, after having been near a corpse in the previous ten days or having been near "corruption" in the previous fourteen days). Also available in Eugene Lane, *Corpus Monumentorum Religionis Dei Menis (MNRDM)* Etudes préliminaires aux religions orientales dans l'Empire romain 19 (Leiden, The Netherlands: E. J. Brill, 1971-78), 1§13, with bibliography. Parker (*Miasma*, 332-51) discusses the Cyrene Cathartic Laws, with translation and

commentary. The inscription was discovered in 1922 at the Roman baths at Cyrene and subsequently published in *Supplementum Epigraphicum Graecum* (Amsterdam: J. C. Gieben, 1979), 9§72. Parker (*Miasma*, 336) translates pertinent lines 16-20 of A of the inscription: "The woman in childbed shall pollute the house . . . she shall not pollute [the person who is outside the house], unless he comes in. Any person who is inside shall be polluted for three days, but shall not pollute anyone else, not wherever this person goes." Lines 1-23 of B detail ritual procedures for women's expected course of life: prenuptial, nuptial, pregnancy. Parker's Appendix 3, "Problems concerning 'Enter Pure from': Requirements in Sacred Laws," discusses what had been constituted "contact" in matters of pollution stemming from women, especially in matters related to λέχος (bed).

14. Parker (*Miasma*, 100-102) points to examples of such late laws as found in *Lois sacrées de l'Asie Mineure*, ed. Franciszek Sokolowksi (Paris: E. Boccard, 1955), 54.7-8, 91.16, 119.3 and *Lois sacrées des cités Grecques, supplément*, ed. Franciszek Sokolowski (Paris: E. Boccard, 1962), 55.5. See also Porphyry, *De Abstentenia* 2.50, and Heliodorus, *Aethiopica* 10.4.5.

15. Parker, *Miasma*, 32-73; see also 352-56 on ideas of pollution ἀπὸ λέχους (from contact with the marriage bed) or ἀπὸ γυναικός/ἀπ' ἀνδρός (from contact with a woman/man).

16. For Greek rituals concerning maidens, including discussion of the Iphegenia legend and especially Artemis festivals at Ephesus, see Ken Dowden (*Death and the Maiden: Girls' Initiation Rites in Greek Mythology* [London: Routledge, 1989]), who quotes (p.40) from *On the City of the Ephesians* by Xenophon of Ephesus, on a procession of boys and girls who honor the hero Habrokomes and the goddess Artemis. On magical protection, see Roy Kotansky, "A Magic Gem Inscribed in Greek and Artificial Phoenician," *Zeitschrift für Papyrologie und Epigraphik* 85 (1991):237-38. The Greek lines read: ἀπόλυσον πάντα δαίμονα Σεφφάρας 'Αμμιᾶ (Release every daimōn from Sepphara [daughter of] Ammia[s]).

17. David G. Martinez (*P. Michigan XVI: A Greek Love Charm from Egypt (P.Mich. 757)*, Michigan Papyri 16; American Studies in Papyrology 30 [Atlanta: Scholars Press, 1991], 48) wrote: "Like the unburied (ἄταφοι) and those who die violently (βιοθάνατοι), the ἄωροι cannot enter Hades, but must remain in a state of restless waiting and wandering until their destined time is fulfilled, a fact which makes them especially valuable for the purposes of magic, because of both their availability and hostility."

18. Erwin Rohde, *Psyche: The Cult of Souls and Belief in Immortality among the Greeks*, 7th ed., trans. W. B. Hillis (New York: Harcourt, Brace, 1925), 586-88 (Appendix 3) and 593-95 (Appendix 7). A terse example of this combination is reproduced in Lattimore, *Themes*, 185: κλαύσατ' ἄωρον ἐμὴν ἡλικίαν ἄγαμος (weep for my untimely, unwedded youth; *SEG* 1§567.16). See in Frey (*Corpus Inscriptionum Iudaicarum*, §984) an epitaph from Tiberias for an ἄγαμος woman who is seventy years old. See also Johnston, "The *Aôrê* and Reproductive Failure," in *Restless Dead*, 184-99.

19. *De Anima* 56.8 speaks also of *animas immaturas et innuptas* (souls of the untimely dead and unmarried); see J. H. Waszink, *Quinti Septimi Florentis Tertulliani De Anima: Edited with Introduction and Commentary* (Amsterdam: J. M. Meulenhoff, 1947), 573-74. As Waszink noted about the ἄγαμοι and ἄτεκνοι, "neither group possesses any progeny to render them the customary honours after death." See comments on Waszink and further literature in Arthur Darby Nock, "Tertullian and the *Ahori*," in *Essays on Religion and the Ancient World, Selected and Edited, with an Introduction, Bibliography of Nock's Writings, and Indexes by Zeph Stewart* (Cambridge, Mass.: Harvard University Press, 1972), 2:712-719.

20. See Franz Cumont, *Lux Perpetua* (Paris: Librarie Orientalise Paul Geuthner, 1949), 303-341. See observations of Auguste Bouché-Leclercq (*L'Astrologie Grecque* [Paris: E. Leroux, 1899], 403) on this theory of "course of life" as presented in Plato *Timaeus* 89 B-C. As translated by R. G. Bury (*Plato: Timaeus, Critias, Cleitophon, Menexenus, Epistles*, Loeb Classical Library [London: William Heinemann, 1929]) Plato writes, "For in its structure every disease resembles in some sort the nature of the living creature. For, in truth, the constitution of these creatures has prescribed periods of life for the species as a whole, and each individual creature likewise has a naturally predestined term of life (ζῷον εἱμαρμένον), apart from the accidents due to necessity (ἀνάγκη)." The Ptolemy text continues with a phrase of explanation: nonviolent and natural death occurs whenever those [powers] taking authority over death happen to be naturally at their own unique tropics, being superseded by none of the powers which inflict evil and create a strangely unusual end (ὅταν οἱ τὴν κυρίαν τοῦ θανάτου λαβόντες ἐπὶ τῆς οἰκείας φυσικῆς ἰδιοτροπίας τύχωσιν ὄντες, ὑπὸ μηδενὸς καθυπερτερηθέντες τῶν κακῶσαι καὶ ἐπιφανέστερον ποιῆσαι τὸ τέλος δυναμένων). This is slightly rephrased a line later as, κυριεύσωσιν οἱ κακοποιοί (the evil-working things hold authority). For the *Circle of Petosiris* see Bouché-Leclercq, *L'Astrologie grecque*, 538-39; 88-90 (figs. 44 and 45). The circle contains, on the bottom, the two types of death: μέγας θάνατος (noble, honorable death) and μικρὸς θάνατος (horrendous, unhonorable death). Bouché-Leclercq found ancient exemplars of these two types: Achilles, King David (μέγας); Hector, Goliath (μικρός). Firmicus Maternus and Vettius Valens include the patriarch Abraham along with Petosiris, Nechepso, Critodemus, and Orpheus as the early and potent founders of astrological knowledge; see Jeffrey S. Siker, "Abraham in Graeco-Roman Paganism," *Journal for the Study of Judaism* 18 (1991): 188-208. See Bouché-Leclercq (*L'Astrologie grecque*, 88-89) for general systems of arranging seasons and years in accordance with phenomena, both natural and unnatural. For the strange and marvelous being told as a results of encounters with the recently dead, see Theodore Hopfner (*Griechisch-ägyptischer Offenbarungszauber*, Studien zur Palaeographie und Papyruskunde 21, 23 [Amsterdam: Verlag Adolf M. Hakkert, 1921], 1§262) on the writer Phlegon of Trailes, who reports in his Περὶ θαυμασίων (*On Marvels*) a story from the time of Philip of Macedon. The story deals with the activities of a Machates and the recently dead Philinnion. "Strange and serious" events take place, as she, undead, starts going each night to

the room of Machates. This is investigated, and eventually Philinnion dies "again"; trans. in William Hansen, *Phlegon of Tralles' Book of Marvels* (Exeter: University of Exeter Press, 1996), 25-28.

21. Trans. by D. J. Harrington in James Charlesworth, *Old Testament Pseudepigrapha*, 2:354. This tradition develops a theme of the willingness of Seila (the daughter's attributed name) to die an exemplary death in sacrifice. The text seems to bring in elements of the *Akedah* (Isaac's willingness to die) or Iphigenia's death. See Ovid (*Metamorphoses* 13.463): "[Iphigenia speaking:] Take, see my noble blood. We need not wait. Into my throat or bosom plunge your blade. . . . She finished, and the whole assembly shed the tears she would not shed. The priest himself, weeping, against his will, drove his blade home, piercing the breast she offered. On the ground, her knees failing, she sank and held her look of fearless resolution to the last; and she took trouble, even as she fell, to wrap what should be kept in privacy, and guard the honour of her chastity" (trans. A. D. Melville, *Ovid: Metamorphoses* [Oxford: Oxford University Press, 1987], 308-309). See Pausanias (Περιήγησις 1.32.5) for stories of the self-sacrifice of Makaria, daughter of Herakles, and observations about pictorial scenes of this death in Frank Brommer, *Herakles II: Die unkanonischen Taten des Helden* (Darmstadt: Wissenschafliche Buchgesellschaft, 1984), 139-40.

22. Margaret Alexiou and Peter Dronke, "The Lament of Jephtha's Daughter: Themes, Traditions, Originality," *Studi Medievali* 12:2 (1971): 819-863. Grave inscriptions are examined in more detail in Ewald Griessmair, *Das Motive der Mors Immatura in den griechischen metrischen Grabinschriften*, Commentationes Aenipontanae, Bd. 17 (Innsbruck: Universitätsverlag, 1966). Griessmair extensively studies a variety of ways in which ἄωρος θάνατος (untimely death) is depicted, lamented, and inscribed on tombstones. See also Horbury and Noy (*Jewish Inscriptions of Graeco-Roman Egypt*, 106), who comment that "ἄωρος is common in epitaphs from Egyptian sites (Boyaval; it is the most popular adjective of all in the necropolis at Kom Abu Billu), and is by no means confined to the very young." The oldest Egyptian Jews about whom it is used are a woman from Demerash age about 35 and a man age 50. At Kom Abu Billu, it is applied to a woman of 82. It occurs twice in the LXX: Wisdom 4:5 applies it to branches broken off before maturity, at the opening of an epitaph-like passage on the early death of a righteous man, and Isaiah 65:20 contrasts ἄωρος (early and untimely) and πρεσβύτης (after many long years). Philo (*Opific.* 104) and Clement of Alexandria (*Stromata* 6.16.144) quote a poem of Solon, who says that someone who dies in the tenth (and last) of the "ages of man" would not be ἄωρος.

23. Alexiou and Dronke, "The Lament," 826-30. The Simonides epigraph has a word play between νύμφεια (marriage-bed) and φερσέφονης θάλαμος (bridal chamber of Persephone). The Errina epigraph is dated to the fourth century BCE.

24. Alexiou and Dronke, "The Lament," 835.

25. Alexiou and Dronke, "The Lament," 839. The first lines are emphatic, parallel ellipses: γάμος δὲ ὁ θάνατος, θρῆνος δὲ ὁ ὑμέναιος (But the wedding, death; the dirge, the wedding song). In beautifully developed fashion, Bion of Smyrna (*Adonidis Epitaphium* 88-89) offers similar notions: οὐκέτι δ' Ὑμήν

Ὑμήν, οὐκέτ᾽ ἄειδεν ἐὸν μέλος, ἀλλ᾽ ἔλεγ᾽, αἰαῖ αἰαῖ καὶ τὸν "Αδωνιν ἔτι πλέον ἢ Ὑμέναιον (no longer, no longer does she sing her song, Hymen, Hymen, but Woe, Woe, the Adonian song much more than the Hymenian). For a panoply of references to similar metaphors and images ("interruzione del canto nunziale"), see Marco Fantuzzi, *Bionis Smyrnaei Adonidis Epitaphium*, ARCA Classical and Medieval Texts, Papers and Monographs 18 (Liverpool: Francis Cairns, 1985), 126-28.

26. Pack of howling creatures in Apuleius *Metamorphoses* 11.2. In the syncretist "Isis = many different deities" material, Proserpina is mentioned: "terrible with the howls of midnight, whose triple face has power to ward off all the assaults of ghosts and to close the cracks in the earth." For easy reference, see *The Ancient Mysteries: A Sourcebook: Sacred Texts of the Mystery Religions of the Ancient Mediterranean*, ed. Marvin W. Meyer (San Francisco: Harper & Row, 1987), 177-78.

27. On apotropaic banquets, see Lewis Richard Farnell (*Cults of the Greek States* [Oxford: Clarendon Press, 1896], 2:511), who writes, "The banquets of Hekate seem to have been offerings made, not to the lunar goddess, but rather to the mistress of spirits, in order to avert evil phantoms from the house. None of the household would touch the food. It was offered on the thirtieth day, which was sacred to the dead." Farnell refers to Plutarch (*Quaestiones Conviviales* 708 F): ὥστε πασχειν τοὺς δειπνίζοντας, ἃ πάσχουσιν οἱ τῇ Ἑκάτῃ καὶ ἀποτροπαίοις ἐκφέροντες τὰ δεῖπνα, μὴ γευομένους αὐτοὺς μηδὲ τοὺς οἴκοι (so that it happens that the ones who eat, upon carrying out those things which were prepared for the banquet *vis-à-vis* Hekate and the warding-off things, neither themselves taste them nor allow their house to eat). On the thirtieth day, see Robert Garland (*The Greek Way of Death* [Ithaca, N.Y.: Cornell University Press, 1985], 38-40), who writes (p.40): "*Triakostia* are associated with the worship of Hekate as well as with the tendency of the dead. The word was also the name for a ritual performed regularly each month, either on the thirtieth day or on the death-day of the deceased." On the mix of Hekate with spirits, see the humor in Lucian (*Philopseudes* 39), who pokes fun at superstition with the line: τέρατα γοῦν καὶ δαίμονας καὶ Ἑκάτας ὁρᾶν μοι δοκῶ (I believe that I see terrors and daimōns and Hekates!). For specifics about food and sacrifices at such banquets, see Franz Joseph Dölger (*ΙΧΘΥΣ: Der Heilige Fisch in den antiken Religionen und im Christentum*, 2d ed. [Münster in Westfalen: Verlag der Aschendorffschen Verlagsbuchhandlung, 1928], 2:328), who comments that types of fish or fish-emblems were dedicated to Hekate, because Hekate indeed was the corpse consumer, the blood drinker, and the heart/flesh devourer (*sarcophagus*). For an early depiction of Hekate as part dog, eating the corpses of fallen humans, see Emily Vermeule, *Aspects of Death in Early Greek Art and Poetry*, Sather Classical Lectures 46 (Berkeley: University of California Press, 1979), 109 (fig. 26). On the goddess as Evil Crescent Moon, see Farnell, *Cults*, 2:514. On ὀξυθύμια (refuse presented [burned] as an offering to Hekate) for a house haunted, see Farnell, *Cults*, 2:600 n.22.

28. Rohde, *Psyche*, 592. See also Ernst Tabeling (*Mater Larum: Zum Wesen der Larenreligion*, Frankfurter Studien zur Religion und Kultur der Antike 1 [Frankfurt am Main: V. Klostermann, 1932], 30-35) for relationship of Greek Hekate to Roman *Mater Larum* in regard to Μορμών, Γοργώ, Λάμια, and Γέλλω (all monsters and night terrors). These creatures are often depicted in masks, most especially Γοργώ; see A. David Napier, *Masks, Transformations and Paradox* (Berkeley: University of California Press, 1986), 91-108. Jean-Pierre Vernant ("La figure des dieux I: Gorgo," in *Figures, idoles, masques* [Paris: Julliard, 1990], 87) wrote that, in a subversion of features of human appearance, there can be expressed, by means of a strangely "unquieting effect," a monstrosity that oscillates between two axes: the horror of the terrifying, the absurd ridiculousness of the grotesque. On the masks of Gorgon/Medusa and the personal name Gorgo or Gorgias, see R. Merkelbach, "ΓΟΡΓΟΣ, ΓΟΡΓΩ," *Zeitschrift für Papyrologie und Epigraphik* 8 (1971): 70. For Γελλώ see Rohde, *Psyche*, 594, citing Zenobius, *Paroemiographus* 3.3; also 590-93 (appendix 6). Hekate herself is also described as a virgin and μουνογενής (only-born), which gives her a unique position of power and mediation between the divine and humans (specifically, women); see Froma I. Zeitlin ("Signifying Difference: The Myth of Pandora," in *Women in Antiquity: New Assessments*, ed. Richard Hawley and Barbara Levick [London: Routledge, 1995], 63), citing *Hymn to Hekate* 450-52.

29. Farnell (*Cults*, 2:550) wrote, "With the same form and attributes she is present on a Nolan vase in a representation of the setting forth of Triptolemus with the gifts of corn. The other persons present are Demeter, Proserpina, probably Artemis, and Hades, so that Hekate is here associated with the Eleusinian divinities of vegetation and the lower world." In such iconography, the figure with two torches alternates between identification as Artemis and as Hekate. Farnell reported that it is often difficult to tell them apart. See also H. C. Youtie and Campbell Bonner ("Two Curse Tablets from Beisan," *Transactions and Proceedings of the American Philological Association* 73 [1937]: 45), who wrote, "There is an important difference between the earlier curse tablets, such as the older Attic *katadesmoi* published by Wünsch, and those which date from the late Hellenistic and Roman periods. The Attic specimens of early date invoke the infernal deities well known in classical literature, Pluto, Kore, the Moirai, Hermes Chthonios, Hekate, the Erinyes, the Pracidikai. Later these invocations are transformed by an influence which is in the main Oriental with some Egyptian elements. Of the old divine and demonic names, some continue in use, particularly Hermes and Hekate; but to these are added Iao, El, Ereschigal, Nephtho, the provenance of which is known, and other names with a foreign sound, but not certainly explicable by means of any known language."

30. Sophie Lunais, *Recherches sur la Lune* 1: *Les auteurs de la fin des guerres puniques à la fin du règne des Antonins*, Études préliminaires aux religions orientales dans l'empire romain 72 (Leiden, The Netherlands: E. J. Brill, 1979), 142 for further references. Hekate's triple image receives several names also in Latin literature: *tergemina* (three-born-at-birth) (Virgil *Aeneid* 4.511), *triceps* (three-headed)] (Ovid *Metamorphoses* 7.194), *triplex* (three-fold) (Ovid

182 — Chapter 6

Fasti 1.387), and *triformis* (three-formed) (Ovid *Metamorphoses* 7.94,177). Her triple nature persisted to become the image of a neoplatonic triad: Hekate, a fine membrane, separating Father and Intellect; see John D. Turner, "The Figure of Hekate and Dynamic Emanationism in *The Chaldean Oracles*, Sethian Gnosticism, and Neoplatonism," *Second Century* 7:4 (1989-1990): 221-32. On Hekate as Cosmic Soul in Chaldean Oracles, see Hans Lewy, *Chaldean Oracles and Theurgy: Mysticism, Magic and Platonis in the Later Roman Empire*, ed. Michael Tardieu (Paris: Études Augustiniennes, 1978), 47-55.

31. For Hekate as nursing deity see Theodora Hadizisteliou Price, *Kourotrophos: Cults and Representations of the Greek Nursing Deities*, Studies of the Dutch Archaeological and Historical Society 8 (Leiden, The Netherlands: E. J. Brill, 1978), 192. In late Orphic literature she had the epithet Kourotrophos (*Orphic Hymns* 1.8 and 12.8). She appears as such on a frieze in Lagina in Asia Minor. The particular presentation of Hekate by Hesiod is a well-known exception to traditions of her as uncanny and infernal; see Jenny Strauss Clay, "The Hekate of the Theogony," *Greek, Roman, and Byzantine Studies* 25 (1984): 27-38. Hesiod's positive view of the goddess is possibly the fruit of his etymological method for explaining the meaning of divinity names. Hekate is intimately linked with the "good will" of Zeus toward humans, a play on the words Ἑκάτη and ἕκητι Διός (willingness of Zeus). For Προθυρία see Farnell, *Cults*, 2:516. For relation to Genetyliis see Price, *Kourotrophos*, 127. Hesychius reports that dogs (Hekate's animal) were sacrificed to Genetyllis for safe deliveries of babies.

32. Farnell, *Cults*, 2:556. Christopher A. Faraone (*Talismans and Trojan Horses: Guardian Statues in Ancient Greek Myth and Ritual* [New York: Oxford University Press, 1992], 7-8) discusses such Hekataia and apotropaia at the thresholds of homes. He mentions that semi-archaic statuettes of Hekate were common house protectors and wrote that "the prototype of the triformed *hekataion* appears to have been the statue of Hekate Epipyrgidia (On the Tower) designed by Alkamenes, which was apparently set up on or near the old Mycenaen tower (*pyrgos*) that overlooked the main entrance to the Athenian acropolis." Faraone observes that *Hekataia* are reported in private homes (Aristophanes, *Vespae* 804) and before gates of cities and at the crossing of three roads (*triodos*).

33. *Curse Tablets and Binding Spells from the Ancient World*, ed. and trans. John Gager (New York: Oxford University Press, 1992), 239. From this sample (his §132) Gager translates: "For it is the stone of Hermes. It works even on dreams and it drives away apparitions by virtue of its repellent power. And it is a powerful phylactery against the anger of one's master once the image of the figure of Hekate or of the Gorgon is carved into it. Anyone who wears it will never succumb to spells, thunder, or lightning, nor be wounded by evil demons. It makes its wearer invulnerable to suffering and it also releases from all forms of pollution [μιάσματα] and curses [καταδέσμοι] . . . it works to ward off all life-threatening spells and to release (the wearer) from all forms of pollution and curses, like an antidote." See also Erica Reiner (*Astral Magic in Babylonia*, Transactions of the American Philosophical Society 85, pt. 4 [Philadelphia: American Philosophical Society, 1995], 124) on the Sumerian "pregnancy stone" and beads made from

semiprecious stones meant to protect from evils wrought by demons and witches. Compare Sarah Iles Johnston ("Defining the Dreadful: Remarks on the Greek Child-Killing Demon," in *Ancient Magic and Ritual Power*, Religions in the Graeco-Roman World 129 [Leiden, The Netherlands: E. J. Brill, 1995], 383-85) on *lithica* literature, especially the first century B.C.E. Damigeron-Evax *lithica* with its instructions on minerals and rocks meant to protect women and infants as well as protect against night terrors. Other *lithica* prescribe still more stones for protection, including galactite, which protects an infant from the *horrida mulier* (terrible woman).

34. O. Gruppe, *Griechische Mythologie und Religionsgeschichte*, Handbuch der klassischen Altertums-Wissenschaft in systematischer Darstellung 5 (München: C. H. Beck'sche Verlagsbuchhandlung, 1906), 760-61. See also J. H. Waszink, *"Mors immatura,"* in *Opuscula Selecta* (Leiden, The Netherlands: E. J. Brill, 1979), 109 and *Paulys Real-Encyclopädie der classischen Altertumswissenschaft*, ed. Georg Wissowa and W. Kroll, Neue Bearbeitung (Stuttgart, Germany: J. B. Metzler, 1905), s.v. "Nekromantie," by T. Hopfner, 2219. A binding spell is found in Gruppe, (*Griechische Mythologie*, 761 n.8), a spell text from Carthage: ἐξορκίζω σε νεκυδαίμων ἄωρε (I adjure you, Nekydaimōn! Untimely dead!).

35. Lloyd, *Science, Folklore, and Ideology*, 100. On the influence of the moon, see Lunais, *Recherches sur la Lune*, 74. The notion of lunar influence was criticized by the medical writer, Soranus of Ephesus, who decried the variety of previous errors in medical literature. See Lloyd, *Science, Folklore, and Ideology*, 170.

36. Aubert, "Threatened Wombs," 421-49.

37. Another tradition of Herakles is of interest here: the "awakening Herakles" (ἡ τοῦ Ἡρακλέους ἔγερσις) and the ceremony at Tyre held in honor of him. See discussion in Farnell, *Greek Hero Cults*, 168-69; compare cautions of Walter Burkert, *Ancient Mystery Cults* (Cambridge, Mass.: Harvard University Press, 1987), 75-76. Lattimore (*Themes*, 77) offers a Greek example of a mother's mourning wails being able to "waken" (ἐγείρω) her deceased child.

38. See Hopfner (*Griechisch-ägyptischer Offenbarungszauber*, 2§46) on magicians who accomplish their feats quite specifically in accompaniment with their *own* ἔκστασις (ecstacy) or ἐνθουσιασμός (frenzy). In magic, it typically is the worker of the magic who enters into ecstacy, not the audience.

39. A healer or potent savior might have taken what he wanted. Pherecydes of Athens tells the story of how the marvel-working Melampus, on healing the daughters of King Proteus from their ten-year affliction of madness, takes as wife one of them, Iphianassa. See Dowden, *Death and the Maiden*, 77, 229 n.15. A text of this account is available in Felix Jacobi, *Fragmente der Griechischen Historiker* (Leiden, The Netherlands: E. J. Brill, 1957), §3 F114. The story in Herodotus (2.42, 47, 49, 123, 144) is considerably different. The cure of the daughter is contingent on a property settlement by Proetus with Melampus. On saviors and healers, wise men and prognosticators who receive their due reward (including Joseph son of Jacob, Elijah, and Elisha), see Cristiano Grottanelli, "Saviours of the Eastern Mediterranean in Pre-Classical Times," in *La soteriolo-*

gia dei culti orientali nell'Impero Romano: Atti del collòquio internazionale, ed. Ugo Bianchi and M. J. Vermaseren, Études Préliminaires aux Religions Orientales dans l'Empire Roman 92 (Leiden, The Netherlands: E. J. Brill, 1982), 649-70. See P. Michigan inv. 3690 as discussed by R. Merkelbach ("Die Heroen als Geber des Guten und Bösen," *Zeitschrift für Papyrologie und Epigraphik* 1 [1967]: 97-99), in which are the lines: τοὺς θ˜ ἥρως σέβεσθ᾿ ὡς ἡμεῖς ἐσμεν οἱ ταμίαι τῶν κακῶν καὶ τῶν ἀγαθῶν ("and pay honor to the heroes, since we are the distributors of evil things and of good things"). Benefaction by heroes is often somewhat quid pro quo.

40. Selvidge (*Women*, 48) nicely presents the broader state of the terminology: "Soranus, in his first-century monumental *Gynaeciorum*, lists three words used to describe menstruation: καταμήν, ἐπιμήν, and κάθαρσις. Plutarch, a contemporary of Soranus, labels the monthly flow as ἐμμηνοίς ἡμερῶν περιόδοις and ἐμμήνοις καὶ καθαρσίους. . . . Hippocrates refers to it as ῥοῶ γυναικείω . . . and in another work poetically calls menstruation γυναικείων ἄγωγον. . . . Diodorus characterizes it as τὰς κοιλιὰς τὰς ρεούσας φαρμάκῳ. . . . In the context of illness Aristotle uses αἱμορροίς . . . and σφόδρα αἱμτώδης. . . . Normal menstruation is termed αἷμα τοῦ περιτώματος and μηνιώδους περιτώματος."

41. According to Selvidge (*Women*, 48), "πηγή is never used to describe abnormal or normal menstruation. . . . Comparison with the LXX version of Leviticus yields very different results."

42. See Howard Eilberg-Schwartz ("Creation, Classification, and the Genealogy of Knowledge," in *The Savage in Judaism: An Anthropology of Israelite Religion and Ancient Judaism* [Bloomington: Indiana University Press, 1990]), who suggests about the unique material in Leviticus that, since a menstruating woman could not conceive, intercourse with her is considered highly impure (Leviticus 18:19). The list of things proscribed in this part of Leviticus include adultery, sex with a menstruating woman, bestiality, male homosexuality, and sacrificing children to Molech (19:21). Eilberg-Schwartz suggests a logic behind this list, that all these are reproductive threats. There may have been an idea that menstruation was antithetical to fertility. Creative fertility was paramount, and resulted in a diversity of regulations ranging from those forbidding boiling a kid in his mother's milk, to prohibiting taking a mother bird and her fledglings from the nest at the same time, to denying killing an animal and its offspring on the same day.

43. See Thomas F. Mathews (*The Clash of Gods: A Reinterpretation of Early Christian Art* [Princeton, N.J.: Princeton University Press, 1993], 63-64) for later Christian iconography's transformation of the actual healing encounter. Jesus and the woman turn to each other, making eye contact before or as the healing happens. This is seen in (1) a painting from Catacomb of Saints Petrus and Marcellinus (340 C.E.), depicting Christ with torso twisted around toward her and his arm and hand are extended back toward her (he recognizes her touch as it happens); (2) a relief of this incident on a sarcophagus fragment from Catacomb of Saint Callixtus, where Christ turns toward the woman and, as she touches the hem, extends his hand down to her head, touching her.

7

Mark 6:1-13, 30-31:
Without Honor in the Πατρίς;
Traveling among the Οἰκίαι of Others

In this chapter, different aspects of the anomalous frightful come to light. Mark 6:1-13 tells two stories about the relationship of Jesus and his disciples to human institutions: home (οἰκία) and homeland (πατρίς). The first account (6:1-6) relates an experience of Jesus in his own πατρίς. In the second account (6:7-13) Jesus sends out the Twelve into the οἰκίαι of others, a story that actually has a second conclusion in 6:30-31, after its apparent end at 6:13. These two concluding verses come after a lengthy interruption about John the Baptist and Herod Antipas in 6:14-29 (to both of which I return in the next chapter). The two verses of the second conclusion end with a geographic focus, εἰς ἔρημον (in the desert; 6:31), a phrase repeated in the following verses (6:32-33) in a transition to the next story about five thousand men who receive a largesse in the desert. Use of the preposition εἰς (in/into), as in the phrase εἰς ἔρημον, stands out in the composition of Mark 6:1-13, stories about travel, city, and family. Jesus enters εἰς πατρίδα (in the fatherland; 6:1); he sends the Twelve εἰς ὁδόν (in the road; 6:8) and εἰς οἰκίαν (in the house; 6:10); finally, he takes the twelve εἰς ἔρημον (6:31, 32). Travel is depicted here: departure, arrival, departure. Mark 6:1-13 has Jesus and the disciples in motion as they are on the road, working through a circuit of activity (designated in 6:6, περιῆγεν τὰς κώμας κύκλῳ [in a circular path he traveled about he towns]). The net result of these narratives of travel is that activity starts from civilization (πατρίς) and migrates to wilderness (ἔρημος). This general movement fits into a broader narrative scheme of 6:1-44, since in 6:35-44 there is a concluding highpoint in the story about bestowing a *largesse* to hungry people, specifically in the ἔρημος (desert). Jesus and the disciples are shown to be wanderers in these accounts, a characteristic that begins with the reception of Jesus in his πατρίς and continued in the way that the disciples are sent on a mission.[1]

In 6:1-6 Jesus enters into his πατρίς, a location emphasized by its repetition in the travel narration (πατρίδα αὐτοῦ) and in a proverb attributed to Jesus in 6:4 (πατρίδι αὐτοῦ). This location offers connotations of citizenship, loyalty, family origins, and possible features of civic responsibilities, indemnities, immunities, and liabilities. Cities and towns were not just matrices of tradition or even relationships between the living and the dead. They also represent the separation between wild and inhabited places, functioning as engines of culture and, more narrowly, a means to resolve matters of guilt, retaliation, and reconciliation.[2] Belonging or not belonging to a city had serious consequences for an individual, his family, or especially his associates and hangers-on. Mark does not specifically identify the city or town in 6:1, and nothing about the place *per se* is emphasized. We are not led to wonder, "why this particular city," because there is nothing about it that appears of interest to the narrator. Instead, we are led to wonder what will happen to Jesus in the situation where people know him. Unlike Matthew and Luke, Mark uniquely highlights these aspects by a threefold description in 6:4: ἐν τῇ πατρίδι αὐτοῦ καὶ ἐν τοῖς συγγενεῦσιν αὐτοῦ καὶ ἐν τῇ οἰκίᾳ αὐτοῦ (in his home city and in his people-group and in his family).[3] Jesus is familiar to the πάτρις, and with his disciples in tow he returns to his home and presents his σοφία and his δυνάμεις in a situation of competition and conflict. This story presents the idea that the abilities and qualities of Jesus are under discernment, and he is found unconvincing and without honor, his wisdom and works implausible to this audience.[4] This becomes the model that he presents to his disciples, who have their own πατρίδες and οἰκίαι to think about. As wanderers with no guarantee that their benefactions will be honored in situations of competing beliefs, they are sent off to the homes of strangers and, eventually, into the wilderness.

Family and city were preoccupations in every sector of ancient civilization. At the time of the Gospel of Mark, πατρίς was a generic translation for *res publica*.[5] A meaning like this in 6:1 indicates that affairs of public life and family are at hand. With this thematic aspect, there now appears the next way that Jesus is pictured and that the anomalous and uncanny are represented. The meaning of πατρίς is narrower than πόλις, bringing an emphasis on social belonging, or public benefaction, civil belonging, criminal reconciliation, and religious organization. No details are given or implied about what the πατρίς of

Jesus signifies: a family business, a family religious involvement, or a unique benefaction to or from someone. A synagogue is located here, a simple and somewhat underdeveloped narrative setting for the event of Jesus teaching. In this synagogue, on some unspecified Sabbath, Jesus speaks to an unspecified audience (referred to as πολλοί), teaching them about an unspecified topic, and extracting from them a response of awe and bewilderment (ἐξεπλήσσοντο) to his teaching (σοφία) and miracles (δυνάμεις), the content of which, although impressive to his audience, remains undisclosed. Such sketchy contents direct a reader's attention to the few concrete details that are given. They are emphasized by the absence of so much else. These narrative emphases are two: (1) how impressive the unnamed audience considers the σοφία it thinks bestowed upon Jesus and the δυνάμεις it sees worked "through his hands," and (2) the refusal of the same, unnamed audience to believe that anything of importance is indicated by such σοφία and δυνάμεις, as so witnessed. In the story, the implausibility is based very specifically on audience familiarity with the family history of Jesus, with the consequence that Jesus marvels at their disbelief and therefore performs "few miracles." There is no recognition of Jesus as a member of a family or school of sages and workers of anomalies (see appendix G, "Families of Holy Men"). Indeed, he is recognized as merely ordinary, without any credentials, the implication being that his family history disqualifies him from being worthy of belief. These narrative turns articulate the idea that the power and authority that Jesus demonstrates publicly are not derived from any source recognized or acknowledge by those who witness him. This is a theme of uncertainty, a theme that is highlighted when Jesus, on the basis of such questionable authority, sends forth his own disciples, most likely to experience exactly what he is experiencing. The significance of this is that, in Mark, the mission of the disciples is based solely on the words of a man by whom, previously, they were terrorized and confused. In their limited experience of him, they certainly see that he has no external, authoritative source for his enterprise, such as a family of origin, a commission, a calling, a previous mentor, or even a synagogue benefactor.[6] We must wonder why these disciples are following this man.

That the audience of Jesus might recognize his σοφία (wisdom) is not unusual. Wisdom was a part of any number of traditions. Such traditions had long been discussed, and brought under comparative study, and even brought through revivals of such comparative study.[7] Σοφία, though often embedded in stable institutions, was not infrequently also identified with traveling sages who represent an accumulation of divine power or an opportunity to resolve local conflicts of divine powers. Porphyry thought Apollonius of Tyana was a ἀνὴρ σόφος (wise man).[8] Origen (*Contra Celsum* 6.41) thinks that Apollonius was a φιλόσοφος (philosopher) and μάγος (magician), since he was a sage and worker of powerful anomalies. Origen believes that the origin of Apollonius' power was *disreputable*, though not unbelievable. Much in the way that the fellow members of his πάτρις (fatherland) receive Jesus, so also Origen had ἀπιστία (faith) in regard to Apollonius. The traditions Origen knew about Apollonius gave him all the information he needed to remain unconvinced. The information likely included the esoteric and mystical inquiries Apollonius was said to have accomplished. Philostratus (*Apollonius* 3.41) reports that Apollonius and his associate, Damis, interviewed exotic Indian σόφοι (wisemen) about ἀστρικὴ μαντεία (astrological divination), an investigation not only into σοφία but also into magical controls over uncertainties. Four books about divination were the result, at least according to Moiragenes (*Apollonius* 3.41), an author whose ἀπομνημονεύματα (remembrances) about Apollonius was important information for Origen. Compositions like ἀπομνημονεύματα (remembrances) have reports of both a sage's wisdom (σοφία) and his powerful acts (δυνάμεις).[9] These two traits are often linked together, since σοφία in these cases is very much implicated in the performance of miracles or in the settling of anomalously frightening events. The latter was done by explaining unfortunate stellar conjunctions, predicting future bad outcomes, or resolving omens of ill fortune. The memoirs of Moiragenes gave Origen the material he needed to support his conviction about the truly corrupt nature and debased origin of the φιλοσοφία and μαγεία of Apollonius. He did not deny that φιλοσοφία and μαγεία were actually exhibited, at least as far as his reception of the reports about them are concerned. He simply questioned their true meaning. Likewise, the people in the πατρίς of Jesus do not deny the reality of his σοφία and δυνάμεις; they simply do not hold them in high regard and do not believe them sufficient reason to act with faith in Jesus. Their response is an example of how the performance and plausibility of Jesus the traveling sage was dismissed. This kind of dismissal points to a more general and well-known cultural phenomenon: the problem of conflict between one person's displayed wisdom and another's rejection of that wisdom.

There are accounts of the words and deeds of powerful individuals (ἀπομνημονεύματα) in magical traditions. In *PGM* 13.965, Euenos is identified as the author of such an account, which apparently contained information about magical acts and, in particular, information about the unique, mysterious, wise, and powerful Egyptian and Syrian terms and pronunciations for the ἅγιον ὄνομα (holy name). Eastern areas of Egypt and Syria here identified, along with the theme of ancient or archaic letters, are to be noted, because both are part of a tradition wherein wisdom and the performance of powerful acts were thought typical of ancient and distant cultures, especially eastern cultures. Apollonius is an example of a traveling sage, displaying wisdom and power, while traveling through many exotic areas.[10] His wisdom and power are continually juxtaposed with those of the East, and usually juxtaposed to the benefit of his reputation. He is not dismissed in the way Jesus is dismissed in his πάτρις (fatherland). In spite of this, Apollonius and Jesus (Mark 6:2) have similar effects on their audiences. Not only the Indian sages are amazed at Apollonius,[11] but so too are the Egyptian sages during a colloquy. These latter exhibit ἔκπληξις (astonishment) when they hear the marvelous discourses of Apollonius (Philostratus *Apollonius* 6.12). The derivative of this substantive is from the same root as the Markan ἐξεπλήσσοντο (Mark 6:2), or the way in which the πάτρις of Jesus perceives him.

Pliny summarized how Pythagoras and Democritus were exposed to the magical wisdom of distant lands.[12] In their cases, in contrast to Jesus, when they returned to their cities they were not dismissed. Their accumulated wisdom and power was instead quite persuasive. Their reputation increased later, especially because of popular beliefs about the influence of exotic foreign wisdom upon them. In his *Philopseudes,* Lucian tells many stories of foreign sages or miracle workers: an ἀνὴρ βαβυλώνιος τῶν χαλδαίων (a Babylonian man from the Chaldeans); a Ὑπερβόρεον (a Hyperborean); an exorcist identified as τὸν Σύρον τὸν ἐκ Παλαιστίνης (the Syrian from Palestine). The provenance of these characters is especially to be noted, because the extremities and boundaries of the world, especially the East, were commonly considered areas from which unusual abilities might emerge. These foreign wisdoms were compared and evaluated for to their quality, as being better or worse than Greek wisdom. Judgment about the value of Egyptian versus Indian wisdom was a reasonable rhetorical and sophistical pastime. With such comparisons, convictions would typically settle on the superiority of Greek παιδεία (culture).[13] In a story about an Egyptian who had been exiled from Memphis because of murder, Philostratus (*Apollonius* 6.5) emphasizes the superiority of Empedoclean and Pythagorean over Egyptian purity rites. This demonstrates how Greek wisdom and culture (παιδεία), comparatively viewed, could seem more potent in the arena of the anomalous frightful (in this case, purification from the guilt of homicide). Not knowing whether beneficence or maleficence might result illustrates uncertainty in such a story. The quest becomes what purification process would work, both to decrease anomaly and to truly expurgate μίασμα (defilement). Who could accomplish this? What σοφία (wisdom) might make this benefaction possible? When, and at what cost? What if one chooses an inferior wisdom? As for Mark 6:1-6, just how is one to know whether the wisdom and miracles of Jesus should be compelling enough to cancel out ἀπιστία (unbelief)? How is one (that is, a potential disciple) to know if the wisdom and powerful anomalies of Jesus create a firm enough base from which to undertake one's own effort at "being sent" and having ἐξουσίαν τῶν πνευμάτων τῶν ἀκαρθάρτων (authority over the unclean spirits; 6:7)?

According to Philostratus, Vardenes gave to Apollonius of Tyana what Jesus never had: a letter of introduction for various local authorities. Apollonius encounters these authorities and uses the letter. In it, Vardenes said that Apollonius is an ἄνδρα ῾Ελληνά τε καὶ θεῖον (a man divine and Greek),[14] or "wise" and a "worker of miracles." In matters of uncertainty about divine power and of whom divine power might favor, this is no small compliment. In Philostratus, these basic themes of the anomalous frightful become literary themes expressive of contemporary culture wars (Greek versus Barbarian). To have the Egyptian Vardenes praise Apollonius for being a man of power is an apt rhetorical flourish for the author, Philostratus, who himself was an aspiring Hellenist. Stories about letters of introduction show how someone who traveled, and gained a reputation for wisdom and power, could be so convincing that others took up and promoted his cause. These stories show the trustworthiness of the sage as well as his believability, especially if suspicions arise about him. In this case, Apollonius has his own detractors who precede him in his travels, warning foreigners and various σόφοι to stay away from him (Thrasyllabus in *Apollonius* 6.7, 9 and Stratocles of Pharos in *Apollonius* 6.10). Their critical campaign created suspicion about Apollonius, although Apollonius reportedly was able to overcome it in nearly every situation.

Mark 6:1-13 mentions no such external support for Jesus, a notable absence. No benefactors, authorities, or letters of introduction from government officials, religious authorities, schoolmasters, or synagogue presidents vouch for Jesus or promote his cause.[15] Jesus is returning home here, but he is now a representative of something new, and this something new is not recognized by his people as a something in which they might believe. For them, Jesus is not an exemplar of anything convincing. As a result, an air of the pathetic attends the activity of Jesus in his πάτρις and then on the road with his disciples. Jesus seems vulnerable, because his wisdom and miracles cannot gain the trust of others. These story elements compel a reader to ask, "Why is it that nobody notices what is supposed to be so important about Jesus?" At this crucial point in the career of Jesus, when he models for his disciples the effect he has on others, and then asks them to attempt to effect the same, the reader may rightly begin to wonder if now would not have been a good time for cleverness or some trickster characteristic of Jesus to become more apparent.[16] Instead, everything remains all the more mysterious as these stories show Jesus withdrawing, strangely, from civilization to the wilderness.

Travel narratives often bring out noticeable differences between places, or between a traveler's orientation and that of the places visited. In its grandest and most polarized forms, this theme includes legendary places at geographical extremes of the world that, when summarized, present competing traditions. A more subtle use of the theme is found in reports about travelers from different places, well-known for their traits and traditions, who offer to others some type of competing wisdom that seems in content both dubious and foreign. In Mark, though Jesus is visiting the town of his family, he is not doing so as a favored son or notable person. He is on a continuing series of travels that happens to include this stop, and he moves on past this place. In the town of his family his reputation for wisdom and mighty deeds is not the reputation of a man who is well known, or even the reputation of a man recognized as a teacher. Instead, he seems a stranger, one who is startling enough that public opinion about him is uncertain and must be generated anew. His actions compel the general public in the synagogue to decide that he is not, after all, wise and powerful in a familiar or persuasive way, but instead is a character to be disbelieved, with actions and words to be treated as foreign. Here we have a confrontation of opinion, not between neighbors but between town residents and a newly arrived traveler, whose reception is like that of a stranger, although his personal roots lie buried in this πάτρις.

In Mark 6:1-6 there is nothing said about exactly how Jesus impressed his audience. This narrative, instead of showing how a conflict in wisdom or a conflict of opinion might have matured and come about, shows instead a complete failure of Jesus to convince and to argue effectively or cleverly in order to persuade the public. The narrative gives an explanation, suggesting this failure was due to public familiarity with

Jesus. Given the depth of this failure, we need to know what was at stake in competition between wisdoms or traditions. As a content for this failure, we need to know why opponents argued over which wisdom or divine power might be most effective. Conclusions to arguments like these indicate resolutions about how to manage divine power, benefaction, fear, uncertainty, and, in general, all elements of the anomalous frightful.

Competition between wisdoms and opinions could be fierce. Stories about sages traveling through cultures, and their travels through circles of different locales, include accounts of their confrontation with ideas different than theirs and, sometimes, their integration of foreign elements into their own schemes. Two examples from Philostratus are useful for examining this phenomenon. Although these texts should be placed in their proper setting, that of the second sophistic and that of Philostratus himself, these examples show what competing wisdoms and cultures could involve and what was at stake in the proper handing of the anomalous frightful. These two examples have quite specific content. They report particulars that one wishes were present in Mark when Jesus appears as a traveler in his πάτρις and when his reception shows that he is not of their opinion and, therefore, remains strange to them. Even the familiarity of Jesus to his πάτρις solidifies his rejection, making him unconvincing and compelling him to move on.

Dionysus was a subject of disagreement between Greeks, between Greeks and Indians, and among Indians themselves.[17] A report in Philostratus (*Apollonius* 3.14), purportedly penned by Apollonius himself, tells how surprised he is to have found erected in India statues of the Dionysus of Limnae and the Dionysus of Amyclae, along with images of Athena Polias and the Apollo of Delos. Greek ritual was enacted at these cult shrines, including use of fire and celebration of the ὀμφαλός (navel of the earth). Greeks claimed Dionysus to be the son of Semele and Zeus, based (according to Philostratus) on evidence found at Delphi, and it was said that some Delphinians personalized their relationship to Dionysus and Demeter when they wore divine images (ἄγαλμα) as fashion accouterments, thinking the gods so to nourish (τρέφω) them (Philostratus, *Apollonius* 5.20). But Indians who dwelt in the Caucasus, by the river Cophen, claimed that Dionysus was actually an Assyrian visitor. And elsewhere, Indians who dwelt between the Indus and the Hydraotes claimed that Dionysus was in fact the son of the Indus River. They said that the Theban Dionysus[18] had roamed wildly (φοιτάζω) after this Indian Dionysus, a tale that depicts the Greek Dionysus as intoxicated with desire for the Indian. Since the Indians claimed that the very real Mount Nysa was the home of their Dionysus, they allowed for a smaller mountain next to it to be the home of the Theban Dionysus. To this traditional source, the Indian Dionysus was greater, more plausible, and more believable (πιστός) than the Greek.[19]

Similarly, Herakles was debated.[20] There was a somewhat well-known vase-scene of Herakles, son of Amphityron, stealing the tripod from the Delphic priestess. An inscription elaborates on the scene, reporting how the priestess simply responds to this behavior by saying, "This is the Herakles of Tiryns and not that of Canopus." Tiryns is about twenty miles due west of Epidaurus, and Canopus is near Alexandria, making this an example of a confrontation between Greek Herakles *and* Egyptian Herakles.[21] In another source, during a symposium with an Indian king, Apollonius is told by the king about the difference between the Theban and the Egyptian Herakles. The discussion concludes in the king's high praise for his own Indian σόφοι, high praise for the Egyptian Herakles, and a jibe at the Greeks.[22] Identification of what is local or foreign, believable or incredible, is a major theme in these narratives. Within this kind of context, the σοφία or δυνάμεις of a traveler may be convincing or annoying. Provision of such unusual manifestations may or may not have caused reconsideration of local identity, values, or claims. This was exactly the risk faced by every traveling sage or worker of anomalies.

More so than with Dionysus, who along with Herakles was an inspiration for kings and military leaders, Herakles became a model for imitation for those σοφοί who traveled, especially in regard to wisdom, decision-making, and virtuous lifestyle. Lucian quipped that Peregrinus had wrongly welcomed (ἀσπάζομαι) an immolation based none other than on the example of Herakles.[23] Philostratus reports how an Egyptian Gymnos named Thespesion explained to Apollonius an Egpytian interpretation of the Ἡρακλέα composed by Prodicus, which has a story about Herakles' decision between κακία (evil) or ἀρετή (virtue), each choice symbolized by women.[24] The interpretation of this legend according to Thespesion is that it is up to the seeker to make a choice between Egyptian wisdom (virtue) or Indian wisdom (vice).[25] In the culture wars between or within Egyptian, Indian, or Greek σόφοι, use of the tradition of Herakles demonstrates how a nonlocal σοφία might be amended or summarily dismissed.

These examples show what was at stake in the experience of Jesus in a συναγωγή in his πάτρις. Jesus presents his words and deeds in a context that accepts neither with πιστία. The conflict of Jesus with these people is not about whether he had wisdom or performed miracles. Instead, it is about what these things mean, and whether Jesus is salient, persuasive, or seminal for the beliefs of those in the synagogue. Although not a grand culture conflict such as that between Greek and Egyptian wisdom, the story presents a similar conflict, as it represents a tussle precisely between the wisdom and powerful deeds of Jesus, who traveled, and the expectations and understanding of wisdom and powerful deeds held by people in his πάτρις. In Mark, no doubt is voiced in public opinion that Jesus actually displays σοφία and power. This impression is, however, immediately juxtaposed with a discommendation of Jesus. He is dismissed. His wisdom and powerful deeds purchase no conviction. No changes in local beliefs are made because of his visit. Indeed, no argument is reported about any belief, and it is as if Jesus is completely stonewalled here. In a curious reversal of the theme of acclamation and wonder because of his miracles, Jesus himself ἐθαύμαζεν διὰ τὴν ἀπιστίαν (marvels at their disbelief, 6:6). Incredulity and a lack of πιστία flourish because, whatever the strength of the wisdom or power presented by Jesus, it does not overcome locals' commitments to their own beliefs.[26]

The relatives of Jesus are familiar with him, and familiarity blocks (σκανδαλίζομαι) them from πιστία. This kind of disbelief, based on a recognition of somebody's family history, is exhibited in Demosthenes. In his attempt to demolish Aeschines' credibility, he points to Aeschines' family and childhood background: "In your childhood you were reared in abject poverty. You helped your father in the drudgery of a grammar-school, grinding the ink, sponging the benches, and sweeping the school-room, holding the position of a menial, not a free-born boy." The same kind of criticism was leveled against Epicurus, a σόφος who had a reputation for traveling and for separating himself from the civilized areas of humankind. In his stories about Epicurus, Diogenes Laertius reported that Posidonius, Sotion, and Dionysius of Halicarnassus told false tales about Epicurus. They said that in his childhood he "used to go around with his mother to cottages and read charms (σὺν τῇ μητρὶ περιιόντα αὐτον ἐς τὰ οἰκίδια καθαρμοὺς ἀναγινώσκειν), and assist his father in his school for a pitiful fee; further, that one of his brothers was a pander and lived with Leontion the courtesan; . . . that he was not a genuine Athenian citizen." This particular attack attempted to undermine Epicureans, who had a reputation for speaking against citizen involvement in the πόλις and for not exercising any concern about *res publica* (πάτρις). Epicurus reportedly instructed his disciples to live anonymously (λάθε βιώσας), which would have meant to avoid all matters of state (*Sententia Vaticanae* 58).[27] Diogenes Laertius (10.119) reports that Epicurus, in his work, Περὶ βίων, taught that a philosopher οὐδὲ πολιτεύσεται (is not to get involved with politics). Since this is a pronounced aspect of their philosophy, Epicureans were often not well received by others. To their opponents they were emblematic of a life of misanthropy, displacement, confusion, or exile. To be branded "Epicurean" meant to be living under a curse, hounded from one πάτρις to another, from one οἶκος to another, apparently godless (rootless and hearthless). This is a description of exactly what was *not* expected either from philosophical wandering or through satisfactory purifications (καθαρμοί) that could benefit others, and is a remarkably apt description of what would be the apparent experience of Jesus.[28]

Criticism against Epicurus, that when a boy he went with his mother ἐς τὰ οἰκίδια (house to house), implies that his adult behavior was really a repetition of his dishonorable boyhood behavior, including house-to-house pandering and colportage. This criticism was formed to target specific behavior of Epicureans, whom others felt intruded into their οἰκίαι. There is here also evident a complete lack of confidence in this σόφος on the basis of its spokesman's previous family history. This rejection is similar to how the σοφία and δυνάμεις of Jesus are acknowledged by his audience, yet the πιστία that they mean anything important never develops, because of their knowledge and opinion of his family.

House-to-house traveling gave one the appearance of being a busybody (περίεργος) and of meddling (πολυπραγμονέω), two things against which Epictetus (*Discourses* 3.22.97) warns. A letter attributed to Diogenes "the Cynic" criticizes a mission done house-to-house instead of to a whole city.[29] Such a mission seems too involved with other people's private affairs. Epictetus (*Discourses* 3.22.100) asks the students, Τί δὲ σοι καὶ τοῖς ἀλλοτρίοις (what does your business have to do with theirs?). The philosopher suggests that a traveling sage is not a "queen bee" but a "drone" (κηφήν), having no license to command anybody to do anything. As a result, he is to be patient and enduring (ἀνεκτικός). Like any autonomous, traveling, independent σόφος, the Cynic needed to know how to live serenely while having nothing, being naked, having no home, living in poverty, and living without a city.[30] Accomplishing this was to be based on the Cynic's belief that he is guided by θεός (Epictetus, *Discourses* 3.22.53). The Cynic is to call only upon Zeus who has sent him, especially when faced with human opposition (Epictetus, *Discourses* 3.22.23, 57). Most importantly, he is to be able to give a speech or diatribe whenever chance permits, just as Socrates had been able to do (Epictetus, *Discourses* 3.22.25).

Such a traveler faced problems similar to those faced by exiles, who were considered hapless and hopeless. Teles refutes arguments that exile induces one to have fewer τέχναι (skills) or less ἀρετή (virtue). He wondered what good it would be to live and eat where one was born, if that place were rotten and falling to pieces.[31] Another theory held that exile is indeed not an evil, because exiles enjoyed a release from what is human but not from what is natural (φύσει). This former includes quite specifically πάτρις (fatherland) and οἶκος (home).[32] Musonius Rufus expressed similar feelings, claiming that exile is only a shift of one πάτρις for another, one οἶκος (house) for another (*That Exile Is Not an Evil* 6,26). Dio Chrysostom reports that Stoics thought a πόλις (city) to be a group of people living under νόμος (law). Whether they belonged to one πόλις (city) or to another, or to none, is secondary. In this argument, νόμος (law) is a universal and abstract phenomenon, to be distinguished from the narrow legal matters of any specific πόλις (city). Accordingly, an individual's πόλις (city) is conceptualized as a type of niche that fits into a broader κόσμος (cosmos). Chrysippus thought the κόσμος (cosmos) a σύστημα (interrelated network) consisting of heaven and earth as well as of θεοί (gods) and ἀνθρώποι (humankind). The κόσμος is like a container, in which all humans live regardless of origin or people group. Within it, individuals have their real and most permanent home, if only they become wise enough to realize it. From a very different school (Epicurean), Diogenes Oenoanda's wall inscription has yet a similar view, as the opinion is expressed there that the whole γῆ (earth) is a single πάτρις for every person, just as the whole κόσμος is a single οἶκος.[33]

Autonomous and traveling σόφοι who worked powerful anomalies (medical miracles), from Elijah or Democedes to Hellenistic philosophers or divine men, needed to learn how to manage and validate a life that did not find its warrant from membership in a single area, city, dynasty, family, temple, court, or bureaucracy.[34] Often validation for the individual enterprise is theological, the object of belief ranging from the YHWH of Elijah to the θεός of Epictetus. In Mark, there is no similar theological validation or object of belief reported for the Twelve, when Jesus sends them out. He calls them, he sends them out two by two, and ἐδίδου αὐτοῖς ἐξουσίαν τῶν πνευμάτων τῶν ἀκαρθάρτων (gave them authority over the unclean spirits). No particular teaching or wisdom is taught them before this task. Jesus instructs them to wear the costume of autonomous wanderers who travel the ὅδοι (roads, ways). This costume is an indication of what to expect: a condition similar to exile. On coming to another's οἶκος, they are to remain there. For how long? It is not said. If they are not received at any particular τόπος (place), they are to perform an apotropaic act toward it, shaking off the dust from their feet, and this will be a μαρτύριον (witness) to that place. Is this act meant to be a sign of contempt or a threat of retaliation? We are not told. To whom, specifically, is it a witness? Who would avenge the rejection of the wanderers? It is never said.³⁵ The narrative ends in 6:12-13 with a summary of some activities of the Twelve, about which Mark has reported no previous instruction by Jesus: καὶ ἐξελθόντες ἐκήρυξαν ἵνα μετανῶσ-ιν καὶ δαιμόνια πολλὰ ἐξέβαλλον, καὶ ἤλειφον ἐλαίῳ πολλοὺς ἀρρώσ-τους καὶ ἐθεράπευον (and going out, they preached that they should repent, and they cast out demons, and anointed with oil many who were sick, and cured them). What does ἐξουσία τῶν πνευμάτων τῶν ἀκαρθάρ-των mean? Mark does not report that Jesus teaches his disciples anything about this authority before bestowing it on them. We are not even told in the name of what god or power this is to be done. And from what are individuals to turn when they "repent"? Nothing is reported previously about what, if anything, Jesus teaches his disciples about this. The disciples use oil in their healing practices, but Mark does not report that their master has so instructed them. The use of oil here seems the use of a tangible and somewhat reliable healing material, or a step away from the apparently simplistic healing practices of Jesus.³⁶ At the regathering of "the apostles" (6:30-31), when they report to Jesus what they have done and taught, Jesus offers no specific response at all to their account of themselves. Instead, he invites them to travel *further* away from inhabited areas, from πάτρις and οἰκίαι.

Having no place in a πάτρις, and travelling through another's οἶκος, was not unknown. Exiles and wanderers validated their situations, sometimes with long, theoretical explanations. Yet, at least, they had explanations. In Mark, the commission to wander follows immediately on the account of the dismissal of Jesus in his own πάτρις. To the disbelief of those in the synagogue, Jesus makes no counter-argument. He shows to his disciples no model of rebuttal and offers no method to secure a better hearing. Rather than apparent civil or religious success, the chief validation for the disciples turns out to be the ἐξουσία that Jesus gives them. Yet what kind of authority is it that they receive from a man of whom they have already felt terrified and who demonstrates no cleverness in overcoming disbelief in his wisdom and miracles? This major episode about discipleship and commission to mission contains, at its heart, a large uncertainty. The disciples are, strangely, invited to follow Jesus, under these apparently unsettling conditions, on a course away from the civilized world, without much explanation. Why should they "go"? What are they expected to accomplish? By all reasonable expectations of the time, this course would provide little in the way of recognizable εὐεργε-σία (benefaction). There is no methodical plan in the disciples' mission but, instead, a burst of unpredictable activity, the only certainty being that Jesus asks them to undertake it. There is little evidence here of a properly commissioned mission, or even of a coherent enterprise of exile-like wandering to the homes of other people. There are only the "many" who are "coming and going."

Notes

1. Graham Anderson (*Sage, Saint, and Sophist: Holy Men and Their Associates in the Early Roman Empire* [London: Routledge, 1994], 223) argues that Jesus falls "within the parameters of the wandering holy man in general."

2. See Alfred Haldar (*The Notion of the Desert in Sumero-Akkadian and West-Semitic Religions*, Uppsala Universitates Årsskrift 1950:3 [Uppsala: A.B. Lundequistska, 1950]) for Scriptural traditions and related parallels on the dichotomy "inhabited places" and "wilderness." For much later and different traditions about the same polarity, see Albert Henrichs ("The Sophists and Hellenistic Religion: Prodicus as the Spiritual Father of the Isis Aretalogies," *Harvard Studies in Classical Philology* 79 [1975]: 139-58 on εὐεργεσία and a Greek distinction between θηριώδης (wild) and ἥμερος (civilized). Individuals who wandered between cities, or separated themselves from cities, raised questions about their place within the civilized universe. A later promoter of Epicurus said that the philosopher was ἡμερότητος καὶ αὐταρκείας (civilized yet self-sustaining; *Sententiae Vaticanae* 36); see Cyril Bailey, *Epicurus: The Extant Remains* (Oxford: Clarendon Press, 1926), 110. This one school emphasized ἀταραξία, ἀφοβία, and ἀπονία (calm, absence of fear, and imperturbability) raising questions about how this was to be done without dependence on or involvement in the civilized πόλις; see J.-A. Festugière, *Épicure et ses dieux*, Mythes et Religions 19 (Paris: Presses Universitaires de France, 1968), 47. For a review of the essential ideas of urban areas as means to resolve guilt and reparation, see Joseph Rykwert, *The Idea of a Town: The Anthropology of Urban Form in Rome, Italy and the Ancient World* (Cambridge, Mass.: MIT Press, 1988). Exile was a chief ingredient in the guilt and reconciliation processes of many cities, sending convicted criminals to wander among and between other people's cities. Stoics and Cynics often discussed this condition, and also the condition of

being in the κόσμος while dwelling (or not) among πόλεις; see Hans Friedrich August von Arnim, *Stoicorum Veterum Fragmenta* [Leipzig, Germany: B. G. Teubner, 1903-1924], 2§526-529. See also Musonius Rufus, *That Exile is Not an Evil*, in *Musonius Rufus: The Roman Socrates*, ed. Cora E. Lutz, Yale Classical Studies 10 (New Haven, Conn.: Yale University Press, 1947), 68-77. Philostratus (*Apollonius* 6.5) discusses the case of a man who was exiled from Memphis because of his unintentional slaying of a citizen of Memphis. For these local Egyptians, the punishment for φόνος is being exiled to stay with the *Gymnoi* until guilt is cleansed and the offender is καθαρμός. Here the exile is described as "wandering" (ἀλύω).

3. This threefold description emphasizes what appears in other sources, which do not have this more expansive terminology for family or city belonging, to be a simpler, proverbial saying. See Luke 4:24 (οὐδείς δεκτός προφήτης ἔστιν ἐν τῇ πατρίδι αὐτοῦ); *Gospel of Thomas* 31 ("Jesus said, No prophet is acceptable in his village; no physician works cures on those who know him"); *P.Oxy* 1.6 (Λέγει ' Ι[σοῦ]ς οὐκ ἔστιν δεκτός προφήτης ἐν τῇ π[ατ]ρίδι αὐτ[ο]ῦ οὐδὲ ἰατρὸς ποιεῖ θεραπείας εἰς τοὺς γεινώσκοντας).

4. For an example of exactly opposite feelings held by a community about an individual, see William Horbury and David Noy, *Jewish Inscriptions of Graeco-Roman Egypt, With an Index of the Jewish Inscriptions of Egypt and Cyrenaica* (Cambridge: Cambridge University Press, 1992), §39. This inscription from Leontopolis (Tell el-Yehoudieh), from the mid-second century B.C.E. to the early second century C.E., reads: "When he had already accomplished a span of fifty-three years, the all-subduer himself carried him off to Hades. O sandy earth, how notable a body you cover: that which had the soul of Abramaos, most fortunate of men. For he was not without honour in the city, but was crowned in his wisdom with a communal magistracy over all the people."

5. Hugh J. Mason, *Greek Terms for Roman Institutions: A Lexicon and Analysis*, American Studies in Papyrology 13 (Toronto: Hakkert, 1974), s.v. πατρίς. See Glen W. Bowersock (*Augustus and the Greek World* [Oxford: Oxford University Press, 1965; repr., Westport, Conn.: Greenwood Press, 1981], 85-100) for an overview of new developments in cities and in civic life under Augustus, affecting all areas under Roman control.

6. This situation resembles that of the original calling of the disciples to follow, as described by Whitney Taylor Shiner, *Follow Me! Disciples in Markan Rhetoric*, Society of Biblical Literature Dissertation Series 145 (Atlanta: Scholars Press, 1995), 183. About those stories Shiner writes that "given the typical functions of call stories to expound the values of a life of wisdom or to demonstrate the power or superiority of a teacher, the Markan call stories are peculiar in the lack of motivation provided for the fisherman's decision to follow Jesus." This remains an issue through much of Mark. Why, exactly, are the disciples following Jesus?

7. Oswyn Murray, "Herodotus and Hellenistic Culture," *Classical Quarterly* 22 (1972): 200-213.

8. In general on sages and divine power, see Richard Reitzenstein (*Hellenistische Wundererzählungen*, 2d ed. [Stuttgart: B. G. Teubner, n.d.; repr., Darmstadt: Wissenschaftliche Buchgesellschaft, 1963], 42), in reference to Apollonius of Tyana. For Mark, the primary fact is the δύναμις of Jesus and the subsequent effect that this has on his reputation and character as a man to whom having proximity means having proximity to divine power. Gail Corrington (*The "Divine Man": His Origin and Function in Hellenistic Popular Religion*, American University Studies, series 7: Theology and Religion 17 [New York: Peter Lang, 1986], 89) writes, on the figure of the divine man and his traits of power, that "what this set of characteristics shows is that, if human beings were accorded divinity, be they king or philosopher, or legendary heroes, they were credited with the two traits so prized by the Hellenistic world, power (δύναμις) and, related to that power, a kind of 'secret wisdom' (σοφία) leading to salvation (σωτηρία)." Porphyry writes about Apollonius in *De abstinentia* 2.34, on the basis of a lost writing of Apollonius, his Περὶ θυσιῶν.

9. Origen, *Contra Celsum* 6.41; see Reitzenstein, *Wundererzählungen*, 40. On such ἀπομνημονεύματα as sources for Jesus, see Justin Martyr, *Dialogue with Trypho* 106.3 and *Apology* 66.3 and 67.3. On such a source for Diogenes Laertius on ancient philosophers, see *Favorin von Arelate: Der erste Teil der Fragmente: Memorabilien und Omnigenum Historia*, ed. Eckhart Mensching, Texte und Kommentare 3 (Berlin: Walter de Gruyter, 1963). On how ἀπομνημονεύματα report the relation of δύναμις to the essential character of the power-wielder, or his ἀρετή, see Vincenzo Longo, *Aretalogie nel mondo greco, 1: Epigrafi e papiri*, Università di Genova Facoltà di Lettere: Pubblicazioni dell'Istituto di Filogia Classica, 29 (Genova: Istituto di Filologia Classica e Medioevale, 1969), 25, 94 and S. Eitrem, *Some Notes on the Demonology in the New Testament*, Symbolae Osloenses 12 (Oslo: A. W. Brügger, 1950), 19. Stobaeus *(Eclogues* 2.62.15 in Arnim, *Stoicorum Veterum Fragmenta*, 3§278) comments on the relation of δύναμις to ἀρετή and Plutarch (*De virt. mor.* 3 in Arnim, *Stoicorum Veterum Fragmenta*, 1§202) describes τὴν ἀρετήν τοῦ ἡγεμονικοῦ τῆς ψυχῆς διάθεσίν τινα καὶ δύναμιν γεγενημένην ὑπὸ λόγου (the virtue of the controlling faculty of the soul is a kind of disposition and power constituted by means of reason).

10. For one eastern area, see Philostratus (*Apollonius* 6.1), who writes, Αἰθιοπία δὲ τῆς μὲν ὑπὸ ἡλίῳ πάσας ἐπέχει τὸ ἑσπέριον κέρας, ὥσπερ ᾽Ινδοὶ τὸ πρὸς ἔω (Ethiopia covers the western wing of the entire earth under the sun, just as India does the eastern wing). The model and exemplar of such traveling sages is also evident in Philostratus (*Vitae Sophistarum* 487-88), who mentions some events of the life of Dio of Prusa, specifically calling him a σόφος. Philostratus compares Dio to Apollonius of Tyana and Euphrates of Tyre. All are wanderers and live as if in exile. All argue and harangue audiences when necessary.

11. Philostratus (*Apollonius* 3.42) relates that Indian sage Iarchas is surprised to find out that Apollonius' divinatory expertise is so powerful that the traditional use of oracles to settle feelings of presentiment could now be abandoned.

12. Pliny, *Natural History* 25.13. Diogenes Laertius (9.35) indicates that he saw (or supposed that he saw) books by Democritus containing reports of his trips to Egypt, to Persia and the "Chaldeans," to the "Red Sea," to India, and to Ethiopia.

13. For one such colloquy, see Philostratus (*Apollonius* 6.12), who retails an account by Damis concerning Apollonius, Thespesion (Egyptian), and Nilus. On the proposed superiority of Greek culture, see Jaap-Jan Flinterman (*Power, Paideia & Pythagoreanism: Greek Identity, Conceptions of the Relationship between Philosophers and Monarchs and Political Ideas in Philostratus' Life of Apollonius* [Amsterdam: J. C. Giben, 1995], 90-106) on Apollonius in relationship to barbarians, truly Greek heroes, and Roman institutions (emperors). Greek superiority is never far below the surface of the stories, especially in the long accounts of Indian marvels, compared to which the victories of Alexander are greater.

14. Philostratus *Apollonius* 2.17. Some thought traveling sages had special powers to speak. Philostratus (*Vita Sophistarum* 616) reports that Polemo was acclaimed a θεῖος ἀνήρ (divine man) because of such gifts. Eunapius (*Vitae Philosopharum* 454) suggests that the book Philostratus wrote about Apollonius should really be titled, Ἐπιδημίαν ἐς Ἀνθρώπους Θεοῦ (A Visit of God to Humanity).

15. On questions of such authority and benefaction, especially for teaching, see David Daube, "By What Authority Doest Thou These Things?" in *The New Testament and Rabbinic Judaism*, School of Oriental and African Studies, University of London: Jordan Lectures in Comparative Religion, 1952 (London: University of London/Athlone Press, 1956), 217-23.

16. That is, cleverness such as that of Antilochus in Homer (*Iliad* 23.319-25), who knows the "right tricks" and has the "skill" (δόλος) to grasp success. See Marcel Detienne and Jean-Pierre Vernant (*Les ruses de l'intelligence: La mètis des grecs* [Paris: Flammarion, 1974], 52) for traditions of terms pertaining to such skills and cleverness: αἱμύλος (wheedling, wily), ἀπάτη (trick, fraud, deceit), δόλος (cleverness), κέρδος (gained advantage), μηχανή (contrivance), ποικιλία (versatility), τέχνη (skill, cunning of hand). On this nature, and on its ability to save conflict with others from defeat by clever and outrageous behavior, see Cristiano Grottanelli ("Tricksters, Scapegoats, Champions, Saviors," *History of Religions* 23 [1984]: 117-39), who briefly defines the trickster (p.120): "Tricksters are breakers of rules, but, though they are often tragic in their own specific way, their breaking of rules is always comical. This funny irregularity is the central quality of the trickster; and what makes the anomie comical is the trickster's lowliness . . . when a human being, he never ranks high, and his power lies in his witty brain or in some strange gift of nature." Grottanelli refers to the first-century C.E. Latin poet Phaedrus and his translation of Aesop's fables for a primary example of a story about a trickster (located in a fable entitled *Pompeius et miles*), citing also (p.136) the Homeric *Hymn to Hermes* as a literary precedent for ideas about cleverness, ideas that eventually influenced the development of the Roman god Mercury. Prometheus was also to be included among these precedents

(p.133), a divine power "criminal and savior, guilty and heroic, impure and sacred, antagonist and mediator."

17. On the disagreement between Greeks, see Philostratus, *Apollonius* 6.20. Apollonius argues that many mystery religions could be coldly criticized if one were of a mind to do so. On the disagreements between Indians and Greeks, see Philostratus, *Apollonius* 2.9.

18. For the terminology, see already Euripides (*Bacchae* 1-2): Διὸς παῖς . . . Θηβαίων χθόνα Διόνυσος.

19. See Euripides (*Bacchae* 15) for the Greek Dionysus making his way to India through Bactra (*Bāhlīka*). See W. W. Tarn (*Alexander the Great* [Cambridge: Cambridge University Press, 1948], 2:45-46) especially on the Greek Peripatetics' discussion about Nysa as a town versus Nysa as a mountain. Seán Freyne (*Galilee from Alexander the Great to Hadrian, 323 B.C.E. to 135 C.E.: A Study in Second Temple Judaism*, University of Notre Dame Center for the Study of Judaism and Christianity Series 5 [South Bend, Ind.: University of Notre Dame Press, 1980], 270) discusses links between Nysa and Scythoplis (Beth She`arim) and the development of Dionysus worship at the latter. Plutarch (*Quaestiones Conviviales* 6:1-2.) reports an interpretation of the *Sukkot* as a Dionysian festival. *Pace* Plutarch, Tacitus (*Histories* 5.5) firmly denies that Dionysus would have anything to do with YHWH. These all represent international competition among mythographies.

20. Philostratus, *Apollonius* 2.23. Herakles is an all-purpose heroic figure, for good or ill; see C. Picard, "Hercule, héros malheureux et. . .bénéfique," in *Hommages à Jean Bayet*, ed. Marcel Renard and Robert Schilling, Collection Latomus, 70 (Bruxelles-Berchem, Belgium: Latomus Revue d'études latine, 1984), 561-68.

21. Pausanias, Περιήγησις 10.13.8; see Lewis Richard Farnell, *Greek Hero Cults and Ideas of Immortality*, Gifford Lectures 1920 (Oxford: Clarendon Press, 1921; repr. 1970), 135-36.

22. The story is that the Egyptian Herakles, with the help of some Dionysus, attacks the area of India that contains true sages (οἱ ἀτεχνῶς σοφοί). Being sages, they foil the attack by playing dead. Lured in too close, the heroes are driven off by the Indian sages who, jumping into action, throw lightening, thunderbolts, and other missiles of destruction at the divine heroes. On this occasion Herakles loses his golden shield. The sages, finding the shield left behind, admire it and the *ekphrasis* upon it. The *ekphrasis* depicts Herakles marking the frontiers of the world at Gadira, using the mountains for pillars, and drawing in the outer ocean into the inner sea (at Gibraltar). The Indian sages honor Herakles by dedicating the shield as an offering. Greek Herakles in Isocrates (*Philippus* 114, 116) is a benefactor specifically of and *only* of Greek culture. In this light, he is later pictured an ancestor of Philipp of Macedon; see Tarn, *Alexander the Great*, 2:403. The context in Isocrates might be entitled, "Against the Barbarian and for Greek *Homonoia*." Pausanias (9.11.1) mentions a statue of Greek Herakles called Πρόμαχος, just outside of the Electra Gate at Thebes; see Farnell, *Greek Hero Cults*, 146.

23. Lucian, *De morte Peregrini* 21; see Hans Dieter Betz, *Nachfolge und Nachahmung Jesus Christ im Neuen Testament*, Beiträge zur historischen Theologie 37 (Tübingen, Germany: J. C. B. Mohr, 1967), 129. The joke Lucian makes throughout this piece depends on the extremely dubious wager made by Peregrinus when he concocted his plan to commit suicide by immolation. The irony of the joke is heightened in Lucian's satire by comparisons of Peregrinus to Proteus, Herakles, Empedocles, the Indian Phoenix, and Cynic philosophers in general. Elsewhere, in his account of Demonax, Lucian claims for this philosopher the same kind of virtuous body and comprehensive intellect as Herakles had; or, a near perfect correspondence in quality of character to that of the heroic Herakles; see Lucian, *Demonax* 1.

24. Philostratus (*Apollonius* 6.10) describes the story as a ζωγραφία (painting) in words; see W. K. C. Guthrie, *The Sophists* (Cambridge: Cambridge University Press, 1971), 278.

25. The virtuous choice involves an inner disposition to turn away from a personal desire for τῦφος, (μηδὲ ἀλαζόνα εἶναι μηδὲ τύφου θηρατήν [neither to be prideful nor a hoarder of vanity]); see Philostratus, *Apollonius* 6.10. The word τῦφος has a double meaning of "vanity" and "illusion," and is an important term in Cynic traditions. The impact of the option for vice against the option for virtue is depicted in another story about Herakles' decision, in this case a decision between two twin mountain peaks. One is βασιλείας ἄκρα, sacred to Ζεὺς βασιλεύς; the other is ἄκρα τυραννική, called Τυφῶνος ἄκρα. Here Typhon symbolizes τῦφος, or illusion, obscurity, and vain self-overestimation (or, in mythographic terms, Chaos). On this and further descriptions of this image from Dio Chrysostom (Περὶ βασιλείας) see Donald R. Dudley, *A History of Cynicism: From Diogenes to the 6th Century* A.D. (London, 1937; repr., Hildesheim: Georg Olms, 1967), 56-57. The word play is between Τυφῶν and τῦφος. The tradition of Zeus-Typhon conflict undergirds this view of choice of philosophical lifestyle. Elsewhere a letter attributed to Crates claims Herakles the inspiration for doing away with δόξα. See Ps.-Crates 8 (*To Diogenes*), in *The Cynic Epistles: A Study Edition*, ed. Abraham J. Malherbe, Sources for Biblical Study 12 (Missoula, Mont.: Scholars Press, 1977), 58. Δόξα is similar to the play on the term τῦφος, as both terms refer to philosophical opinion too ineptly complicated. A letter attributed to Diogenes uses Herakles as an example of truly overcoming the adversities of poverty and disease, and not just the simpler adversities of "water serpents, bulls, lions, cerberuses"; see Ps.-Diogenes (*To Timomachus*) 36, in *The Cynic Epistles*, 148-53.

26. The verb θαυμάζω (to wonder at) is rightly identified as rare in Mark by Timothy Dwyer (*The Motif of Wonder in the Gospel of Mark*, Journal for the Study of the New Testament Supplement Series 128 [Sheffield: Sheffield Academic Press, 1996], 123-24), although Dwyer does nothing much with the irony of this description in Mark 6:6. On ways and means of expressing and maintaining belief, see T. C. W. Stinton ("*Si credere dignum est*: Some Expressions of Disbelief in Euripides and Others," *Proceedings of the Cambridge Philological Society* 202 [1976]: 60-89), especially for discussion and numerous

examples of how it is expressed that a παράδοξος might be "true" (apt in detail and fitting in likeness), but not "believable."

27. On public involvement by Epicureans, see *Epicurea*, ed. Hermann Usener (Stuttgart: B. G. Teubner, 1887), §552. Citations for this bit of Epicurean teaching include Plutarch, *Life of Pyrrhus* 20 (πολιτείαν φευγόντες); Lactantius, *Divine Institutes* 3.17.3 (*ignauum prohibet accedere ad rem publicam);* and Augustine, *Contra Academicos* 3.35 (*nec tu debuisti administrare rem publicam, quia Epicuri uisum est non esse faciendum*). On λάθε βιώσας (hidden life) see Fragment §86 in Bailey, *Epicurus*, 138. See also Usener (*Epicurea*, §551) for a history of how this Epicurean proverb is quoted and criticized. One supporter argued that it was said falsely about Epicurus, ἔθετο δόγμα μὴ φυσει εἶναι τὸν ἄνθρωπον κοινωνικόν τε καὶ ἥμερος (he established it as a principle that humans were by nature neither community-minded nor civilized; Themistius, *Orations* 26). Philostratus (*Apollonius* 8.28) uses the Epicurean proverb (λάθε βιώσας) in a word play with ἀποβιώσας (dissolve away from life), telling how Apollonius exits from mortal life by a "dissolution." See also *Sententia Vaticanae* 58: Ἐκλυτέον ἑαυτοὺς ἐκ τοῦ περὶ τὰ ἐγκύκλια καὶ πολιτικὰ δεσμωτηρίον (We must release ourselves from the prison of affairs and politics).

28. Lucian (*Alexander* 46) describes Epicurean life as living ὡς ἀσεβῆ καὶ ἄθεον (as an impious atheist), parallel to living life under a curse; that is, never to be received under another's roof, never to share fire or water, and always to be driven to wandering (ἀλύω). The concept of "uncleanness" in these descriptions is to be viewed along with the ironic complaints made against Epicurus and his mother, pictured as having sold καθαρμοί (purifications) door to door. On this description and the satire it evokes, see Roy D. Kotansky, "Greek Exorcistic Amulets," in *Ancient Magic and Ritual Power*, ed. Marvin Meyer and Paul Mirecki, Religions in the Graeco-Roman World 129 (Leiden, The Netherlands: E. J. Brill, 1995), 252-53. Plato (*Republic* 364B-E; trans. H. D. P. Lee, *Plato: The Republic*, Penguin Classics [Baltimore: Penguin Books, 1955], 95) describes house calls made by purifiers and exorcists: "There are itinerant evangelists and prophets who knock at the door of the rich man's house, and persuade him that they have some kind of divine power, and that any wrong that either he or his ancestors have done can be expiated by means of charms and sacrifices and the pleasure of the accompanying feasts; while if he has any enemy he wants to injure he can for a small fee damage him (whether he is a good man or not) with their spells and incantations, by which they profess to be able to persuade the gods to do their will. In support of all this they cite the evidence of the poets. Some, in support of the easiness of vice, quote Hesiod: 'Evil can men attain easily and in companies: the road is smooth and her dwelling near. But the gods have decreed much sweat before a man reaches virtue' and a road that is long and hard and steep. Others quote Homer on turning aside the gods—'The very gods are capable of being swayed. Even they are turned from their course by sacrifice and humble prayers, libations and burnt offerings, when the miscreant and sinner bend the knee to them in supplication.' Or they may produce a whole collection of books or ritual instructions written by Musaeus and Orpheus, whom they call descen-

dants of the Moon and the Muses; and they persuade not only individuals but whole communities that, both for living and dead, remission and absolution of sins may be had by sacrifices and childish performances, which they are pleased to call initiations, and which they allege deliver us from all ills in the next world, where terrible things await the uninitiated."

29. Ps.-Diogenes 36.20, in *The Cynic Epistles*, 149. Other Cynics thought and operated differently. Anacharsis visited individuals, appearing at the doors of their houses as a ξένος (stranger); see Ps.-Anacharsis 2.19, in *The Cynic Epistles*, 38.

30. Epictetus, *Discourses* 3.22.45. *Palatine Anthology* 7.65 recalls that Diogenes lived life using the weapons of self-sufficient sobriety (αὐτάρκους ὅπλα σαοφροσύνας).

31. Teles Περὶ φυγῆς 21H-22H; see *Teles [The Cynic Teacher]*, ed. and trans. Edward O'Neil, Texts and Translations 11: Graeco-Roman Religion 3 (Missoula, Mont.: Scholars Press, 1977), 21-23.

32. Plutarch *De exilio* 600E; see Arnim, *Stoicorum Veterum Fragmenta*, 1§371.

33. Dio Chrysostom, *Orations* 36.20; Arnim, *Stoicorum Veterum Fragmenta*, 3§329. Stobaeus (*Eclogues* 1.184) reports the thinking of Chrysippus; Arnim, *Stoicorum Veterum Fragmenta*, 2§527. Diogenes, Oenoanda 25.2; see A. Long and D. N. Sedley, *The Hellenistic Philosophers* (Cambridge: Cambridge University Press, 1987), 2§22P. Diogenes discusses those who are strangers and those who are not strangers; see C. W. Chilton, *Diogenes of Oenoanda: The Fragments* (Oxford: Oxford University Press, 1971), 11.

34. See Grottanelli ("Saviours of the Eastern Mediterranean") for Herodotus 3.129-138 on Democedes. Grottanelli discusses Elisha, Melampus, Epimenides, Pythagoras, and Empedocles, speaking of an "Iron Age crisis" and a subsequent development of autonomous healer and/or saviors whose autonomy is in strict separation from kings and other traditional authorities. These figures are reported sometimes to have been the only ones able to heal kings, to whom they did not belong as subjects.

35. I do not discuss here the Markan variant that parallels Matthew 10:15, which gives an etiological reason for the ματύριον, based on a theory of an eschatological Day of Judgment (Amen, truly I say to you, there will be more mercy for Sodom and Gomorrah in the day of judgment than for that city).

36. Samuel Daiches, *Babylonian Oil Magic in the Talmud and in the Later Jewish Literature*, Jews' College, London, Publications 5 (London: Jews' College, 1913). Eitrem (*Some Notes on the Demonology*, 23-24) states that Jesus "acts as a person with an authority quite different from that of an ordinary magician or exorcist, and with greater effect than is attained by a θεῖος ἀνήρ (divine man) or an emperor." The authority of Jesus is different from these other because Mark reports nothing about Jesus' discourses on the divine, his utterance of magical formulae, or his use of magical accouterments. Narrative elements like these would have better completed a picture of Jesus as a magical practitioner, even if that picture were meant to be *skiagraphic* (just "a rough but plausible sketch").

8

Mark 6:14-29:
Antipas, John,
and Fear of Retaliation
Because of Violent Death

Mark 6:14-29 relates information about a leader identified as a βασιλεύς (king), a term used in Mark here and also in chapter fifteen, where Jesus is identified as βασιλεύς τῶν 'Ιουδαίων (king of the Jews).[1] Herod Antipas is here called a *king*, which is a curious emphasis since Herod Antipas was never a king of anything.[2] Identifying him in this way creates the means for three basic sections of this story to unfold, through use of the key word βασιλεύς, a term that has many political, religious, and philosophical connotations. Each event in the story turns on the opinions or actions of this βασιλεύς. So, for fifteen verses, the Markan narrative loses sight of Jesus. Instead, we find here a tale about a worried, foolish, and rash "king." This character is a prime actor in a melodrama about fear of retaliation due to political violence through assassination (or βιαιοθανασία). When Antipas hears about the miracles of Jesus, he does not think of beneficial acts in the countryside. Instead, he thinks of the prophet whom he had violently killed. In his mind, the miracles indicate a response from his victim.

Mark 6:14a reports that a rumor went out because of the δυνάμεις (miracles) of Jesus and the disciples. The phrase φανερὸν γὰρ ἐγένετο τὸ ὄνομα αὐτοῦ (for his name had become public) indicates that the δυνάμεις are to be linked to Jesus (in this case, τὸ ὄνομα αὐτοῦ = Jesus). The explanations of these anomalous works that follow in 6:14b-15, however, do not show that others in this story understood that the object in dispute here is actually Jesus. Instead, the mere fact of miracles done out in the wilderness and among the villages, takes on a disrupting and

substantial life of its own. Three options are offered as current explanations for what those confronted with such news reports thought was going
on: καὶ ἔλεγον ὅτι ᾽Ιωάννης ὁ βαπτίζων ἐγήρερται ἐκ νεκρῶν καὶ διὰ
τοῦτο ἐνεργοῦσιν αἱ δυνάμεις ἐν αὐτῷ. ἄλλοι δὲ ἔλεγον ὅτι ᾽Ηλίας
ἐστίν, ἄλλοι δὲ ἔλεγον ὅτι προφήτης ὡς εἷς τῶν προφητῶν (and they
were saying that John the Baptist had risen from the dead and because of
this powerful miracles were being worked by him. Yet others said that he
was Elijah, and still others that he was a prophet like one of the
prophets).[3] In spite of the variety of choices suggested in the story for
interpreting the miracles, it is the opinion of the βασιλεύς alone that in
fact moves this story on. Whomever to others it seems was performing
δυνάμεις, Antipas is convinced it is John the Baptist. Why? Because he
had John beheaded, and therefore it is Antipas who would be the object
of any subsequent revenge, should a postmortem John appear to retaliate
for his unjust and untimely death. In short order within Mark 6:14-18, the
reader is provided with two ideal types: Βασιλεύς and Βιαιοθανασία.
βιαιοθανασία (violent death), by its very nature a graphic and irreversible
human experience, is naturally a metaphor for anything that was anomalously frightful. Vettis Valens (*Anthologiarum Libri* 94.1), links violent
death with φυγαδεία (exile) and presents it as an experience typically
caused by ὁ τοιοῦτος ἡγεμονικὸς τυραννικός (a certain kind of tyrannical
leadership). The first ideal type, Βασιλεύς, is of utmost importance for
grasping the irony in this story and framing the second.

There are numerous places in the Hellenistic world to look for
common expectations of a king and especially of an ἀγαθὸς βασιλεύς
(good king). The concept of νόμος ἔμψυχος (internalized law) was a
robust ideal in the propaganda of kings. It can be traced from speeches of
Themistius back to Plato and Isocrates. The latter speculated on the
concept of law as it "dwells with" (κειμένων) the king.[4] The king has a
τρόπος (manner) of law. As another rhetorician puts it, the most beautiful
κοινὸς νόμος (common law) stems from the ἡγεμονία (intentional self)
of the βασιλεύς (king),[5] emphasizing what Plato (*Laws* 714A) suggests,
that νόμος (law) was a νοῦ διανομή (regulation of mind). While writing
of Cyrus, Xenophon (*Cyropaedia* 8.1.21-22) observes that a good leader
(βασιλεύς) keeps an eye on the law (βλέποντα νόμον . . . ἐνόμισεν) as he
becomes law for his subjects. Aristotle (*Politics* 1284a13), observing why
democracies ostracize certain powerful men, explains that such individuals are like θεοί (gods) among humans and, consequently, are not able to
live as equals in a state, αὐτοὶ γάρ εἰσι νόμος (for they are themselves
law). Elsewhere (*Nicomachean Ethics* 1132a22), Aristotle writes that

when plaintiffs and defendants go before a judge, they do so because ὁ δικαστὴς βούλεται εἶναι οἷον δίκαιον ἔμψυχος (the judge was thought to act justly, having internalized the law). These concepts of the βασιλεύς are also linked to the king as ποιμής[6] or *pastor*, an idea that broadens the notion of how a βασιλεύς embodies justice and law. Archytas, Diotogenes, and Ekphantus show how the concept of internalized law became widespread in the world of the Gospel of Mark (see appendix H, "Νόμος ῎Εμψυχος).

A βασιλεύς who embodies δική καὶ νόμος (justice and law) exudes ἀρετή (virtue). This belief is well-represented in inscriptional and papyrological witnesses.[7] The ideal βασιλεύς was expected to exhibit σωφροσύνη, μεγαλομερεία, νήφων, ἀδωροδοκία, δικαισύνη, εὐνόμια, ἐπιεικεία, φιλοτιμία, πρόνοια, εὔνοια, πίστις, φιλανθρωπία, εὐγνωμοσύνη, ἔλεος, εὐμένεια, and φιλοστοργία (temperateness, lavishness, sobriety, incorruptibility, justice, good order, fairness, honor, foresight, kindness, faithfulness, love of people, candor, mercy, kindness, and affection). He was to offer asylum and would thus be called Σωτήρ, Εὐεργέτης, and Βοηθός (Savior, Benefactor, and Helper), titles actually taken by Ptolemaic kings. Musonius Rufus details the duties of such an ἀγαθὸς βασιλεύς, including among his duties the distribution of benefaction, acts of justice, promotion of what is good, and especially behaving with σωφροσύνη (moderation). Philodemus, in his Homeric exegesis, depicts the good king according to several vignettes from Homer.[8] Use of these older texts to comment on immediately contemporary politics is also to be seen in the composition of the *Temple Scroll*. This latter evidence stems from the time of Alexander Jannaeus, when Jewish foreign relations with Nabateans and Parthians reached critically active levels.[9] In this political context, a notion of Judean kingship developed, arguably evident in *Temple Scroll* 57-59.[10] In yet a very different tradition, the kingly figures of David and Solomon are compared to Orpheus in some rabbinic texts. In these cases, the ἀγαθὸς βασιλεύς is likened to a shepherd and musician. As such, he is represented as having ἀρετή (virtue) of soul.[11]

Such is the strength of the many and varying strands of thought about kingship. Within this milieu of awareness of and preferences for kings, Mark 6:17-20 reports about the kind of relationship Antipas, the so-called βασιλεύς, has with the Baptist. It is complicated and politically volatile. The story has it that Antipas feared the living John, εἰδὼς αὐτὸν ἄνδρα δίκαίον καὶ ἅγιον (knowing him to be just and holy). Josephus (*Antiquities* 18.117) gives a different account of this story yet also stresses the kind of relationship that Antipas has with John, that the virtue of John opposed the vice of Antipas. For Josephus, the actions of Antipas against John are actions done against an ἀγαθὸς ἀνήρ (divine man) who had done nothing more than exhort the Jews toward virtue, righteousness, and godliness. Unjust actions by a βασιλεύς (king) loom large in both these presentations, receiving extensive thematic development in two accounts with different accents. In Mark, the behavior of the βασιλεύς falls far below standard, and Antipas seems an ἀδικίος βασιλεύς (unjust king). Comparison to Josephus shows how Mark skillfully paints this portrait.

Josephus (*Antiquities* 18.117-118) writes that Antipas had John killed because the Baptist, due to his πίθανον (persuasiveness), had developed too large a following. The historical veracity of this account is highly disputed because of the probability that it contains a Christian interpolation on the matter of John's baptismal method and preaching. Nonetheless, it is reported that John threatened Antipas with civil unrest (στάσις). The subsequent police action of the Antipas of Josephus is pictured as that of an installed authority under Roman rule (an ἄρχων or *magistratus*) who does not want Roman reprisals against him because of poor management of his allotment (his "fourth"). In an earlier account (*Antiquities* 18.109-115), Josephus tells us the story about how the daughter of Aretas, at the time when Antipas was beginning to scheme to leave her and marry Herodias, saw what Antipas was trying to do. She slips away, going back to her father. Reporting the imminent divorce of herself by Antipas (so that he might marry Herodias), she infuriates her father Aretas against Antipas. Eventually war breaks out, and the entire army of Antipas is lost. In Josephus, the downfall of Antipas is due not to an outside, autonomous prophet like John, but to the anger of Aretas and his daughter, once divorce is threatened and the misbehavior of Antipas creates a public humiliation.

Things are quite different in Mark. Antipas seizes John and locks him in prison because of things John has said to Antipas about his marriage to Herodias, "the wife of Philip his brother (ἀδελφός)" (6:17). John announced to Antipas that it was not permitted for him (οὐκ ἔξεστιν σοι) so to marry.[12] In doing so, he allies himself with Aretas, the father of the first wife of Antipas. An alignment of this sort would appear to be a direct assault by an autonomous and wandering figure (the Baptist) against the interdynastic politics of Antipas. It is personal, one man against another. If Antipas were to take any steps to retaliate against John, it would not be because of potential social unrest caused by John, but solely because of his very personal and unjust disposition against a "righteous and holy" man. Given the situation narrated in Mark, the acts of Antipas are heightened in their audacity, as acts of the unjust against the just. The character of Antipas is thereby colored as vice-ridden and cowardly.[13]

The audacious misbehavior of Antipas is illustrated in the strange account of how it comes about that Antipas actually kills the Baptist, and for what reasons. Mark reports a εὐκαίρος ἡμέρα: the birthday celebration of this βασιλεύς. Historically, leaders of varying types celebrated, or had celebrated for them, their birthdays, with varying effect. In the *fasti* of the *Feriale Duranum*, the birthdays of several emperors and notable leaders are marked for celebration by the army.[14] The decree of the proconsul and provinces of Asia in 9 B.C.E., concerning the adjustment of sacral calendars to the γενέθλιον of Augustus, calls for some of the most extreme effects contingent on the birthday celebration of a human leader.[15] Other birthdays were noted, including one at the very same Priene for Lysimachos in 286 B.C.E., one of the earliest witnesses to the development of Hellenistic kingship. Earlier Plato (*Alcibiades* 121C) notes that a custom in Persia intriguing to Greeks is the celebration of the γενέθλια of its king. A decree of 239 B.C.E. at Canopus in Ptolemaic Egypt instructs that γενέθλια be celebrated for the βασιλεύς, along also with the date when he had inherited his βασιλεία from his father. Antiochus I Commagene in 69 B.C.E. initiated a series of birthday celebrations throughout his cities and villages,[16] erecting also in those places a series of representations of himself in δεξίωσις (handshake) with Zeus-Oromasdes-Apollo, Mithra-Helios-Hermes, Artagenes-Herakles-Ares. His kingdom became a unique experiment among eastern dynasties that dealt with Rome and the east, especially Parthia. Depictions of δεξίωσις are symbolic of Antiochus I making peace with eastern neighbors. Antipas would later try to play a similar role under Rome, commissioned by Tiberias as a diplomate in affairs concerning Rome and Parthia.[17]

Given the key word βασιλεύς here in Mark, it seems likely that the report about this birthday celebration is meant to evoke traditional themes of powerful royalty, international diplomacy, and kingly glory. Such themes are not foreign to the Hellenistic world, including the history of Judea/Galilee with eastern neighbors. But the power of royal office, leadership in international diplomacy, and kingly glory are all things with which Antipas historically had little or no part. This portrait of Herod Antipas is a pointed satire that paints the character of Antipas with a poignant negative irony.

In Mark, a feast (δεῖπνον) is reported. Those in attendance with

Antipas are his μεγιστᾶνες (courtiers), χιλίαρχοι (officers), and πρῶτοι (leaders) of Galilee (6:21),[18] the first and third from whom he likely extracted his income under the authority of Rome, with the assistance of the second. This story can be compared to the report of a feast given by Antipas for Vitellius and the Parthian king Artabanus (Josephus, *Antiquities* 18.102-103), at the middle point of a bridge over the Euphrates River. In that story, Antipas was surrounded by actually important, international figures. In the Markan scene, he is surrounded by local aspirants to power. His birthday celebration is the celebration of a self-promoting upstart. He appears minor and trivial, a characterization that makes the actions that follow even more grotesque.

Antipas' stepdaughter, described as a κοράσιον in 6:22, dances (ὀρχησαμένη) at the festivities. This particular εὐκαίρος ἡμέρα (festival day) turns out for Antipas to be his undoing. Extremely pleased with her performance, he desires to give her a gift. From elsewhere we have reports about how, sometimes, kings needed to be restrained in their gift giving. A notable story of such restraint is told by Plutarch, who reports at least twice on the interaction of the κωμῳδιοποιός Philippides and King Lysimachus. In another case of gift-giving, Philostratus reports how Severus was pleased with performances of the sophist Hermocrates and δωρεάς τε αἰτεῖν ἀνῆκεν (granted him the privilege of asking for presents). Subsequently the clever answers of Hermocrates fit his character and honor the emperor. Hadrian, many times pleased with the sophist Polemo, gave him many gifts of money and free rights of travel (Philostratus, *Vitae Sophistarum* 533).[19] In these scenes, the gifts of the βασιλεύς fit the performance and the person performing. In light of this, the account in Mark makes Antipas look all the more ridiculous.

Taking weighty oaths in the presence of all, he swears to give, to a girl who merely dances for him, anything she asks, even up to half of his βασιλεία, which again is ironic because Antipas did not *have* a βασιλεία. What he had wasn't his to give away, since in the first place it was given to him by Augustus as an allotment. Speaking with her mother, the girl is instructed to ask for the head of John the Baptist on a πίναξ (platter). Immediately[20] she does just this. Appalled and grieved by his impetuous oaths, Antipas does what she requests. In turn, she gives the head to her mother. John's disciples come for his body and bury his remains.

The key action of this part of the story turns on the rash and irreversible oath of a βασιλεύς. The account can be compared to that of Jephtha (Judges 11), whose daughter's lament in Pseudo-Philo I have previously discussed. Jephtha takes an oath (Judges 11:30) to the Lord, to kill and thus make an offering of the first person whom he sees emerging from his own home, should it be allowed him to return victorious from the territory of the Ammonites. The person he then sees is his daughter, his only child. In Scripture Jephtha makes his rash oath while the Spirit of the Lord is on him. But Pseudo-Philo takes a different approach and comments on the rashness of this oath: "And God was very angry and said, 'Behold Jephtha has vowed that he will offer to me *whatever meets him* first *on the way*; and now if a dog should meet Jephtha first, will the dog be offered to me? And now let the vow of Jephtha be accomplished against his own firstborn, that is, against the fruit of his own body, and his request against his only-begotten.'"[21] Trapped, Jephtha becomes a pathetic creature. His rash action involves an impulsive oath.

Without oath taking, a similar rash action in the heat of conflict is also reported to have ruined the life of Poemander, who took up a stone previously used in the ritual *Nuktelion* and angrily threw it down from a fortification, intending to hit and kill Polycrithus. He missed and hit his son Leucippus, tragically killing him instead. Consequently Poemander was sent into exile.[22] These rash actions of heroic figures can help to interpret the action of Antipas in Mark. The stories tell of terrible and frustrating results stemming from the impulsive acts of rulers. When these men act in this way, the aftermath includes perplexing uncertainty and fear. In the case of Antipas, the rash action creates a situation that is most tragic (the death of John the Baptist) and for the most trivial of reasons, all leading to an outcome that seems absurd. The story juxtaposes the fearful impact of a violent death, an act in other texts associated with the disposition of a tyrant, with the dithering of an aspirant to power. The theme of violent death and its expected bad outcome is greatly emphasized.

The beheading of John in this account can be seen against two backgrounds. First, in the Roman empire decapitation was a relatively swift and painless death (if done correctly), reserved for Roman citizens. In a section entitled "On the Cornelian Law Concerning Assassins and Poisoners," Paulus in his *Opinions* wrote that "for these crimes it as been decreed that capital punishment shall be meted out to persons of superior rank; humble persons, however, are either crucified or thrown to wild beasts."[23] The distinction between swift as opposed to painful (and drawn out) capital punishment is evident. Class distinction makes the difference. Even after the *Constitutio Antoniana* in 212 C.E., when the right of citizenship became far more widely available to many more people, decapitation was reserved for *honestiores*, "senators, soldiers and others in the emperor's service, and members of municipal councils, with their families."[24] In light of this, it is tempting to see the decapitation of John as an example of a mode of death reserved for respected citizens. Yet in this story it is not Antipas who seeks such a sentence; rather, it is the dancing stepdaughter who demands it. Mark does not here focus on a decent quality of death for John by Roman lights but, instead, on the removal of his head so that it could be given to the girl, who passed it on to her mother (6:28).

In light of this unusual use of John's head under these circumstances, we should examine a second background, in which decapitation is viewed as an act of atrocious death, even as σπάραγμα (tearing). In Greek sensibilities, beheading is viewed as a barbaric act, done by the likes of Scythians or Celts. Conversely, the last sentence of the LXX psalter contains a unique notice of David's beheading of Goliath, a giant who cursed Israel and brought disgrace on the people of God (Psalm 151:7). Whereas in that account the beheading is very much a cleansing response to an earlier disgrace, to other sensibilities this beheading could very likely have been the occasion for a curse upon the city responsible for the execution. Margaret Visser comments on the usual form of such stories that view violent acts such as beheading as impurities.

> A city which has been seriously harmed by an enemy, either an invading foreigner or a turbulent member of its own citizen body, finally has its enemy in its power; the hostile person is a prisoner of war, has taken sanctuary, or is dead. The city exacts its revenge, usually stoning or beheading the helpless enemy, or similarly mutilating his corpse. Plague and pollution follow, until a god, usually Delphic Apollo, is asked for an explanation. The god replies that the city is suffering because its dead enemy requires remembrance and propitiation. The people whom he had originally wronged must now treat him as a hero it they wish to be released from his curse. The plague is lifted when worship for the enemy is instituted, and the hero continues to be honored down to the "present day."[25]

The uncanny nature of decapitation is to be noted, and this nature also appears in some Roman sources. One report about the fate of Pompey, after his failed resistance to Caesar, says that he was killed in the court of Ptolemy, before his wife and children. The decapitation of his corpse follows. The writer emphasizes that such an atrocity is unheard of before then.[26] Even so, Caesar honors the severed head appropriately. By the accounts given in *De viris illustribus*, it seems that generally Romans may not have objected to killing a helpless prisoner, especially one considered a traitor (the fate of Appius Claudius in *De Viris Illustribus* 21). Nor, at least in their ancient history, apparently did they object to crucifying the bodies of prisoners, even already killed prisoners, charged with treason.[27] But to Greeks, beheading and other disfigurement of a corpse was aberrant. In Plutarch (*De Iside et Osiride* 358E), legends about a dismemberment of Horus or a decapitation of Isis are disgusting. It is an uncanny and terrible end when King Pyrrhus of Epirus is killed during an attack on Argos by a blow to the head. Traditions of Dionysus Zagreus, Orpheus, Adonis, and Pentheus contain beheadings, stonings, and in general the mutilation of their cadavers. Orpheus, decapitated, continues to talk. These are all essentially the most terrible of events.[28] As traditions, their content is different from the Markan story of the beheading of John the Baptist. Yet there is a link in accent between them; the anomalous frightful pervades them both through themes of dismemberment. These traditions report uncanny and atrocious deaths of individuals whose destiny, because of the death, becomes uncertain and fearful. Such individuals are potentially either dangerous to those responsible for their death, or beneficial to those who honor them and respond correctly in ritual. This, then, is a main contribution of these deaths to the anomalous frightful: the violence is especially gruesome and creates a great pollution, initiating a most volatile situation of unavenged death.

Antipas thinks that reports about events out in the wilderness and among the villages are reports about John the Baptist "raised" (ὃν ἐγὼ ἀπεκεφάλισα Ἰωάννην, οὗτος ἠγέρθη [6:16]). The cowardly king worries about retaliation by the man he unjustly killed, whom he now thinks to be wandering about, attempting some type of sedition against him; so, at least, he interprets the δυνάμεις. Here we find an atrocious βιαιοθανασία (violent death) based on the overt stupidity of a king (βασιλεύς) who is trivial, marginal, and foolish. The beheading is a type of σπαραγμός, or a desecrative rending of the flesh, as also will be the σταύρωσις (crucifixion) later in Mark. It is a focused presentation of uncertainty, terror, and strangeness. In this case, the object of uncertainty, terror, and strangeness is a violent and untimely death.

Notes

1. βασιλεύς in 6:14, 22, 26, 27. βασιλεία in 6:25. The quotation of Antipas in 6:23, μου βασιλείας. The one exception to the usage in chapters 6 and 15 is in 13:9, followers to be dragged ἐπὶ ἡγεμόνων καὶ βασιλέων.

2. In the setting of his lavish temple to Apollo, Augustus, on hearing the dispute between successors and claimants of Herod's kingdom (Josephus, *Antiquities* 17.298-299), settles the matter by appointing to Antipas "one-quarter" of Herod's territory, so that he might receive revenue from that area, from Galilee, and from Peraea (*Antiquities* 17.318-319). Josephus (*Antiquities* 17.224; *War* 2.22) is clear that, at this adjudication, Antipas had in fact been contending for the βασιλεία of Herod. Antipas definitely wanted to be βασιλεύς. When Gaius Caligula believes him to be a seditious conspirator, he takes away Antipas' "one-fourth" and adds it to the βασιλεία of Agrippa (*Antiquities* 18.252). Before him, a kingdom; after him, a kingdom. It is fair to say that, of all the things Antipas ever was, never was he a βασιλεύς. See Emil Schürer (*The History of the Jewish People in the Age of Jesus Christ*, ed. Geza Vermes, Fergus Millar, and Martin Goodman, rev. ed. [Edinburgh: T & T Clark, 1986], 1:341) for title of Antipas strictly as Tetrarch, as inscriptions from Cos and Delos show. Roger Aus (*Water Into Wine and the Beheading of John the Baptist*, Brown Judaic Studies 150 [Atlanta: Scholars Press, 1988], 41-42) reiterates these facts, suggesting that behind the Mark 6:21 birthday banquet of Antipas is the tradition of Esther 1:2-3. Based on Esther Rabbah, Ahasuerus becomes Antipas and Queen Vashti becomes John the Baptist. I should not want to endorse these poignant guesses.

3. The comments of Richard A. Horsley ("'Like One of the Prophets of Old': Two Types of Popular Prophets at the Time of Jesus," *Catholic Biblical Quarterly* 47 [1985]: 435-63) may or may not be pertinent to this phrase in Mark. The two types of prophet are "oracular" and "action," and information about them is primarily from Josephus. Horsley argues that the type of prophet meant in Mark 6:15 is likely someone such as one of the contemporary, Judean prophets. Yet the narrative here has no interest in developing any choice other than what it is that Antipas thinks, whether there were contemporary prophets or not. See Klaus Berger (*Die Auferstehung der Propheten und die Erhöhung des Menschensohnes: Traditionsgeschichtliche Untersuchungen zur Deutung des Geschickes Jesu in frühchristlichen Texten*, Studien zur Umwelt des Neuen Testaments 13 [Göttingen: Vandenhoeck und Ruprecht, 1976], 17-18) for description of materials external to Josephus about contemporary expectations for prophets. Berger rightfully notes that terminology for the appearances of *prophets* parallels that for resurrection of the *dead* (p.18). He also notes from Justin (*Apology* 52.10) the juridical theory that Christian martyrs will appear to and devastate those who killed them, just as, in a future judgment day, Jesus will appear to and devastate his murderers.

4. Isocrates 1.36. For the history of these concepts see G. J. D. Aalders, "ΝΟΜΟΣ ΕΜΨΥΧΟΣ," in *Politeia und Res Publica: Beiträge zum Verständnis von Politik, Recht und Stadt in der Antike, dem amdenken Rudolf Starks gewidmet*, ed. Peter Steinmetz, Palingenesia, Monographien und Texte zur klassischen Altertumswissenschaft 4 (Wiesbaden: Franz Steiner Verlag, 1969), 315-29. On the ἀγαθὸς βασιλεύς see Musonius Rufus, *That Kings Also Should Study Philosophy* 35; *Musonius Rufus: The Roman Socrates*, ed. Cora E. Lutz, Yale Classical Studies 10 (New Haven, Conn.: Yale University Press, 1947), 64. The text is from Stobaeus, *Eclogues* 4.7.67. On νόμος ἔμψυχος see William Klassen, "The King as 'Living Law' with Particular Reference to Musonius Rufus," *Studies in Religion/Sciences Religieuses* 14 (1985): 63-71.

5. Anaximenes *Rhetorica ad Alexandrum* 1420a 19-20; see Aalders, "ΝΟΜΟΣ ΕΜΨΥΧΟΣ," 318.

6. In Archytas (Περὶ νόμου καὶ δικαιοσύνη, in *The Pythagorean Texts of the Hellenistic Period*, ed. Holger Thesleff, Acta Academiae Aboensis, Series A: Humaniora: Humanistiska Vetenskaper, Socialvetenskaper, Teologi 30 no. 1[(Åbo: Åbo Akademi, 1965], 36 ll.2-5) the ἀληθινὸν ἄρχοντα (true leader) is like a ποιμήν (shepherd). Philo (*Legatio ad Gaium* 44) writes of βουκόλοι, αἰπόλοι, νομεῖς, and ἀγελάρχαι (herdsmen, goatherds, shepherds, and herd-keepers).

7. W. Schubart, "Das hellenistische Königsideal nach Inschriften und Papyri," *Archiv für Papyrusforschung* 12 (1937): 1-26.

8. Musonius Rufus, *That Kings Also Should Study Philosophy*, in *Musonius Rufus, the Roman Socrates*. Philodemus (Περὶ τοῦ καθ᾽ Ὅμηρον ἀγαθοῦ βασιλέως) covers such topics as the hubris of kings before gods, the proper use of leisure time by kings (συμποσίαι), the proper use of self-praise, and the best way to conduct military affairs; see Oswyn Murray, "Philodemus on the Good King According to Homer," *Journal of Roman Studies* 55 (1965): 161-82.

9. Menahem Stern, "Judaea and Her Neighbors in the Days of Alexander Jannaeus," *Jerusalem Cathedra* 1 (1981): 22-46.

10. These columns of the *Temple Scroll* stand out from their context in the manner in which they refer to God, especially in a complete lack of second person address in them. Unlike the text before and after this section in the *Scroll*, these chapters show virtually no link to Scriptures, other than reference to Exodus 18:21. See Andrew M. Wilson and Lawrence Wills, "Literary Sources of the *Temple Scroll*," *Harvard Theological Review* 75 (1982): 275-88. On this unique document illustrating the development of a theory of kingship in Hellenistic Judea, see M. Hengel, J. H. Charlesworth, and D. Mendels, "The Polemical Character of 'On Kingship' in the Temple Scroll: An Attempt at Dating 11QTemple," *Journal of Jewish Studies* 37 (1986): 28-38. Parallels can be drawn between this portion of the *Temple Scroll* and the story of the Seven Banquets in the *Letter of Aristeas*; see D. Mendels, "'On Kingship' in the 'Temple Scroll' and the Ideological *Vorlage* of the Seven Banquets in the 'Letter to Philocrates'," *Aegyptus* 59 (1979): 127-36. Oswyn Murray ("Aristeas and Ptolemaic Kingship," *Journal of Theological Studies* 18 [1967]: 337-71 argues that Seven Banquets section is to be explained only on the basis of the history of the Ptolemaic dynasty. For a

theory of quite different influences on this particular genre of theory about kingship, see W. W. Tarn, *The Greeks in Bactria and India* (Cambridge: Cambridge University Press, 1951), 414-36 ("Excursus: The Milindapanha and Pseudo-Aristeas").

11. Sandra R. Shimoff ("Hellenization among the Rabbis: Some Evidence from Early Aggadot Concerning David and Solomon," *Journal for the Study of Judaism* 18 [1991]: 168-87) identifies a "Greek Orphic model"with elements of "Hellenistic hairstyle, Hellenistic social mores, Hellenistic coins, Hellenistic culinary excesses, royal world dominion, and Solomon's throne" as found in a few key texts: (1) *Second Treatise of the Great Seth*, (2) *Testimony of Truth*, and (3) earlier in 11QPsᵃ col. XXVIII line 5. In this latter Qumran text, the coiffures of the brothers of David are mentioned: "tall of stature (*hgbhîm bqwmtm*) and handsome by their hair (*hypîm bš`rm*)"; see J. A. Sanders, *The Dead Sea Psalms Scroll* (Ithaca, N.Y.: Cornell University Press, 1967), 97. The LXX Greek text varies significantly from the Qumran Hebrew text, as it leaves out much of the material that points to a "Greek Orphic model." See Sanders (*Dead Sea Psalms Scroll*, 98) on the picture of David as a Hellenistic king. Textual material from Qumran is some of the earliest evidence of a literary depiction of David as an Orpheus. Pictorial representations of this association are also known, including a mosaic from Jerusalem with David as an Orpheus. Shimoff points to rabbinic texts on the hairstyle of David: bKid. 76b, bSan. 49 and bSan. 21a ("Rab Judah states in Rab's name: David had four hundred children, all the offspring of beautiful women, all with hair trimmed in front and locks growing long, and all sat on golden chariots, and went at the head of armies, and they were the strong men of the house of David that went to terrorize opposing armies"). In visual styling, proper coiffure is essential to represent correctly a royal figure.

12. Josephus (*Antiquities* 18.109-111) reports that Antipas was long married to the daughter of Aretas, the Arab king of Petra. While on the way to Rome, Antipas lodges with his half-brother, Herod (in Mark designated "Philip"). This half-brother's mother is the daughter of Simon the High Priest. When Antipas visits, Herod is then married to Herodias, who herself is the daughter of Aristobulus (the brother of both Antipas and Herod the half-brother). Herodias is also the sister of Agrippa the Great. It is easy to see how enmeshed these dynastic families became, due to political marriages; family lines are difficult to follow. See Richard D. Sullivan (*Near Eastern Royalty and Rome, 100-30 B.C.*, Phoenix Supplementary Volume 24 (Toronto: University of Toronto Press, 1990), appendix called "Stemma 8: Judea" for a complete genogram of the family. The confusion between Mark's Philip and Josephus' Herod the half-brother is discussed by Harold Hoehner, *Herod Antipas*, Society for New Testament Studies Monograph Series 17 (Cambridge: Cambridge University Press, 1972), 131-36. John's comment to Antipas may be compared to that of another autonomous figure, Herodes, who once wrote a message to Cassius the proconsul of Asia, on hearing of his plans for treason: Ἡρώδης Κασσίῳ, ἐμάνης (Herodes to Cassius: You are insane!); see Philostratus, *Vitae Sophistarum* 565. Antipas' actions toward the Baptist are not unlike those of Dionysius I (of Syracuse) toward the

comic, satirical poet Antiphon of Rhamnus. Philostratus (*Vitae Sophistarum* 500) reports how a remark made by Antiphon to Dionysius, that the best bronze is found in Athens and not in Italy, leads to Dionyius' trumping up charges of treason against Antiphon and summarily executing him.

13. Mark reports that Antipas wants to kill John, but fears him too much to do so. Instead, he keeps John, watching over him closely and listening to him gladly, either "doubting much" of what John said or "being spurred on to do much" from what he said. A textual problem in this strange story of Antipas' relationship to John consists in the need to decide between the reading πολλὰ ἐποίει (he did much) or πολλὰ ἠπόρει (he doubted much); see Campbell Bonner ("Note on Mk 6:20," *Harvard Theological Review* 37[1944]: 41-44) for a full review of all the curious ideas that have been proposed to resolve this textual problem. These include speculation about Hellenistic Greek semiticisms and an Aramaic *Vorlage* for Mark. They also include suggestions about lost words in the textual transmission. Alex Pallis (*Notes on St. Mark and St. Matthew*, new ed. [London: Oxford University Press, 1932], 19-20) suggests that the original text is πολλὰ ἃ ἐποίει and that the penultimate word of the verse, αὐτοῦ, is anaphoric to a hypothetical, previously unstated substantive, ὄχλος (based on the notion that Antipas did not fear *John* but, instead, feared the "*crowd*" that honored John). Bonner proposed that the meaning of the verb ἠπόρει comes out of philosophical schools, meaning not "he doubted" but "he disputed." Bonner's suggestion that John is to Antipas as other wise men, teachers, counselors, soothsayers, prophets, or inventors of new arts are to other kings and leaders bears investigation, but its relevance seems minor, given the other major facts of this story. Yes, John is an autonomous agent, much as Cristiano Grottanelli ("Saviours of the Eastern Mediterranean in Pre-Classical Times," in *La soteriologia dei culti orientali nell'Impero Romano: Atti del colloquio internazionale*, ed. Ugo Bianchi and Maarten. J. Vermaseren, Études Préliminaires aux Religions Orientales dans l'Empire Roman 92 [Leiden, The Netherlands: E. J. Brill, 1982]) describes from the centuries previous to this. But no, there is no indication that Antipas is interested in collecting autonomous agents like John to assist him in some way. He has John locked up because he wants John dead, though he can't manage to do that himself. See also David Alan Black ("The Text of Mk 6:20," *New Testament Studies* 34 [1988]: 141-45) for discussion of the adverb πολλὰ linked with participle ἀκούσας, on the basis of Mark's use of πολλὰ. The translation then is a simple, "he doubted."

14. It is more likely that γενέσια means "birthday" and not "accession day," as is suggested in Hoehner, *Herod Antipas*, 160 n.5. Schürer already holds this view in *History of the Jewish People*, 1:346 n.26. This is not just *any* birthday, like one in a papyrus letter discussed by Adolf Deissmann (*Light from the Ancient East*, 4th ed., trans. Lionel R. M. Strachan [London: Hodder & Stoughton, 1922], 184); this is the birthday of a minor aspirant. For birthdays and anniversaries in the military see John Hegeland, "Roman Army Religion," *Aufstieg und Niedergang der römischen Welt* ii/16.2 (1978): 1481-84.

15. Ehrenberg and Jones, *Documents Illustrating the Reigns of Augustus and Tiberius*, §98. This event is the occasion of a famous use of εὐαγγελίον. In this inscription, the term means the "proclamation" of the birthday celebration as a readjustment of sacred calendars.

16. For the birthday of Lysimachos see *Orientalis Graeci Inscriptiones Selectae*, ed. W. Dittenberger (Leipzig, Germany, 1903-1905), §11. For translation see Stanley M. Burnstein (*The Hellenistic Age from the Battle of Ipsos to the Death of Kleopatra VII*, Translated Documents of Greece and Rome 3 [Cambridge: Cambridge University Press, 1985], §10): "And also sacrifices shall be made each year by all the priests and priestesses throughout the city and all the citizens shall wear wreaths, and both the priests and the board of magistrates shall conduct a procession with all the citizens on the birthday of King Lysimachos." Christian Habicht (*Gottmenschentum und griechische Städte*, 2d rev. ed., Zetemata 14 [München: Verlag C. H. Beck, 1970], 38-39) describes yearly sacrifices and coronation processions attendant to this celebration. On Persian customs see Schürer (*History of the Jewish People*, 1:3476 n.26) for literary and papyri sources for birthdays of notables. For the decree at Canopus see Dittenberger, *Orientalis Graeci Inscriptiones Selectae*, §56.5-6. For the Antiochus I Commagene decree, see Dittenberger, *Orientalis Graeci Inscriptiones Selectae*, §383; Burnstein (*Hellenistic Age*, §48) translates: "With regard to the permanence of religious rites, suitable arrangements I made in order that together with the sacrifices which the ancient and common law required also new festivals for the worship of the gods and our honors will be celebrated by all the inhabitants of my kingdom. For my body's birthday, Audnaios the sixteenth, and for my coronation. . . . In the future, I have ordered that each month one (day) equivalent to the aforementioned—for my birthday the sixteenth and for my assumption of the diadem the tenth—shall always be honored by the priests." Similar also were the birthday celebrations for Ptolemy V, for which celebration instructions are given in the last lines of the Rosetta Stone (Burnstein, *Hellenistic Age*, §103). Birthday celebrations for this dynastic founder were to continue forever. This inscription begins with an emphasis on the receipt by Ptolemy V of the βασιλεία from his father. Kingship, when conceived as inheritance, is propagated as an unavoidable historical advance. The apocryphal *Letter of Solomon* reported in Eupolemus, written with a thorough Egyptian political milieu in mind and addressed to a "Vaphres the βασιλεύς of Egypt," emphasizes Solomon's receipt of the βασιλεία from his father David and, then, his subsequent cultic license to build a temple and initiate cult proceedings there; see Carl R. Halladay, *Fragments from Hellenistic Jewish Authors* 1: *Historians*, Texts and Translations 20; Pseudepigrapha Series 10 (Chico, Calif.: Scholars Press, 1983), 119 l.10.

17. The "handshake" (δεξίωσις) is discussed in Jacques Duchesne-Guillemin, "Iran and Greece in Commagene," in *Études Mithriaques: Actes du 2e Congress International, Téhéran*, ed. Jacques Duchesne-Guillemin, Acta Iranica 17 (Tehran-Leiden, 1978), 187-99. On multiple references in divine names see the astrological material in Vettius Valens 1.22, his Περὶ σχηματισμῶν κατὰ πλείους, which contains thirty-one similar combinations of named divine entities (technically

known as Πλείων). Rome had begun to move its direct rule farther east: to Palmyra at the time of Tiberias, to Commagene on the Euphrates by 72 C.E., to the kingdom of Agrippa II by the early 90s C.E., and to the kingdom of Nabataea (especially Petra) at its defeat in 106 C.E.; see Fergus Millar, "Empire, Community and Culture in the Roman Near East: Greeks, Syrians, Jews and Arabs," *Journal of Jewish Studies* 38 (1987): 146.

18. Hugh J. Mason, *Greek Terms for Roman Institutions: A Lexicon and Analysis*, American Studies in Papyrology 13 (Toronto: Hakkert, 1974), s.v. μέγιστος (= [*pontifex*] *maximus* or simply *princeps viri*); Χιλίαρχος (= *tribunus militum*); Πρῶτος (= *princeps senatus*; *ordinarius*; [*amicus*] *primae admissionis*; [*centurio*] *prior*). According to Séan Freyne (*Galilee from Alexander the Great to Hadrian, 323 B.C.E. to 135 C.E.: A Study in Second Temple Judaism*. University of Notre Dame Center for the Study of Judaism and Christianity Series 5 [South Bend, Ind.: University of Notre Dame, 1980], 270), these are all designations for bureaucrats within the administration of Antipas.

19. Lysimachus is the same king who in 286 B.C.E. initiated birthday celebrations in his own honor. When pleased with his performance, Lysimachus asked Philippides, τίνος σοι τῶν ἐμῶν μεταδῶ (which one of my possession may I share with you?). The just answer of the comic poet is, μόνον ὦ βασιλεῦ μὴ τῶν ἀπορρήτων (anything, O king, except your secrets); see Plutarch, *De curiositate* 517B; reported with slightly different wording in *De garrulitate* 508C. Philippides had a reputation for righteous actions, as he once made fun of the self-promotion of Demetrius Poliorcedes; see Plutarch, *Demetrius* 11-12. Eunapius (*Vitae Philosopharum* 455) considered the reign of Severus particularly fortunate because of the number of virtuous philosophers during that time (and, no doubt from another perspective, the number of expert sophists). On Hermocrates see Philostratus, *Vita sophistarum* 611: "[Hermocrates responded], 'Crowns and immunities and meals at the public expense, and the consular purple and the high-priesthood our great-grandfather bequeathed to his descendants. Why then should I ask from you today what I have so long possessed? However, I have been ordered by Asclepius at Pergamum to eat partridge stuffed with frankincense, and this seasoning is now so scarce in our country that we have to use barley meal and laurel leaves for incense to the gods. I therefore ask for fifty talents' worth of frankincense, that I may treat the gods properly and get proper treatment myself.' Then the Emperor gave him the frankincense with approving words, and said that he blushed for shame at having been asked for so trifling a gift" (trans. Wilmer C. Wright, *Philostratus and Eunapius: The Lives of the Sophists*, Loeb Classical Library [Cambridge, Mass.: Harvard University Press, 1961], 277).

20. Mark vividly uses terminology for the sudden turn of events in this passage: εὐθὺς μετὰ σπουδῆς . . . ἐξαυτῆς [immediately with vigor . . . quickly].

21. Ps.-Philo, *Liber Antiquitatum Biblicarum* 39:11; trans. D. J. Harrington in *The Old Testament Pseudepigrapha*, ed. James Charlesworth (Garden City, N.Y.: Doubleday, 1983), 2:353.

22. Plutarch, *Quaestiones Graecae* 299C-D. This account of Poemander is analyzed by Ken Dowden (*Death and the Maiden: Girls' Initiation Rites in Greek Mythology* [London: Routledge, 1989], 59-60) in light of the Iphigenia pattern ("Aulis Myth"), which follows a common outline: (1) *A man*, conceivably the temple founder . . . (2) (shot a deer and thereby) *angered a divinity* (Artemis), (3) *who sent tribulation* (plague and/or famine) (4) *so that a prophet pronounced that the man must sacrifice his daughter to the divinity* (Artemis). The pattern includes an unintentional or rash action that has horrendous results of impurity and unfathomable suffering.

23. Trans. Naphtali Lewis and Reinhold Meyer, *Roman Civilization: Sourcebook II: The Empire* (New York: Columbia University Press, 1955), 549.

24. Thomas Wiedemann, *Emperors and Gladiators* (London: Routledge, 1992), 69. The whole section of Wiedemann's book titled "Executing Criminals" (pp. 68-97) is of relevance here, referring to many episodes of crucifixion and death by wild beasts, burning, or torture, as well as beheadings and distinctly Roman comments about the difference between painful and swift capital punishment.

25. On the rending of flesh, see Margaret Visser, "Worship Your Enemies: Aspects of the Cult of Heroes in Ancient Greece," *Harvard Theological Review* 75 (1982): 409. For Scythian beheading of enemies with subsequent posting of the head on a pole above the victor's home as an apotropaic measure, see Herodotus 4.103. For Celtic treasuring of the heads of enemies, sometimes embalming them and keeping them in special chests, see Diodorus 5.29.4.

26. *De Viris Illustribus* 72: "After the death of Crassus, Pompey ordered Caesar to disband his army, but was driven from the city when Caesar approached prepared for battle. Defeated at Pharalia, he fled to Ptolemy at Alexandria. Septimius, an officer of Ptolemy, stabbed Pompey in the side with a sword in the sight of Pompey's wife and children. The head was cut from his lifeless body; such an action had been unknown before this time [*quod usque ad ea tempora fuerat ignoratum*]. The rest of the body, thrown into the Nile and burned on a funeral pile by Servius Codrus, was buried in a tomb with this inscription: Here lies Pompey the Great. Pompey's head, wrapped with an Egyptian covering, was presented along with a ring to Caesar by Achillas, an attendant of Ptolemy. Caesar could not keep back tears, and he took care that the head was burned with many very costly perfumes" (trans. Walter K. Sherwin, *Deeds of Famous Men [De Viris Illustribus]* [Norman: University of Oklahoma Press, 1973], 179-81.

27. One story concerns how Tarquinius Superbus had hung on crosses the cadavers of men whom he killed because they disobeyed his orders. According to another account, the men were dead because they killed themselves *en masse*. These tales are handed down through the *Annals* of Cassius Hemina and appear in Servius' commentary on the *Aeneid* as well as in Pliny (*Natural History* 36.15.107). In either story, the crucifixions are an act of vengeance. The account of the crucified men as suicides displays the belief that crucifixion would ward off the vengeance inherent in these suicides. The suicides are presented quite explicitly as acts of retaliation against the suiciders' enemy, Tarquinius Superbus.

For details see Yolande Grisé, "Pourquoi 'retuer' un mort? Un cas de suicide dans la Rome royale," in *Mélanges d'Études anciennes offerts à Maurice Lebel*, ed. Jean-Benoît Caron, Michel Fortin, and Gilles Maloney (St.-Jean-Chrysostôme, Québec: Les Éditions du Sphinx, 1980), 267-81.

28. Herodotus (9.78-90) reports that general Pausanias described it as a typical barbarian atrocity avoided by Greeks as a form of legal punishment. Plutarch (*Pericles* 28.2-3) defends the reputation of the Athenian statesman, saying that never had he ever consented to the deaths of captured Samians by having had them hit on the head. Stories about King Pyrrhus of Epirus vary. The blow came either by a roof tile thrown down on him by a woman, or by the sword of a soldier of Antigonos, who lopped off his head in one fell swoop. Either way, an impurity is produced in so doing; see Visser, "Worship Your Enemy," 407. In the story about the roof tile, the outcome is that an oracular response from the gods tells the Argives to build a sanctuary to Demeter on the spot where Pyrrhus fell (Pausanias 1.14.7-8). Plutarch (*Pyrrhus* 34) mentions that after he was beheaded by the soldier Zopyrus (who did a bad job at it, needing to hack Pyrrhus' neck and ligaments to pieces in order to get the head separated from the body), the son of Antigonos (Alcyoneus) came running up, recognizes the face on the decapitated head, takes it to his father, and throws it before his father's feet. Antigonos angrily receives the head from his son and, upset, chases his son from his presence by beating him with his royal scepter. Then, in good Greek fashion, he treats properly all the remains of Pyrrhus. One version of the story of Orpheus' decapitation had it that, in full Dionysian frenzy, the Maenads had ripped his head right off his body. Together with his lyre, the head then floated across the sea to Lesbos, was found by a fisherman, and was placed in an underground cave at Antissa; see Walter Burkert, *Homo Necans:The Anthropology of Ancient Greek Sacrificial Ritual and Myth*, trans. Peter Bing (Berkeley: University of California Press, 1983), 202. On the relationship of Maenads to cultic acts σπάραγμα and ὠμοφάγια, see Eric R. Dodds, *The Greeks and the Irrational* Sather Classical Lectures 25 (Berkeley: University of California Press, 1951), 270-80. For oracles from a severed head, see Jan N. Bremmer, *The Early Greek Concept of the Soul* (Princeton, N.J.: Princeton University Press, 1993 [1987]), 46-47.

9

Mark 6:32-44:
Temporary Largesse in the Desert

Codex Alexandrinus labels its capitulation of this account, Περὶ τῶν πέντε ἄρτων, emphasizing the little that, multiplied, becomes huge.[1] Five verses of transition (6:30-34) prepare for the inclusion of this story about a wilderness feast of abundant food. Mark 6:30-31 recapitulates and concludes the account of the followers of Jesus being "sent." The gathering of these "apostles" to Jesus in the ἔρημος (desert) after their wandering (6:30) completes a trajectory that shows the activity of Jesus and his disciples moving from πατρίς to οἰκία to ἔρημος (fatherland to home to desert), or from what is ἥμερος (civilized) to what is θηριώδης (wild).[2] The δώδεκα once sent (ἀποστέλλω) are here again with Jesus and called ἀπόστολλοι (apostles, 6:30).[3] Once given instruction by Jesus (παρήγγειλεν), they now report back (ἀπήγγειλαν) to him their activities, a time of summary review (πάντα ὅσα ἐποίησαν καὶ ὅσα ἐδίδαξαν). Mark also notes the way in which Jesus tends to conduct his affairs with his followers: κατ᾽ ἰδίαν (privately). They all rest a little (ὀλίγον), for many (πολλοί) have surrounded them who οὐδὲ φαγεῖν εὐκαίρουν (they did not have opportunity to eat), pictured as ceaselessly moving (ἦσαν γὰρ οἱ ἐρχόμενοι καὶ ὑπάγοντες πολλοί [there were many, coming and going]). Immediately after this, 6:32-33 in its summation repeats words and phrases from the previous two verses (κατ᾽ ἰδίαν [privately], εἰς ἔρημον τόπον [in a desert place], ὑπάγοντες/ὑπάγοντας, πολλοί [many coming, going])[4]. The briefest of boat rides is mentioned (6:32). Sanae Masuda correctly detects abundant Markan redaction throughout this transition.[5]

Mark 6:32-33 is a quick narrative bridge that continues a complex line of action that starts in 6:1. It includes the relationship of Jesus to cultural institutions of family lineage (πατρις), the relationship of Jesus to his disciples while moving from ἥμερος (civilization) to ἔρημος

225

(wilderness), the account of Antipas and John with its foolish king (βασιλεύς) and the threat of retaliation, and a recapitulation of Jesus with his disciples amid many people in ceaseless motion. There is a double reaffirmation (6:31, 32) that what is to happen next takes place specifically in the ἔρημος. What follows focuses expressly on leadership (kingship) and εὐεργεσία (benefaction),[6] but also more. An omission in the narrative is conspicuous and a key to the interpretation of this account. That is, it describes *no celebration* of a capable or messianic king who has finally arrived and who will hear and grant benefactions (ἐπαγγελία or ὑποσχέσις, promises or pollicitations). The narrative does not include any honoring of such a king's φιλοδοξία (love of glory) or of his provision of marvelous abundance.[7] But for one notable exception, there is not present here usual contemporary terminology for statements about and instructions for benefaction.[8] Instead, the entire scene ends when Jesus εὐθύς (immediately) sends his disciples on a boat trip εἰς τὸ πέραν (across) while he goes up into a mountain (6:45). Mark describes no acclamation for a benefaction of largesse. It is not even evident that Jesus in any way at first intends to feed the multitudes himself, or that the multitudes suspect that, when sated, Jesus has fed them. Consequently, it remains uncertain just what the eating in the wilderness inaugurates,[9] or ends, or whether it does either. There is so much food, so little public notice of its provider, and so little indication that a gift is bestowed, or even what such a gift might signify.

Leadership is accented in this story by a proverbial similitude in 6:34, sometimes attributed to Numbers 27:17: ἐσπλαγχνίσθη ἐπ᾽ αὐτούς ὅτι ἦσαν ὡς πρόβατα μὴ ἔχοντα ποιμένα (he had compassion on them, since they were like sheep without a shepherd).[10] The verb σπλαγχνίζομαι is rare outside of scriptural traditions, the substantive σπλάγχνον instead being somewhat more common.[11] This reflection about sheep in Mark 6:34 is not necessarily a citation of scripture, yet the possibility that it is piques a reader's interest. In scripture, YHWH is sometimes described literally as a shepherd (Genesis 48:15, 49:24; Psalm 23:1, 80:1) or pictured by analogy as such (Psalm 68:7, 23:3; Isaiah 40:11, 49:10; Jeremiah 50:19; Ezekiel 34). In its various forms, it is not an uncommon scriptural theme. A king imagined as a shepherd was, at the time of the Gospel of Mark, a well-known political and literary convention.[12]

Specific scriptural references to God as a shepherd do not always combine with them specific references to God as a king. References that do combine them are more common in later texts, where benefaction is not so much attributed to God as to God's Messiah. An eschatological depiction of a future messiah who will be a shepherd of the people of the Lord occurs in 4Q521 1.ii.1-14, a text worth quoting at some length.

> He will not turn aside from the Commandments of the holy Ones. (3) Take strength in His service, (you) who seek the Lord. (4) Shall you not find the Lord in this, all you who wait patiently in your hearts? (5) For the Lord will visit the Pious Ones (*Hasidim*) and the Righteous (*Zaddakim*) will He call by name. (6) Over the Meek will His Spirit hover, and the Faithful will He restore by His power. (7) He shall glorify the Pious Ones (*Hasidim*) on the Throne of the Eternal Kingdom. (8) He shall release the captives, make the blind see, raise up the do[wntrodden.] (9) For[ev]er will I cling [to Him . . .], and [I will trust] in His Piety (*Hesed*), (10) and [His] Goo[dness . . .] of Holiness will not delay. . . . (11) And as for the wonders that are not the work of the Lord, when He . . . (12) then He will heal the sick, resurrect the dead, and to the Meek announce glad tidings. (13) . . . He will lead (*ynhl*) the [Holy Ones; He will shepherd (*yr`h*) [th]em.[13]

The messiah is to rule, having a throne and an eternal kingdom. The *adventus* of this anointed person and the subsequent, fortuitous cascade of eschatological events would display a cosmological power. The chthonic, marvelous, and fearful entities *mqrwnê mym wnhlîm* (fountains of water and the rivers) would witness the miraculous new dispensation of this messiah in the world (4Q521 5.3). The "Spirit of God" would "hover" over the people instead of over the waters.[14] Inclusion in this text of the poor, the captives, the blind, the disabled, the wounded, the dead, and the preaching of good news to the poor point to eschatological renewal as described in Isaiah 35:3-6 and 61:1-4. Messianic justice is metaphorically linked to re-creation and a cosmic new First Day of creation. The messiah as a shepherd emerges out of these metaphors, within this traditional symbolic field of eschatological renewal. As a pastoral metaphor from Qumran, it has been rightly compared to Isaiah 49:8-12 and Ezekiel 34:23.[15]

Isaiah 49 speaks of YHWH himself answering his people. It is he who established the land, he who says to prisoners, "Come out," he who says to those in darkness, "Show yourselves," he who feeds the people "along the ways," and he who gives to them the "bare heights" for their "pastures." Ezekiel 34:23 promises, "I will set up over them one shepherd, my servant David, and he shall feed them: he shall feed them and be their shepherd. And I, the Lord, will be their God, and my servant David shall be prince among them; I, the Lord, have spoken" (NRSV). Comparison of lines from 4Q521 to Ezekiel 34 raises numerous general questions about messianic expectations, and about the exact nature of the messianic shepherd in 4Q521. Metaphors of the shepherd and of the people as a flock that appear in these sources had long been proverbial, expressing a variety of common theological ideas and expectations. How such a proverbial idea is presented in any given text is the more accessible subject for interpretation. The Greek translation of Ezekiel 34:11-16 depicts YHWH specifically providing voμή (pasture). The wording of the text raises questions of aretalogy and the broad ancient understanding of divine powers who, in general, were thought to be shepherds. What follows is an oracle of eschatological fulfillment.

> For thus says the Lord God: I myself will search for my sheep and will seek them out. As shepherds seek out their flocks when they are among their scattered sheep, so I will seek out my sheep. I will rescue them from all the places to which they have been scattered on a day of clouds and thick darkness. I will bring them out from the peoples and gather them from the countries, and will bring them into their own land; and I will feed them on the mountains of Israel, by the watercourses, and in all the inhabited parts of the land. I will feed them with good pasture (ἀγαθή), and the mountain heights of Israel shall be their pasture (μάνδρα);[16] there they shall lie down in good grazing land, and they shall feed on rich pasture (νομὴ ἀγαθή) on the mountains of Israel. *I myself will be the shepherd of my sheep, and I will make them lie down, says the Lord God*[17]. I will seek the lost, and I will bind up the injured, and I will strengthen the weak, but the fat and the strong I will destroy. I will feed them with justice (NRSV).

Use of the word voμή in the Greek translation is notable, especially in light of the additional aretalogical statement found only in the LXX version Ezekiel 34:15: ἐγὼ εἰμι κύριος (I am the Lord). To rephrase these elements in other terms, the κύριος is νόμιος (Lord is shepherd).

The kingly nature of the shepherding messiah in 4Q521 may have implications for the royal house of David, if Ezekiel 34 influences 4Q521. Generally, the substance of the eschatological dispensation under the possibly Davidic, kingly messiah is to be future fullness and well-being. It is to be miraculous in sustenance, and it is to come directly from God, as an intervention in the universe that in 4Q521 was pictured as a kind of re-creation.[18] Although it is a unique text spared from oblivion by the caves at Qumran, 4Q521 contains eschatological themes that were widespread, having enjoyed a diverse development in different places.

They appear in Babylonian texts about the *Nisan* renewal festival. In relation to that festival, an Akkadian festival ritual text describes Beltiya, the consort of Bel, as she "who brings complaints, who defends, who impoverishes the rich, who causes the poor to become wealthy, who fells the enemy who does not fear her divinity, who releases the prisoner, grasps the hand of the fallen."[19] Re-creation could be centered on the temple and care of the temple, or on the coming of a New Year or New Age. It ever is a divine action and is miraculous, full of plentitude and leisure and, in some cases, erotic satiation. It is difficult to overestimate how far these ideas permeate ancient religious thought in every direction, in whatever particular form they assume.[20]

These were the powers of deities. Near Eastern kings themselves, messiah or not, had also long held such abilities. The theme of such salvific abilities was linked to the metaphor of a fruitful tree. Such a "Tree of Life" has its companion symbol in the "Water of Life," and in one Akkadian text is called the *kiškanu* tree. It is described as having the appearance of lapis lazuli and is situated on top of the Deep (*Apsu*). A king might not only have been considered a guardian of such a tree and water, but also one who possesses them. In one iconographic scene, Gudea king of Lagash holds the same vase of abundance as that held by the god Enki. The Sumerian King Šulgi is called "a datepalm planted by the waterditch" and "a cedar rooted by abundant water" (see appendix I, "Tree and Water"). The idea of "Water of Life" is related also to an "Elixir of Life," both in turn related to the color white (λευκός) or to white color found in the glistening quality of an oiled stone. Günther Zuntz finds these latter ideas in the way the Orphic Golden Tablets use ὕδωρ (water) and relate it to the Lake of Remembrance (Μνημοσύνη).[21]

Such royal and messianic imagery was remarkably persistent, making its way everywhere, especially into Jewish and early Christian currents.[22] A Thanksgiving hymn from Qumran offers praise in just these terms.

> Thy righteousness is established forever . . . I praise Thee, O Lord, for Thou placest me by a source of flowing streams in a dry ground and a spring of water in a parched land and a drink for the garden . . . Thou settest in the desert the planting of the cypress and the plane tree together with the larch for Thy glory; trees of life on the mysterious fountain concealed amongst all the trees by the water. And they shall be for the purpose of making the sprout to bud for a perpetual plantation.[23]

The last lines of this hymn are much like a paradise tradition that Holger Thesleff identifies in a variety of Greek literary sources. He calls one variant of this tradition the "Eleusinian-type." Its notion of paradise is

> flowering meadow, or grass, on the banks of the Oceanus river, in the
> land of the setting sun, inhabited by those chosen by the gods, to spend
> an everlasting life of bliss. That this place is thought to be located on
> the western extremes of the earth is evident from many facts, such as the
> presence of Zephyr (the western wind), which usually brings fine
> weather and which here acts as a sort of breeze.[24]

We have already encountered this idea of utopia and how it influenced an
account in Plutarch's *Sertorius*, which describes a unique journey to the
Isles of the Blessed as a trip to a place of moderate rainfall, gentle
breezes, healthful air, little seasonal change, fertile soil, abundant crops,
and little need for agricultural toil.[25]

Desire for abundance, whether utopian or eschatological or seasonal
in nature, meant desire for nearness and accessibility to material provision. Both the fear resulting from proximity to divine power and the
uncertainty of maintaining divine favor are important elements of the
anomalous frightful. When a human is thought to be the bearer of divine
power, then proximity and accessibility are especially paramount. A main
feature of Near Eastern scenes of the presentation of the king to his
people, the king's *availability*, is to be found also among depictions of
Hellenistic kings and Roman emperors. The *Ara Pacis* of Augustus, a
unique monument celebrating and depicting the new *imperium* of Rome
and its leading man, contains a powerful and ideal scene of the king's
ἀπάντησις (public presentation).[26] Like the sons of Asclepius who save
those in trouble, a good king, because he is accessible, saves from peril
those who come before him.[27] Augustus himself was worshiped within
this framework. He became *Aeternitas Augustus*, an ever-present
benefactor.[28] The *Res Gestae Divi Augusti* incorporate all of this, even
reviewing the many different sacred roles that Augustus had filled, roles
that outline his presence and benefaction in almost every domain of
human affairs.[29] The *adventus* of a benefactor like this emperor became
the vehicle of administrative action, if not also the possibility of utopian
bliss. Claudius Mamertinus later (1 January 362 C.E.) describes such an
event in the winter of 290/291 C.E.

> All the fields were filled with crowds not only of men rushing to see,
> but with herds of beasts leaving their remote pastures and woods; the
> peasants vied with each other in reporting what they had seen to all the
> villages. Altars were lit, incense thrown on, libations poured, sacrificial

victims slain.[30]

The *adventus* of this tetrarch or emperor occurs with similar motifs as those found earlier in Mark 6:32-33, including the crowds, the fields (open spaces), and rumors abounding through the villages.

The "Feeding of Five Thousand" should be understood within this entire context of eschatological renewal, shepherding benefactors, and fresh availability of access to divine favor. Others have noted this already, although they often add other, dubious observations. The view that this feeding is a eucharistic, theological narrative is common, and often based on comparisons of Mark 6 to John 6; it has been critically examined by G. H. Boobyer.[31] Such a view understands the feeding as an eschatological, messianic, and divine favor, at the very least an indication of some sort of soteriological inauguration. Such themes existed in a variety of forms and were quite persistent and popular throughout many ancient cultures. Robert M. Grant recognized these by comparing both the miraculous feedings and parables of amazing fertility to Greek and Roman theories of the Golden Age.[32] Richard I. Pervo refined the comparisons further.[33] But even with this material in hand, the problem in Mark is that, given the contextual potential for symbolism of abundance, messianic lordship, eschatological satiation, or the Golden Age, Mark does not properly report a benefaction that would have been recognized as such.

In Mark, when the disciples recognize the late hour in the wilderness with the ceaselessly moving crowd, they recommend to Jesus that he dismiss the crowd into areas where they might purchase food. By this report, they do not have in mind a εὐεργεσία or *largesse*. But apparently, neither did Jesus intend that for himself, for he tells the disciples, Δότε αὐτοῖς ὑμεῖς φαγεῖν (You give them something to eat, 6:37). It happens that distribution of free bread was one of the best-known institutions of Hellenistic cities.[34] Even so, the Markan story does not indicate that Jesus wants to draw attention to himself by feeding the multitude or to show himself a benefactor in any way. Δότε (give) is a *hapax legomenon* here in Mark. It is the exact form of δίδωμι (give) that appears in numerous Greek inscriptions of benefaction, largesse, and festive distributions of food.[35] It is the disciples who are being asked to become benefactors. To his instruction, they reply with a brief review of the economic problem involved with the purchase of such a largesse, speaking about the amount of δηναρίαι (*denarius*) needed. On his questioning, they reveal to him that they have but five loaves (ἄρτοι) and two fish (ἰχθύες).

This description of the food available is reminiscent of a basic menu, elsewhere summarized as ἄρτος, οἶνος, and ὄψον (bread, wine, and prepared food [protein]), mentioned in a variety of literary references.[36] It is practical food, representative in Mark of the basic need for sustenance. Symbols of necessary sustenance like ἄρτος and ἰχθύς appear elsewhere. Artistic depictions of Greek banquet scenes show round objects, or ἄρτοι. Such scenes spread throughout the Hellenistic world and were used in a variety of symbolic illustrations.[37] Bread also represents economic conditions in general, which throughout the Empire at this time oscillated from abundance to dearth of food.[38] Fear of food shortage was ever present, and Juvenal (*Satires* 10.78-81) jokes that people of the Empire cared only for bread and spectacles. Pervo outlines how social divisions created unequal food availability, with the rich always having better access to food than the poor.[39] Yet in Mark there is no commentary on contemporary economic conditions. Jesus does not propose that he become a benefactor, even to those who are poor. The disciples suppose that the crowds are able to shop and buy what they need, so the crowds are not indigent. Jesus then has the disciples organize the crowd to recline for a meal. The setting is rich in abundance (συμπόσια συμπόσια ἐπὶ τῷ χλωρῷ χόρτῳ), a special gathering within a robust and verdant field, or an oasis. On blessing the bread and breaking it for distribution, Jesus gives it to his disciples, who pass out pieces of bread and bits of fish so that everyone eats until sated. The opportunity for a possible public acknowledgment of the benefaction particularly from Jesus is lost. Instead, his disciples perform the action. Nobody other than the disciples seems to know that Jesus is linked to the food.

The account in Mark *could*, deliberately, have compared Jesus, the one capable of shepherding the people who were without a shepherd, to Antipas, the foolish king and bad shepherd. It *could*, deliberately, have shown Jesus to be a benefactor, or at least it *could* have identified him publicly as a source of divine benefaction.[40] It does none of these things. Here we have a nuanced facet of the anomalous frightful, uncertainty pertaining to a divine grant of the necessities of life. In this story Jesus himself creates the uncertainty, since he does not act according to expectations. Given the context of abundance, eschatological renewal, and expectations for full stomachs, why is it that Jesus does not step into the public eye as a σωτήρ (savior)? Why is the benefaction so occluded? Turning five loaves and two fish into a meal for five thousand, with twelve baskets of bread and fish left over as πληρώματα (full measures), seems important, but for what? The story ends with a statement about the amount of abundance accomplished: the size of the largesse. The previous sentence places a mysterious twist on of all this, stating how five loaves became an even-numbered δώδεκα (twelve), or perhaps an ἄρτιον πλήρωμα (even-numbered fullness). The power of Jesus over matters of eschatological fullness and εὐεργεσία (benefaction) appears to be trivial compared to some other, hidden meaning. Yet what is this meaning? We are never told. Standard expectations for food are met, but the public aspect of benefaction is sidestepped. In so reporting, the narrative leaves the reader uncertain about this new meaning of divine favor, and therefore anomaly again pervades the narrative.

Notes

1. Henry Barclay Swete, *The Gospel According to Saint Mark: The Greek Text with Introduction, Notes and Indices*(London: Macmillan, 1898), xlviii.
2. Mark never makes a play on ἔρημος (wild) and ἥμερος (wilderness); yet it should be kept in mind, an apposite opposition that a reader might easily have understood. Similarly, we may see an unstated but possible link of ἄρτος (bread) to ἄρτιος (complete, full).
3. Ernst Bammel ("The Feeding of the Multitude," in *Jesus and the Politics of His Day*, ed. Ernst Bammel and C. F. D. Moule [Cambridge: Cambridge University Press, 1984], 212) discusses the shifting terminology in Mark for the followers of Jesus: μαθηταί, ἀπόστολοι, δώδεκα. Bammel considers the terminology in 6:30 (ἀπόστολοι) intrusive, a poor attempt by the redactor to fashion a link with 6:7 (linking δώδεκα to ἀποστέλλειν). Mark 6:7 is the last account of Jesus and the disciples before the long narrative about Antipas and John.
4. These are terms common elsewhere in Mark: κατ᾽ ἰδίαν in 4:34, 7:33, 9:2, 9:38, 13:3; εἰς ἔρημον τόπον in 1:35, 1:45; ὑπάγοντες/ὑπάγοντας (and variants) in 1:44, 2:11, 5:19, 5:34, 6:38, 7:29, 8:33, 10:21, 10:53, 11:2, 14:13, 14:21; πολλοί in numerous places.
5. Sanae Masuda, "The Good News of the Miracle of the Bread: The Tradition and Its Markan Redaction," *New Testament Studies* 28 (1988): 191-219.
6. Paul Veyne (*Bread and Circuses: Historical Sociology and Political Pluralism*, abridged ed., trans. Brian Pearce [London: Allen Lane/Penguin Press, 1990], 85) writes that "Euergetism is a union of three 'themes'—patronage; the more or less symbolic *largesses* that politicians confer out of their own pockets, by virtue of their office (*ob honorem*); and funerary liberalities and foundations. . . . Euergetism is manifested in the form of pious donations or foundations, choergic monuments in which a liturgist becomes a patron in order to express and perpetuate his glory in a building, public subscriptions (ἐπίδοσις) and public promises of *largesses*, called pollicitations, and the generosity shown by

magistrates who meet the expenses of their offices out of their own pockets, or offer liberalities in honour of the function they have assumed." The hymns of Isidorus offer a routine description of Isis: ζωῆς εὑρέτρια πάσης. This description is related to Isis as εὑεργέτεια καρπῶν, one of the first Greek epithets for Isis. The sophistic play on themes here is between Food-Provider and Founder-of-Culture; see Vera F. Vanderlip, *The Four Greek Hymns of Isidorus and the Cult of Isis*, American Studies in Papyrology 12 (Toronto: A. M. Hakkert, 1972), 38. For the phrase τὸ μέγεθος τῆς σῆς εὑεργετείας (the bounty of your benefaction) describing Isis, see lines 3-4 of the aretalogy published in Yves Grandjean, *Une nouvelle arétologie d'Isis à Maronée*, Études préliminaires aux religions orientales dans l'Empire Roman 49 (Leiden, The Netherlands: E. J. Brill, 1975), 17. Iconography of the Isis-Osiris-Harpocrates family system often includes symbols of εὑεργετείας, primarily a horn of abundance held in the left hand; see Vincent Tran Tam Tinh, "Etat des études iconographiques relatives à Isis, Sérapis et Sunnaoi Theoi," *Aufstieg und Niedergang der römischen Welt* ii/17.3 (1979): 1710-38. Benefit (εὑεργέτεια) and salvation (βοήθεια) were hallmarks of any theory of divine intervention, even appearing in Euhemerist interpretation; see Diodorus Siculus 6.6.1 on a Euhemerist view of Castor and Pollux, their campaign with the Argonauts, and their appearance as ἐπιφανεῖς βοηθοί (manifesting, helping deities). Judged by such valor, they are construed "sons of Zeus."

7. Klaus Bringmann, "The King as Benefactor: Some Remarks on the Ideal Kingship in the Age of Hellenism," in *Images and Ideologies: Self-Definition in the Hellenistic World*, ed. Anthony Bulloch, Erich S. Gruen, A. A. Long, and Andrew Stewart; Hellenistic Culture and Society 12 (Berkeley: University of California Press, 1993), 15. Aristotle (*Rhetoric* 1361a28) described an expected and usual procedure of acclamation: the ὁ δυνάμενος εὑεργετεῖν (the one who is able to supply benefactions) is worthy of τιμή (honor). For the use of φιλοδοξία (fondness of giving) to describe the virtue of a civic benefactor from Kyme in the first century B.C.E., see S. R. Llewelyn and R. A Kearsley, *New Documents Illustrating Early Christianity, 7: A Review of the Greek Inscriptions and Papyri Published in 1982-83* (Macquarie University, N.S.W.: Ancient History Documentary Research Centre, 1994), §10.10.

8. Klaus Bringmann and Hans von Steuben, *Schenkungen hellenistischer Herrscher an griechische Städte und Heiligtümer* 1: *Zeugnisse und Kommentare* (Berlin: Akademie Verlag, 1995), 3: ἀνατιθέναι, διδόναι, ἐπιδιδόναι, καταδιδόναι, δωρεῖσθαι, χαρίζεσθαι, ἐπαγγέλλειν, or ὑπισχεῖσθαι (dedicate, give, contribute as a benevolence, assign to, bestow gifts, extend grace, make promises, commit by promising). Their text number 284 (E 1) records a public benefaction for Eirenias, who received from King Eumenes II Soter a great gift that he then took back to his city. Apparently, Eirenias had talked Eumenes into supporting a local event: ". . . he, having spoken with all zeal and having inspired him to increase what had been promised (κατὰ τὴν ἐπαγγελίαν) and to assume the costs (δαπάνας) of the completion of the honors (τιμῶν) himself so that the People's gratitude toward its benefactors (εἰς τοὺς εὑεργέτας) might be made manifest (εὑχαριστίαν φανεράν) to all and that the supplies for what had been specified be from the resources of

the king" (trans. Stanley M. Burnstein, *The Hellenistic Age from the Battle of Ipsos to the Death of Kleopatra VII*, Translated Documents of Greece and Rome 3 [Cambridge: Cambridge University Press, 1985], §40.

9. Bammel ("Feeding of the Multitude," 238) suggested about abundant feeding that "the event must have made its impression on those who took part. The masses follow Jesus. . . . Indeed, the Feeding could be taken as the beginning of the revival of the wondrous events of the desert time, as part of a sequence of actions which would culminate in 'salvation'." Bammel recognized that in the traditions, Jesus withdraws after the feeding instead of pushing forward into messianic fulfilment. He suggested that the withdrawal of Jesus dashed the "popular eschatology" of the crowds.

10. Numbers 27:17 LXX reads ὡσεὶ πρόβατα οἷς οὐκ ἔστιν ποιμήν (as a flock for whom there is no shepherd). This is repeated in 2 Chronicles 18:16, with only slight variation in the LXX: ὡς πρόβατα οἷς οὐκ ἔστιν ποιμήν. The second part of the Greek phrase in Mark 6:34 may be a participial translation of the relative clause from Hebrew Numbers 27:17. It is not a LXX citation. The saying in 2 Chronicles is in an entirely different context from that of Numbers (King Jehoshaphat and prophet Micaiah), and parallels leader (ἡγούμενος / *ᵃdônnîm*) to shepherd (ποιμήν / *sō'n*). The variability of settings gives away the ease with which this saying is used proverbially. Both Numbers and 2 Chronicles use the proverb to reflect on kingship (Jehoshaphat) or leadership (Joshua/Nun). In both cases, the pastoral image includes an environment of fields, mountains, or wilderness. In 2 Chronicles the Lord sends off the congregation in safety, each one εἰς τὸν οἶκον αὐτοῦ ἐν εἰρήνη (into his own home in peace). Bucolic reverie and frank soteriological safety (bread and water, not heaven) are essential in the 2 Chronicles pastoral imagery.

11. The verb is a favored term in Mark in picturing an inner disposition of Jesus. As an emotional arousal of some type for Jesus, see Mark 1:41; 6:34; 8:2; 9:22. Some of the clearer indications that this emotion is one of compassion include Mark 1:41, where the term is followed by the statement of Jesus about his willingness to help out in a difficult situation, θέλω, καθαίσθητι; Luke 7:13, where the term is linked to a statement of consolation by Jesus to the widow of Nain, μὴ κλαῖε; Matthew 9:36, the entirely different synoptic parallel to Mark 6:34, where the term is linked to a description of the flock (ὄχλοι) as ἐσκυλμένοι καὶ ἐρριμμένοι (harassed and helpless). The substantive σπλάγχνον is better attested in a broader range of literature: Wisdom 10:5 with an image of σπλάγχνον for one's child; Herodas *(Mimiambi* 1.56) with the phrase ἐκύμηνε τὰ σπλάγχνα ἔρωτι καρδίην ἀνοιστρηθείς (the deep feelings seethe once the heart is goaded to love).

12. Archytas (Περὶ νόμου καὶ δικαιοσύνη, in *The Pythagorean Texts of the Hellenistic Period*, ed. Holger Thesleff, Acta Academiae Aboensis, Series A: Humaniora: Humanistiska Vetenskaper, Socialvetenskaper, Teologi 30, no. 1 [Åbo: Åbo Akademi, 1965], 36 ll.2-5) likens the ἀληθινὸν ἄρχοντα to a ποιμήν. Also Philo (*Legatio ad Gaium* 44) speaks of βουκόλοι, αἰπόλοι, νομεῖς, and ἀγελάρχαι. See also Suetonius (*Tiberias* 32.2), who labels Tiberias *bonus pastor*,

and Cassius Dio (57.10), who describes Tiberias as κύριος and shepherd.

13. Trans. Robert H. Eisenman, and Michael O. Wise, *The Dead Sea Scrolls Uncovered: The First Complete Translation and Interpretation of 50 Key Documents Withheld for Over 35 Years* (Shaftesbury, Dorset: Element, 1992), 23.

14. The specifics of line 1.ii.6 include a combination of cosmogonic terms (the Spirit hovering) that describe a messianic presentation of God to the people. Terms here are yoked together previously only in the creation account of Genesis 1:2; see James D. Tabor and Michael O. Wise, "4Q521 'On Resurrection' and the Synoptic Gospel Tradition: A Preliminary Study," *Journal for the Study of the Pseudepigrapha* 10 (1992): 153.

15. Tabor and Wise, "4Q521," 158.

16. LXX Ezekiel 34:14 is one of only two places that μάνδρα translated *nwh* (dwelling place). The other is 1 Chronicles 17:7, where Nathan tells David that David was to be king, having been *taken out of the pasture* (μάνδρα) by YHWH.

17. LXX Ezekiel 34:15 considerably expands this verse: ἐγὼ βοσκήσω τὰ πρόβατά μου καὶ ἐγὼ ἀναπαύσω αὐτά, καὶ γνώσονται ὅτι ἐγώ εἰμι κύριος (I will be shepherd of my sheep and I will give them rest and they will know that I am Lord).

18. Psalm 78:21 contains a taunt about the people of God who sinned against God, not believing that God could produce in the wilderness a table or, even as water had once gushed from a rock struck by Moses, "give bread and provide meat for His people." These seemed impossible things. They are a type of abundance of eschatological renewal.

19. Trans. A. Sachs, "Akkadian Rituals," in *Ancient Near Eastern Texts Relating to the Old Testament*, ed. James B. Pritchard, 3d ed. (Princeton, N.J.: Princeton University Press, 1969), 332.

20. See Martin L. West (*Early Greek Philosophy and the Orient* [Oxford: Clarendon Press, 1971], 191) for an Iranian tradition about Yima, the first man, who lived for 1,000 years that were a "golden age" of prosperity and abundance. Theories of successive ages, full either of regression or of evolution, were quite prevalent; see Bodo Gatz (*Weltalter, goldene Zeit und sinnverwandte Vorstellungen*, Spudasmata 16 [Hildesheim, Germany: Georg Olms, 1967], 24-25) on time frames and themes of παλιγγενεσία [regeneration]. Themes of cosmic renewal found their way into philosophical schemes of individual rebirth and mysterious awakening into wisdom; see Fred Burnett, "Philo on Immortality: A Thematic Study of Philo's Concept of παλιγγενεσία," *Catholic Biblical Quarterly* 46 (1984): 447-70. On a very different but yet seminal conjunction of renewal at the New Year and salvation, see J. B. Segal (*The Hebrew Passover: From the Earliest Times to A.D. 70*, London Oriental Series 12 [London: Oxford University Press, 1963], 126-28) on Passover in the month of Nisan.

21. See Günther Zuntz (*Persephone: Three Essays on Religion and Thought in Magna Graecia* [Oxford: Clarendon Press, 1971], 385-91) on λευκὸς ὕδωρ (bright water) in Homer, and ξεστοὶ λίθοι (glistening stones) described as λευκοί in *Odyssey* 3.408. Zuntz also traces the material to Akkadian stories about the *kiškanu*-tree, mentioning Matthew 17:2 and its description of the whiteness of

Jesus as "like light" (ὡς τὸ φῶς), an image unique to Matthew.

22. See the history of these symbols in Jean Daniélou, *Primitive Christian Symbols*, trans. D. Attwater (Baltimore: Helicon Press, 1964), 25-41 ("The Vine and the Tree of Life"). Earlier and widespread persistence of such royal themes is detailed in Moshe Weinberg, *Social Justice in Ancient Israel and in the Ancent Near East* (Jerusalem: Magnes Press, 1995), 45-56 ("Justice and Righteousness as the Task of the King") and 57-76 ("Justice and Righteousness as the Task of the Eschatological King").

23. *Thanksgiving Hymns* 8:1-6, trans. Menahem Mansoor, *The Thanksgiving Hymns*, Studies in the Texts of the Desert of Judah 3 (Grand Rapids, Mich.: William B. Eerdmans, 1961), 153.

24. Holger Thesleff, "Notes on the Paradise Myth in Ancient Greece," *Temenos* 26 (1982): 132.

25. John Ferguson, *Utopias of the Classical World* (Ithaca, N.Y.: Cornell University Press, 1975), 157

26. Mario Torelli, *Typology and Structure of Roman Historical Reliefs*, Jerome Lectures, 14th series (Ann Arbor, Mich.: University of Michigan Press, 1982), 54. This occurs in the *domus* scene.

27. Menander Rhetor (Περὶ ἐπιδεικτικῶν II.1-2 [βασιλικὸς λόγος] 375.10) suggests such a comparison by saying, "Just as the sons of Asclepius rescue the sick, just as fugitives obtain security in the inviolate precincts of divine power—for we make no attempt to drag anyone away—so also he who comes into the sight of the emperor is freed from his perils (τῶν δεινῶν)" (trans. in *Menander Rhetor*, ed. D. A. Russell and N. G.Wilson [Oxford: Clarendon Press, 1981], 89). Ideals of kingship and eschatological expectations among Christians, Jews, Egyptians, Iranians, Stoics, and others had something in common: they expected divine beneficence to overflow into the human arena and eliminate the anomalous frightful.

28. See Harold Axtell (*The Deification of Abstract Ideas in Roman Literature and Inscriptions* [Chicago: University of Chicago Press, 1907], 33-34) for the first use of this in Spain. Concepts and terms of eternal time varied in their florid use. A Jewish inscription from Rome translates *l`ôlm* with εἰς τὸν ἄπαντα χρόνον; see Jean-Baptiste Frey, *Corpus Inscriptionum Iudaicarum* (Rome: Pontificio Istituto di Archeologia Cristiana, 1936; repr., New York: KTAV, 1975), 2§820. Doro Levy ("AION," *Hesperia* 13 [1944]: 263-314) carefully describes a banquet scene (κλίνη = eating = benefaction and safety) found in a mosaic at Antioch-on-the-Orontes, which features four figures: Παρω(ι)χημένος, Ἐνεστώς, Μέλλων, and Αἰών (Past, Present, Coming, and Forever). According to Levy, "the name Aion may well be used often as a mere attribute, since its essence is nothing else than the first quality from immemorial times assigned by philosophy to the primeval divine being; furthermore, Aion is the quality which religion and mysticism assign to the supreme deity, under whatever name worshipped" (p.307).

29. *Res Gestae Divi Augusti* 7, ostensibly a quotation from the sire himself: *Pontifex maximus, augur, XV virum sacris faciundus, VII virum epulonum, frater arvalis, sodalis Tatius, fetialis fui.* See P. A. Brunt and J. M. Moore, *Res Gestai*

Divi Augusti: The Achievements of the Divine Augustus (Oxford: Oxford University Press, 1967), 50: "It was a mark of Augustus' special position that he belonged to all these colleges; the most eminent Romans in the Republic seldom held more than one priesthood." The Greek text transliterates many of these Latin terms, but translates a few: *pontifex maximus* = ἀρχιερεύς; *sodalis Titius* = ἑταῖρος Τίτιος.

30. Trans. Fergus Millar, *The Emperor in the Roman World (31 B.C. - A.D. 337)* (Ithaca, N.Y.: Cornell University Press, 1977), 32-33. Panegyric was a good place to fabricate ideals for propaganda, rather than reporting simple and mundane reality. Millar noted the correspondence of this report to Plutarch (*Sertorius* 22.2), who reported that the citizens of Spanish cities had greeted an arrival of Quintus Caecilius Metellus Pius in the 70s B.C.E., with altars and sacrifices.

31. G. H. Boobyer ("The Eucharistic Interpretation of the Miracles of the Loaves in St. Mark's Gospel," *Journal of Theological Studies*, n.s. 3 [1952]: 161-71) correctly argued that neither the vocabulary nor the ideas in Mark 6:35-44 represent in the least an early "eucharist." The explanation of the bread and fish in Mark 8:14-21, where one might have expected to find such indications, indicates nothing at all about a "eucharist." Links to the festival of Passover or to some tradition of substitution (one body for another), or those things that seem essential for some relevant meaning of "eucharist" are not evident here.

32. Robert M. Grant, *The Problem of Miraculous Feedings in the Graeco-Roman World*, Center for Hermeneutical Studies in Hellenistic and Modern Culture: Protocol of the 42d Colloquy, 14 March 1982 (Berkeley: Graduate Theological Union and University of California Press, 1982), 1-15. Grant shows a background to this gospel material that consists of traditions about the Golden Age, scriptural traditions about Eden, and apocalyptic scenarios about new wine and grand banquets.

33. Richard I. Pervo "PANTA KOINA: The Feeding Stories in the Light of Economic Data and Social Practice," in *Religious Propaganda and Missionary Competition in the New Testament World: Essays Honoring Dieter Georgi*, ed. Lukas Bormann, Kelly Del Tredici, and Angela Standhartinger, Novum Testamentum Supplement. 74 (Leiden, The Netherlands: E. J. Brill, 1994), 163-94. In this belabored study Pervo takes Mark's stories as statements of early, practical theology about how the poor were to be treated within primitive Christian communities. He also sees in them a "nascent sacramental theology" (p.193), based on their utopian dimensions; specifically, a coming utopia that was not contingent on the benefactor emperor, but on Christ. A view of the feeding as a nascent sacramental meal might find support in the analysis of Erwin R. Goodenough (*Jewish Symbols in the Greco-Roman Period, 5: Fish, Bread, and Wine*, Bollingen Series 27 [New York: Pantheon Books, 1956], 41-50), who said that fish often represent a "sacramental or eucharistic food." Yet Goodenough's propensity to find mystical meaning in many types of evidence may make such an interpretation dubious.

34. Veyne (*Bread and Circuses*, 99) writes that "No better example could be imagined for examining the problem of euergetism. 'The Rhodians,' writes Strabo, 'are concerned for the people in general, although their rule is not democratic; still, they wish to take care of their multitude of poor people. Accordingly, the people are supplied with provisions and the needy are supported by the well-to-do, by a certain ancestral custom. . . .' One year at Priene, the 'supply of corn falling short,' a citizen named Moschion, 'seeing that the situation was urgent, and cherishing a devotion for the people which forbade him to wait to be asked, presented himself spontaneously before the Assembly and, in his own name and that of his Brother,' distributed corn at four drachmas the measure (an extremely low price at the time). . . . He performed what was called a παράπρασις, a cut-price sale for charity."

35. Bringmann and von Steuben, *Schenkungen hellenistischer Herrscher*, s.v. Δότε. This verb in this particular form is the critical technical term in inscriptional acclamations of or inscriptional instructions for benefaction. Δότε does not appear in the second feeding, in Mark 8:1-9.

36. See Crawford H. Greenewalt (*Ritual Dinners in Early Historic Sardis*, University of California Publications: Classical Studies 17 [Berkeley: University of California Press, 1978], 38-39) for a list of numerous references. Archaeological work at ancient Sardis uncovered utensils and dishes paralleling this basic triad of daily menu items.

37. See Goodenough (*Jewish Symbols in the Greco-Roman Period*, 5:62-76) specifically on widespread use of "round objects" and their meaning as bread.

38. Peter Garnsey and Richard Saller, *The Roman Empire: Economy, Society and Culture* (Berkeley: University of California Press, 1987), 83-103.

39. Pervo, "PANTA KOINA," 185: "In the Mediterranean world as a whole, the higher one was upon the social scale, the more likely one was to benefit from such distributions. When limitations existed, those excluded were the poor rather than the rich. Nor was family size a normal consideration. The vast majority of benefactions, one-time or ongoing, was restricted to (usually male) members of the citizen body. Only rarely did these gifts embrace resident aliens, slaves, children, or women."

40. See Frederick W. Danker (*Benefactor: Epigraphic Study of a Graeco-Roman and New Testament Semantic Field* [Saint Louis: Clayton Publishing House, 1982], 317), who wrote that benefactors were uniformly recognizable as "people or deities of uncommon excellence precisely because of their outstanding character or the service that they render or both."

10

Mark 6:45-53:
Jesus, Walking on the Ocean,
Appears as a Ghost

Prepositional phrases dominate the opening, middle, and closing of this account. The first verses contain εἰς τὸ πλοῖον (into the boat; 6:45), εἰς τὸ πέραν πρὸς βηθσαϊδάν[1] (across over the expanse to Bethsaida; 6:45), εἰς τὸ ὄρος (into the mountain; 6:46), and end with an elucidation of geographical dichotomy: the disciples are ἐν μέσῳ τῆς θαλάσσης (in the middle of the ocean) while Jesus is ἐπὶ τῆς γῆς (upon the land; 6:47). Subsequent actions are dominated by prepositional phrases: πρὸς αὐτούς (to them; 6:48), παρελθεῖν αὐτούς (to pass them by; 6:48), ἐπὶ τῆς θαλάσ-σης (on the ocean; 6:48, 49), μετ᾽ αὐτῶν (with them; 6:50), and πρὸς αὐτούς (to them; 6:51). Trajectories of contrasting geographical settings are painted, one for the Disciples, one for Jesus.

> Disciples: εἰς τὸ πλοῖον →εἰς τὸ πέραν πρὸς βηθσαϊδάν → ἐπὶ τῆς θαλάσσης → ἐπὶ τῆς γῆς (into the boat →across over to Bethsaida → upon the ocean → upon the land)
> Jesus: εἰς τὸ ὄρος (ἐπὶ τῆς γῆς) → ἐπὶ τῆς θαλάσσης → ἐπὶ τῆς γῆς (into the mountain [on the land] → on the ocean → on the land)

After 6:52, with its unusual prepositional phrase attached to a verb of perception (οὐ γὰρ συνῆκαν ἐπὶ τοῖς ἄρτοις [for they did understand the meaning of the loaves]),[2] the phrase ἐπὶ τῆς γῆς (on the land) is repeated after the verb διαπεράω (go across; 6:53). This initiates a closing section (6:53-56), presenting an activity summary with yet more depiction of motion and travel: ὅπου ἂν εἰσεπορεύετο εἰς κώμας ἢ εἰς πόλεις ἢ εἰς ἀγρούς (to whatever various towns, cities, or fields he went;(6:56). On the whole, this second boating narrative has a rounded form: ἐπὶ τῆς γῆς →

ἐπὶ τῆς θαλάσσης → ἐπὶ τῆς γῆς (on the land →on the ocean →on the land). The text is metaphorically rich, and it is easy to see why, while pursuing the meaning of this land/sea complex, other interpreters have examined both scriptural and Greek epic sagas of sea crossings or even New Testament resurrection narratives (see appendix J, "Sea Stories").

Contained here within this small ring structure are elements encountered in the first boating narrative: Sea, Wind, Night, and Storm.[3] Though it is not reported that the boat is sinking, those in the boat in 6:48 are fiercely laboring in their driving progress across the water (ἐν ἐλαύνειν).[4] The night setting (ὀψίας γενομένης [it became late] as in 4:45) is expanded with an exact time description: περὶ τετάρτην φυλακὴν τῆς νύκτος (at the fourth watch of the night; 6:48), and the nighttime danger is more acute because of the lack of a saving power in the boat, as Jesus stays behind on a mountain. When Jesus does finally enter into the boat, the wind stills (ἐκόπασεν ἄνεμος, as in 4:39). As in the first boating narrative, the response of those in the boat is bewilderment, here described differently: καὶ λίαν [ἐκ περισσοῦ] ἐν ἑαυτοῖς ἐξίσταντο (and they were tremendously and ecstatically amazed; 6:51).[5] The phrase ἐν ἑαυτοῖς (within themselves) emphasizes the wonder of the event, identifying the ecstasy not in Jesus but in the witnesses of his activities.

The triptych format of this second boating narrative carries in its center part the strange and unusual event of Jesus, deep in the night, appearing to those in the boat as a φάντασμα (ghost) while he walks on the θάλασσα (ocean). The appearance seems not to be deliberate on his part, since he wants to walk by apparently without the knowledge of those in the boat (καὶ ἤθελεν παρελθεῖν αὐτούς, 6:48). The sea is a beast, a place of conflict, and a place the dead. An appearance of a φάντασμα in this context deserves review because of its narrow focus as a particular event of the anomalous frightful.

Jesus miraculously walking on the sea is, as Adela Yarbro Collins observes, one of three usual interpretive points identified in this passage by commentators. The other two usual points are (1) interpretation of this story as a generic boating rescue, and (2) interpretation of this story as the report of an epiphany. On the basis of comparisons to materials in Greek mythography and in Scripture, the walking *per se* is assessed by Collins as an indication of divine power over the sea. In light of stories about Persian and Hellenistic kings and the use of those stories later in the Roman imperial propaganda, Collins interprets the walking as an *exemplum* "for the (humanly) impossible and for the arrogance of the ruler aspiring to empire."[6] Stories about Xerxes, Cyrus II, and Alexander[7]

include impressive water crossings, performed either by technological feat (floating bridges) or mysterious responses on the part of nature to the powerful leader (the sea "recognizes" Alexander and makes it possible for him to go across). Either way, military victories are made possible when the protagonists "walk" over or through the water. Transposed into Roman propaganda, the taming of the sea became a theme for the promotion of *imperium*. The person so promoted is thought favored and with the ability to compel divine benefaction and favor on his own behalf.[8] I shall not, however, focus on the walking *per se* but, instead, on the perception by the disciples in the boat of that walking, a perception reported with noticeable deliberateness in this story. The deliberateness is focused through use of the term φάντασμα [ghost], a word with a robust and allusive meaning.

Symbolically, water is ever chthonic, subject to myriad mythographic treatments, including its use for the placement of chthonic elements at specific locales on earth.[9] Beyond the sea there are fiery substances, which when they manifest themselves on earth or through water, are the basic, perceivable events from which develop theories of how the underworld makes its way to our surface world. Besides the obvious case of volcanos, a chief example of a doorway between worlds was identified at Lake Palikoi in Sicily, with its jets of volcanic gases. This ancient evidence attracted the attention of Peter Kingsley, a researcher who reports about his search through ancient philosophical opinions that equate Hades with fire.[10] Sicilian volcanic activity and the resultant geography of caves are critical aspects of what was understood as a type of elemental, central fire in the earth.[11] Plato points to the same ῥύαξ (volcanic steam jet) phenomenon at Sicily, and summarized the tradition of a tiered cosmos with a verse from Homer that suggests a deeper pit (βάρεθρον, called Τάρταρος by "older poets") lies underneath the χθών [earthy underground].[12] The tiers are illustrated in Homer in various ways, sometimes with an indication of a journey between them. Prayers of Penelope to Artemis indicate such. She pleads that a storm wind might lift her up from one level and carry her away on dark pathways to the mouths of Okeanos, that is, on through to the entrance of the Land of the Dead.[13]

Theories of a cosmic hydrology emerge from these depictions. In particular, Plato indicates how it was commonly thought that water from the deepest, chthonic places flows into observable and navigable, but dangerous, θαλάττας τε καὶ λίμνας καὶ ποταμοὺς καὶ κρήνας (oceans and seas and rivers and springs).[14] The tiers of deepness are explained with theories of flow, and different subterranean bodies of water are identified:

᾿Ωκεάνος, Λίμνη ᾿Αχερουσιάς, Πυριφλεγέθων, Στύγιον, and Κωκυτός [Oceanus, Acherusian Lake, Pyriphlegethon River, Stygian River, and Cocytus River, or River of Wailing Shrieks].[15] These locations have specific meanings for the post-death experience of souls (ψυχαί). Each deceased person is prepared (κομίζω) by an entity (identified as a δαίμων) for his or her entrance into a specific chthonic locale, with subsequent punishments or purifications resulting.[16] Such places of punishment are not simply for average humans. Pausanias (Περιήγησις 1.17.4-5) reports a tale about Theseus and Peirithous, that they were imprisoned in the Cocytos by the Thesprotian king. Here, these chthonic places are imagined as real geographical locations that can literally imprison. The Acherusian Lake is said to be right next to the Cocytos and the River Acheron, and is called ὕδωρ ἀτερπέστατον (most abominably detestable water). Herodotus passes on stories of a Νεκυομαντήιον (oracle for evoking the dead) on this River Acheron. These reports show how the underworld and its deceased inhabitants were thought available at specific places to those living above, *all in conjunction with water*.[17] A link between the ocean and the chthonic world means that the sea, as a specific type of place, retains an air of troubling difficulty. Pausanias (Περιήγησις 1.33.-4) reports that ᾿Ωκεάνος (Ocean) is the father of Νέμεσις (Nemesis), a tradition that links sea (Θάλασσα) with vengeance (Νέμεσις). From the point of view of the anomalous frightful, this is all a remarkably apt conjunction of elements: death, the dead, ghosts, ocean, revenge, and chaos.

Kingsley identifies Pythagorean tradition in much of the Platonic material. He notes that Lake Avernus in Italy, next to Cumae, three hundred miles north of Syracuse, and at the tip of the Bay of Naples, was thought to be in the vicinity of the Pyriphlegeton, the water in it actually the water of the Styx.[18] Lake Avernus was observed to be exceptionally pure and still. Cults of Persephone at Syracuse and at Cumae are suggested by Kingsley to be indications of an ancient belief that Naples and Syracuse are linked by a series of underground passages and channels of fire. More specifically, Pindar (*Pythian Ode* 1.18-20) proposes that Typhon is pinned underneath Mount Etna, held down at each end by Cumae and Syracuse. Otto Gruppe reviewed ancient theory that extrapolated from geographies and produced various mythographies about traditional divine entities. He refers to such examples as morning stars setting "into the sea" or gods in the sea who maintain an aspect of the sun "setting into the water" (see appendix K, "Mythographic Geography"). Egyptian Typhon in particular retains a curious mix of both lordship over the starry sky (*PGM* 4.265-266: Σε τὸν ἄνω μέσον τῶν ἄστρων Τυφῶνα δυνάστην, σε τὸν ἐπὶ τῷ στερεώματι δεινὸν ἄνακτα, σε τὸν φοβερὸν καὶ τρομερὸν καὶ φρικτνὸ ἐόντα ["You are midpoint of the stars above, master Typhon; you are dreaded lord over the stars; you are fearful and dreadful and terrifying"]) and chthonic, watery authority.[19] To the Phoenician and Syrian Ba`al Zaphôn, similar attributes are attached.[20] Greek Typhon was once deeply engaged in a variety of conflicts among the divine powers, the chthonic against the Olympian.[21]

Specific identifications of what was chthonic include identification of people, places, and things that are representative of it, gateways for it, or participants in it. Invocations to Hades that include specific commands to rivers, seas, lakes, fountains[22] show patently the linking of the underworld to worldly, watery locales. Besides in general the θάλασσα (ocean), there were several different places where the chthonic opened out into the world above. These include Ankara (between Nysa and Tralles), Argos "Hippoboton," Ephura in Thesprotia, Herakleia Pontica, Hermione, Hierapolis in Phrygia, Phigaleia, Taenarus, Thymbrion (between Magnesia and Myus), and Troizen.[23] Lake Avernus was thought water of the Styx, a type of water that Aristophanes calls an ἄβυσσον.[24] Silius Italicus (13.397) reports that some called on souls to perform magical operations at this very water. Pausanias (Περιήγησις 2.37.5) reports stories about a body of water identified as the Alkyonian Lake, through which Dionysus had a κατάβασις (descent) in order to rescue Selene from Hades.[25] The quality that characterizes the Avernian and Alkyonian waters is dead calm, and serpent-creatures live in them (this could mean either real snakes or fantastic and monstrous beasts). Salt (sea) water was used in cultic rites pertaining to chthonic powers,[26] sometimes related to Poseidon and his battles, as suggested in Pausanias Περιήγησις 1.26.5-6.[27]

Water with its full traditional and mythgraphic connotations is implicated in a variety of different oracular and magical operations.[28] Prophecies by Nereids are specific and irreversible,[29] and so it is that in Euripides (*Orestes* 360) Glaucus observes, Νηρέως προφήτης ἀψευδὴς θεός (prophet of the Nereid, an absolutely truthful god). Artemidorus (*Oneirocriticus* 2.39) says that ᾿Ωκεανὸς καὶ Τηθὺς φιλοσόφοις καὶ μάντεσι μόνος ἀγαθοί (Ocean and [his wife] Tythus are good only to philosophers and prophets), their august and terrifying appearances in dreams usually are invariant predictions of death. Other oracular figures related to water are the Okeanides Metis and Idyia as well as the Nereides Panope, Themisto, Pronoe, and Polynoe.[30] Pausanias (Περιήγησις 7.21.3-6) describes a shrine of Poseidon at Patai, next to which was a sanctuary

for Demeter. In front of the shrine was a spring with an infallible oracle.[31]
The same author (3.23.8 and 3.26.1) describes the lake of Ino near the
Acropolis at Patai (Ino, nurse of Dionysus). It is small and very deep, and
near it was a sanctuary at which oracular pronouncements came to
sleeping inquirers.[32] Even without a specially constructed oracle nearby,
springs were still celebrated. The springs of the Jordan River made an
ideal site for a temple to Augustus.

As controllable water in small spaces (springs, wells) was ideal for
various ritual operations, so also was water that was held in magic bowls.
PGM 4.154[33] describes a particular magical operation in which one
attaches oneself to Helios (συσταθεὶς πρὸς τὸν Ἥλιον) by lying on the
roof at midday. After specific actions are taken, this invocation follows:
Κραταιὲ Τυφῶν, τῆς ἄνω σκηπτουχίας σκηπτοῦχε καὶ δύνάστα θεὲ θεῶν,
ἄναξ . . . γνοφεντινάκτα, βρονταγωγέ, λαιλαπετέ, νυκταστράπτα,
ψυχροθερμοφύσησε, πετρεντινάκτα, τειχοσεισμοποιέ, κοχλαζοκύμων,
βυθοταραξοκνίνσε (O mighty Typhon, ruler of the realm above and
master, god of gods, lord. . . .O dark's disturber, thunder's bringer,
breather-forth of hot and cold, shaker of rocks, wall-trembler, boiler of the
waves, disturber of the sea's great depth"). One addressing the deity in
this way takes on the power and persona of Helios, reiterating a legend of
Typhon in conflict with Osiris, all in close conjunction with symbols of
water. The unusual epithet Bolchoseth (βολχοσήθ, *PGM* 4.2025) in a
spell written by Pitys in his letter to King Ostanes (*PGM* 4.2006-2125),
a spell to acquire the assistance of a νεκυδαίμων [spirit of the dead], may
be a reference to Seth/Typhon.[34] The particular magical operation reported
here relates Typhon, a chthonic power of stormy and dangerous water,
with dead humans. It is well to remember that magical operations such as
these do not deal with just any dead, but notably with those dead that we
have met above, the ἄωροι, βιαιοθάνατοι, and ἄταφοι.[35]

Ideas about the bodily appearance of these and other dead circulated.
Propertius (*Elegies* 4.1.106) speaks of *umbrave quae magicis mortua
prodit aquis*.[36] Conceptualization of the dead as shadowy or apparitional
was widespread in the Hellenistic world,[37] as discussed by Apollodorus
of Athens in his Περὶ θεῶν.[38] He comments on some ideas from Homer,
that souls appear flittering and as though one sees them while dreaming,
as described in the *Odyssey* 11.222 (ψυχὴ δ᾿ ἠΰτ᾿ ὄνειρος ἀποπταμένη
πεπότηται [like a dream, flits away, hovering to and fro]),

Ὑποτίθεται γὰρ τὰς ψυχὰς τοῖς εἰδώλοις τοῖς ἐν τοῖς κατάπτροις
φαινομένοις ὁμοίας καὶ τοῖς διὰ τῶν ὑδάτων συνισταμένοις, ἃ καθάταξ

ἡμῖν ἐξείνασται καὶ τὰς κινήσεις μιμεῖται, στερεμινώδη δ᾽ ὑπόστασιν οὐδεμίαν ἔχει εἰς ἀντίληψιν καὶ ἀφήν. ὅθεν αὐτὰς βροτῶν εἴδωλα καμόντων λέγει (He suggests that souls are like the images appearing in mirrors, which each time they present to us imitate things that move, yet have no solid extension for apprehension or gripping. For this reason, he says "Images of mortal dead.").

Images on reflecting surfaces are like the appearance of the dead. These images appear strange and unexplainable. Timarchus explains in Plutarch (*De deo Socrates* 22), with regard to his visions of Hades and the shadowy images there, that when he saw them, he did not know εἴτε ἐγρήγορεν εἴτ᾽ ὠνειροπόλει (whether he was wide awake or dreamt). With yet another play on the idea of reflections in water, from Boeotia there comes a report of a less famous account of Narcissus, that he thinks that the reflection at which he peers in the spring is that of his deceased twin sister and not of himself.[39] The observations of Apollodorus in his Περὶ θεῶν (On the Gods) are made with regard to Homeric lines from *Iliad* 23.72 (disembodied souls of the dead) and from *Odyssey* 11.475 (πῶς ἔτλης ῎Αϊδόσδε κατελθέμεν, ἔνθα τε νεκροὶ ἀφραδέες ναίουσι, βροτῶν εἴδωλα καμόντων; [how dare you come down to Hades, where the unheeding dead dwell, phantoms of men outworn]).[40] The dead are described as shadows in *Odyssey* 10.495 (τοὶ δὲ σκιαὶ ἀΐσσουσιν [indeed, shadows are darting back and forth]). The appearance of the souls of the deceased is described in *Odyssey* 11.204-209 as an appearance as if seen in a dream (So she spoke, and I pondered in heart, and was fain to clasp the spirit of my dead mother. Thrice I sprang towards her, and my heart bade me clasp her, and thrice she flitted from my arms like a shadow or a dream, and pain grew ever sharper in my heart)[41] and *Odyssey* 11.219-221 (For the sinews no longer hold the flesh and the bones together, but the strong might of blazing fire destroys these, as soon as the life leaves the white bones, and the spirit, like a dream, flits away, and hovers to and fro).[42] Suitable as a theme of tragic encounters in epic, in Vettius Valens (2.13) it is said that a clever person who can successfully predict events through horoscopes is successful ὑπὸ δαιμονίων καὶ ὑπὸ φαντασίας εἰδώλων (by means of daimons and by means of images of apparitions).[43] Apparitional images leave the perceiver caught between imagination and vague evidence, between dreaming and waking. Discerning them is an uncanny affair, partly because the stakes for discerning correctly seem as high as the level of uncertainty.[44]

In his study of the ancient Greek idea of ψυχή (soul), Erwin Rohde emphasizes the idea's development through the experience of recalling dream images.[45] His approach is supported, but clarified, by Walter F. Otto, who points out abundant ancient evidence for encounters with the dead that does *not* imply a dreamer's Doppelgänger, one popular theory for explaining ghosts in human perception.[46] One ancient theory has it that the *animus* of a sleeper is stronger during sleep, when the body is as though dead. Some ancients thought that the semi-dead state would give great celerity to recalling the past, to comprehending the present, and to foreseeing the future.[47] Pindar states that a part of humans that lived forever after death, the αἰῶνος εἴδωλον, has an insubstantial appearance like the appearance of objects in dreams (ἀτὰρ εὐδόντεσσιν ἐν πολλοῖς ὀνείροις δείκνυσι τερπνῶν ἐφέρποισαν [but to ones sleeping through many dreams show the approach of delights].[48] The term εἴδωλον means the appearance and the substance of the deceased.[49] It is reported about Ostantes that his cosmic hierarchy began with the eternal god, from whom emerged other powers in descending order: (1) titans, (2) daimons, (3) earth-born ones, (3) young warriors/divinities (κουρῆτας), (4) heroes, (5) divine entities (εἴδωλα θεῖα), and (6) little human daimons (δαιμόνια τῶν ἀνθρώπων).[50]

The term εἴδωλον, useful in description of divine and human forms, has a meaning similar to the term ψυχή.[51] The ψυχή is depicted in Greek funereal art as a miniature replica of the individual, "endowed with wings to account for its swift daimonic flight, retaining some powers of memory and emotion."[52] It flutters, hovers, and darts like a dragonfly.[53] Human perception of apparitional figures, as indicated by descriptions of κολοσσοί (gigantic statues) and ψυχαί (souls), is described with reference to dream (ὄνειρος) images, εἴδωλα, σκιαί and φάσματα (images, shadows, appearances).[54] An evocation of an uncanny, dreamy sensibility seemed typically to follow these apparitional experiences wherever they are reported or discussed. Plato (*Phaedo* 81c-d) tells us how, in then current folklore, φάντασμα is a primary synonym of εἴδωλον: περὶ ἃ δὴ καὶ ὤφθη ἄττα ψυχῶν σκιοειδῆ φάντασμα, οἷα παρέχονται αἱ τοιαῦται ψυχαὶ εἴδωλα (even around which [tombs] certain things of souls are seen: shadowy apparitions; that is, as those types of things which are like souls being apprehended as ghosts).

A synonym of φάντασμα is φάσμα. The LXX uses the terms φάντασμα and φάσμα to translate *ḥzzyôn* (vision, oracle). In Numbers 16:30 Moses promises that, in retaliation, the Lord will appear as a φάσμα (apparition) to the families of Korah, Dathan, and Abiram, in order suddenly to destroy them. The destruction by this φάσμα takes on characteristics of the chthonic: the mouth of the earth opens to swallow them, taking them down to Hades (ἀνοίξασα ἡ γῆ τὸ στόμα αὐτῆς κατατπίεται αὐτους . . . καὶ κατβήσονται ζῶντες εἰς ᾅδου [the earth opened, its mouth swallowed them. . .and, while still alive, they descended to Hades]). In Job 20:8 there is a comparison in Zophar's description of the wicked, in the way they will suddenly vanish: ὥσπερ ἐνύπνιον (in a manner similar to a dream). . . ὥσπερ φάσμα νυκτερινόν (in a manner similar to a night time apparition). This description of insubstantial existence makes good use of themes of dream images and fluctuating apparitional temporality. In Job 33:15, Elihu's answer to Job makes a similar use of φάσμα, when Elihu describes the way God speaks: ἐν μελέτη νυκτερινῇ [ὡς φάσμα in Codex Alexandrinus], ὡς ὅταν ἐπιπίπτη δεινὸς φόβος ἐπ᾽ ἀνθρώπους (in ominous, nocturnal threat [like apparitions], as when terrible fear falls upon humans). With compositional skill many themes of the anomalous frightful are woven together in these wisdom texts.

Wisdom 17:4 (φάσμα [apparition]) and 17:14 (φάντασμα [apparition]) are in a unique literary context that might adequately be entitled, "Encomium to God's Judgment."[55] The themes are meticulously put together. They include numerous aspects of the anomalous frightful: "captives of darkness . . . prisoners of long night . . . dark curtain of forgetfulness . . . terrible alarm . . . fear . . . terrifying sounds . . . no illumination for the hateful Night." In 17:4, we find a description of the appearance of φάσματα ἀμειδήτοις κατηφῆ προσώποις (dismal apparitions with gloomy faces), entities of some kind, though not deceased persons. In 17:14 the term φάντασμα describes the anomalous frightful: τὰ τέρασιν ἠλαύνοντο φαντασμάτων, τὰ δὲ τῆς ψυχῆς παρελύοντο προδοσίᾳ, αἰφνίδιος γὰρ αὐτοῖς καὶ ἀπροσδόκητος φόβος ἐπεχθη (and now were driven by monstrous specters, and now were paralyzed by their souls' surrender, for sudden and unexpected fear overwhelmed them). In this case, some type of discrete entities are implied, perhaps even actual ghosts. Often φάσμα and φάντασμα occasion a panoply of themes about fear, agitation, uncertainty, distress, panic, and terror.

Josephus used the term φάντασμα to describe angelic visitations or images recalled from dreaming.[56] Generally Josephus uses the term φάσμα in connection with divine power that is frightening due to the threat of terrible danger. In *War* 6.296, Josephus offers an account of how φάσμα τι δαιμόνιον ὤφθη μεῖζον πίστεως (a certain daimonic apparition was seen, one that perhaps only the credulous would believe). The apparition involves chariots in the air and armed battalions riding the clouds, all in conjunction with an impending attack on the Jerusalem temple.[57] In *War*

7.438, an account of Jonathan (one of the Sicarii) reports how he promised followers εἰς τὴν ἔρημον σημεῖα καὶ φάσματα δείξειν (to show signs and apparitions in the desert). None of these passages presents angry ghosts or other dead, but they do emphasize the anomalous frightful.[58] In these sources, the terminology tends to be used without emphasis on the underworld and its specific inhabitants.[59]

In very different sources, the terms φάσμα and φάντασμα are linked specifically to the underworld and its inhabitants, and more generally with terrors and ill portents.[60] Hekate is linked to the ghostly, as in the phrase ἑκατικὰ φάσματα (Marinus, *Vita Procli* 28). She is also addressed in ways as were chthonic monsters Γοργὼ καὶ Μορμὼ καὶ Μήνη[61] καὶ πολύμορφε.[62] Elsewhere, coincidences of Hekate with Baubo (βαυβώ) highlight the yelping sound of dogs, which sound the root βαυ suggests.[63] Baubo is in one place a giant nocturnal specter.[64] All of these figures are terrible and the origin of night terrors, and their terrors involve ghosts and the unhappy dead. Gorgo, who is monstrous, is chthonic.[65] She is the consort of Acheron. Rohde suggests that figures identified as "mothers of the underworld" are developed along the lines of Gorgo and of Hekate.[66] Referring to other entities in this class, Γελλώ and Ἔμπουσα, he proposes that they coincide in their shape-shifting[67] and night roaming, as well as in their status as night terrors and dangers to children.[68] Philostratus (*Apollonius* 2.4) renders a story about a moonlight walk of Apollonius and friends, during which a φάσμα Ἐμπούσης spooks them. It oscillates in its form, sometimes vanishing from sight. The last line of the account emphasizes that the entity is a φάσμα, which goes away shrieking ὥσπερ τὰ εἴδωλα (just like a ghost).[69] Just like Gorgo, Mormor, Gello, and Empousa, Hekate herself appears in the upper world as an εἴδωλον (image), or as a terrible figure surrounded by εἴδωλα (images). Helen in Euripides (*Helena* 596) exclaims, "O, Phosphorescent Hekate has sent me a kindly φάσμα," in the next phrase clarified as a νυκτίφαντον (night appearance). Rohde refers to a full description of Hekate: εἴτ᾽ ἐνύπνιον φάντασμα φοβῇ χθονίας θ᾽ Ἑκάτης κῶμον ἐδέξω (or you fear during sleep an apparition of the chthonic and receive a reveling band of Hekate).[70] Hekate wanders the night with the restless dead (ἀώροι) (*PGM* 4.2731). In a spell addressed to her, she is invoked, δεῦρ᾽ Ἑκάτη . . . πυρίπνοα φάσματ᾽ ἔχουσαν (Come, Hekate! . . . having fire-breathing apparitions) (*PGM* 4.2728). It is at least once reported of Gello that she too, originally being ἄωρος, is a φάντασμα (Zenobius 3.3). Hekate and like entities who are specifically linked with φάσματα are threats to humans.[71]

Appearances of ghosts do not occur only within these specific traditional contexts with various monstrous figures. Elements of the anomalous frightful recur elsewhere. Herodotus (*History* 6.69) tells a story about how a φάσμα of an ancient hero impregnated a woman, a story full of dire consequences.[72] The εἴδωλον of Melissa is the subject of several reports. Murdered by her husband, Periander (*History* 3.50), she became the subject of strange doings reported in relation to a lost treasure of gold. Her appearance at the Νεκυομαντήιον on the River Acheron in Thesportia is reported (*History* 5.92). In other stories, the φάσμα of Aristeas is sighted at different times at Proconnesus and Cyzicus, speaking with townsfolk and, once, giving instructions that a βωμός be set up for Apollo (*History* 4.14-15). Josephus (*War* 7.452) reports the dreadful fate of Catullus, who spent his last days haunted by the εἴδωλα of the ones he had murdered. He ends confined to a sick bed, racked with pain, eventually eaten alive by worms.[73] The emperors Nero and Otho experienced similar ghostly events of retaliation,[74] and the ghost of the emperor Caligula was said to have haunted the house in which he was murdered (Suetonius, *Gaius Caligula* 59).

Plato (*Phaedo* 81c-d) adumbrates how it was thought that εἴδωλα/φάντασμα circulated περὶ τὰ μνήματά τε καὶ τοὺς τάφους (around the graves and the tombs). Pausanias (Περιήγησις 6.6.7-9) provides the story of how Euthymus, a boxing champion, was the first human able to fight off the δείματα ἀπὸ τοῦ δαίμονος (terrors from the ghost) at Temesa in Italy. That daimon was the ghost of a shipmate of Odysseus, having been put to death there long ago by stoning. The story is that, until that time, τοῦ καταλευσθέντος ἀνθρώπου τὸν δαίμων οὐδένα ἀνιέναι καιρὸν ἀποκτείνοντα τε ὁμοίως τοὺς ἐν τῇ Τεμέσῃ (the daimon of the slain man had never quit killing those who lived in Temesa, without distinction). When Euthymus defeats him, the ghost is vanguished, καταδὺς ἐς θάλασσαν (sinking [it] in the sea). We see that δαίμονες of the dead are notoriously dangerous, especially if their deaths were violent. A καταποντισμός for them was deemed warranted. Pausanias (Περιήγησις 1.32.4) reports on the ἐκ τῶν δαιμόνων ὀργή (wrath of daimons) in connection with those killed in action during the Battle of Marathon, who are noisy and *exceptionally dangerous* to anyone who happened to hear or see them.

In Mark 6:49, the sighting of Jesus walking on the ocean (θάλασσα), appearing to be a ghost (φάντασμα), is an occasion for these connotations about apparitions to come to the fore, and quite strongly. Apparitions are focused and powerful representations of the anomalous frightful. They constitute a well-known experience of definite, perceptual uncertainty, among other things implying that strange beings are emerging from "below" into the world "above." Whether generically "terrible sightings" or specifically "ghostly sightings," such narratives convey infernal, chthonic, deadly doings. And so we find, in Mark, that those in the boat respond. Subsequently, Jesus approaches them and makes three short statements to them: θαρσεῖτε, ἐγώ εἰμι, μὴ φοβεῖσθε (be bold, I am, be not afraid). He boards, the wind ceases, and those in the boat become "full of ecstasy." Mark's own explanatory voice briefly enters into the story, to tell us (through a γάρ independent clause) that the ecstasy occurs because "they had not understood about the loaves" and because "their hearts were hardened." This narrator's comment and explanation, as George W. Young has belabored to point out, is quite critical of the disciples, and it furthers a specific dynamic at the end of this narrative cycle, that of aggrandizement of the uncertain, as we find here more unexpected and unexplained story elements.[75] Even so, with this narrative intrusion about the state of mind of the disciples, nothing is said about the potent events that take place, and the story glosses over the more than natural terror that humans are likely to have experienced under such circumstances. In Mark, it genuinely seems overly simple that Jesus walks on the sea, attempting to bypass those in the boat and appearing as a strange apparition. An event of such magnitude goes by, with little to no development. No explanations are offered, no reasons are given.

Why does Jesus appear this way? Why is he mistaken for a ghost or for some other form of dead person? We are never told. These essential elements of the story slip by. Once more, Jesus is encountered in a situation of the utterly strange, this time appearing himself to epitomize the anomalous. To those whom he beckons to follow him, he appears as a ghost, a being of dreadful character linked to those entities who might snatch away life at its most vulnerable moment. That is to say, in this account, it is Jesus who is presented as the anomaly and the entity who represents indeterminate fear. Even so, the narrative moves by, quickly leaving this episode behind. Uncertainty prevails; the reader is not given much at all with which to grasp the depth of these unusual events. Although there is here an acme of themes of the anomalous frightful, and therefore a most opportune time to explain what is happening, the story simply concludes. Is there a meaning to these events? If so, what is it? When Jesus appears as a ghost, he colludes with the chthonic. When no explanation is given, a reader is left to be caught between a dream and the reality of the terrible.

Notes

1. Unlike others, I do not make much here of the name, Bethsaida. See Stephen Smith, "Bethsaida via Gennesaret: The Enigma of the Sea-Crossing in Mark 6,45-53," *Biblica* 77 (1996): 349-74. Perhaps geographical names serve Mark for one symbolic function or another. Such a service is beyond what I examine. After all the material that Smith belabors in his article, his conclusion that an arrival at Bethsaida is symbolism for the disciples' finally "getting it" about the universality of the gospel seems rather brilliant speculation.

2. The clause συνῆκαν ἐπὶ τοῖς ἄρτοις includes an unusual use of the preposition ἐπὶ, plus a pleonasm of prepositions. This is the only clause in Mark in which a verb of perception is attached to its object with the preposition ἐπὶ. Two other examples in Mark are similar to this use, but just a: στυγνάσας ἐπὶ τῷ λόγῳ (10:22) and ἐξεπλήσσοντο ἐπὶ τῇ διδαχῇ αὐτοῦ (1:22) or ἐξεπλήσσετο ἐπὶ τῇ διδαχῇ αὐτοῦ (11:18). One can see why George W. Young (*Subversive Symmetry: Exploring the Fantastic in Mark 6:45-56*, Biblical Interpretation Series 41 [Leiden, The Netherlands: E. J. Brill, 1999], 146-84 ["Rhetoric and the Reader"]) draws so much attention to Mark 6:52. Young hears the narrator here talking to the reader and, in so stepping in to comment on the story, enacting a point of view about the "The Fantastic."

3. On the storm theme in this second boating story, see Wendy J. Cotter ("The Markan Sea Stories: Their History, Formation, and Function in the Literary Context of Greco-Roman Antiquity," [Ph.D. dissertation, University of Saint Michael's College, 1991], 105), who claims emphatically that this story does not contain the theme of a hostile sea due to storm. Cotter is predisposed to interpret Hellenistic "victory-at-sea" stories as philosophical examples of how Fortune favors protagonists in a story. Adela Yarbro Collins ("Rulers, Divine Men, and Walking on the Water [Mark 6:45-52]," in *Religious Propaganda and Missionary Competition in the New Testament World: Essays Honoring Dieter Georgi*, ed. by Lukas Bormann, Kelly Del Tredici, and Angela Standhartinger, Novum Testamentum Supplement. 74 [Leiden, The Netherlands: E. J. Brill, 1994], 226) rightfully points out verbal similarities between the wind ceasing in this story and in the first boating narrative, thereby drawing attention to Storm in each. J. Duncan M. Derrett ("Why and How Jesus Walked on the Sea," *Novum Testamentum* 23 [1981]: 330-48) suggests that the disciples, in a boat, were floating about in that area of the Sea of Galilee that was quite shallow, though indeed with sudden underwater drop-offs of deeper trenches. A knowledgeable local person would be able literally to "walk" on the shallows, avoiding the deeps, and yet appear to be hiking across the water.

4. The verb ἐλαύνειν is a nautical term, implying in general a force needed to compel a craft forward against resisting wind and waves. Pollux (*Onomasticon* 1.116) described how a violent thunderstorm (βίαιος ὄμβρος) may drive against a ship (ἐλαυόμενος). Use of the term βασανιζομένος supports the view that, since

the sailors were working hard against the wind, it must have been at least somewhat stormy. Possibly there is also a metaphorical meaning for struggling or laboring against resistance in this story. Luke 8:29 adds a feature to the story about the man in the cemetery who is daimōnized by the Λεγιών, that the daimōn occasionally "drove" him (ἠλαύνετο) into the wilderness. In Wisdom 17:14 those who have φόβος are often "driven" by terrors of ghostly appearances (τὰ μὲν τέρασιν ἠλαύνοντο φαντασμάτων). Pausanias (Περιήγησις 2.6.8-10) tells a story about how, at Temesa, after Euthymus awaits the "onslaught" (ἡ ἔφοδος) by a daimōn of the long-dead sailor who once traveled with Odysseus and now haunts here, then fights and "drives out" (ἐξηλαύνετο) the daimōn from the area. These examples are not nautical, yet they indicate use of the term ἐλαύνειν in various contexts depicting conflict and violence (or its resolution) between active agents. Therefore, perhaps, the depiction in Mark 6:48 focuses on Ἄνεμος as an entity of resistance, possibly as if it were a living entity with disposition and will, or itself daimōnic.

5. Textual variants do not change the essential meaning of this description. Manuscripts A, D, W, and Θ add καὶ ἐθαυμάζον to ἐξισταντο, perhaps because of the appearance together of these terms in Acts 2:7.

6. Collins, "Rulers, Divine Men, and Walking on the Water," 209.

7. For Xerxes, see Herodotus 7.35,56; Dio Chrysostom, *Third Discourse on Kingship* 1.30-31; compare Collins, "Rulers, Divine Men, and Walking on the Water," 218-19; Cotter, "Markan Sea Stories," 298-301. For Cyrus II, see Xenophon (*Anabasis* 1.4.17-18); compare Cotter, "Markan Sea Stories," 301-302. For Alexander, see Cotter ("Markan Sea Stories," 303-309) on the numerous stories reported in Callisthenes, Arrian, and Strabo.

8. See Cotter ("Markan Sea Stories," 178-180) for her summary of principles of how to interpret Hellenistic views of nature and the sea as matters of chance (Τύχη and *Fortuna*). Cotter assessed the whole Hellenistic period in this way, concluding that "most people" in the period held rationalistic views about natural forces and were no longer inherently superstitious or religious about such things. I must conclude otherwise.

9. Otto Gruppe, *Griechische Mythologie und Religionsgeschichte* Handbuch der klassischen Altertums-Wissenschaft in systematischer Darstellung 5 (München: C. H. Beck'sche Verlagsbuchhandlung, 1906), §266. The abundance of materials available is collected and reviewed by Martin Ninck, *Die Bedeutung des Wassers im Kult und Leben der Alten: Eine symbolgeschichtliche Unter-suchung*, Philologus, Supplementband 14, Heft 2 (Leipzig, Germany: Die-terisch'sche Verlagsbuchhandlung, 1921). P. Kyriakou ("ΚΑΤΑΒΑΣΙΣ and the Underworld in the *Argonautica* of Apollonius Rhodius," *Philologus* 139 [1995]: 256-64) reviews locations in proximity to the Underworld as described in the land of the Mariandynoia (*Argonautica* 2.341-407), the Sicilian town Eryx (*Argonautica* 4.912-19), and Libya (*Argonautica* 4.1228-50). In this literature, the θάλασσα itself also is portrayed as a merging upper world and underworld: "The impenetra-ble darkness that engulfed the ship immediately after the departure from Crete, the cloud indistinguishable from infernal haze and gloom, as emblematic of the crew's

continued helplessness" (p.263). See Christine Sourvinou-Inwood (*"Reading"
Greek Death: To the End of the Classical Period* [Oxford: Clarendon Press,
1995], 72-75) on geographical landscapes and ways in which some thought the
underworld flows into our world. According to Sourvinou-Inwood, "the Hades
which Odysseus had visited in the earlier epic would not have been reached
through a journey to the ends of the earth, but descended down to through one of
the entrances to the Underworld (which, it was believed, existed in various parts
of Greece) in a place near Ithaca; this place can only have been Epirus, the
geography of which is reflected in, provided material for the construction of, the
geography of Hades, and in which was eventually situated the oracles of the dead
[*Nekymanteion*]. . . . Pausanius 1.17.5 thought that Homer had used Thesprotian
landscape elements to construct his Underworld . . . the site of the Nekymontaion,
the oracle of the dead, does seem to be not entirely unrelated to the topography of
the Underworld in a way that suggests that the epic tradition had used really
geographical Thesprotian features, because it was describing a real place, where
an entrance to the Underworld was supposed to be situated."

10. Peter Kingsley, *Ancient Philosophy, Mystery, and Magic: Empedocles
and Pythagorean Theory* (Oxford: Clarendon Press, 1995), 36-48.

11. Kingsley, *Ancient Philosophy*, 73.

12. Plato (*Phaedo* 111d-112a) cites Homer, *Iliad* 8.14. See also Apollonius
of Rhodes (*Argonautica* 4:596) on steam belching up in bursts (ῥόοι) from the
Eridanus.

13. *Odyssey* 20.61-65, a beautiful combination of several elements of the
anomalous frightful already discovered: "'Great Artemis, Daughter of Zeus,' she
prayed, for it was to Artemis that the noble lady's thoughts had flown, 'oh for an
arrow from your bow to pierce my heart and take away my spirit in this very hour!
Or let the Storm-Wind [θυέλλα] snatch me up and vanish with me down the ways
of darkness to drop me where the sea runs into the circling Stream of Ocean—just
as the daughters of Pandareus were rapt away by the Demons of the Storm
[θυέλλαι]" (trans. E. Rieu, *Homer: The Odyssey* [London: Penguin, 1946], 305).
See also Sourvinou-Inwood (*'Reading' Greek Death*, 61) who, about the river that
thought to separate Hades, notes that *Iliad* 23.71-74 reports how a shade could not
cross this river (a river not formally named but instead only just called πόταμος,
but that in *Iliad* 8.396 the river is indeed called "Styx"). She wrote about *Odyssey*
10.508-515, that "the rivers have multiplied: Okeanos comes in and so to
Pyriphlegethon and Kokytos as well as Styx, and also Acheron, who is destined
to become eventually *the* river-border separating Hades from the no-man's land
which communicates with the upper world. The appearance of Okeanos and the
elaborated Underworld landscape are the result of the transfer of the entrance to
the Underworld to the ends of the earth and the combination of that imaginary
geography with elements from the Thesprotian landscape around the entrance to
Hades."

14. Plato, *Phaedo* 112c. Plato's use of this material is to be seen in light of
his dialogue's broader interest in the hypothesis of an immortal soul. This material
was part of popular, prevalent thought, here entered into a Socratic dialogue.

15. Plato *Phaedo* 113. See Cornutus *Natura Deorum* 35 for on these bodies of water all in conjunction with Hades, and with legends about Ἄορνος Λίμνη (Lake Avernus).

16. Plato *Phaedo* 113d. Relevant to much of the material previously cited, *Phaedo* 113e does make specific mention of the fate of those who commit certain ἁμαρτήματα, especially φόνους ἀδίκους (unjust murders). The latter end in Tartarus. On the development of these locales in early Christian considerations about afterlife and punishment of souls by God's judgment, see Erik Peterson ("Die 'Taufe' im Acherusischen See," in *Frühkirche, Judentum und Gnosis: Studien und Untersuchungen* [Darmstadt: Wissenschafliche Buchgesellschaft, 1982], who traced the Λίμνη Ἀχερουσιάδα through the *Apocalypse of Peter, Apocalypse of Paul* (Coptic), and *Apocalypse of Moses* 37 (terminology = Ἀχερουσίαν Λίμνη). Peterson thoroughly discusses themes of paradise, third heaven, the archangel Michael, the throne of God, and waters of baptism. The *Apocalypse of Peter* mentions Ἐλυσίος πεδιός, and Petersen aptly compared this to the Second Sibyline §338, αἰώνιον ἀθανάτοισιν Ἐλυσίῳ πεδίῳ, ὅθι οἱ πέλε κύματα μακρὰ λίμνης ἀενάου Ἀχερουσιάδος βαθυκόλπου (eternity with immortals on the Elysian Field, where are large waves of the deep, eternal Acherousian Lake). These conceptions of baptismal water in such early Christian eschatological theories are linked to ἰχθύς imagery and related terminology: *abyssus saeculi; abyssus fallaciae, vanitatis, ignorantiae; fluctus istius saeculi;* βύθος ἀγνωσίας; πέλαγος κακίας; see Robert Eisler, *Orphische-dionysische Mysteriengedanken in der christlichen Antike*, Vorträge der Bibliothek Warburg 1922-1923, II. Teil (Leipzig and Berlin, 1925; repr., Hildesheim: Georg Olms, 1966), 116-23.

17. Herodotus, *History* 5.92. This notion persisted. Strabo (V,4.5) states that Ephoros of Kyme also reported about the νεκομαντεῖον located near the Ἀχερουσία λίμνη; see Felix Jacoby, *Die Fragmente der griechischen Historiker* (Leiden, The Netherlands: E. J. Brill, 1957), §70 No. 134.

18. See Kingsley (*Ancient Philosophy*, 88-95) for Pythagorean material; for Lake Avernus see pp. 98-101.

19. J. Gwyn Griffiths (*The Conflict of Horus and Seth from Egyptian and Classical Sources: A Study in Ancient Mythology* [Liverpool: Liverpool University Press, 1960], 110) translates Plutarch (*De Iside et Osiride* 376E-377A): "It is not correct to believe that Osiris or Isis are water or the sun or the earth or the sky; or again, that Typhon is fire, or drought or the sea; but we should rather assign to Typhon whatever in these is unrestrained and disordered through excesses or defects, and respect and honour whatever is well-ordered and good and beneficial as the work of Isis and as the image and copy and reason of Osiris." Griffiths identified three main classical sources for the account of conflict: Herodotus, *History* 2.62-63 (in Herodotus, Horus = Apollo); Diodorus Siculus 1.11, 21, 25, 88; and, Plutarch, *De Iside et Osiride* 358B19 - 359B20. Gruppe (*Griechische Mythologie und Religionsgeschichte*, 812) suggested that Typhon was originally a chthonic divinity, assimilated to the Egyptian Set, since fire and smoke commonly characterized entrances to the underworld. Material in Manetho shows

a Euhemerist view of Egyptian divine entities (p.97): *de deis et de heroibus, de manibus et de mortalibus regibus qui Aegypto praefuerunt* (on gods and heroes, on spirits of the dead and mortal kings who ruled Egypt). "Whether the *manes* really form a third non-mortal category," Griffiths commented, "is rendered a little doubtful by a subsequent sentence in the same account: *secuta est manium heroumque dominatio*, where the *manes* and *heroes* may be regarded as identical. They are kept apart, however, in other references" (p.97).

20. The other Mt. Casius, known as Ba'al Zaphôn in Syria, where the Orontes meets the Mediterranean, is a primary sacred Mountain identified in ancient eastern texts; see Patrick N. Hunt, "Mount Saphon in Myth and Fact," in *Phoenicia and the Bible: Proceedings of the Conference Held at the University of Leuven on the 15th and 16th of March 1990*, ed. E. Lipinski, Orientalia Lovaniensia Analecta 44: Studia Phoenicia 11 (Leuven, Belgium: Uitgeverij Peeters, 1991), 103-115. This site and legends pertaining to it were employed throughout antiquity. Hunt translated a curse on a treaty stipulation from the Assyrian King Esharhaddon to Ba'lu the King of Tyre that reads, "May *Ba-al sa-me-me* and *Ba-al ma-la-ge-e* and *Ba-al sa-pu-nu* let loose an evil wind on your ships, tear their riggings, and carry away their masts" (p.109). The relation of Ba'al to oceanic anomalies and terrors is strong. The Hellenistic historian Sanchuniathon wrote, "Light, and Fire, and Flame begat sons of surpassing size and might, whose names were applied to the mountains which they occupied; so that from them were named Mount Casius, and Libanus, and Antilibanus" (p.108), taken from Eusebius *Praeperatio evangelica* 1.10.7. Mount Libanus was the mountain of El. A Hellenistic cosmogony of heavenly or chthonic powers involved theories that personified elemental substances linked to manifestations of power and terror. Skylax reports that this mountain was called "The Face of God" (ὄρος θεοῦ πρόσωπον); see Carl Müller, *Geographi Graeci Minores* (Hildesheim: Georg Olms, 1965), 1:78 §104.

21. Following a canonical version of the tradition, the gigantomachy of the Altar of Pergamum depicts Typhon the giant (and serpent) fighting directly against Zeus; see J. J. Pollitt, *Art in the Hellenistic Age* (Cambridge: Cambridge University Press, 1986), 109. In Hesiodic cosmology, Typhon is a monstrous beast, the child of Earth and Tartarus. Defeated by Zeus through thunder and lightening (airy and fiery storm), he is thrown alive into Tartarus (like the Deep), from which place he will forever control the Winds (except the south wind, which was considered gentle). Another version of the story in Apollodorus (1.40) relates that Zeus pursued Typhon to the coast of Syria at Ba'al Zaphôn, at which point Typhon ceased retreat and attacked Zeus, cutting the tendons of Zeus's hands and feet and thereby crippling him. Cadmus, along with Nonnus, distracted Typhon so that Zeus could rush up to heaven in order to continue thunderbolt and lightening warfare. Typhon ran but could not hide: first to Mount Nysa, then to Mount "Blood" in Thrace, and finally to Mount Etna in Italy, where local tradition thought him pinned down underground in defeat. Boetians, proud of their hero Cadmus, dedicated a nearby mountain as Mount Typhion. Greek legends of Titans, Giants, Aloadai, and Typhon are reviewed in H. J. Rose, *A Handbook of*

Greek Mythology, Including Its Extension to Rome (New York: E. P. Dutton, 1959), 58-63. All are monstrous, powerful, and eccentrically anomalous (even by Olympian standards). Rose identified the Aloadai with nightmare terrors as found linked to the entity Ephialtes (p.62), a manifestation of the anomalous frightful.

22. Terms include ποταμοί, θάλασσαι, λίμναι, and πηγαί. Josef Kroll (*Gott und Hölle: Der Mythos vom Descensuskampfe*. Studien der Bilbiothek Warburg Heft 20 [Leipzig, Germany: Bibliothek Warburg, 1932], 475) cites Papyrus Lugd. V and provides numerous parallel passages (including *PGM* 1.272, "the seas and rocks tremble"). Note that these are not mere descriptions, as is the case in Plato (*Phaedo*), but magical operations meant to produce magical outcomes. Also note that the gathering together of these types of watery locales into a one group (ποταμοί θάλασσαι λίμναι πηγαί) is a rhetorical tradition, evident later in instructions by Menander Rhetor (Περὶ ἐπιδεικτικῶν I [Πῶς χρὴ πόλεις ἐπαίειν] 349.26-27) on how to praise the water supply of a city: "Resources of water should be divided into three: πηγαί, ποταμοί, λίμναι"; see Donald. A. Russell and N. G. Wilson, *Menander Rhetor* (Oxford: Clarendon, 1981), 39.

23. See Gruppe (*Griechische Mythologie und Religionsgeschichte*, 815) for complete references. Not only bodies of water or springs gave humans access to chthonic elements, but also caves and pits. The oracle of Trophonius involved a descent into a cave. Callistratus (*Descriptions*: Εἰς Σατύρον 421K) describes a cave near Thebes that contained an elaborate labyrinth of passageways leading to a central chamber. Deep inside the center of the cave is a beautiful statue of a satyr, possibly also previously set up along with an image of Pan embracing Echo; see *Philostratus, the Elder, the Younger, Imagines; Callistratus, Descriptions*, ed. and trans. Arthur Fairbanks, Loeb Classical Library (Cambridge, Mass.: Harvard University Press, 1979), 376-77. Pliny (*Natural History* 2.208) describes a handful of famous caves, chasms, and fiery spots (Soracte near Rome, Sinuessa, Pozzuoli, the temple at Memphitis, Hierapolis in Asia, and Delphi). Prophetic oracles were located in some, by Pliny linked with the power of their overcoming sulfuric fumes. So lethal were the fumes of the Hierapolis cave that only a priest of the cult of Magna Mater could survive them. The symbolism of caves was ever available to represent and communicate with the abyss. Dio Cassius (67.16) reports that Domitian dreamed of a statue of Minerva standing up from its pedestal, mounting a horse, and riding off into a χάσμα (chasm), which is a sure portent (σήμειον) of destruction ahead.

24. Aristophanes, *Ranae* 137. The open sea was commonly thought an Abyss, as in Aeschylus, *Supplices* 470 (ἄβυσσον πέλαγος). The κῆτος (sea monster) that helped the Argos expedition make its way back home disappeared, slithering back into the μέγαν βυθύν (great deep); see Apollonius of Rhodes, *Argonautica* 4.1619.

25. According to Pausanias, "The depth of the Alkyonian Lake is limitless, nor do I know anyone who was ever able by any contrivance whatever to reach down to the bottom. Nero tied together many, many fathoms of rope, with a hanging lead weight and every kind of useful device for experiment, but he was unable to discover any limit to its depth. I have also been told that however calm and still this lake may be to look at [the essential meaning of ἀλκυονιδές], it drags

down anyone who dares to swim across it and sucks him into the depth. Its circuit is not great, in fact under a hundred yards; there are grasses and rushes around its lip. It would be sacrilegious if I publicly reported the night celebrations to Dionysus that take place every year at this lake" (trans. Peter Levi, *Pausanias: Guide to Greece*, rev. ed. [London: Penguin Press, 1981], 1:222. This is a correlation of danger, water, and mystery cult; see Ninck, *Die Bedeutung des Wassers*, 6 n.1. Diodorus (5.3.4) reports that a πηγή (spring) named Κυάνη near Syracuse is the place where Pluto took the abducted Kore into Hades. The site became a place both of individual and of community offerings and sacrifices. The unseen, dark, and chthonic places entered through the water are in 5.5.1 praised during rites for Demeter and Kore as γαίας μελαμφαείς μυχούς (innermost, lightless corner of earth). Josephus (*Antiquities* 15.363-64) reports that Herod the Great built a temple (ναός) in honor of Augustus near Πάνείον, at the foot of Mount Hermon (see Seán Freyne, *Galilee from Alexander the Great to Hadrian, 323 B.C.E. to 135 C.E.: A Study in Second Temple Judaism*, University of Notre Dame Center for the Study of Judaism and Christianity Series 5 [South Bend, Ind.: University of Notre Dame Press, 1980], 271) at the springs of the Jordan River. As Josephus describes it, "In the mountains here there is a beautiful cave, and below it the earth slopes steeply to a precipitous and inaccessible depth, which is filled with still water (βάθος ἀπερρωγὸς ἄβατον, ὕδατος ἀκινήτου πλέον), while above it there is a very high mountain. Below the cave rise the sources (αἱ πηγαι) of the river Jordan. It was this most celebrated place that Herod further adorned with the temple which he consecrated to Caesar" (trans. Ralph Marcus, *Jewish Antiquities, Books xv-xvii*, Loeb Classical Library [Cambridge, Mass.: Harvard University Press, 1980], 176).

26. Gruppe (*Griechische Mythologie und Religionsgeschichte*, 814-815) refers to Mylasa (Asia Minor), Miniteia (due west of Epidaurus), the Athenian Acropolis. See also Strabo (8.8.4) on the lethal water of the Styx, an idea found also in Pliny, *Natural History* 30.149.

27. About the Acropolis, Pausanias reports that "there is a building called the Erechtheion; in front of the entrance is an altar of Zeus the Highest where they sacrifice nothing that breathes, but they put sweet-cakes there and the rite allows not even use of wine. As you go in there are altars of Poseidon, where they sacrifice to Erechtheus as well according to an oracle, and of the hero Boutos, and thirdly of Hephaistos. There are pictures on the walls of the family of the Bautadai, and, the building being double, some sea-water inside in a well. This is not so very surprising: some inland people do have sea-water, as do the Carians of Aphrodisias. But the extraordinary thing about this well is that when the wind blows south a sound of waves comes from it. The mark of a trident is in the rock. They say that these were Poseidon's arguments in the quarrel over the country" (trans. Levi, *Pausanias: Guide to Greece*, 1:74-75). The θάλασσα Ἐρεχθηΐς (Erechthean Sea) was at Athens, a fountain sacred to the hero.

28. Ninck, *Die Bedeutung des Wassers*, 47-99 ("Wasser und Weissagung"). See also Christopher Faraone ("The Mystodokos and the Dark-Eyed Maidens: Multicultural Influences on a Late-Hellenistic Incantation," in *Ancient Magic and*

Ritual Power, ed. Marvin Meyer and Paul Mirecki, Religions in the Graeco-Roman World 129 [Leiden, The Netherlands: E. J. Brill, 1995], 316-25) for review of fresh water springs and healing (implicating nymphs), water-jars, and stories of salvation from fiery death by springs that appear miraculously.

29. Austere perspicacity characterized these water-creatures, whose link to the anomalous frightful was forged through their oracular divine power. Apollonius of Rhodes (*Argonautica* 4:844) describes Nereids as sisters (αὐτοκασίγνητοι) of ever-true and ever-right Thetis. All together, they would perfectly guide the Argonauts between the Scylla and Charybdis. *Orphic Hymn* 24.9-11 declares them the first to show humans the sacred rite (τελετὴν σεμνήν) of Bacchus and Persephone. In some cases, Nereids are a unique intervention after the moment of death, as they guide the deceased to a better destiny and honor the dead. See Arthur Darby Nock, "Nymphs and Nereids," in *Essays on Religion and the Ancient World, Selected and Edited, with an Introduction, Bibliography of Nock's Writings, and Indexes by Zeph Stewart* (Cambridge, Mass.: Harvard University Press, 1972), 2:919-27, on the 328 C.E. Syrian epitaph, Νύμφε κὲ Νερεείδες δέξασθε 'Ονεζάθην (Nymphs and Nereids, receive Onezathe). Nereids and nymphs occasionally "carry off" little children who have died, which is comforting symbolism of blissful destiny for the children. The same honors were attributed to a 22-year-old deceased man on Crete, to whom the Nereids were invited to come to his tomb and, in lament, sing to him the heroic tales of Achilles. *Palatine Anthology* 7.1 reports that Nereids buried Homer. In Roman sarcophagus iconography they appear in conjunction with Oceanus and safe travel to the Isles of the Blessed; see J. M. C. Toynbee (*Death and Burial in the Roman World* [Ithaca, N.Y.: Cornell University Press, 1971], 38): "Others threw open to all human souls the Blessed Isles across the Ocean (reserved in the literary tradition only for heroes), to judge from the constant representation in sepulchral art of Oceanus and of the homeward journey of the happy dead on ships or in the guise of Nereids or Cupids carried safely over the waves on the backs of friendly, frolicsome sea-lions, sea-bulls, sea-horses, sea-griffins, sea-Centaurs, Tritons, dolphins, and other Ocean-born creatures."

30. Ninck, *Die Bedeutung des Wassers*, 48.

31. Of oracular procedures there, Pausanias writes, "They tie a mirror onto some thick kind of cord, and balance it so as not to dip it into the spring, but let the surface of the mirror just touch lightly on the water. Then they pray to the goddess [Demeter] and burn incense and look into the mirror, and it shows them the sick man either alive or dead. The water is as truthful as that" (trans. Levi, *Pausanias: Guide to Greece*, 1:284).

32. See Ninck (*Die Bedeutung des Wassers*, 81-83) for further references to water oracles, including Virgil (*Aeneid* 7.81-107) on the incubation oracle of the Tiburtine nymph, Albunea.

33. A magical letter of Nephotes to Psametchos describes use of a λεκάνης αὐτοπτικός [bowl of divinatory self-revealing], into which a user gazes and spies the τὸν θεὸν ἐν τῷ ὕδατι and then hears this god speak. The result of these operations is to be τὸ παράδοξον (anomalous). In *PGM* 4.223-29 different kinds

of water are stipulated for use in the bowl, depending on the desired magical outcome: "rainwater if you are calling upon heavenly gods, sea water if gods of the earth, river water if Osiris or Sarapis, spring water if the dead" (trans. Edward O'Neil in *The Greek Magical Papyri in Translation, Including the Demotic Spells*, ed. Hans Dieter Betz [Chicago: University of Chicago Press, 1986], 42).

34. Theodor Hopfner, *Griechisch-ägyptischer Offenbarungszauber*, 2 Bd. Studien zur Palaeographie und Papyruskunde 21, 23. (Amsterdam: Verlag Adolf M. Hakkert, 1921), 2:§369.

35. See *Paulys Real-Encyclopädie der classischen Altertumswissenschaft*, Neue Bearbeitung, ed. G. Wissowa and W. Kroll (Stuttgart: J. B. Metzler, 1905), s.v. "Nekromantie," by Theodor Hopfner, with numerous references to his *Griechische-ägyptischer Offenbarungszauber* on these matters.

36. See Ninck, *Die Bedeutung des Wassers*, 56 for summary of this and similar evidence for appearance of supranormal entities in conjunction with magical or oracular operation around water. Ninck notes other vocabulary for such appearances: *umbra mortua, imagines deorum, ludificatione daemonum, simulacrum Mercurii*.

37. See the comprehensive review by Peter W. van der Horst, "Der Schatten im hellenistischen Volksglauben," in *Studies in Hellenistic Religions*, ed. M. J. Vermaseren, Études préliminaires aus religions orientales dans l'empire romain 78 (Leiden, The Netherlands: E. J. Brill, 1979), 27-36.

38. Greek texts from Ninck (*Die Bedeutung des Wassers*, 57 n.1), as found in Stobaeus, *Eclogue* 1.49.

39. Pausanias (Περιήγησις 9.31.6) wrote: "But there is another story about him less well known (though one does hear it), that Narkissos had a twin sister; they were exactly the same to look at with just the same hair-style and the same clothes, and they even used to go hunting together. Narkissos was in love with his sister, and when she died he used to visit the spring; he knew what he saw was his own reflection, but even so he found some relief in telling himself it was his sister's image" (trans. Levi, *Pausanias: Guide to Greece*, 1:376-77). An alternative account, this story emphasizes a reflected image of a mirrored double of a deceased twin.

40. See also Ovid (*Fasti* 5.476): *lubrica prensantes effugit umbra manus*, in an account of Faustulus and Acca seeking out the ghost of Remus.

41. Trans. A. T. Murray, *Homer: The Odyssey*, Loeb Classical Library (Cambridge, Mass.: Harvard University Press, 1930), 401.

42. *Homer: The Odyssey*, 403. For summaries and a myriad of references, see Gruppe, *Griechische Mythologie und Religionsgeschichte*, §276. The theme of reaching out and grasping for a previous resident of Hades appears in a story about the failed attempt by Orpheus to carry up Eurydice, in Ovid (*Metamorphoses* 10.52-58): "The track climbed upwards, steep and indistinct, through the hushed silence and the murky gloom; and now they neared the edge of the bright world, and, fearing lest she faint, longing to look, he turned his eyes—and straight she slipped away. He stretched his arms to hold her—to be held—and clasped, poor soul, naught but the yielding air" (trans. A. D. Melville, *Ovid: Metamorphoses*

[Oxford: Oxford University Press, 1986], 226.

43. Wilhelm Kroll, *Vetti Valentis Anthologiarum Libri* (Berlin: Weidmann, 1908), 67.

44. See Norman W. DeWitt, "Epicurus, Περὶ φαντασίας," *Transactions of the American Philosophical Association* 70 (1939): 420 n.13 for a philosophical discussion of the difference between φάντασμα and φαντασία, citing Diogenes Laertius 7.50. The term φάντασμα has more to do with what is evident to the διανοία as though through ὕπνος. Sleep is continually a useful metaphor for perception, especially for perception of divine power.

45. Erwin Rohde, *Psyche: The Cult of Souls and Belief in Immortality among the Greeks*, 7th ed., trans. W. B. Hillis (New York: Harcourt, Brace, 1925).

46. Walter F. Otto, *Die Manen oder von den Urformen des Totenglaubens: Eine Untersuchung zur Religion der Griechen, Römer und Semiten und zum Volksglauben überhaupt* (Darmstadt: Wissenschaftliche Buchgesellschaft, 1958). The theory revolves around the experience in dreaming of another *Ich* that appears as a Dopplegänger. Otto commented (p.67) about Roman belief, that, by *di manes*, Romans meant a group of dark spirits living in the Deep. Somewhat later this category was affixed to souls of the deceased. *Lemures* and *larvae* are generally indications of the underworld. Otto thought the spirits of the deceased might belong to an older, popular faith in underworld daimōns.

47. Cicero (*De Divinatione* 1.67) continues: *Iacet enim corpus dormientis ut mortui, viget autem et vivit animus. Quod multo magic faciet post mortem, cum omnino corpore excesserit* (for though the sleeping body then lies as it if were dead, yet the soul is alive and strong, and will be much more so after death when it is wholly free of the body; trans. W. Falconer, *Cicero: De Senectute, De Amicitia, De Divinatione*, Loeb Classical Library [Cambridge, Mass.: Harvard University Press,, 1927], 295). Xenophon (*Cyropaedia* 8.7.21) Plato, and Aristotle previously voice this opinion; see Eric R. Dodds (*The Greeks and the Irrational*, Sather Classical Lectures 25 [Berkeley: University of California Press, 1951], 135) for these references. On the earlier influence on these beliefs of a lost text of Democritus (*On Images*), see Eric R. Dodds, "Supernormal Phenomena in Classical Antiquity," in *The Ancient Concept of Progress and Other Essays on Greek Literature and Belief* (Oxford: Clarendon Press, 1973), 161-63.

48. Pindar, frg. 131, quoted in *Paulys Real-Encyclopädie*, s.v. "εἴδωλον," by A. Körte, 2085.

49. See Hopfner ("Nekromantie," in *Paulys Real-Encyclopädie*) for a discussion of the οὐσία of the dead. Hopfner, (*Griechische-ägyptischer Offenbarungszauber* 1§367-68) also describes ancient practices of desecration and mutilation of cadavers in order to effect negative results in the postmortem existence of the deceased.

50. Cosmas of Jerusalem, Ad Carmina S. Gregorii; text in Joseph Bidez and Franz Cumont, *Les Mages hellénisées: Zorastre, Osanès et Hystaspe d'après la tradition grecque* (Paris: Société d'Éditions Les Belles Lettres, 1938), 2:271. See also Pliny, *Natural History* 30.14. Osthanes was reputed to be a technical innovator, who categorized the cosmic hierarchy of substances and entities

according to various specific magical operations. He used to say that there once had been several forms of magic: "he professes to divine from water, globes, air, stars, lamps, basins and axes, and by many other methods, and besides to converse with ghosts and those in the underworld (*praeterea umbrarum inferorumque colloquia*)" (trans. W. H. S. Jones, *Pliny Natural History*, Loeb Classical Library [Cambridge, Mass.: Harvard University Press, 1963], 8:287).

51. See Körte ("εἴδωλον," in *Paulys Real-Encyclopädie*) for full references, and observations about the use of the term in grave inscriptions and defixiones (col. 2085).

52. Emily Vermeule, *Aspects of Death in Early Greek Art and Poetry*, Sather Classical Lectures 46 (Berkeley: University of California Press, 1979), 9. According to Vermeule (p.212 n.12), "In ordinary practice the *psyche* is the visible part of the dead, small enough to escape from limbs ([*Iliad*] 16.856, 12.361), or a wound (14.518); stick on a spear (16.505); settle in the neck (22.325); flow out on the breath (Simonides 52 D); it is weightless like smoke); floats in the arms of the sea (Archilochus 23 D). . . . The shift from *psyche* to *eidolon* to *nekros* is a matter of convenience, like the vision of bodies on the souls of the dead, or warriors with wounds and body armor."

53. Vermeule, *Aspects of Death*, 30-31.

54. Jean-Pierre Vernant ("Figuration de l'invisible et catégorie psychologique du double: Le colossos," in *Myth et pensée chez les Grecs: Études de psychologie historique*, new ed. [Paris: Éditions la Découverte, 1985], 330) argues that the category of the Double presupposes a way of thought quite different from ours. A double is completely different than an image. It is not an object found in nature but neither is it a mental object. It is neither an imitation of an real thing, an illusion of the mind, nor a creation of thought. The double is a reality external to the subject, but by its very appearance it is distinct from familiar objects or everyday surroundings, as it has an unusual character. In his "La figure des morts I: Eídōlon: Du double à image" (in *Figures, idoles, masques*, Conférences, Essais et Leçons du Collège du France [Paris: Julliard, 1990], 34-41), Vernant describes a psycholgoical development of this symbolism and imagery, noting that Herodotus uses the term εἴδωλον in a variety of ways: (1) 5.92, account of how of the deceased Melissa appears an εἴδωλον to Periander; (2) 6.58, account of how the Spartans construct an εἴδωλον of a deceased king for use at his funerary procession; (3) 1.51, account of a Lacedaemonian εἴδωλον of a woman (a statue made of gold and four feet tall) said to be that of the woman who served bread to Croesus. Souls and statues are linked through a complex psychological terminology of imagery, representation, and familiarity. See also Ninck, *Die Bedeutung des Wassers*, 68: "Bild, Traumbild, Wachvision und Totengespenst können alle mit gleichem Ausdruck als 'Erscheinungen', φαντασίαι, φαντάσματα (ὄψεις), visiones, Phantomata etc. bezeichnet werden" (Image, dream, waking-vision and spirit of the dead could all be signified by the same word, such as "appearances," images, apparitions, visions, phantoms, and so on). Ninck offers a full list of comparative references (p.68). Mirror reflections, like shadows, present corporal images without substance, appearing to shimmer or move. See now also D. Felton

(*Haunted Greece and Rome: Ghost Stories from Classical Antiquity* [Austin: University of Texas Press, 1999], 23-24): "The various terms used for ghost in both Greek and Latin do not have very specific denotations. Besides φάσμα and the variant φάντασμα, Greek has several all-purpose words for apparition or ghost, including εἴδωλον and δαίμων. The latter often referred not just to ghosts but to evil spirits who might take possession of a person while εἴδωλον referred to apparitions of all sorts. Several other Greek words for 'ghost' were used rather infrequently— σκιά meant a 'shade' of the dead, and ψυχή often referred not only to the soul but to the phantom of the deceased." The same dexterity and ambiguity of terminology also persists in Latin sources.

55. Μεγάλαι σου αἱ Κρίσεις, only slightly to rearrange the first line of this scriptural composition.

56. For Josephus on angels, *Antiquities* 5.213; 5.277; for dreams, *War* 3.353; *Antiquities* 2.82; for other visions and apparitional experiences, *War* 5.381, *Antiquities* 1:325 (visions Jacob had while fleeing), 3.62, 10.272.

57. Tacitus (*Histories* 5.13) offers a different version while maintaining similar aspects of the anomalous frightful. The historiographic intentions and religious criticisms of Tacitus are clearly in evidence as he discusses the event as a *prodigium*. Jews are a *gens supersitioni obnoxia* and subsequently unable to deal with such portents, as could a proper and proud Roman. *Visae per caelum concurrere acies*, Tacitus writes, *rutilantia arma et subito nubium igne conlucere templum. Apertae repente delubri fores et audita maior humana vox excedere deos; simul ingens motus excedentium* (Contending hosts were seen meeting in the skies, arms flashed, and suddenly the temple was illumined with fire from the clouds. Of a sudden the doors of the shrine opened and a superhuman voice cried: 'The gods are departing': at the same moment the mighty stir of their going was heard). Tacitus reports that few Jews at the time thought these events portended disaster, since their *antiquiis sacerdotum litteris* (ancient holy writings) predicted the outcome of these events to be favorable to them.

58. In Josephus (*War* 6.296), the heavenly armies wait to attack or not; in *War* 7.438, an Exodus and Wilderness Experience is reenacted in order [magically, or the revivification of the Exodus as a type of execration?] to unseat current political and religious authorities.

59. See *Reallexikon für Antike und Christentum*, ed. Theodore Klauser (Stuttgart: Anton Hiersemann, 1976), s.v. "Geister (Dämonen): iv, Volksglaube," by C. D. G. Müller. Section 4 of this dictionary essay reviews differences in appearance of Jewish and non-Jewish daimonic bodies and substances.

60. Dionysius of Halicarnassus (*Antiquitates Romanae* 4.62.5) writes about difficulty interpretating τεράτων τινῶν καὶ φαντασμάτων μέγαλων (certain magnificent prodigies and apparitions).

61. See *PGM* 4.279-284, a love spell addressed to Σελήνη, to whom is attributed a variety of names and functions: giant Hekate, Baubo, Kore, Artemis, "Dog-leader," and august Virgin. See also *PGM* 7.886, in which Hekate/Selene equaled Baubo. Some who constructed horoscopes believed that the influence of Σελήνη (Moon) leads unfortunate souls to unwarranted violent (βιάζω) and hostile

retaliation (ἀντιπράσσω) against friends. Such people suffer greatly and are wracked with pain (ὀδυνάω). They have no fear of death and ἄγονται ὑπὸ δαίμονος (are led by a daimon). See Vettius Valens (6.9, in Kroll, *Vetti Valentis Anthologiarum Libri*, 261 l. 10-13).

62. Epithets found in *Hymnus in Hecatem* 7, ed. Ernst Heitsch, *Die griechsichen Dichterfragmente der römischen Kaiserzeit*. 2d ed. Abhandlungen der Akademie der Wissenschaften in Göttingen, philologisch-historische Klasse, dritte Folge, 49 (Göttingen: Vandenhoeck und Ruprecht, 1963), §54 from Hippolytus, *Refutationes* 4.35.5.

63. Suggested by Rohde (*Psyche*, 590-91), referrmg to *H.Mag.* 1289 (Abel) and to *PGM* 4.1911 for the term βαυκύων. The verb βαυβύζω (bark like a dog) is in *PGM* 36.157. Dogs in the retinue of Hekate are a primary element of the symbolic link that Cornutus (*Natura Deorum* 34) draws between Hekate and Artemis. Cornutus wrote about Artemis with qualities of Hekate: αὐτὴν νυκτὸς καὶ σκότος ὁρωμένην καὶ μεταβάλλουσαν νυχίαν τε καὶ νυκτιπόλοον καὶ χθονίαν ἐκάλεσαν (they call her chthonian, she who rushes headlong through night and darkness and, rushing about, belongs to the night and wanders about by night). So also Apollonius Rhodius (*Argonautica* 3.1213), on Hekate Brimo, who is a δεινὴ θεός (dreadful divinity) and is accompanied by χθόνιοι κύνες (chthonic dogs). The long history of tradition about dogs in relation to attacking, ripping apart, or otherwise terrorizing vulnerable humans in some type of divine conflict is reviewed by Gruppe (*Griechische Mythologie und Religionsgeschichte*, 968-70). Gruppe refers especially to traditions about Aktaion and his death (torn asunder by a pack of his own dogs after being converted by Athena into a stag). Gruppe links these traditions generically to earlier traditions about Dionysus and Osiris, both of whom are mutilated in divine conflict (though not by dogs). See also Lewis Richard Farnell, *Greek Hero Cults and Ideas of Immortality*, Gifford Lectures 1920 (Oxford: Clarendon Press, 1921), 26-27. Noel Robertson ("Hittite Ritual at Sardis," *Classical Antiquity* 1 [1982]: 130-31) wrote, while reviewing evidence for the unusual stature of dogs in ritual and cult and in Hittite sacrifices, "In short, the dog as a creature of superstition or piety was at least as important in Greece as in any other part of the ancient world. . . . Of course there is Hekate, a goddess native to Caria and notoriously linked with dogs and puppies. But so far as the use of dogs and puppies belongs to domestic rites and witchcraft, it is very widely attested throughout the Greek world."

64. *Orphicorum Fragmenta*, ed. Otto Kern (Dublin: Weidmann, 1972), F52. Hekate is γιγάεσσα (giant) in *PGM* 4.2714 and in Lucian (*Philopseudes* 22), in who measures her "half a furlong high." Accounts of appearances of φάσματα (apparitions) at various crucial times often include mention of their large size; see Herodotus (*History* 6.117) for an account of an apparition during the Battle of Marathon: a huge hoplite with an enormous beard appears to Epizelus, an Athenian. Passing him by, the monstrous soldier strikes down the comrade next to him. Since that day, Epizelus was blind. Dio Cassius (55.3) reports that γυνὴ τις μείζων (a certain huge woman) had appeared to Drusus as he was attempting to cross the Albis River to further his conquests. She prevents him, predicting that

his death is at hand. The same author in 68.26 reports that Trajan was led to safety through a window by μείζονός τινος ἢ κατὰ ἄνθρωπον (some entity greater than anything by human standards). In a dream, Ptolemy Soter saw a beautiful young man (Sarapis) of superhuman size (Tacitus, *Histories* 4.83-84: *decore eximi et maiore quam humana specie iuvenem*), recalling *PGM* 4.279-84, with its "giant Hekate." Pliny (*Letters* 7.27) heard reports, generated by Curtius Rufus, about a supposed *phasma* that appears in *mulieris figura humana grandior pulchriorque* (the figure of a most tremendous and beautiful human woman). Felton (*Haunted Greece and Rome*, 30) offers further examples, especially a story from Plutarch (*Dion* 2.1-2), which reports that Dion and Brutus were each warned by apparitions of their imminent deaths. Dion sees a huge female apparition, a "tragic Fury," and Brutus sees a δεινὴν καὶ ἀλλόκοτον ὄψιν (terrible and monstrous vision). When he addresses it, it responds, "I am your own evil daimōn, Brutus" (ὁ σός, ὦ βροῦτε, δαίμων κακός).

65. Apollodorus (Περὶ θεῶν, in Stobaeus, *Eclogue* 1.49) writes Γοργύρα: Ἀχέροντος γυνή (Gorgo: a woman of the Acheron); see Apollodorus 1.5.3. Euripides (*Ion* 1053) refers to her as χθονία Γοργὼ (chthonian Gorgo). Hekate is often called χθονία. Rohde (*Psyche*, 322 n.90) refers to Sophocles *fr.* 7: χθονία καὶ νερτέρων πρύτανις (chthonic ruler of the underworld).

66. Rohde, *Psyche*, 592.

67. See Aristophanes (*Ranae* 289-90) on this quality of Empousa. This includes the acclamation πολύμορφε for Hekate (as well as αἰλόμορφος). Other divine powers having this characteristic are listed by Ninck (*Die Bedeutung des Wassers*, 172): Hera, Hermes, and various "dream and magical gods." Add to this the example of Herakles acclaimed αἰλόμορφε in *Orphic Hymn* 12.3. See also Ninck (*Die Bedeutung des Wassers*, 161-63) for a list and chart of various divinities shifting into various shapes.

68. So thought already in Sappho *fr.* 44; see Rohde, *Psyche*, 592. Lamia and Gello carried off children as well as ἄωροι from this world, as did Keres, Harpies, Erinyes, and Thanatos; compare Sarah Iles Johnston, *Restless Dead: Encounters Between the Living and the Dead in Ancient Greece* (Berkeley: University of California Press, 1999), 173-75. Brimo, too, is νυκτιπόλος in Apollonoius Rhodius, *Argonautica* 3.862.

69. Philostratus (*Apollonius* 1.4) tells of events just before Apollonius' birth. A φάσμα of Proteus approached his mother. Well-known for oscillations in shape, in this case Proteus comes in the guise of an Egyptian δαίμων.

70. Rohde, *Psyche*, 593.

71. Rohde (*Psyche*, 323 n.96) describes Hekate as an ἀνταία θεός (hostile, opposing god), especially as a divinity of the "three-roads" or of the "cross-roads." With φάσματα in tow, Hekate produces an assaultive encounter with the anomalous frightful. Rohde refers to Sophocles *fr.* (Nauck) 311, 368, 492. Pliny *(Natural History* preface 33) quips that *cum mortuis non nisi larvas luctari* (only phantoms fight with the dead).

72. This is a story about Demaratus, who compels his mother to tell him who his father really is. In response she tells him how, while in Ariston's house (ostensibly until then, the father of Demaratus), a ghost approached her "on the third night" and slept with her. The ghost had the exact appearance of Ariston, but was not Ariston. It is later determined to have been Astrobaeus, an ancient hero, whose cult place was nearby.

73. See Thomas Africa ("Worms and the Death of Kings: A Cautionary Note on Disease and History," *Classical Antiquity* 1 [1982]: 1-17) on how such stories of medical nightmares were moralistically applied to figures of certain and vast disrepute.

74. Suetonius, *Nero* 34.5. Nero, having had his mother murdered, was known to have said that he felt plagued by her *speci* (apparition) and by "whips and blazing torches of the Furies." See Suetonius (*Otho* 7), where the *manes* of Galba appears in a dream of Otho, terrifying him. Several more examples may be found in Felton (*Haunted Greece and Rome*, 8-10), including an account from Dio Cassius (78.15) about Caracella, who murdered his brother and then apparently saw phantoms, thinking he was being pursued by the ghosts of his father and brother (ghosts who are, in this terrible perception, armed with swords).

75. George W. Young (*Subversive Symmetry: Exploring the Fantastic in Mark 6:45-56*, Biblical Interpretation Series 41 [Leiden, The Netherlands: E. J. Brill, 1999], 158): "The aside in v.52 is revealed to be a space of contradiction whereby the implied reader is drawn into a dialogical interrogation, a meditation, of both story world characters and narrator alike . . . the device of an unreliable narrator in v.52 serves to emphasize through negation a multiplicity of conflicting views within the story world. For, on the one hand, by gloating over the disciples' *theoria* of reality with condescension and contempt, the narrator funnels the reader's attention back upon the story world's fantastical character: its ontological tensions, antinomy, and bidimensionality. On the other hand, the obscurity and illogic of the rhetorical narrator's voice draws attention to itself, becoming itself an object of criticism and judgment, and is ultimately deemed unreliable. Henceforth, reading Mark becomes an intensely rigorous activity whereby naive trust in the narrator is quickly replaced by guarded suspicion."

11

Waking up to Uncertainty,
Growing Aware of the Uncanny,
. . . and Following Jesus

To wake up to uncertainty in the Gospel of Mark is to grow conscious of anomaly, fear, and the uncanny in Mark and of the need to discern what these frightful things may mean. These things are, indeed, the Gospel's literary elements, and they are not easily explained. That is to say, their meaning is not well explained through literary techniques that gloss over the bits of fear, anomaly, and miasma represented in them. Unless we know the world of the Gospel of Mark, we shall miss these bits, and consequently we shall be blind to what is being represented. Without background information, we shall not even know what it is that we need to do when we read. Mark's literary representations should resist our urge to handle this Gospel merely as a textual code awaiting our responsive *sententia*, or as an evocative myth, or as a literary verisimilitude about important historical events. The reason this text should resist such an urge on our part is simple: fear, dread, anomaly, and uncertainty are not easily rationalized. Rather, it is exactly this content that stumps us, and should stump us, if not make us uneasy. We ought to run out of answers. This is not so because, as with any narrative, a transcendent ambiguity in Mark lies latent in its fiction. Rather it is so because the story in Mark is so strange and, through its quick and inexplicable presentation, is nearly called out to us. The Gospel of Mark elaborates, illuminates, articulates, and extrapolates about people, places and things that are weird and bizarre. And so they ought to seem to us.

This strangeness creates an interesting problem, especially for readers who seek something meaningful from Mark. The Gospel of Mark is an identified, "canonical," Christian text, and regardless of its content is therefore typically read either to maximize Christian theology (the reader

as theologically enfranchised) or to minimize Christian theology (the
reader as theologically disenfranchised). Either kind of reading can be
blind to the anomalous frightful in Mark, which means that either kind of
reading can make mistakes of such magnitude that the essential literary
elements of Mark go unnoticed.

Yet even now, having our eyes opened, the literary themes of
anomaly, fear, and the uncanny still do not lead us blithely to immediate
satisfaction in our theological understanding. We may desire to discover
statements in Mark about the early mission to the Gentiles, or Christology
that promotes the virtue of suffering, or miracles, or the poor, or women,
or how the early church considered thing or another, but we should
discover these only after embracing the more salient elements of Mark.
These elements are those things that the author of Mark brings to our
attention, which I have discussed in detail throughout this book. Once we
become aware of these things, we then may legitimately wonder exactly
how it is that fear and uncertainty may become the raw materials for later
theological constructions. How can the anomalous frightful make possible
a Christology?

But before we worry about theology, let us again review some of the
facts. The suffering of crucifixion is not simply "unfortunate" and a
bothersome outcome; it is a horror of fate. Jesus overpowers the Storm for
salvation; he also terrorizes those who are saved. The vengeful, ghost-
laden Legion is not simply a difficult power; it is a chthonic impurity
typically handled by magic and desperation. The bleeding woman and the
dead girl are not simply unlucky females; they are female symbols of
miasma and anomaly, both of which are undone by a man who seems to
shrug his shoulders and say it is never really a disaster anyway ("She is
not dead, but sleeping"). The hometown of Jesus is not simply an
unsuccessful example of persuasion; it is a story of Jesus failing to
convince the civilized world about the value of his miracles and wisdom.
The sending of the disciples is not a convenient picture about
discipleship; it is the sending of men into an unpredictable, undesirable
life of exile, with little to no sense of what θέος (god) they are working
for or why. The beheading of John is not just an odd political story; it is
a story about the vengeance that the violently killed have on those
responsible of their deaths. The feeding in the wilderness is not a picture
of eucharistic, eschatological sation; it is a social largesse and benefaction
from which its patron inexplicably hides, and then walks away. The
perambulation of Jesus on the ocean while appearing to be a ghost is not
a symbol of victory over death; it is a picture of Jesus appearing to be just

the opposite, not a victor over death but a member of the dead, now undead, a terror-bringing ghost (φάντασμα).

Given these facts of the anomalous frightful, how should we begin to make "theology" out of this Gospel? There must be some way to span the distance between Mark's representation of the anomalous frightful and our ongoing theological conversations. The need to bridge this gap is a problem that is, in fact, already illustrated in the Gospel of Mark. Let us turn to the end of the Gospel. Who would have wanted to "return to Galilee" to see Jesus again, as the "young man" instructs the women at the empty tomb (Mark 16:7)? In Galilee the most bizarre events have taken place, and given these kinds of events before the outrageous death by crucifixion, who would want to return to the scene, repeat them, and then try to extrapolate some meaning from them? As this story has it, are the women not correct in their judgment, to run away in fear from the emptied tomb? They are perhaps the clearest thinkers, given their odd situation and the strange doings that have led up to it. A raised Jesus, at least in the Gospel of Mark, is not someone whom you might want to see again so soon. We can imagine the women reacting along lines that, when the problem of death is apparently now behind this anomaly of a savior, how strange will things now become? What will happen next? Why risk it? Anomalies are not the things that one volunteers to encounter or to take on as a burden.

Likewise, anomalies are not the things from which one wants to construct theology. Yet there is a saving grace within this. True, the women run away, as we also might feel a desire not to make anything of the anomaly that Mark offers us. Yet in Mark, even given the anomaly, we (like the followers of Jesus) are invited to follow Jesus further, and not simply to stop at our confusion about the anomalous frightful in the Gospel. Our attempt to interpret all of this, and to make some sort of meaning of it, would not be unlike a "return to Galilee" to find Jesus again, in spite of the strange things that such a return might inaugurate.

If we try to construct theology out of the Gospel of Mark while paying attention to what needs attention, the anomalous frightful, then we shall not need to bog down in interminably tedious, critical discussions, such as how our "ideology" affects our reading.[1] As I have labored to demonstrate, the Gospel of Mark presents to us material that emphasizes the uncertain, the dreadful, the impure, and the uncanny. It is as if the Gospel were reminding us that our ideology, or whatever kind of mentation we might use to solve riddles and eliminate uncertainty, is from the very first subject to assault by this particular Gospel narrative. This much, I think, is certain. We are then left to wonder how we may interpret this material, and there is nothing more effective than this sense of wonder to help us to identify how our "ideology" wants to compel our interpretation. This wonder is the overarching significance of this kind of material, and this wonder is an integral part of Mark's message, which message probably ought not to be domesticated by our commentary on it. No matter what our ideologies, Mark is in principle against them. We may find, therefore, that between such robust narrative representations of the uncanny and our propositions of theology about those representations is more distance, historical, and theological, than we are apt at first to admit. I can think of no easy way to formulate content like this into *sententiae* or λόγοι about God, as either the Christian or anti-Christian reader is wont to do.

Perhaps this difficulty can be partly accounted for by theories about rhetoric, wherein the sense and image of a character or events involving a character are meant to impress a *feeling* or a *disposition* upon the hearer, not necessarily impress a syllogistic or propositional content. As Longinus (35.5) says, θαυμαστὸν δ᾽ ὅμως ἀεὶ τὸ παράδοξον ("what is amazing is always anomalous"). Often it is that our attention is most fully got by things that don't make sense to us. The need to come to terms with this rhetorical matter becomes a priority, especially when we assume that the figure as represented is of critical importance. Given that our natural tendency is to conclude the work of narrative interpretation with syllogisms, onto exactly what shall we hold in order to create our final propositions when the object we are assessing is the anomalous frightful? When the narrative representation is richly anomalous, and by all appearances deliberately so, and when it seems to convey information about a critical turn of events, then what would we do should it be found that our concluding syllogisms disregard too much of the actual impression of the matter?

The Gospel of Mark is to be embraced with all its representation of the anomalous frightful, from each occurrence to its implication in the pattern of the Gospel as a whole. In so embracing, we shall have difficulty finding in Mark a simple, theological statement about Jesus, the church, or any other single matter. We shall find in Mark a style, a dimension, an aspect, and a tendency that comes into play throughout. It is an adequate interpretation of this style to conclude that it seeks to represent Jesus as a character around whom people felt neither comfortable nor coherent. What was expected did not happen, and the good that did happen seemed to occur wrongly, or in a backwards manner, or inexplicably.

Continuing the Journey

In our work to interpret Mark well, we are wise to be aware of the monumental guesses made by many who study Mark, when they attempt to speak about the kind of material offered in the Gospel. Obsessive readers may look for codes, and romantic readers may look for myth. The latter is such a vague category that those who pursue it seem to offer up but vapors of meaning when they conclude that the Gospel of Mark is a myth of one type or another. Meanwhile, theologically committed readers want to find the verisimilitude, "the truth," offered in the Gospel of Mark. As we weigh these variant approaches, we need some place to stand, from which to begin to make our interpretive judgments. We need only think of the vast chasms opened between current viewpoints, as between Dennis Ronald MacDonald's theory about a Markan use of Homer and Roger David Aus's theory about a Markan use of Midrash,[2] to appreciate the need for common ground as we begin the job of interpreting Mark. For our own relief, let us admit that determination of how or even if the representations in the narrative of the Gospel of Mark are "valid' and "reliable," and for what, is a job dependent on multiple tasks. Not the least important task is an investigation into just what the words, themes, scenes, and characters in Mark might mean in the general context from which they emerge. Pursuit of this task has been a major burden of this book.

I should like to think that, ultimately, the Gospel of Mark might have some of its best interpretive results in the domains of theology. Those who might create finer creations and expressions through use of material from Mark may well be theologians who can negotiate Mark's cultural and historical context, rather than historians and literary critics who have little interest in theology. There is not likely one set of interpretive results about Mark that will prove to be permanently more persuasive than another. The charm of the Gospel of Mark is that, in spite of perennial problems in our interpretation, it seeks to focus and hold our attention on a Jesus who is magnificently anomalous and inexplicable. We are to identify with the women who run away from the emptied tomb in fear, but not permanently. Once we digest the truth that fear and confusion, at least according to Mark, are totally normal responses to Jesus of Nazareth and the things that happen in proximity to him, then we can investigate how that might also be true for us, who are theologically interested readers. And after that, we can explore how it is that, in spite of fear and confusion, we can still follow Jesus to find out what might happen next.

Notes

1. George Aichele, "Text, Intertext, Ideology," in *Jesus Framed* (London: Routledge, 1996), 146-65.

2. Dennis R. MacDonald, *The Homeric Epics and the Gospel of Mark* (New Haven, Conn.: Yale University Press, 2000). Roger David Aus, *"Caught in the Act," Walking on the Sea, and the Release of Barabbas Revisited*, South Florida Studies in the History of Judaism 157 (Atlanta: Scholars Press, 1998) and *Water Into Wine and the Beheading of John the Baptist*, Brown Judaic Studies 150 (Atlanta: Scholars Press, 1988).

Appendix A

Redeeming, Violent Death in Hellenistic Literature

Onias, Eleazar, and the Seven Brothers: In 2 Maccabees 4:30-35, the murder of Onias, lured out of sanctuary, is touted as an example of pagan impiety in contrast to the righteousness of Onias. Reports of the executions of Eleazar and the seven brothers display their virtue. Eleazar dies with honor instead of having dishonored himself by eating pig's flesh. The writer states about him, "This was how he died, leaving his death as an example of nobility and a record of virtue not only for the young but for the great majority of the nation" (2 Macc. 6:31 JB). The spokesman for the seven brothers declares, "We are prepared to die rather than break the laws of our ancestors" (2 Macc. 7:2 JB). The narrative of each successive death mentions some element of redeeming consideration: (1) God would retaliate; (2) the deceased would be raised up by the true King of the world; (3) limbs and tongues could be cut off here in this world, but would be restored in the world to come; (4) all the sons would be restored to their mother in the Day of Mercy. Jan Willem van Henten ("Das jüdische Selbstverständnis in den ältesten Martyrien," in *Die Entstehung der jüdischen Martyrologie,* ed. J. W. Van Henten, Studia Post-Biblica, 38 [Leiden, The Netherlands: E. J. Brill, 1989], 127-61) identified these as central texts of a Jewish martyrology genre. Henten noted that the deaths are embedded in narratives that highlight information about the martyrs' vicarious relation to their people (ἡ ἄγια πόλις, τὸ ἔθνος τῶν Ἰουδαίων, τὸ ἔθνος, τὸ γένος). The deaths are deaths on behalf of a people group. They may have been torturous, but last thing they were was anomalous. 4 Macc. 7:1-4 (OTP) presents Eleazar's death as a philosophical model, thereby driving even further away any uncanny aspect of the death.

> Like an outstanding pilot, indeed, the reason of our father Eleazar,
> steering the vessel of piety on the sea of passions, though buffeted by
> the threats of the tyrant and swamped by the swelling waves of torture,
> in no way swerved the rudder of piety until he sailed into the haven of

deathless victory. No city beleaguered by many devices of all kinds has ever offered such resistance as did that perfect saint. When his sacred soul was assailed with blazing rack and torture, through reason, the shield of his piety, he overcame his besiegers.

Philoctetes: Glen W. Bowersock sketched out traditions about this figure in "The Wounded Savior," *Fiction as History* (Berkeley: University of California Press, 1994), 55-76. Greek stories about Philoctetes reported that he performed a noble deed for Herakles, was then bitten by a snake, had an incurable wound, and was finally abandoned by Odysseus on the island of Lemnos. Later he was the key to victory in the Trojan War. By the third century B.C., stories placed him in Italy, bravely fighting and dying in battle. He became a suffering pariah who was killed as a righteous warrior. Moralizing about his suffering and death was apparently attempted by Peregrinus (Lucian, *Peregrinus* 33). According to Lucian, Peregrinus taught that Philoctetes was an example of dying "to instruct humanity." A notable feature of the Hellenistic and Roman versions of the story has to do with the serpent wound and the death. First there were great cries of pain, then quiet and a stoic acceptance. His death became a model of virtue.

Aesop: Lawrence Wills (*The Quest for the Historical Gospel: Mark, John, and the Origins of the Gospel Genre* [London: Routledge, 1997], 28) suggested that Aesop's death became vicarious:

> [in] the *Life of Aesop* tradition . . . the poet's death results in purification. The immediate result from the death itself is impurity, but the ultimate result is eternal purification by way of propitiating the hero in cult—as ordained by Apollo himself. Moreover, the mode of Aesop's death is itself a purification, in that he dies like a *pharmakos* "scapegoat."

In *Vita G* f.66, before his death Aesop tells a story (λόγος) about the Frog and the Mouse, through which he indicates that his death by the Delphians will be wrong. In this story about unjust murder the Mouse states, νεκρὸς ὢν ζῶντά σε ἐκδικήσω (being dead, I will seek revenge on you the living). It is later reported that, in the very moments of his dying, Aesop laments, ὦ Ζεῦ, τί σε ἠδίκησα ὅτι οὕτως ἀπόλλυμαι (O Zeus! How have I acted unjustly toward you, that I am dying like this?). The wrongness of the death is here emphasized, depicting Aesop a righteous victim.

Appendix B

Ancient Reading of Narrative and Plot

On close reading of narrative and perspicuous plot interpretation in antiquity, see Bowersock, (*Fiction As History*, 8) with a wonderful example.

> In a small but telling way an epigram of the Greek satiric poet Lucillius, from the time of the emperor Nero, illustrates this whole process. The poet addressed a dancer of female roles who afforded general pleasure to viewers by performing mythological ballets according to the stories that everyone knew: πάντα καθ στορίην ρχούμένος, "you danced everything according to the story" (*Palatine Anthology* 11.254). But the satirist is vexed by the dancer's failure to enact the suicide of a figure who was well known to have killed herself after an incestuous affair with her brother. "You had a sword," says the poet, "but yet left the stage alive: that was not according to the story" (το το παρ στορ-ίην).

The most ancient commentary on Mark is found in comments in Origen's *Commentary on the Gospel According to Matthew*. (Texts found in *Commentaire sur l'Évangile selon Matthieu, tome 1: Livres X et XI*, ed. and trans. Robert Girod, Sources Chrétiennes 162 [Paris: Éditions Cerf, 1970].) A scholar of Alexandrian training, Origen sought clarifications and definitions. One may ask, "About what was the passage reporting the poor reception of Jesus in his home city?" The answer is that the passage really contains information about how the church is to conduct its missionary affairs to the extremities of the world (τοῖς ἔθνεσι). (See *Commentary on Matthew* 10.16.45.) One may ask, "Why did Herod think Jesus was John the Baptist raised from the dead?" Origen answered that Herod entertained a misunderstanding of a technical concept called μετενσωματώσις. (See *Commentary on Matthew* 10.20.36.) One may ask, "Why did Jesus occasionally climb into the mountains?" The answer is that the crowds (ὄχλοι) pressured him so to climb. Origen argued that the topography of τὸ ὄρος (mountain) is symbolic in Mark. Being outsiders, the crowd could not follow him (up) there; only his insider disciples could. (See *Commentary on Matthew* 10.4.14.) Origen suggested that in the gospel narrative, inability to follow Jesus up the mountain is analogous to inability to understand his parables. Furthermore, the scene of the disciples βασανιζομένοι in 6:48 (ἦν γὰρ ὁ ἄνεμος ἐναντίος αὐτοῖς) is symbolic of how Christians faced temptations. Origen likened ὁ ἄνεμος to τὸ πνεῦμα τοῦ πονηροῦ, or that evil spirit which tempts Christians. (See *Commentary on Matthew* 11.6.25ff.) All of this meaning is unlocked, decoded, and made evident if readers pay perspicuous attention to the story of the gospels (ὁ μὲν οὖν ἁπλούστερος ἀρκείσθω ἱστορίᾳ). (See *Commentary on Matthew* 11.6.1 for details of this hermeneutical principle.) On this principle, see Jean Pépin, ("Terminologie exégétique dans les milieux du paganisme grec et du judaisme hellénistique," in *La terminologia esegetica nell'antichità* [Bari, Italy: Epiduglia, 1987], 15) reviewing the literal sense of λέξις (speech) in Philo as well as the adjectives ἁπλοῦς (simple) and φανερός (plainly clear) used to describe ἱστορία (written accounts of alleged events).

Ancient commentary and use of Homer developed similar skills, to many different ends. See Robert Lamberton, (*Homer the Theologian: Neoplatonist Allegorical Reading and the Growth of the Epic Tradition* [Berkeley: University of California Press, 1986], 2): "It is difficult to say whether there was ever a time when the *Iliad* and *Odyssey* were *not* viewed as possessing potential to reveal meanings beyond the obvious." Numenius carefully examined select Homeric passages. He noted semantic distinctions between Homeric θέοι and ἀθάνατοι (divinities ad immortals), doing so for the end of promoting his own discussion about Cancer, Capricorn, and the origin and fate of souls (that is, Neo-Platonic views of souls emerging from the Milky Way, through the cave at the tropic of Cancer, and then exiting through the tropic of Capricorn). (See Numenius *Frag.* 31.25 in Édouard des Places, *Numénius: Fragments*, Collection des Universités de France [Paris: Société d'Édition Les Belles Lettres, 1973], 83. In specific response to such a way of reading as this, Origen later criticized what had appeared to be Numenius' promiscuous indulgence in allegorization, not only concerning Homeric tales but also concerning his exegesis of tales about Jesus, Moses, and Jannes and Jambres. (See Origen *Contra Celsum* 4.51; Numenius *Frag.* 10a.) Origen wrote, περὶ τοῦ ᾽Ιησοῦ ἱστορίαν τινα . . . καὶ τροπολογεῖ αὐτήν (a certain story about Jesus . . . and he [Numernius] developed rhetorical flourishes with it). The allegorist Heraclitus wrote that the whole wandering course of [Odysseus], if one considers it carefully, is nothing but a great allegory. [Odysseus] is like some instrument fashioned by Homer from all the virtues; through him Homer teaches us moderation (sagacity) because he detests the vices that destroy mankind. Especially, the pursuit of strange pleasures, as in the land of the Lotus-Eaters, where [Odysseus] fell under its spell.

See Heraclitus Ὁμήρικα Προβλήματα 70.1-3; English translation here by Richard Brilliant, *Visual Narratives: Storytelling in Etruscan and Roman Art* (Ithaca, N.Y.: Cornell University Press, 1984), 60; compare *Héraclite: Allégories d'Homère*, ed. and trans. Félix Buffière, Collection des Universités de France (Paris: Société d'Édition Les Belles Lettres, 1962), §70. The *Tabula Odysseaca* in the Vatican Museum offers a pictorial reading of the *Odyssey* that epitomizes and visualizes the narrative scenes, juxtaposing them to mythic scenes about Poseidon. The visual impact of the scenes is a result of careful selection of narrative materials. (See Brilliant, *Visual Narratives*, 58-59.) For rhetorical instruction, Aelius Theon discussed examples from the *Odyssey* to demonstrate types of narrative accomplishment in the section Περὶ διηγήματος (On Narrative) from his Προγυμνάσματα (School Book Instructions). (See Theon *Progymnasmata* 193 in Spengel, *Rhetores Graeci*, 2:86.) Aelius Aristides reported that he once had been told by Athena that he was in fact both Odysseus and Telemachus! She reminds him that the "tales" in the *Odyssey* are not "idle."(See Aelius Aristides *Orations* 48.42.)

Appendix C

"Waters of Death"

On the "Waters of Death" in the *Gilgamesh Epic* see Reinhard Kratz (*Rettungswunder: Motiv-, traditions-, und formkritische Aufarbeitung einer biblischen Gattung*, Europäische Hochschule Schriften 23 [Frankfurt am Main: Peter Lang, 1979], 54-65), pointing to Job 26:5; Psalms 18:4-5, 10, 15-16; 69:14-15; and 88:3-6; and Ezekiel 26:19-20. The "Waters of Death" appear especially in an Old Assyrian version of the *Epic* in Tablet X (ii.25, 27; iii.50; iv.3); see "Akkadian Myths and Epics," trans. E. A. Speiser, in *Ancient Near Eastern Texts Relating to the Old Testament*, 3d ed., ed. James B. Pritchard (Princeton, N.J.: Princeton University Press, 1969), 90-93. One story (ii.20-27) should be noted.:

> The ale-wife said to him, to Gilgamesh: "Never, O Gilgamesh, has there been a crossing, and none who came since the beginning of days could cross the sea. Only valiant Shamash crosses the sea. Other than Shamash, who can cross (it)? Toilsome is the place of crossing, very toilsome the way thereto, and in between are the *Waters of Death* that bar its approaches! When there, O Gilgamesh, wouldst thou cross the sea? On reaching the *Waters of Death*, what wouldst thou do?"

On death expressed through water terminology, see Nicholas J. Tromp, *Primitive Conceptions of Death and the Nether World in the Old Testament*, Biblica et Orientalia 21 (Rome: Pontifical Biblical Institute, 1969), 59-61. On p.59 Tromp observes that the word $t^e hôm$ never appears with an article, meaning that it became a standard, traditional name. In Ugarit, it is found in *UT* 51:V:20ff: "Then surely she (Anat) set her face towards El at the source of the rivers (in) the midst of the channels of the two oceans (*thmtm*)." See also *UT* `nt:III:19-22: "Speech of wood, whisper of stone, converse of heavens with the Nether World, the deeps (*thmt*) with the stars." Tromp notes that the same word is used in the Genesis 1 creation story, yoked with Darkness. The Deluge later is its chaotic return. Tromp also points to suggestive verses that use the theme: Psalm 107:26, "They mounted up to $š^a mayîm$, went down to the $t^e hômôt$ . . ." and Jonah 2:6, "The $t^e hôm$ was around me." See Herbert G. May

("Some Cosmic Connotations of *Mayim Rabbîm*, 'Many Waters'," *Journal of Biblical Literature* 74 no. 2 [1955]: 9-21), who writes (p.12),

> Yahweh's conquest over the enemies of Israel, whether at the Red Sea, or in the present, or at the beginning of the new age (cf. Isa. 27:1) is a victory over cosmic evil and wickedness, over the demonic, or more properly the dragonic. . . . We may note how in Dan. 7 the four beasts which are the four pagan kingdoms have their origin in the great sea over which, as over the primordial deep in Gen. 1, the winds were active.

On the same terminology in 11QPs^a Psalm 150 and the *Yoser Qedushah* see Moshe Weinfeld, "The Angelic Song over the Luminaries in the Qumran Texts," in *Time to Prepare the Way in the Wilderness: Papers on the Qumran Scrolls by Fellows of the Institute for Advanced Studies of the Hebrew University Jerusalem, 1989-1990*, ed. Devorah Dimant and Lawrence H. Schiffman, Studies in the Texts of the Desert of Judah 16 (Leiden, The Netherlands: E. J. Brill, 1995), 135-37. Matthias Krieg (*Todesbilder im Alten Testament, oder: Wie die Alten den Tod gebildet*, Abhandlungen zur Theologie des Alten und Neuen Testaments 73 [Zürich: Theologischer Verlag, 1988], 601-606), on the Deep and death, cites Job 3:3,4-6 but also Psalm 88:5-12, "I am counted among those who go down to the Pit. . . . You have put me in the depths of the Pit, in the regions dark and deep. Your wrath lies heavy on me, and you overwhelm me with all your waves. . . . Every day I call on you, O Lord; I spread out my hands to you. Do you work wonders for the dead? Do the shades rise up to praise you? Is your steadfast love declared in the grave, or your faithfulness in Abaddon? Are your wonders known in the darkness, or your saving help in the land of forgetfulness" (NRSV). Compare to these lines from Psalm 88 lines from *PGM* 4.1460-1464, where a similar combination of the underworld and forgetfulness is presented: "O Primal Chaos, Erebos, and you O awful water of the Styx, O streams, O Lethe, Hades' Acherousian pool, O Hekate and Pluto and Kore, and chthonic Hermes, Moirai, Punishments" (trans. E. O'Neil in *Greek Magical Papyri in Translation*, ed. Hans Dieter Betz [Chicago: University of Chicago Press, 1986], 66). In the unspeakable whirlpools (ἀπροφατοι δίναι) of Acheron, λήθη (amnesia) sweeps over a person's ψυχή (soul). This is the abode of the ὑποχθόνιοι (underworld entities); see Apollonius Rhodius, *Argonautica* 1.644-645. *Palatine Anthology* 7.25 suggests that Teos, after death, lived alone in Acheron, dwelling in the Λήθης δόμων (House of Forgetfulness).

Appendix D

Chains and Haunted Houses

Pliny (*Epistles* 7.7) reports a story about a haunted house, with the chains in which a man was buried playing a large role in the after-death experience of the man, who appears as a ghost.

> At one time in Athens there was a roomy old house where nobody could be induced to live. In the dead of night the sound of clanking chains would be heard, distant at first, proceeding doubtless from the garden behind of the inner court of the house, then gradually drawing nearer and nearer, till at last there appeared the figure of an old man with a long beard, thin and emaciated, with chains on his hands and feet . . . Athenodorus did not raise his eyes or stop his work, but kept his attention fixed and listened. The sounds gradually grew nearer, and finally entered the room where he was sitting. Then he turned round and saw the apparition. It beckoned him to follow, but he signed to it to wait and went on with his work. Not till it came and clanked its chains over his very head would he take up a lamp and follow it. The figure moved slowly forward, seemingly weighed down with its heavy chains, until it reached an open space in the courtyard. There it vanished. Athenodorus marked the spot with leaves and grass, and on the next day the ground was dug up in the presence of a magistrate, when the skeleton of a man with some rusty chains was discovered. The remains were buried with all ceremony, and the apparition was no more seen.

The man is buried in chains, perhaps already bound before his death and buried that way. Chains are a chief part of this story, mentioned five times. This translation appears in Lacy Collison-Morley, *Greek and Roman Ghost Stories* (Chicago: Argonaut, 1912). See also D. Felton (*Haunted Greece and Rome: Ghost Stories from Classical Antiquity* [Austin: University of Texas Press, 1999]), who mentions Lucian (*Philopseudes* 15) on ghosts who are afraid of noise of bronze or iron; Pausanius (9.38.5) for how inhabitants of Orchomenos stop a dangerous ghost by burying its bones, making a bronze statue of it, and then fastening the statue with iron to a rock; Plutarch (*Cimon* 1.6) on haunted baths at Chaeronea, where are heard sounds of ghosts groaning and rattling chains. Felton (p. 9) reviews stories about threatening revanants, including Livy (3.58.11) in which the ghost of the slain Verginia roams from house to house and never rests until all the people involved in her death are brought to justice; *Aeneid* 1.353-7, in which the murdered Sychaeus appears to Dido in her sleep, saying that her brother Pygmalion was the one who killed him, and warning her to flee; Apuleius (*Metamorphoses* 9.29), in which a discarded wife arranges for a ghost to kill her husband; Apuleius (*Metamorphoses* 9.31), in which the ghost of murdered husband appears to his daughter in her sleep, revealing his wife's complicity in his murder.

See also *Testament of Solomon* (1:13) for a very different sort of binding, in this case the binding of nefarious powers, especially (5:11-13) on Asmodeus, who is bound with iron and put into the service of fabricating vessels for the temple. Binding had different meanings, depending on history and context of the nonhuman entity depicted as bound. In our sources, weird and dangerous entities generally are described as bound or in need of binding. This is a consistent theme of the anomalous frightful. For an apocalyptic scenario, see Revelation 20:1, depicting an angel descending from heaven to the δράκοντα (= Διάβολος = Σατανας) with a key to the Abyss and a ἅλυσιν μεγάλην (great prison). The angel grabs the beast, binds it for 1,000 years, and throws it into the Abyss, locking the door behind it and sealing it up. See also 1 Enoch 21:7 on the ἀβύσσος (abyss) with great fire and burning. The Ethiopic version expands the description of this place, so that it "had a cleavage that extended to the last sea, pouring out great pillars of fire." The place is the δεσμωτήριον (prison) of the angels, in which they are locked up αἰῶνος εἰς τὸν αἰῶνον (forever). 11QPsApᵃ col. iv lines 8-9 (trans. E. Isaac in *The Old Testament Pseudepigrapha*, ed. James Charlesworth [Garden City, N.Y.: Doubleday, 1983]), 1:24) states about wickedness that "the Lord [will impris]on you in the lowest [Sheo]l [and close upon you do]rs of iron." See Bilhah Nitzan, *Qumran Prayer and Religious Poetry*, trans. Jonathan Chipman, *Studies on the Texts of the Desert of Judah* 12 (Leiden, The Netherlands: E. J. Brill, 1994), 234.

Appendix E

Divinities Affecting Women

Harpocrates: For a detailed foray into the syncretism, see Maria Totti, "Der griechisch-ägyptische Traumgott Apollon-Helios-Harpokrates-Tithoes in zwei Gebeten der griechischen magischen Papyri," *Zeitschrift für Papyrologie und Epigraphik* 73 (1988):287-96 and "ΚΑΡΠΟΚΡΑΤ-ΗΣ ΑΣΤΡΟΜΑΝΤΙΣ und die ΛΥΧΝΟΜΑΝΤΕΙΑ," *Zeitschrift für Papyrologie und Epigraphik* 73 (1988): 297-301. Tithoes protected humans while they slept (that is, protection against night terrors), sometimes called Τοτοῆς Θεοδαίμων ῞Υπνος, as on a votive relief from Amphipolis.

Meliouchos: See Christine Harrauer (*Meliouchos: Studien zur Entwicklung religiöser Vorstellungen in griechischen synkretistischen Zaubertexten*, Wiener Studien, Beiheft 11: Arbeiten zur Antiken Religionsgeschichte 1 [Wien: Verlag der Österreichische Akademie der Wissenschaften, 1987], 77) on how Harpocrates (especially in Ptolemaic times) had qualities similar to Apollo-Horus (Diodorus Siculus, 1.25.7: "Horus, which when translated turns out to be whom we call Apollo"). This Apollo (*PGM* 6.35-36) is Phoibos son of Leto who elsewhere is also acclaimed φιλαίματος (Lover of Blood; Aeschylus, *Septem contra Thebas* 45). As Harrauer suggests as a proper interpretation for *PGM* 6.35, Meliouchos-Harpocrates as a night-roaming creature (νυκτερόφοιτος) is also a *Heilgott*. She notes that in Herakleapolis Magna in Egypt, there is a Herakles *Gestalt* in iconography. Harpocrates closely fits into this syncretism, as statues and coins make him out to be like this Herakles. Harrauer suggests that a pastiche of Meliouchos-Horus and Melqart was then current, and that both are solar deities and had *Heraklesgestalten*. Herodotus linked the Tyrian and Egyptian Herakles figures (*History* 2.43-44). Plutarch *De Iside et Oside* 41 mentions the astronomical meaning of the sun-god figures, including as a possible result of this conglomerate divinity's actions the phrase πηγαῖς ὑπὸ βίας καὶ ῥώμης περαινομέναις (fountainous source shut off by force and might). See Corinne Bonnet ("Héraclés en orient: Interprétations et syncrétismes," in *Héraclès: D'une rive à l'autre de la Méditerranée: Bilan et perspectives: Actes de la Table Ronde de Rome*, ed. C. Bonnet and C. Jourdain-Annequin, Études de philologie, d'archéologie et d'histoire anciennes 28 [Bruxelles: Institut Historique Belge de Rome, 1992], 165-98) for an overview of the widespread and complex syncretism of Herakles with Melqart as witnessed in (1) Tyre and the Syro-Phoenician coast, where Herakles is a figure of ambiguity: male and female, human and divine, civilized and wild; and Melqart is a similar figure (a heroic king; here the iconographic features of Herakles begin to surface in Melqartian representations); (2) the Transjordan; (3) the Decapolis and Arabia; (4) Haran, where an Arameo-Arabic culture produced iconographic features of a classical Herakles, especially including the "apotropaic" character of the Twelve Works (statues of Herakles were often placed at borders, near colonies, at gates, and elsewhere, to ward off trouble). On the Herakles Δωδεκάεθ-λος (Twelve Labors) in iconography, see Frank Brommer, *Herakles: Die zwölf Taten des Helde in antiker Kunst und Literatur*, 5th ed. (Köln: Böhlau, 1986), 53-63. On exportation of Herakles-Melqart to the Phoenician colony of Gades, with discussion of aniconic cult, swine taboo, and this Herakles as divine guardian, see Lewis Richard Farnell (*Greek Hero Cults and Ideas of Immortality*, The Gifford Lectures 1920 [Oxford: Clarendon Press, 1921], 167-68.

Ὀρθία or Ὀρθωσία: David G. Martinez (*P. Michigan XVI: A Greek Love Charm from Egypt (P.Mich. 757)*, Michigan Papyri 16; American Studies in Papyrology 30 [Atlanta: Scholars Press, 1991], 37) argues that Ὀρθία or Ὀρθωσία were variations of Artemis' name. For Artemis' identification with Hekate/Selene, see Theocritus 2.33 and *PGM* 4. 2523, 2720f., 2816.

βαυβω: See Martinez, *P. Michigan XVI*, 38. This name, originally associated with Demeter's tradition and cult, came to represent also Hekate. See *PGM* 4. 2709-2784, a love-spell addressed to Σελήνη (Moon) to whom is attributed a variety of names and functions: giant Hekate, Baubo, Kore, Artemis, "dog-leader," august virgin, and so on. See also *PGM* 7. 886 (Hekate/Selene = Baubo). See Maurice Olender ("Aspects of Baubo: Ancient Texts and Contexts," in *Before Sexuality: The Construction of Erotic Experience in the Ancient Greek World*, ed. David M. Halperin, and others (Princeton, N.J.: Princeton University Press, 1990), 83-113, esp. pp.100-104 on conjunctions of nocturnal Hekate and her Baubo, Demeter, Demeter's nurse, Demeter's nurse's lizard, female toads in magic, the night terrors Gello (Γελλώ), Mormo (Μορμών), Gorgon (Γοργώ), Empousa (Ἔμπουσα), and Lamia (Λάμια), old women, ugliness, and obscene gestures.

Coptic NOURE: Martinez (*P. Michigan XVI*, 38) comments on the Greek form of this term, νοηρε, probably for the Coptic *noure* (vulture), a bird thought to be only of the female sex and thus sacred to a number of goddesses, including Hekate-Selene.

Ερεσχιγαλ: Martinez (*P. Michigan XVI*, 38) comments on this Babylonian goddess equated with Hekate-Persephone. Κούρη Περσεφόηη (Queen Persephone) in magical texts is associated with the Babylonian underworld goddess Ereschigal (*PGM* 7.984), who herself is associated with Hekate (*PGM* 70). See especially Hans Dieter Betz ("Fragments from a Catabasis Ritual in a Greek Magical Papyrus," *History of Religions* 19 [1979-1980]: 288-89) on phrases in *PGM* 70.5: Ἑκάτης ᾽Ερεσχιγάλ (Hekate Ereschigal) and ἐγώ εἰμί ᾽Ερεσχιγάλ (I am Ereschigal).

Ο ὑροβόρος: Martinez (*P. Michigan XVI*, 38) comments on this name for a "serpent swallowing the end of its tail," including the variant ἀκρουροβόρε. The diagram of a serpent forming a circle by biting its tail occurred in magical papyri (*PGM* 7 col. xvii) and especially in amulets. As a symbol of eternity, resurrection, and the underworld, the image is mainly connected with Helios-Osiris, but on a secondary level may also be associated with the moon and thus with Hekate, as is the case in the invocation, Κόρη Ἑκάτη ἀκρουροβόρη Σελήνη (Kore, Hekate, Moon-Serpent-Tail-Swallowing).

Appendix F

Gynecological Health

Campbell Bonner (*Studies in Magical Amulets Chiefly Graeco-Roman,* University of Michigan Studies, Humanistic Series 49 [Ann Arbor: University of Michigan Press, 1950], 85) comments on amulets with magical formulas for women's health safety, including diagrams of the uterus. "We may therefore treat it as definitely proved," Bonner writes,

> that the vessel shown on these amulets is a conventionalized representation of the uterus, and that the lines proceeding from its top represent the Fallopian tubes, the others the ligaments that hold the organ in place. The various deities shown in connection with the design are to be regarded just as in other amulets; they exercise control over the department of human life to which the amulet ministers. In some cases the appropriateness of the individual deities is obvious. Isis as a guardian of women and Harpocrates as a divine infant are naturally associated with the functions of reproduction, and the comical dwarf Bes is known to have been regarded, even from dynastic times, as a protector of children. The goddess Thueris, who sometimes appears among the deities in the upper field, was apparently a guardian of pregnant and nursing women.

For texts invoking protection from pregnancy see *Curse Tablets and Binding Spells from the Ancient World* (ed. and trans. John Gager [New York: Oxford University Press, 1992], §24): SIDE A: "We bind (*Kallistrate) the wife of (*Theophemos) and Theophilos, son of Kallistrate, and the children/slaves of (*Kalli)strate, both Theophemos and (*Eustratos) the brother. . . . I bind their souls and their deeds and their entire selves and all their belongs. . . ." SIDE B: ". . . and their penis and their vagina and Kantharis and Dionysios, son of (*Kantharis) both themselves and their soul and deeds and all their entire selves and their penis and unholy vagina." This is a curse so that pregnancy does not occur. Gager's §108 pertains to finds from Tell Sandahannah in Palestine and includes bound lead figurines with targeted phallic and mastitic body areas that are subject to cursing for resulting anomaly (nonfunction).

Christopher A. Faraone (*Talismans and Trojan Horses: Guardian Statues in Ancient Greek Myth and Ritual* [New York: Oxford University Press, 1992], 46) discusses Near Eastern evidence for "house amulets used to avert demonic attacks from pregnant women and newborn infants. Wall plaques depicting the notorious Assyrian demons Pazuzu and Lamashtu contain similar incantations."

Joseph Naveh and Shaul Shaked (*Magic Spells and Formulae: Aramaic Incantations of Late Antiquity* [Jerusalem: Magnes Press, 1993], §27) translate a good example of an amulet meant to protect against these very dangers.

> And by the rod of Moses and by the front-plate of Aaron the High Priest and by the signet-ring of Solomon and . . . of David and by the horns of the altar and by the nam[e] [of] the living and existent God: that you should be expelled, (you,) [the evil] [s]pirit and the evil assailant and every evil des[troyer] from the body of Marian daughter of [Sarah] and the *fetus* that is in her belly from th[is day] to eternity, Amen, Amen, Selah.

Pliny (*Natural History* 30.6) reports how amulets inscribed with the fish *mora* (the fish that used to plague Roman boats), were worn in order to arrest miscarriages and, by reduction in prolapses of the uterus, in order to allow the fetus to attain full maturity. See Tal Ilan (*Jewish Women in Greco-Roman Palestine: An Inquiry into Image and Status*, Texte und Studien zum antiken Judentum 44 [Tübingen, Germany: J. C. B. Mohr, 1995], 116) on Jewish thoughts about dangers of childbirth. A curious example is found in Mishnah *Shabbath* 2.6, which suggests that women died in childbirth because of "three transgressions": (1) not obeying laws of the menstruant; or (2) not obeying laws of the dough-offering; or (3) not obeying the laws about lighting the Sabbath lamp. Although these are not cases of malevolent entities or magical attack, the presence of the anomalous frightful is quite clear in this passage. Obedience and subsequent benefaction (or not) always create a tentativeness at being caught between being saved or destroyed, between being aided or ignored.

For infant care in general, see Price, *Kourotrophos* for a complete account of the long history of Near Eastern, Egyptian, Greek, and Hellenistic cults and iconography of female (and some male) deities who watch over pregnancy, delivery, and neonatal care. Fear of terrible loss of the infant due to nefarious forces was widespread and can be traced from Lilith to Gello. See Sarah Iles Johnston ("Defining the Dreadful: Remarks on the Greek Child-Killing Demon," in *Ancient Magic and Ritual Power*,

J. Brill, 1995]) for the names of more such stealing creatures and aversion techniques to use against them. Gail Corrington (*Her Image of Salvation: Female Saviors and Formative Christianity* [Louisville, Ky.: Westminster/John Knox Press, 1992], 94) notes epithets for Isis pertinent to these issues: Isis *bubastis* (for women of childbearing age); Isis *puellaris* (for girls before menstruation); Isis *lochia* (for women in childbed).

Appendix G

Families of Holy Men

See Graham Anderson (*Sage, Saint, and Sophist: Holy Men and Their Associates in the Early Roman Empire* [London: Routledge, 1994], 113-14) for accounts of "holy men" who continue the family line of business. "A holy man or religious virtuoso," Anderson writes, "might belong to a family which had held hereditary priesthoods, as in the case of both Josephus and the Emperor Elagabalus; and at least some other sacred virtuosi also had a father-to-son occupation" (p.113). For the claims of Josephus about his family background, see *Vita* 1.2. For Elagabalus as a hereditary priest of the Ba`al of Emesa, see Herodian 5.3.4. Among other examples, Artemidorus saved dream-interpretation tricks of the trade for his son (*Oneirocriticon* 4 *praef.*), and Titus Flavius Ulpianus boasted that his father, grandfather, and three uncles also had been prophets; see *Didyma* 2: *Die Inscriften*, ed. Albert Rehm [Berlin: Staatliche Museen zu Berlin, 1941-58], 277.

Walter Burkert (*The Orientalizing Revolution: Near Eastern Influence on Greek Culture in the Early Archaic Age*, trans. M. Pinder and W. Burkert, *Revealing Antiquity* 5 [Cambridge, Mass.: Harvard University Press, 1992], 43-44) comprehensively lists other families of "holy men": (1) the Melampodidae, to whom Teisamenos was related (Herodotus 9.33-36); (2) the Iamidae from Olympia and the Klytiadae (both related; both survived for centuries) (Pindar *Odes* 6); (3) the Telmissians in Caria, who were a "mantic family [γένος]" (Arrian *Anabasis* 2.3.3-4); (4) the Eumolpidae and the Kerykes, priest-families in Eleusis for about 1,000 years; (5) a certain Timotheus, a mantic, who traveled to Egypt with Ptolemy I (Plutarch, *De Iside et Osiride* 28.362a; Tacitus, *Histories* 4.83-84); (6) Polemainetos, being childless, chose Thrasyllos to be his successor and bequeathed to him his "art," his books, and his money; subsequently, Thrasyllos became rich and his own children continued to bicker over his huge estate years after his death (Isocrates, *Aiginetikos* 19.5.45); (7) the mother of the orator Aeschines is characterized by Aeschines' bitter enemy, Demosthenes, as a witch-like priestess of arcane mysteries; according to an inscription, she is from a family of seers in the tradition of Amphoras (her father and brothers were practicing seers) (Demosthenes 19.249; 18.120, 259-60; *Supplementum Epigraphicum Graecum* 16 §193); (8) King Ptolemy Philopater decreed in 210 B.C.E. that all those who practiced Dionysiac mysteries in Egypt had to register in Alexandria and to declare "from whom they have received the sacred things, up to three generations"; (9) secret knowledge is to be passed on only to actual sons in *PGM* and alchemical writings (*PGM* 4.475); (10) physicians passed information down through sons; the best known, the Asclepiades (*Supplementum Epigraphicum Graecum* 16 §326 inscription mentioning this family). Burkert quotes (p.44) from the Hippocratic Rule (νόμος): "Holy things are shown to holy men; such things are not permitted for the profane until they are initiated through the rites of knowledge." Often this meant family. According to Burkert,

> Precisely this connection of sacred skills with family tradition and the mandate of esotericism can already be found in cuneiform documents. These contain extensive information about many kinds of seers and practitioners of magic. Even in the ordinary crafts the son takes over the art from the father so that the true craftsman is called the "son of the master craftsman" (*mâr ummani*); the Codex Hammurapi makes the learning of a craft a de facto adoption. On the Tyskiewicz bowl found in Italy, Phoenician artists signed as "sons of the foundrymen." Correspondingly, a true seer was a "son of a seer"; in his incantation he presented himself as "the knowing one, son of the master craftsman."

Appendix H

Νόμος Ἔμψυχος

Archytas (Περὶ νόμου καὶ δικαιοσύνη [On Law and Justice], in *The Pythagorean Texts of the Hellenistic Period*, ed. Holger Thesleff, Acta Academiae Aboensis, Series A: Humaniora: Humanistiska Vetenskaper, Socialvetenskaper, Teologi 30 no. 1 [Åbo: Åbo Akademi, 1965], 33 1.8) write, νόμων δὲ ὁ ἔμψυχος βασιλεύς, ὁ δ᾽ ἄψυχος γράμμα. πρᾶτος ὢν ὁ νόμος (On the one hand, the king has internalized the law, while on the other, he has not internalized letters, since the law is practice [and not theory, as is letters]).

Diotogenes (Περὶ βασιλείας [On Rulership], in *The Pythagorean Texts of the Hellenistic Period*, 71 1.22) comments, ὁ δὲ βασιλεύς ἤτοι νόμος ἔμψυχος ἐντι ἢ νόμιμος ἄρχων (for the king is either truly the 'law internalized,' or he is a leader [acting] in accordance with law) and (p.72 1.23) ὁ δὲ βασιλεύς . . . καὶ αὐτὸς ὢν νόμος ἔμψυχος (So the king . . . is also himself law internalized).

Ekphantos (Περὶ βασιλείας [On Rulership], in *The Pythagorean Texts of the Hellenistic Period*, 80 1.22) finds αἴτε νόμος αἴτε βασιλεὺς διέποι τὰ κατ᾽ αὐτώς (either law or king manage things just so) and (p.81 1.9) prescribes achievement of the best virtue for τὸν ἐπὶ τᾶς γᾶς βασιλέα (the king over the land) on the basis of the virtues κατ᾽ ὠρανόν (in accordance with heaven).

Dates of these writings are debated, although general ideas developed in them have a long history before and beyond Pythagorean traditions. Erwin R. Goodenough ("The Political Philosophy of Hellenistic Kingship," *Yale Classical Studies* 1 [1928]: 55-102) sees them as an influence on Philo and therefore places them in the third and second centuries B.C.E.. See the debate between L. Delatte (*Les traités de la Royauté d'Ecphante, Diotogéne et Sthénidas* [Liége, 1942]) and Holger Thesleff (*An Introduction to the Pythagorean Writings of the Hellenistic Period*, Acta Academiae Aboensis, Series A: Humaniora: Humanistiska Vetenskaper, Socialvetenskaper, Teologi 24, no. 3 [Åbo: Åbo Akademi, 1961]). Delatte claimed that the treatises were from the second century C.E..

Thesleff agreed with the dating proposed by Goodenough. The argument
continues between Thesleff and Walter Burkert in *Pseudepigrapha* I, ed.
Kurt von Fritz, Entretiens sur l'antiquité classique 18 (Vandoeuvres-
Geneve: Fondation Hardt, 1972), 57-87 and 23-55, respectively. Taking
up Burkert's challenge, Thesleff tried to show that one could date the
treatises early solely on the basis of their philosophical content. Kingship
was highly regarded, and the idea of νόμος ἔμψυχος [internalized law] is
an example of such high regard. Emile Bréhier (*Les idées philosophiques
et religieuse de Philon d'Alexandria* [Paris: Librarie Alphonse Picard,
1908], 144-45) questions the direct relationship between the Pythagorean
texts and Philo. He outlines instead a Stoic influence on Philo, specifically in *Quaestiones et solutiones in Genesin* 57. In that text is an
allegorical discussion about the meaning of the Two Guardians over
Paradise in Genesis 3:24 (the Cherubim and the Fiery Sword). Philo
argues that the cherubim themselves represent two parts of the nature of
God, the ποιητικός (creative) and the βασιλικός (sovereign). In theoretical
terms, the first is θεός (God: beneficent and kind) and the second is
κύριος (Lord: law-giving and chastising). Bréhier notes a parallel to this
typology in the Stoic Cornutus (*De Natura Deorum*), specifically in the
allegories there about Χάρις [Grace] and Δική [Justice]. Stoics used
Χάρις as a term synonymous with εὐεργέτημα [benefaction], *gratia*, and
beneficium; see Hans Friedrich August von Arnim, *Stoicorum Veterum
Fragmenta* (Leipzig, Germany: B. G. Teubner, 1903-1924), s.v. Χάρις.
In kingly propaganda, all of these qualities identify the person of the
βασιλεύς and his giving of gifts. See also Philo (*De Vita Mosis* 1.162) on
God's destiny for Moses to be νόμος ἔμψυχος καὶ λογικός (rational, with
law internalized [in him]). In Philo, Moses is depicted not as a βασιλεύς
specifically but as a ἡγεμών and νομοθέτης (leader and lawgiver). Other
Jewish authors writing in the Hellenistic milieu emphasize the virtue of
Moses specifically as a βασιλεύς; see Eupolemus (Περὶ τῶν ἐν τῇ
Ἰουδαίᾳ βασιλέων [On the Kings in Judea]) as cited in Clement of
Alexandria (*Stromateis* 1.23.153).

Appendix I

Tree and Water

To understand this royal imagery one must start with Geo Widengren, *The King and the Tree of Life in Ancient Near Eastern Religion (King and Saviour IV)*, Uppsala Universitets Årsskrft, 1951:4 (Uppsala: A.-B. Lundequistska Bokhandeln, 1951). See also Irene J. Winter ("The King and the Cup: Iconography of the Royal Presentation Scene on Ur III Seals," in *Insight through Images: Studies in Honor of Edith Porada*, ed. Marilyn Kelly-Buccellati, *Bibliotheca Mesopotamica* 21 [Malibu, Calif.: Undena Publications, 1986], 252-65) on iconography of ancient Mesopotamian kings as those who give justice and benefaction. See Widengren (*King*, 5-6) for the *kiškanu* tree on the Deep. On the King Gudea scene see Widengren, *King*, 24.

Ancient Mesopotamian images of kings were more than symbolic reminders. They were used in rituals of consecration, installation, and maintenance, each ritual an activity of calling favor from the gods on a city; see Irene J. Winter, "'Idols of the King': Royal Images as Recipients of Ritual Action in Ancient Mesopotamia," *Journal of Ritual Studies* 6 (1992): 13-42. On King Šulgi see Widengren, *King*, 42. The nature of Tammuz is depicted with various botanical specimens: tamarisk, the cedar, and the *hašur*-tree. One text reads: "Tamarisk, reedbush, tree, grown on the pure heaven and earth; At your holy roots, o cedar, at your foliage, o *hašur*-tree, has the consecrated water for the goddess Ninahakuddu the *apkallu* brought with pure hand" (p.48). On Šulgi, Samuel Noah Kramer ("Sumerian Hymns," in *Ancient Near Eastern Texts Relating to the Old Testament*, ed. James B. Pritchard, 3d ed. [Princeton, N.J.: Princeton University Press, 1969], 586) translates a hymn for him in which several themes that I have discussed are presented.

I, the king, a hero from the (mother's) womb am I,
I, Šulgi, a mighty man from the day I was born am I

King of the four corners (of the universe) am I,
Herdsman, shepherd of the blackheads [Sumerians] am I . . .

Especially pertaining to the king as Tree and Water, or having power over these, we may note these lines:

On that day, the storm howled, the tempest swirled,
Northwind (and) Southwind roared eagerly,
Lightning devoured in heaven alongside the seven winds,
The deafening storm made the earth tremble,
Ishkur thundered throughout the heavenly expanse,
The winds on high embraced the waters below,
Its (the storm's) little stones, its big stones,
Lashed at my back.
(But) I, the king, unafraid, uncowed,
Like a young lion (prepared to) spring I shook myself loose.

Appendix J

Sea Stories

For the influence of Scripture on Mark, see William Richard Stegner, "Jesus' Walking on the Water: Mark 6:45-52," in *The Gospels and the Scriptures of Israel*, ed. Craig A. Evans and W. Richard Stegner, JSNT Supplement Series, 104; Studies in Scripture in Early Judaism and Christianity 3 (Sheffield: University of Sheffield Press, 1994), 212-34. The prepositional phrases in Mark remind Stegner of LXX Exodus 14:16 (ἐπὶ τῆς θαλάσσης, the place over which Moses stretches out his hands). Stegner outlines verbal parallels between Exodus 14 and Mark (θαρσεῖτε in Exodus 14:13, Mark 6:50; ἐγώ εἰμί (κύριος) in Exodus 14:18, Mark 6:50).

Beyond Stegner, see now the far more extensive study of these ideas by Roger Aus (*"Caught in the Act," Walking on the Sea, and the Release of Barabbas Revisited*, South Florida Studies in the History of Judaism 157 (Atlanta: Scholars Press, 1998), 55), who suggests that the διαπεράσαντες in Mark. 6:53 stems from the Hebrew term, `'br, to cross over (the Red Sea) in Exodus 15:16. For proof, Aus cites *Exodus Rabbah* Beshallah 22/7 on Exodus 15:1 (chant the Song before God on that night when Israel crossed [ `'br]), *'Avot Rabbi Natan* A 33 (Rise, go across [`'br]!), and *Mek* Shirata 9 (Until your people pass over, taken to mean passing over the Sea. Aus notes that Jesus praying at a mountain is like Moses praying at a mountain before the Sea-Crossing, a particular tradition developed by Josephus (*Antiquities* 2.320-49) with embellishments on the Sea-Crossing (in Josephus, the topography is written as, "between inaccessible cliffs and the sea; for it was the sea in which terminated a 'mountain' [ὄρος] . . . thine is the sea, thine the mountain that encompasseth us"). Mark has the disciples ἐν μέσῳ τῆς θαλάσσης (6:47), hypothetically the same phrase as found in Exodus 14:16, 22, 27, 29 and 15:19. Jesus as a ghost (φάντασμα) Aus compares to traditions about God flying, riding, or fluttering (as a bird) over chaotic waters. Aus reviews traditions that link the Messiah to God's Spirit at the creation, showing creative benefaction in later divine control over the Waters. These are interesting literary comparisons, but limited in application. I do not to attempt to show some tradition or other to be behind the Markan accounts, but rather that the θάλασσα (ocean) is important because it is often a narrative occasion used to elucidate themes of fear and benefaction.

For these themes in Homer, see Roy D. Kotansky, ("Jesus and Heracles in Cádiz [τὰ Γάδειρα]: Death, Myth, and Monsters at the 'Straits of Gibraltar' [Mark 4:35-5:43]," in *Ancient and Modern Perspectives on The Bible and Culture: Essays in Honor of Hans Dieter Betz*, ed. Adela Yarbro Collins, Scholars Press Homage Series 22 [Atlanta.: Scholars Press, 1998], 160-229) for a highly developed view, focused on earlier stories in Mark 4:35-5:43, and their form in hypothetical pre-Markan traditions. I should argue that the second boating narrative is lexically and thematically linked to the earlier stories in Mark, as they stand now, through use of the participle διαπεράσαντος (crossing over; Mark 5:21, 6:53) and similar prepositional phrases, especially εἰς τὸ πέραν (to the far boundary; 4:35, 5:1, 5:21 and 6:45). I avoid guesses about pre-Markan tradition and its specific form or content. Kotansky compares Mark's εἰς τὸ πέραν to a Greek mythographic τὸ πέραν (known boundaries of the cosmos). This comparison points to a narrative geography not pertinent to Galilee, but representative instead of the Straits of Gibralter, the Atlantic Ocean, and points due east (a place construed as the end of the world, where cosmic "Rivers of Ocean" flowed). Traditions in the *Odyssey* and the *Argonautica* are critical here, as are traditions about Herakles and the herds of Geryon. (Kotanksy opines that in Mark the herds change from cattle to swine perhaps due to the influence of a swine taboo in a Phoenician cult of Herakles-Melqart known to be in operation near the Straits of Gilbralter). Kotansky points to Greek mythographic themes of the Storm (Pherecydes 3 frg. 18a), of monstrous creatures in or near the Ocean, of stormy waters near steep cliffs, and of Ocean calms (*Odyssey* 5.452, 7.319, 13.75-77, 10.86; *Argonautica* 4.1249). He suggests that "journeys to the mystic lands [τὸ πέραν] in the epic tradition bring the hero and his crew face-to-face with the divine in many forms; nymphs, spirits, and sorceresses; unnamed demons (δαίμονες), ungainly monsters, and unknown races of divine people populate the lands of epic heroes" (p.180) and that "the epic voyage to a mythic land [τὸ πέραν] brings the hero into close contact with the world of the supernatural, that of Afterlife and the Beyond, in a word, a land not associated with normal existence; it is thus at once a magic land of blissful immortality and the domain of the less fortunate dead" (p.185). Much of Kotansky's work was

intensely criticized by his respondent, David Aune ("Jesus and the
Romans in Galilee: Jews and Gentiles in the Decapolis," in *Ancient and
Modern Perspectives on the Bible and Culture*, 230-51), who noted that
"the many journeys of individuals and groups to the realm of the dead in
Mediterranean mythologies unfailingly make it perfectly obvious to the
hearers and readers that a perilous visit to the dreaded underworld is in
view, yet the stories in Mark 4:35-5:43 require allegorical manipulation
to elicit such an underworld journey" (p.249). Indeed comparisons of
literature have enduring value only if undertaken with the utmost care.

For a hypothetical literary influence of traditions of the resurrection
of Jesus on Markan sea stories, see Patrick J.Madden, *Jesus's Walking on
the Sea: An Investigation of the Origin of the Narrative Account*, Beihefte
zur Zeitschrift für die neutestamentliche Wissenschaft und die Kunde der
älten Kirche 81 (Berlin: Walter de Gruyter, 1997). To no one's surprise,
there are narrative similarities between accounts of resurrection and
accounts of a ghosts walking on the sea. The "Taxonomies of Appearance" Madden develops should be taken simply as more evidence for how
the uncanny and the anomalous suit and befit matters of death, the
underworld, and nefarious doings.

Appendix K

Mythographic Geography

Otto Gruppe (*Griechische Mythologie und Religionsgeschichte*, Handbuch der klassischen Altertums-Wissenschaft in systematischer Darstellung 5 [München: C. H. Beck'sche Verlagsbuchhandlung, 1906], 811] offers the insight, referring to φαέθων (son of Helios) in mythography and various strands of cosmology. In Orphic cosmology, φαέθων could be named Πρωτόγονος (First Created), a son of Αἰθέρος (Aither); see *Orphicorum Fragmenta*, ed. Otto Kern (Dublin: Weidmann, 1972), F73. See Erwin Rohde (*Psyche: The Cult of Souls and Belief in Immortality among the Greeks*, 7th ed., trans. W. B. Hillis [New York: Harcourt, Brace, 1925], 111 n.35) on Hesiod (*Theogony* 987-99) and the relation of φαέθων to Aphrodite, her translation of him to a chthonic hero in her temple (making him a νηοπόλος μύχιον [inner-most niche temple-keeper]), and the relation of his new position to other θεοὶ μύχιοι, and μύχιοι as "dwellers in the earth." Apollonius of Rhodes (*Argonautica* 4.598) tells the story of how φαέθων fell from the chariot of Ἥλιος into the deeps of the Eridanus River. This locale is described in vivid detail.

> Thence they entered the deep stream of Rhodanus, which flows into Eridanus; and where they meet there is a roar of mingling waters. Now that river, rising from the ends of the earth [γαίης κ μυχάτης], where are the portals and mansions of Night [πύλαι κα δέθλια Νυκτός], on one side bursts forth the upon the beach of Ocean, at another pours into the Ionian sea, and on the third through seven mouths sends its stream to the Sardinian sea and its limitless bay. And from Rhodanus they entered stormy lakes [λίμνας], which spread throughout the Celtic mainland of wondrous size (trans. R. C. Seaton, *Apollonius Rhodius, The Argonautica*, Loeb Classical Library (Cambridge, Mass.: Harvard University Press, 1919).

Photius identified μυχόπεδον (abyss) as γῆς βάθος (very deep earth), which is also Ἅιδης (Hell). Gruppe (*Griechische Mythologie und Religionsgeschichte*, 956-59) suggests that the model for the φαέθων is a

mix of eastern traditions about the Morning Star: φωσφόρος (from
Carthage through Phoenicia); `aštoret; Aziz (often related to Ares); and,
hêlal (from Isaiah 14:12, the king of Babylon, a term that is perhaps a
calque on an Assyrian term for "shining one"). Elsewhere in epic, Ocean
and Sun are related in the journey of the deceased suitors of Penelope,
whom Hermes leads "past Ocean Stream, past the Gates of the Sun, past
the Region of Dreams" (Odyssey 24). See also Albrecht Dieterich
(NEKYIA: Beiträge zur Erklärung der neuentdeckten Petrusapoakalypse
[Leipzig, Germany: B. G. Teubner, 1893], 25-26) on the ἐρυθρὰ θάλασσα
(Indian Ocean) and the circuit of the sun, addressing notions of the
expanse of the sun's course from India in the east to Spain and the
Atlantic in the west (λίμνη περικαλλής [Homer, Odyssey 3.1]; also
῝Ηλιος λίμνη). Dieterich cites (p.26) a fragment of Aeschylus, lines
found in Strabo (1.2.27): φοινικόπεδόν τ' ἐρυθρᾶς ἱερὸν, χεῦμα
θαλάσσης, χαλκοκέραυνόν τε παρ' Ὠκεανῷ, λίμναν παντοτρόφον
Αἰθιόπων, ἵν' ὁ παντόπτας ῝Ηλιος αἰεὶ, χρῶτ' ἀθάνατον κάματόν θ'
ἵππων, θερμαῖς ὕδατος, μαλακοῦ προχοαῖς ἀναπαύει (The sacred flood
of the Red Sea with its bed of scarlet sands, and the mere on the shore of
Oceanus that dazzles with its gleam of brass and furnishes all nourishment
to Ethiopians, where the Sun, who sees all things, gives rest to his tired
steeds and refreshes his immortal body in warm outpourings of soft water;
trans. John R. S. Sterrett, The Geography of Strabo, Loeb Classical
Library (Cambridge, Mass.: Harvard University Press, 1917). Joseph
Fontenrose, ("Typhon among the Arimoi," in The Classical Tradition:
Literary and Historical Studies in Honor of Harry Caplan, ed. Luitpold
Wallach [Ithaca, N.Y.: Cornell University Press, 1966], 64-82) demonstrates the near eastern (Lydian, Syrian, Palestinian) influence on much
of the Typhon myth. "Arimoi" is the term used by Strabo to describe the
Arameans. Properly, Fontenrose mentions that "multiple localization of
a mythical scene is frequent" (p.71), especially in conflict myths.
Traditions have the conflict taking place in many different locales,
showing how different narrative characters and locales can serve to
represent divine conflict, cosmological principles, and the resolution of
cosmic strife. Gruppe (Griechische Mythologie und Religionsgeschichte,
812) cites Herodotus 3.5 and its report that Typhon was buried in Lake
Serbonis, a body of water about sixty miles west of Gaza and created by
the Serbonian Bank. This is one of the two mountains called Mt. Casius.
Gruppe suggested the Phoenician siphôn is behind Typhon. The place in
Scripture is called Ba`al Saphôn. Typhon discovered the body of Osiris
and, after cutting it into fourteen parts, scattered it. The story stayed vivid.

(*Chaeremon: Egyptian Priest and Stoic Philosopher: The Fragments Collected and Translated with Explanatory Notes* Études préliminaires aux religions orientales dans l'empire romain 101 [Leiden, The Netherlands: E. J. Brill, 1984], §4) for Chaeremon's criticism of practitioners of magic arts who tried to compel Typhon to magically re-scatter this divine body. Along similar infernal lines, Chaeremon notes that magicians regularly attempted to discover the ἀπόρρητον (secrets) of ' Αβύδος (Abydos), to unlock the κρύπτα (hidden things) of Isis, and to stop the "solar bark," all events that would be amazing acts of power, as well as demonstrations of the anomalous frightful. Tertullian (*De Anima* 57.1, perhaps following Pliny) includes an Egyptian king Typhon among well-known magicians Ostanes, Dardanus, Damigren, Necatanebus, and Bernice, all of them inventors of the magic that dealt specifically *ahori* and *biaiothanati*; see J. H. Waszink, *Quinti Septimi Florentis Tertulliani De Anima: Edited with Introduction and Commentary* (Amsterdam: J. M. Meulenhoff, 1947), 575-76. The name "Typhon" enters here into a tradition of strange doings. Typhon as a water-god, and not as a legendary king, is found in symbolism at Apollinopolis, in which he is speared while in the form of a hippopotamus by the second phase of the moon, which was represented as a man with a falcon face. See Van der Horst (*Chaeremon*, §17D) on reports about this in Porphyry, *De cultu simulacroroum* fr. 10.

Bibliography

Aalders, G. J. D. "ΝΟΜΟΣ ΕΜΨΥΧΟΣ." 315-29 in *Politeia und Res Publica: Beiträge zum Verständnis von Politik, Recht und Stadt in der Antike, dem amdenken Rudolf Starks gewidmet*, edited by Peter Steinmetz. Palingenesia, Monographien und Texte zur klassischen Altertumswissenschaft 4. Wiesbaden: Franz Steiner Verlag, 1969.

Africa, Thomas. "Worms and the Death of Kings: A Cautionary Note on Disease and History." *Classical Antiquity* 1 (1982): 1-17.

Aichele, George. *Jesus Framed.* London: Routledge, 1996.

Alexiou, Margaret and Peter Dronke. "The Lament of Jephtha's Daughter: Themes, Traditions, Originality." *Studi Medievali* 12, no. 2 (1971): 819-63.

Alkier, Stefan. *Urchristentum: Zur Geschichte und Theologie einer exegetischer Disziplin*. Beiträge zur historischen Theologie 83. Tübingen, Germany: J. C. B. Mohr, 1993.

Annen, Franz. *Heil für die Heiden: Zur Bedeutung und Geschichte der Tradition vom besessenen Gerasener (Mk 5,1-20 parr.)*. Frankfurter Theologische Studien 20. Frankfurt am Main: Josef Knecht, 1976.

Asmis, Elizabeth. "*Psychagogia* in Plato's *Phaedrus.*" *Illinois Classical Studies* 11 (1985-1986): 153-72.

Athanassakis, Apostolos N. *The Orphic Hymns: Text, Translation, and Notes*. Texts and Translations 12; Graeco-Roman Religions Series 4. Missoula, Mont.: Scholars Press, 1977.

Attridge, Harold and Robert Oden. *Philo of Byblos: The Phoenician History: Introduction, Critical Text, Translation, and Notes*. Catholic Biblical Quarterly Monograph Series 9. Washington, D.C.: Catholic Biblical Association, 1981.

Aubert, Jean-Jacques. "Threatened Wombs: Aspects of Ancient Uterine Magic." *Greek, Roman and Byzantine Studies* 30, no. 3 (1988): 421-49.

Audollent, Augustus. *Defixionum Tabellae*. Paris: Albert Fontemoing, 1904; repr., Frankfurt/Main: Minerva, 1967.

Aune, David E. "Jesus and the Romans in Galilee: Jews and Gentiles in the Decapolis." 230-51 in *Ancient and Modern Perspectives on the Bible and Culture: Essays in Honor of Hans Dieter Betz*, edited by Adela Yarbro Collins. Scholars Press Homage Series 22. Atlanta: Scholars Press, 1998.

Aus, Roger David. *"Caught in the Act," Walking on the Sea, and the Release of Barabbas Revisited*. South Florida Studies in the History of Judaism 157. Atlanta: Scholars Press, 1998.

Axtell, Harold. *The Deification of Abstract Ideas in Roman Literature and Inscriptions*. Chicago: University of Chicago Press, 1907.

Bammel, Ernst. "The Feeding of the Multitude." 211-40 in *Jesus and the Politics of His Day*, edited by Ernst Bammel and C. F. D. Moule. Cambridge: Cambridge University Press, 1984.

Batto, Bernard F. "The Sleeping God: An Ancient Near Eastern Motif of Divine Sovereignty." *Biblica* 68, no. 2 (1987): 153-76.

Bauernfeind, Otto. *Die Worte der Dämonen im Markusevangelium*. Beiträge zur Wissenschaft vom Alten und Neuen Testament, dritte Folge, Heft 8. Stuttgart: Verlag W. Kohlhammer, 1927.

Belo, Fernando. *A Materialist Reading of the Gospel of Mark*. Trans. Matthew J. O'Connell. Maryknoll, N.Y.: Orbis Books, 1981.

Benz, Ernst. *The Mystical Sources of German Romantic Philosophy*. Trans. Blair R. Reynolds and Eunice M. Paul. Pittsburgh Theological Monographs new series 6. Allison Park, Pa.: Pickwick Publications, 1983.

Berger, Klaus. "Hellenistische-heidnische Prodigien und die Vorzeichen in der jüdischen und christlichen Apokalyptik." *Aufstieg und Niedergang der römische Welt* ii/23 nr. 2 (1988): 1428-69.

Bethe, Eric. *Pollucis Onomasticon*. Sammlung Wissenschaftlicher Commentare: Lexicographi Graeci 9. Stuttgart: Teubner, 1987.

Betz, Hans Dieter. "Fragments from a Catabasis Ritual in a Greek Magical Papyrus." *History of Religions* 19 (1979-1980): 287-95.

———. "Jewish Magic in the Greek Magical Papyri (*PGM* VII.260-271)." 46-63 in *Envisioning Magic: A Princeton Seminar and Symposium*, edited by Peter Schäfer and Hans G. Kippenberg. Studies in the History of Religions (*Numen* Book Series) 75. Leiden, The Netherlands: E. J. Brill, 1997.

———. *The Greek Magical Papyri in Translation, Including the Demotic Spells*. Chicago: University of Chicago Press, 1986.

Bialik, Hayim Nahman and Yehoshua Hana Ravnitzky, eds. *The Book of Legends (Sefer Ha-Aggadah): Legends from the Talmud and*

Midrash. Trans. William G. Braude. New York: Schocken Books, 1992.

Bietenhard, Hans. "Die syrische Decapolis von Pompeius bis Traian." *Aufstieg und Niedergang der römischen Welt* ii nr. 8 (1978): 220-51.

Blackburn, Barry. *Theios Anēr and the Marcan Miracle Traditions: A Critique of the* Theios Anēr *Concept as an Interpretative Background of the Miracle Traditions Used by Mark*. Wissenschaftliche Untersuchungen zum Neuen Testament, 2. Reihe 40. Tübingen, Germany: J. C. B. Mohr, 1991.

Bloch, Raymond. *Les Prodiges dans l'Antiquité (Grèce, Étrurie et Rome)*. Mythes et Religions. Paris: Presses Universitaires de France, 1963.

Bloch-Smith, Elizabeth. *Judahite Burial Practices and Beliefs about the Dead*. Journal for the Study of the Old Testament Supplement Series, 123; JSOT/ASOR Monograph Series 7. Sheffield: University of Sheffield Press, 1992.

Boardman, John. "'Very Like a Whale': Classical Sea Monsters." 73-84 in *Monsters and Demons in the Ancient and Medieval Worlds: Papers Presented in Honor of Edith Porada*, edited by Ann E. Farkas, Prudence Harper, and Evelyn Harrison. Franklin Jasper Walls Lectures 10. Mainz am Rhine: Verlag Philipp von Zabern, 1987.

Bonner, Campbell. *Studies in Magical Amulets Chiefly Graeco-Roman*. University of Michigan Studies, Humanistic Series 49. Ann Arbor: University of Michigan Press, 1950.

Bonnet, Corinne. "Héraclés en orient: Interprétations et syncrétismes." 165-189 in *Héraclès: D'une rive à l'autre de la Méditerranée: Bilan et perspectives: Actes de la Table Ronde de Rome, 15-16 septembre 1989 à l'occasion du cinquantenaire de l'Academia Belgica, en hommage à Franz Cumont, son premier président*, edited by Corinne Bonnet and C. Jourdain-Annequin. Études de philologie, d'archéologie et d'histoire anciennes/Studies over oude filologie, archeologie en geshiedenis 28. Bruxelles: Institut Historique Belge de Rome, 1992.

Boobyer, G. H. "The Eucharistic Interpretation of the Miracles of the Loaves in St. Mark's Gospel." *Journal of Theological Studies* n.s. 3, no. 2 (1952): 161-71.

Bouche-Leclercq, André. *L'Astrologie Grecque*. Bruxelles: Culture et Civilzation, 1899.

———. *Histoire de la Divination dans l'Antiquité*. Bruxelles: Culture et Civilization, 1879.

Bowersock, Glen W. *Augustus and the Greek World.* Oxford: Oxford
    University Press, 1965.
————. *Fiction as History: Nero to Julian.* Sather Classical Lectures 58.
    Berkeley: University of California Press, 1994.
————. *Martyrdom and Rome.* Wiles Lectures, Queen's University of
    Belfast 1993. Cambridge: Cambridge University Press, 1995.
Boyce, Mary and Franz Grenet. *A History of Zoroastrianism* 3:
    Zoroastrianism under Macedonian and Roman Rule. Handbuch der
    Orientalistik, erste Anteilung: Der nahe und der mittlere Osten 8:
    Religion, erster Abschnitt: Religionsgeschichte des alten Orients 2,
    2. Leiden, The Netherlands: E. J. Brill, 1991.
Bremmer, Jan. "'Effigies Dei' in Ancient Greece: Poseidon." 35-41 in
    Effigies Dei: Essays on the History of Religions, edited by Dirk Van
    der Plas. Studies in the History of Religions (Supplements to *Numen*)
    51. Leiden, The Netherlands: E. J. Brill, 1987.
Bringmann, Klaus. "The King as Benefactor: Some Remarks on the Ideal
    Kingship in the Age of Hellenism." 7-24 in *Images and Ideologies:
    Self-Definition in the Hellenistic World,* edited by Anthony Bulloch,
    Erich S. Gruen, A. A. Long, and Andrew Stewart. Hellenistic
    Culture and Society 12. Berkeley: University of California Press,
    1993.
Bringmann, Klaus and Hans von Steuben. *Schenkungen hellenistischer
    Herrscher an griechische Städte und Heiligtümer* I: *Zeugnisse und
    Kommentare.* Berlin: Akademie Verlag, 1995.
Bronner, Leila Leah. *From Eve to Esther: Rabbinic Reconstructions of
    Biblical Women.* Louisville, Ky.: Westminster John Knox Press,
    1994.
Brunt, P. A. and J. M. Moore. *Res Gestae Divi Augusti: The Achieve-
    ments of the Divine Augustus.* Oxford: Oxford University Press,
    1967.
Burkert, Walter. *Ancient Mystery Cults.* Carl Newell Jackson Lectures
    1982. Cambridge, Mass.: Harvard University Press, 1987.
————. *Greek Religion.* Trans. John Raffan. Cambridge, Mass.: Harvard
    University Press, 1985.
————. *Homo Necans: The Anthropology of Ancient Greek Sacrificial
    Ritual and Myth.* Trans. Peter Bing. Berkeley: University of Califor-
    nia Press, 1983.
————. *The Orientalizing Revolution: Near Eastern Influence on Greek
    Culture in the Early Archaic Age.* Trans. M. Pinder and W. Burkert.
    Revealing Antiquity 5. Cambridge, Mass.: Harvard University Press,

1992.

Burnstein, Stanley. *Agatharchides of Cnidus* On the Erythraen Sea. Hakluyt Society Second Series 172. London: Hakluyt Society, 1989.

———. *The Hellenistic Age from the Battle of Ipsos to the Death of Kleopatra VII.* Translated Documents of Greece and Rome 3. Cambridge: Cambridge University Press, 1985.

Campany, Robert Ford. *Strange Writing: Anomaly Accounts in Early Medieval China.* SUNY Series in Chinese Philosophy and Culture. Albany: State University of New York Press, 1996.

Cancik, Hubert. "Libri fatales: Römishce Offenbarungsliteratur und Geschichtstheologie." 549-76 in *Apocalypticism in the Mediterranean World and the Ancient Near East,* edited by David Hellholm. Tübingen, Germany: J. C. B. Mohr, 1983.

Carson, Anne. "Putting Her in Her Place: Woman, Dirt, and Desire." 83-113 in *Before Sexuality: The Construction of Erotic Experence in the Ancient Greek World,* edited by David M. Halperin, John L. Winker, and Froma I. Zeitlin. Princeton, N.J.: Princeton University Press, 1990.

Castle, Terry. *The Female Thermometer: 18th-Century Culture and the Invention of the Uncanny.* New York: Oxford University Press, 1995.

Childs, Brevard. "The Enemy from the North and the Chaos Tradition." *Journal of Biblical Literature* 78 (1959): 187-98.

Chilton, C. W. *Diogenes of Oenoanda: The Fragments.* Oxford: Oxford University Press, 1971.

Clay, Diskin. "Sailing to Lampsacus: Diogenes of Oenoanda, New Fragment 7." *Greek, Roman, and Byzantine Studies* 14 (1972): 49-59.

Collins, Adela Yarbro. "Mysteries in the Gospel of Mark." 11-23 in *Mighty Minorities? Minorities in Early Christianity—Positions and Strategies: Essays in Honour of Jacob Jervell on His 70th Birthday,* edited by D. Hellholm, H. Moxnes, and T. Seim. Oslo: Scandinavian University Press, 1995.

———. "Rulers, Divine Men, and Walking on the Water (Mark 6:45-52)." 207-227 in *Religious Propaganda and Missionary Competition in the New Testament World: Essays Honoring Dieter Georgi,* edited by Lukas Bormann, Kelly Del Tredici, and Angela Standhartinger. Novum Testamentum Supplementum 74. Leiden, The Netherlands: E. J. Brill, 1994.

Collison-Morley, Lacy. *Greek and Roman Ghost Stories.* Chicago: Argonaut, 1912.

Corrington, Gail. *The "Divine Man": His Origin and Function in*

Hellenistic Popular Religion. American University Studies Series 7: Theology and Religion 17. New York: Peter Lang, 1986.

―――. *Her Image of Salvation: Female Saviors and Formative Christianity.* Louisville, Ky.: Westminster/John Knox Press, 1992.

Cotter, Wendy J. "The Markan Sea Stories: Their History, Formation, and Function in the Literary Context of Greco-Roman Antiquity." Ph.D. diss., University of Toronto, St. Michael's College, 1991.

Cumont, Franz. *Lux Perpetua.* Paris: Librarie Orientalise Paul Geuthner, 1949.

―――. *Recherches sur le symbolisme funéraire des Romains.* Haut-Commissariat de l'État Français en Syrie et au Liban, Service des Antiquités: Bibliothèque archéologique et historique 35. Paris: Paul Geuthner, 1942; repr., New York: Arno Press, 1975.

Daniélou, Jean. *Primitive Christian Symbols.* Trans. D. Attwater. Baltimore: Helicon Press, 1964.

Danove, Paul L. *The End of Mark's Story: A Methodological Study.* Biblical Interpretation Series 3. Leiden, The Netherlands: E. J. Brill, 1993.

Daremberg, C. and E. Saglio, eds. *Dictionnaire des Antiquités d'après les Textes et les Monuments.* Paris: Librarie Hachette, 1877; repr. Graz: Akademische Druck und Verlagsanstatt, 1962. S.v. "Katapontismos," by G. Glotz.

Dawson, Lorne. "Otto and Freud on the Uncanny and Beyond." *Journal of the American Academy of Religion* 57, no. 2 (1988): 283-311.

Day, John. *God's Conflict with the Dragon and the Sea: Echoes of a Canaanite Myth in the Old Testament.* University of Cambridge Oriental Publications 35. Cambridge: Cambridge University Press, 1985.

Deissmann, Adolf. *Light from the Ancient East.* 4th ed. Trans. Lionel R. M. Strachan. London: Hodder & Stoughton, 1922.

Derrett, J. Duncan M. *The Making of Mark: The Scriptural Bases of the Earliest Gospel* 1: *From Jesus' Baptism to Peter's Recognition of Jesus as the Messiah.* Shipston-on-Stour, Warwickshire: Drinkwater, 1985.

―――. "Why and How Jesus Walked on the Sea." *Novum Testamentum* 23, no. 4 (1981): 330-48.

DeWitt, Norman W. "Epicurus, Περὶ φαντασίας." *Transactions of the American Philological Association* 70 (1939): 414-27.

Dickie, Matthew W. "The Fathers of the Church and the Evil Eye." 9-34 in *Byzantine Magic*, edited by Henry Maguire. Washington, D.C.:

Dumbarton Oaks Research Library and Collection; Cambridge, Mass.: Harvard University Press, 1995.

Dieterich, Albrecht. *Abraxas: Studien zur Religionsgeschichte des spätern Altertum.* Festschrift für Hermann Usener. Leipzig, Germany: Teubner, 1891.

————. *NEKYIA: Beiträge zur Erklärung der neuentdeckten Petrusapoakalypse.* Leipzig, Germany: B. G. Teubner, 1893.

Dittenberger, Wilhelm. *Orientalis Graeci Inscriptiones Selectae.* 3rd ed. 1903-1905. Hildesheim, Germany: Georg Olms, 1986.

————. *Sylloge Inscriptionum Graecarum, 4 Bde.* 4th ed. 1920; repr., Hildesheim, Germany: Georg Olms, 1960.

Dodds, Eric R. *The Greeks and the Irrational.* Sather Classical Lectures 25. Berkeley: University of California Press, 1951.

————. "Supernormal Phenomena in Classical Antiquity." In *The Ancient Concept of Progress and Other Essays on Greek Literature and Belief.* Oxford: Clarendon Press, 1973.

Doudna, John Charles. *The Greek of the Gospel of Mark.* Journal of Biblical Literature Monograph Series 12. Philadelphia: Society of Biblical Literature and Exegesis, 1961.

Dowden, Ken. *Death and the Maiden: Girl's Initiation Rites in Greek Mythology.* London: Routledge, 1989.

Drijvers, Hans. J. W. "After Life and Funerary Symbolism in Palmyrene Religion." 709-772 in *La Soteriologia dei culti orientali nell'Impero Romano: Atti del Colloqio Internazionale, Roma 24-28 Settembre 1979,* edited by Ugo Bianchi and M. Vermaseren. Études préliminaires aux religions orientales dans l'Empire Romain, 92. Leiden, The Netherlands: E. J. Brill, 1982.

————. *Cults and Beliefs at Edessa.* Études préliminaires aux religions orientales dans l'Empire Romain, 62. Leiden, The Netherlands: E. J. Brill, 1980.

Duchesne-Guillemin, Jacques. "Iran and Greece in Commagene." 187-99 in *Études Mithriaques: Actes du 2e Congress International, Téhéran,* edited by Jaceques Duchesne-Guillemin. Acta Iranica 17. Tehran-Leiden, 1978.

Dunbabin, Katherine M. D. and Matthew W. Dickie. "*Invidia Rumpantur Pectora*: The Iconography of Phthonos/Invidia in Graeco-Roman Art." *Jahrbuch für Antike und Christentum* 26 (1983): 7-37.

Dyck, Andrew R. "The Fragments of Heliodorus Homericus." *Harvard Studies in Classical Philology* 95 (1993): 1-65.

Eilberg-Schwartz, Howard. *The Savage in Judaism: An Anthropology of*

Israelite Religion and Ancient Judaism. Bloomington: Indiana University Press, 1990.

Eitrem, S. *Some Notes on the Demonology in the New Testament.* Symbolae Osloenses 12. Oslo: A. W. Brøgger, 1950.

Elliott, J. K. *The Language and Style of the Gospel of Mark: An Edition of C. H. Turner's "Notes on Marcan Usage" Together with Other Comparable Studies.* Supplements to Novum Testamentum 71. Leiden, The Netherlands: E. J. Brill, 1993.

Fantuzzi, Marco. *Bionis Smyrnaei Adonidis Epitaphium.* ARCA Classical and Medieval Texts, Papers and Monographs 18. Liverpool: Francis Cairns, 1985.

Faraone, Christopher A. "The Mystodokos and the Dark-Eyed Maidens: Multicultural Influences on a Late-Hellenistic Incantation." 297-333 in *Ancient Magic and Ritual Power*, edited by Marvin Meyer and Paul Mirecki. Religions in the Graeco-Roman World 129. Leiden, The Netherlands: E. J. Brill, 1995.

―――. *Talismans and Trojan Horses: Guardian Statues in Ancient Greek Myth and Ritual.* New York: Oxford University Press, 1992.

Farnell, Lewis Richard. *The Cults of the Greek States.* Oxford: Clarendon Press, 1896.

―――. *Greek Hero Cults and Ideas of Immortality.* Gifford Lectures 1920. Oxford: Clarendon Press, 1921.

Felton, D. *Haunted Greece and Rome: Ghost Stories from Classical Antiquity.* Austin: University of Texas Press, 1999.

Ferguson, John. *Utopias of the Classical World.* Ithaca, N.Y.: Cornell University Press, 1975.

Festugière, André-Jean. *Épicure et ses dieux.* Mythes et Religions 19. Paris: Presses Universitaires de France, 1968.

―――. *Personal Religion Among the Greeks.* Sather Classical Lectures 26. Berkeley: University of California Press, 1954.

Fink, R. O., A. S. Hoey, and W. F. Snyder. "The *Feriale Duranum.*" *Yale Classical Studies* 7 (1940): 1-222.

Fitzgerald, John T. and L. Michael White. *The* Tabula *of Cebes.* Texts and Translations 24; Graeco-Roman Religion Series. 7. Chico, Calif.: Scholars Press, 1983.

Fontenrose, Joseph. "Typhon among the Arimoi." 64-82 in *The Classical Tradition: Literary and Historical Studies in Honor of Harry Caplan*, edited by Luitpold Wallach. Ithaca, N.Y.: Cornell University Press, 1966.

Fowler, Robert M. *Loaves and Fishes: The Function of the Feeding*

Stories in the Gospel of Mark. Society of Biblical Literature Dissertation Series 54. Chico, Calif.: Scholars Press, 1981.

Freud, Sigmund. "The Uncanny." *The Standard Edition of the Complete
Psychological Works of Sigmund Freud* 17, edited and translated by
James Strachey. London: Hogarth Press, 1974.

Frey, Jean-Baptist. *Corpus Inscriptioum Iudaicarum: Recueil des
inscrtiptions juïves qui vont du IIIe siècle avant Jésus-Christ au VIIe
siècle de notre ère* 1: *Europe*. Sussidi allo Studio delle Antichità
Cristiane 1.1. Roma: Pontifico Istituto di Archeologia Cristiana,
1936.

———. *Corpus Inscriptionum Iudaicarum: Recueil des inscrtiptions
juïves qui vont du IIIe siècle avant Jésus-Christ au VIIe siècle de
notre ère* 2: *Asie-Afrique*. Sussidi allo Studio delle Antichità
Cristiane 3. Roma: Pontifico Istituto di Archeologia Cristiana, 1952.

Freyne, Seán. *Galilee from Alexander the Great to Hadrian, 323 B.C.E.
to 135 C.E.: A Study in Second Temple Judaism*. University of Notre
Dame Center for the Study of Judaism and Christianity series 5.
South Bend, Ind.: University of Notre Dame Press, 1980.

———. *Galilee, Jesus and the Gospels: Literary Approaches and
Historical Investigations*. Philadelphia: Fortress Press, 1988.

———. "Jesus and the Urban Culture of Galilee." 597-622 in *Texts and
Contexts: Biblical Texts in Their Textual and Situational Contexts:
Essays in Honor of Lars Hartman*, edited by T. Fornberg and David
Hellhom. Oslo: Scandinavian University Press, 1995.

Frisch, Amos. "Jerusalem and Its Parallels: Five Cities with Jerusalem in
the Bible." *Abr-Nahrain* 32 (1994): 80-95.

Frymer-Kensky, Tikva. *In the Wake of the Goddesses: Women, Culture,
and the Biblical Transformation of Pagan Myth*. New York: Free
Press, 1992.

Gager, John. *Curse Tablets and Binding Spells from the Ancient World*.
New York: Oxford University Press, 1992.

García Moreno, Luis A. "Paradoxography and Political Ideals in Plutarch's *Life of Sertorius*." 132-58 in *Plutarch and the Historical
Tradition*, edited by Philips A. Stadter. London: Routledge, 1992.

Garland, Robert. *The Greek Way of Death*. Ithaca, N.Y.: Cornell
University Press, 1985.

Gatz, Bodo. *Weltalter, goldene Zeit und sinnverwandte Vorstellungen*.
Spudasmata 16. Hildesheim: Georg Olms, 1967.

Giannini, Alexander. *Paradoxographorum Graecorum Reliquiae*.
Classici Greci e Latini: Sexione Texti e Commenti 3. Milano: La

Nuova Italia, 1967.

Girod, Robert. *Origenes Commentaire sur l'Évangile selon Matthieu.* Sources Chrétiennes 162. Paris: Éditions du Cerf, 1970.

Goldin, Judah. *The Fathers According to Rabbi Nathan.* Yale Judaica Series 10. New Haven, Conn.: Yale University Press, 1955; repr., New York: Schocken Books, 1974.

Goodenough, Erwin R. *Jewish Symbols in the Greco-Roman Period* 5: *Fish, Bread, and Wine.* Bollingen Series 27. New York: Pantheon Books, 1956.

Grandjean, Yves. *Une nouvelle arétalogie d'Isis à Maronée.* Études Préliminaires aux Religions Orientales dans l'Empire Roman 49. Leiden, The Netherlands: E. J. Brill, 1975.

Grant, Robert M. *The Problem of Miraculous Feedings in the Graeco-Roman World.* Center for Hermeneutical Studies in Hellenistic and Modern Culture: Protocol of the 42d Colloquy, 14 March 1982. Berkeley: Graduate Theological Union and the University of California Press, 1982.

Grisé, Yolande. "Pourquoi retuer un mort? Un cas de suicide dans la Rome royale." 267-81 in *Mélanges d'Études anciennes offerts à Maurice Lebel,* edited by Jean-Benoît Caron, Michel Fortin, and Gilles Maloney. St.-Jean-Chrysostôme, Québec: Les Éditions du Sphinx, 1980.

Grottanelli, Cristiano. "Saviours of the Eastern Mediterranean in Pre-Classical Times." 649-70 in *La soteriologia dei culti orientali nell'Impero Romano: Atti del colloquio internazionale,* edited by Ugo Bianchi and M. J. Vermaseren. Études Préliminaires aux Religions Orientales dans l'Empire Roman 92. Leiden, The Netherlands: E. J. Brill, 1982.

————. "Tricksters, Scapegoats, Champions, Saviors." *History of Religions* 23 (1984): 117-39.

Gruppe, O. *Griechische Mythologie und Religionsgeschichte.* Handbuch der klassischen Altertums-Wissenschaft in systematischer Darstellung 5. München: C. H. Beck'sche Verlagsbuchhandlung, 1906.

Güttgemanns, Erhardt. *Fragmenta semiotico-hermeneutica: Eine Texthermeneutik für den Umgang mit der Hl. Schrift.* Forum Theologicae Linguisticae: Interdisziplinäre Schriftenreihe für Theologie und Linguistik. 9. Bonn: Linguistica Biblica, 1983.

Habicht, Christian. *Gottmenschentum und griechische Städte.* 2d rev. ed. Zetemata 14. München: Verlag C. H. Beck, 1970.

Haldar, Alfred. *The Notion of the Desert in Sumero-Akkadian and West-*

Semitic Religions. Uppsala Universitates Årsskrift 1950:3. Uppsala: A. B. Lundequistska, 1950.

Halkin, Léon. *La supplication d'action de grâces chez les Romains.* Bibliothèque de la Faculté de Philosophie et Lettres de l'Université de Liège 128. Paris: Société d'Édition Les Belles Lettres, 1953.

Hansen, William. *Phlegon of Tralles' Book of Marvels.* Exeter: University of Exeter Press, 1996.

Harrauer, Christine. *Meliouchos: Studien zur Entwicklung religiöser Vorstellungen in griechischen synkretistischen Zaubertexten.* Wiener Studien 11: Arbeiten zur Antiken Religionsgeschichte 1. Wien: Verlag der Österreichische Akademie der Wissenschaften, 1987.

Hegeland, John. "Roman Army Religion." *Aufstieg und Niedergang der römischen Welt* ii/16, nr. 2 (1978): 1470-1505.

Heil, John Paul. *Jesus Walking on the Sea: Meaning and Gospel Functions of Matt 14:22-33, Mark 6:45-52 and John 6:15b-21.* Analecta Biblica 87. Rome: Pontifical Institute Press, 1981.

Heitsch, Ernst. *Die griechsichen Dichterfragmente der römischen Kaiserzeit.* 2d ed. Abhandlungen der Akademie der Wissenschaften in Göttingen, philologisch-historische Klasse, dritte Folge 49. Göttingen: Vandenhoeck & Ruprecht, 1963.

Hengel, Martin. *Crucifixion in the Ancient World and the Folly of the Cross.* Trans. by John Bowden. Philadelphia: Fortress Press, 1977.

Hengel, Martin, J. H. Charlesworth, and D. Mendels. "The Polemical Character of 'On Kingship' in the Temple Scroll: An Attempt at Dating 11QTemple." *Journal of Jewish Studies* 37, no. 1 (1986): 28-38.

Henten, Jan Willem van. "Das jüdische Selbstverständnis in den ältesten Martyrien." 127-61 in *Die Entstehung der jüdischen Martyrologie,* edited by J. W. Van Henten. Studia Post-Biblica 38. Leiden, The Netherlands: E. J. Brill, 1989.

Hock, Ronald F. "Why New Testament Scholars Should Read Ancient Novels." 121-38 in *Ancient Fiction and Early Christian Narrative,* edited by Ronald F. Hock, and others. Society of Biblical Literature Symposium Series 6. Atlanta: Scholars Press, 1998.

Hopfner, Theodor. *Griechisch-ägyptischer Offenbarungszauber, 2 Bd.* Studien zur Palaeographie und Papyruskunde 21, 23. Amsterdam: Verlag Adolf M. Hakkert, 1921.

Hopkins, Keith. *Death and Renewal.* Sociological Studies in Roman History 2. Cambridge: Cambridge University Press, 1983.

Horbury, William, and David Noy. *Jewish Inscriptions of Graeco-Roman*

Egypt, With an Index of the Jewish Inscriptions of Egypt and Cyrenaica. Cambridge: Cambridge University Press, 1992.

Hornum, Michael B. *Nemesis, the Roman State, and the Games.* Religions in the Graeco-Roman World 117. Leiden, The Netherlands: E. J. Brill, 1993.

Horst, Pieter Willem van der. *Chaeremon: Egyptian Priest and Stoic Philosopher: The Fragments Collected and Translated with Explanatory Notes.* Études prélimiaires aux religions orientales dans l'empire romain 101. Leiden, The Netherlands: E. J. Brill, 1984.

———. "Der Schatten im hellenistischen Volksglauben." 27-36 in *Studies in Hellenistic Religions,* edited by M. J. Vermaseren. Études prélimiaires aus religions orientales dans l'empire romain 78. Leiden, The Netherlands: E. J. Brill, 1979.

Hufford, David. *The Terror That Comes in the Night: An Experience-Centered Study of Supernatural Assault Traditions.* Publications of the American Folklore Society, new series 7. Philadelphia: University of Pennsylvania Press, 1982.

Hunt, Patrick N. "Mount Saphon in Myth and Fact." 103-15 in *Phoenicia and the Bible: Proceedings of the Conference Held at the University of Leuven on the 15th and 16th of March 1990,* edited by E. Lipinski. Orientalia Lovaniensia Analecta 44; Studia Phoenicia 11. Leuven, Belgium: Uitgeverij Peeters, 1991.

Ilan, Tal. *Jewish Women in Greco-Roman Palestine: An Inquiry into Image and Status.* Texte und Studien zum antiken Judentum 44. Tübingen, Germany: J. C. B. Mohr, 1995.

Isaac, Benjamin. "The Roman Army in Jerusalem and Vicinity." 635-40 in *Studien zu den Militärgrenzen Roms III: 13. Internationaler Limeskongreß, Aalen 1983.* Forschungen und Berichte zur Vor- und frügeschichte in Baden-Württemberg 20. Stuttgart: Konrad Theiss Verlag, 1986.

Johnston, Sarah Iles. "Defining the Dreadful: Remarks on the Greek Child-Killing Demon." In *Ancient Magic and Ritual Power,* edited by Marvin Meyer and Paul Mirecki. Religions in the Graeco-Roman World 129. Leiden, The Netherlands: E. J. Brill, 1995.

———. *Restless Dead: Encounters Between the Living and the Dead in Ancient Greece.* Berkeley: University of California Press, 1999.

Jones, A. H. M. *The Greek City from Alexander to Justinian.* Oxford: Clarendon Press. 1940.

Jonker, Gerdien. *The Topography of Remembrance: The Dead, Tradition and Collective Memory in Mesopotamia.* Studies in the History of

Religion (*Numen* Book Series) 68. Leiden, The Netherlands: E. J. Brill, 1995.

Kermode, Frank. *The Genesis of Secrecy: On the Interpretation of Narrative.* Charles Eliot Norton Lectures 1977-1978. Cambridge, Mass.: Harvard University Press, 1979.

Kern, Otto. *Orphicorum Fragmenta.* Dublin: Weidmann, 1972.

Kettenbach, Günter. *Einführung in die Schiffahrtsmetaphorik der Bibel.* Europäische Hochschulschriften, Reihe XXIII: Theology 512. Frankfurt am Main: Peter Lang, 1994.

Kiefer, René. "Traditions juives selon Mc 7,1-23." 675-88 in *Texts and Contexts: Biblical Texts in Their Textual and Situational Contexts: Essays in Honor of Lars Hartman,* edited by T. Fornberg and David Hellholm. Oslo: Scandinavian University Press, 1995.

Kingsley, Peter. *Ancient Philosophy, Mystery, and Magic: Empedocles and Pyhagorean Theory.* Oxford: Clarendon Press, 1995.

Kirk, G. S. and J. E. Raven. *The Presocratic Philosophers.* Cambridge: Cambridge University Press, 1962.

Klassen, William. "The King as 'Living Law' with Particular Reference to Musonius Rufus." *Studies in Religion/Sciences Religieuses* 14, no. 1 (1985): 63-71.

Knox, Wilfred L. *The Sources of the Synoptic Gospels 1: St. Mark,* edited by Henry Chadwick. Cambridge: Cambridge University Press, 1953.

Koets, Peter John. Δεισιδαιμονία: *A Contribution to the Knowledge of Religious Terminology in Greek.* Purmerend, The Netherlands: J. Muusss, 1952.

Kotansky, Roy. "Greek Exorcistic Amulets." 243-77 in *Ancient Magic and Ritual Power,* edited by Marvin Meyer and Paul Mirecki. Religions in the Graeco-Roman World 129. Leiden, The Netherlands: E. J. Brill, 1995.

———. "Jesus and Heracles in Cádiz (τὰ Γάδειρα): Death, Myth, and Monsters at the 'Straits of Gibraltar' (Mark 4:35-5:43)." 160-229 in *The Bible and Culture: Ancient and Modern Perspectves,* edited by Adela Yarbro Collins. Atlanta: Scholars Press, 1998.

———. "Two Inscribed Jewish Aramaic Amulets from Syria." *Israel Exploration Journal* 41, no. 4 (1991): 267-81.

Kraeling, Carl Hermann. *Gerasa: City of the Decapolis: An Account Embodying the Record of a Joint Excavation Conducted by Yale University and the British School of Archaeology in Jerusalem (1928-1930), and Yale University and the American Schools of Oriental Research (1930-1931, 1933-1934).* New Haven, Conn.:

American Schools of Oriental Research, 1938.

———. *The Synagogue*. Excavations at Dura-Europos Conducted by the Yale University and the French Academy of Inscriptions and Letters: Final Report 8: 1. New Haven: Yale University Press, 1956; repr., New York: KTAV Publishing House, 1979.

Kratz, Reinhard. *Rettungswunder: Motiv-, traditions- und formkritische Aufarbeitung einer biblischen Gattung*. Europäische Hochschulschriften, Reihe xxiii: Théologie 123. Frankfurt am Main: Peter Lang, 1979.

Krieg, Matthias. *Todesbilder im Alten Testament, oder: Wie die Alten den Tod gebildet*. Abhandlungen zur Theologie des Alten und Neuen Testaments 73. Zürich: Theologischer Verlag, 1988.

Kroll, Josef. *Gott und Hölle: Der Mythos vom Descensuskampfe*. Studien der Bilbiothek Warburg 20. Leipzig, Germany: Bibliothek Warburg, 1932.

Kroll, Wilhelm. *Vetti Valentis Anthologiarum Libri*. Berlin: Weidmann, 1908.

Kyriakou, P. "ΚΑΤΑΒΑΣΙΣ and the Underworld in the *Argonautica* of Apollonius Rhodius." *Philologus* 139, no. 2 (1995): 256-64.

Laird, Andrew. "Fiction, Bewitchment and Story Worlds: The Implications of Claims to Truth in Apuleius." 147-74 in *Lies and Fiction in the Ancient World*, edited by Christopher Gill and T. P. Wiseman. Austin: University of Texas Press, 1993.

Lane, Eugene N. *Corpus Monumentorum Religionis Dei Menis (MNRDM)*. Études préliminaires aux religions orientales dans l'empire romain 109. Leiden, The Netherlands: E. J. Brill, 1976.

Lattimore, Richard. *Themes in Greek and Roman Epitaphs*. Urbana: Univeristy of Illinois Press, 1962.

Levi, Peter. *Pausanias: Guide to Greece*. Rev. ed. London: Penguin, 1981.

Levy, Doro. "AION." *Hesperia* 13, no. 4 (1944): 263-314.

Lewis, Naphtali. *The Interpretation of Dreams and Portents*. London: Samuel Stevens, 1976.

Lichtheim, Miriam. *Ancient Egyptian Literature: A Book of Readings*. Berkeley: University of California Press, 1980.

LiDonnici, Lynn R. *The Epidaurian Miracle Inscriptions: Text, Translation and Commentary*. Texts and Translations 36; Graeco-Roman Series 11. Atlanta: Scholars Press, 1995.

Lindemann, Andreas. "Die Öesterbotschaft des Markus: Zur theologischen Interpretation von Mark 16.1-8." *New Testament Studies* 26

(1980): 298-317.

Lloyd, G. E. R. *Polarity and Analogy: Two Types of Argumentation in Early Greek Thought.* Cambridge: Cambridge University Press, 1966; repr., London: Bristol Classical Press, 1992.

———. *Science, Folklore and Ideology: Studies in the Life Sciences in Ancient Greece.* Cambridge: Cambridge University Press, 1983.

Lommatzsch, C. H. E. *Origenis Commentarius in Proverbia Salomonis. Origenis Opera Omnia* 13. Berlin: Haude et Spener, 1841.

Longo, Vincenzo. *Aretalogie nel mondo greco, 1: Epigrafi e papiri.* Pubblicazioni dell'Istituto di filologia classica dell'Università di Genova 29. Genova: Istituto di Filologia Classica e Medioevale, 1969.

Lunais, Sophie. *Recherches sur la Lune, 1: Les auteurs de la fin des guerres puniques à la fin du règne des Antonins.* Études préliminaires aux religions orientales dans l'empire romain 72. Leiden, The Netherlands: E. J. Brill, 1979.

Lutz, Cora E. *Musonius Rufus: The Roman Socrates.* Yale Classical Studies 10. New Haven, Conn.: Yale University Press, 1947.

Luz, Menahem. "A Description of the Greek Cynic in the Jerusalem Talmud." *Journal for the Study of Judaism* 20, no. 1 (1986):49-60.

McClenon, James. *Wondrous Events: Foundations of Religious Belief.* Philadelphia: University of Pennsylvania Press, 1994.

Macdonald, L. "Inscriptions Relating to Sorcery in Cyprus." *Proceedings of Society of Biblical Archaeology* 13 (1890-1891): 160-90.

MacDonald, Dennis R. *The Homeric Epics and the Gospel of Mark.* New Haven, Conn.: Yale University Press, 2000.

MacRae, George. "Miracles in the *Antiquities* of Josephus." 129-47 in *Miracles: Cambridge Studies in Their Philosophy and History,* edited by C. F. D. Moule. London: A. R. Mowbray, 1965.

Mack, Burton L. *A Myth of Innocence: Mark and Christian Origins.* Philadelphia: Fortress Press, 1988.

Madden, Patrick J. *Jesus's Walking on the Sea: An Investigation of the Origin of the Narrative Account.* Beihefte zur Zeitschrift für die neutestamentliche Wissenschaft und die Kunde der älten Kirche 81. Berlin: Walter de Gruyter, 1997.

Malbon, Elizabeth Struthers. *Narrative Space and Mythic Meaning in Mark.* San Francisco: Harper & Row, 1986.

Malherbe, Abraham J. *The Cynic Epistles: A Study Edition.* Society of Biblical Literature Sources for Biblical Studies 12. Atlanta: Scholars Press, 1986.

Mansoor, Menahem. *The Thanksgiving Hymns*. Studies in the Texts of the Desert of Judah 3. Grand Rapids, Mich.: William B. Eerdmans, 1961.

Martin, Luther H. "Artemidorus: Dream Theory in Late Antiquity." *Second Century* 8, no. 2 (1991): 97-108.

———. "Secrecy in Hellenistic Religious Communities." 101-121in *Secrecy and Concealment: Studies in the History of Mediterranean and Near Eastern Religions*, edited by Hans G. Kippenberg and Guy S. Stroumsa. Studies in the History of Religions (*Numen* Book Series) 75. Leiden, The Netherlands: E. J. Brill, 1995.

Martinez, David G. *P. Michigan XVI: A Greek Love Charm from Egypt (P.Mich. 757)*. Michigan Papyri 16; American Studies in Papyrology 30. Atlanta: Scholars Press, 1991.

Mason, Hugh J. *Greek Terms for Roman Institutions: A Lexicon and Analysis*. American Studies in Papyrology 13. Toronto: Hakkert, 1974.

May, Herbert G. "Some Cosmic Connotations of *Mayim Rabbîm*, 'Many Waters'." *Journal of Biblical Literature* 74, no. 2 (1955): 9-21.

Meagher, John C. *Clumsy Construction in Mark's Gospel: A Critique of Form- and Redaktionsgeschichte*. Toronto Studies in Theology 3. New York: Edwin Mellen Press, 1979.

Mendels, D. "'On Kingship' in the 'Temple Scroll' and the Ideological *Vorlage* of the Seven Banquets in the 'Letter to Philocrates'." *Aegyptus* 59 (1979): 127-36.

Meyers, Eric. "Galilean Regionalism: A Reappraisal." 115-31 in *Approaches to Ancient Judaism 5: Studies in Judaism and Its Graeco-Roman Context*, edited by William Scott Green. Brown Judaic Studies 32. Atlanta: Scholars Press, 1985.

Millar, Fergus. *The Emperor in the Roman World (31 B.C.-A.D. 337)*. Ithaca, N.Y.: Cornell University Press, 1977.

———. "Empire, Community and Culture in the Roman Near East: Greeks, Syrians, Jews and Arabs." *Journal of Jewish Studies* 38, no. 3 (1987): 143-64.

Mitropoulou, Elpis. *Kneeling Worshipers in Greek and Oriental Literature and Art*. Athens: Glauchi, 1975.

Momigliano, Arnaldo D. "Religion in Athens, Rome and Jerusalem in the First Century B.C." 1-18 in *Approaches to Ancient Judaism 5: Studies in Judaism and Its Graeco-Roman Context*, edited by William Scott Green. Brown Judaic Studies 32. Atlanta: Scholars Press, 1985.

Morgan, Michael A. *Sepher Ha-Razim: The Book of Mysteries*. Texts and

Translations 25: Pseudepigrapha Series 11. Chico, Calif.: Scholars Press, 1983.

Müller, Carl. *Geographi Graeci Minores*. Hildesheim, Germany: Georg Olms, 1965.

Murray, Oswyn. "Aristeas and Ptolemaic Kingship." *Journal of Theological Studies* 18 (1967): 337-71.

————. "Philodemus on the Good King according to Homer." *Journal of Roman Studies* 55 (1965): 161-82.

Musurillo, Herbert A. *The Acts of the Pagan Martyrs: Acta Alexandrinorum*. Oxford: Clarendon Press, 1954.

Naveh, Joseph and Shaul Shaked. *Amulets and Magic Bowls: Aramaic Incantations of Late Antiquity*. Jerusalem: Magnes Press, 1985.

————. *Magic Spells and Formulae: Aramaic Incantations of Late Antiquity*. Jerusalem: Magnes Press, 1993.

Ninck, Martin. *Die Bedeutung des Wassers im Kult und Leben der Alten: Eine symbolgeschichtliche Untersuchung*. Philologus, Supplement-Band 14, Heft 2. Leipzig, Germany: Dieterich'sche Verlagsbuchhandlung, 1921.

Nitzan, Bilhah. *Qumran Prayer and Religious Poetry*. Trans. Jonathan Chipman. Studies on the Texts of the Desert of Judah 12. Leiden, The Netherlands: E. J. Brill, 1994.

Nock, Arthur Darby. *Essays on Religion and the Ancient World, Selected and Edited, with an Introduction, Bibliography of Nock's Writings, and Indexes by Zeph Stewart*. Cambridge, Mass.: Harvard University Press, 1972.

Noy, David. *Jewish Inscriptions of Western Europe* 1: *Italy (Excluding the City of Rome), Spain and Gaul*. Cambridge: Cambridge University Press, 1993.

————. *Jewish Inscriptions of Western Europe* 2: *The City of Rome*. Cambridge: Cambridge University Press, 1995.

Olender, Maurice. "Aspects of Baubo: Ancient Texts and Contexts." 83-113 in *Before Sexuality: The Construction of Erotic Experience in the Ancient Greek World*, edited by David M. Halperin, John L. Winkler, and Froma I. Zeitlin. Princeton, N.J.: Princeton University Press, 1990.

O'Neil, Edward. *Teles [The Cynic Teacher]*. Texts and Translations 1; Graeco-Roman Religion 3. Missoula, Mont.: Scholars Press, 1977.

Otto, Walter F. *Die Manen oder von den Urformen des Totenglaubens: Eine Untersuchung zur Religion der Griechen, Römer und Semiten und zum Volksglauben überhaupt*. Darmstadt: Wissenschaftliche

Buchgesellschaft, 1962.

Overbeck, Franz. *Christentum und Kultur: Gedanken und Anmerkungen zur modernen Theologie.* 2d ed. 1919; repr., Darmstadt: Wissenschaftliche Buchgesellschaft, 1963.

Paschall, Dorothy May. "The Vocabulary of Mental Aberration in Roman Comedy and Petronius." Ph.D. diss., University of Chicago, 1939. Repr. as Language Dissertations 27 in *Supplement to Language: Journal of the Linguistic Society of America* 15:1 (January-March 1939); repr., New York: Krauss, 1966.

Peabody, David Barrett. *Mark as Composer.* New Gospel Studies 1. Macon, Ga.: Mercer University Press, 1987.

Perdrizet, Paul. *Negotium Perambulans in Tenerbris: Études de démonologie gréco-orientale.* Publications de la Faculté des Lettres de l'Université de Strasbourg 6. Strasbourg: Faculté des Lettres de l'Université de Strasbourg, 1922.

Perry, Ben. *Aesopica: A Series of Texts Relating to Aesop or Ascribed to Him or Closely Connected with the Literary Tradition That Bears His Name 1: Greek and Latin Texts.* Urbana: University of Illinois Press, 1952.

Pervo, Richard I. "PANTA KOINA: The Feeding Stories in the Light of Economic Data and Social Practice." 163-94 in *Religious Propaganda and Missionary Competition in the New Testament World: Essays Honoring Dieter Georgi*, edited by Lukas Bormann, Kelly Del Tredici, and Angela Standhartinger. Novum Testamentum Supplements 74. Leiden, The Netherlands: E. J. Brill, 1994.

Pesch, Rudolph. *Der Besessene von Gerasa: Entstehung und Überlieferung einer Wundergeschichte.* Stuttgarter Bibelstudien 56. Stuttgart: KBW Verlag, 1972.

Pomeroy, Sarah B. *Goddesses, Whores, Wives, and Slaves: Women in Classical Antiquity.* New York: Schocken Books, 1975.

Preisendanz, Karl. *Papyri Graecae Magicae: Die Griechischen Zauberpapyri.* Leipzig, Germany: Teubner, 1928.

Price, Theodora. Hadizisteliou. *Kourotrophos: Cults and Representations of the Greek Nursing Deities.* Studies of the Dutch Archaeological and Historical Society 8. Leiden, The Netherlands: E. J. Brill, 1978.

Reiner, Erica. *Astral Magic in Babylonia.* Transactions of the American Philosophical Society 85, no. 4. Philadelphia: American Philosophical Society, 1995.

Remus, Harold. *Pagan-Christian Conflict over Miracle in the Second Century.* Patristic Monograph Series 10. Philadelphia: Philadelphia

Patristic Foundation, 1983.

Robert, Louis. *Le Martyre de Pionios, Prêtre de Smyrne,* edited by G. W. Bowersock and C. P. Jones. Washington, D.C.: Dumbarton Oaks Research Library and Collection, 1994.

Robinson, James M. *The Problem of History in Mark.* Studies in Biblical Theology 21. London: SCM Press, 1957.

Robinson, John A. and M. R. James. *The Gospel According to Peter, and the Revelation of Peter: Two Lectures on the Newly Recovered Fragments Together with the Greek Texts.* London: C. J. Clay, 1892.

Rohde, Erwin. *Psyche: The Cult of Souls and Belief in Immortality among the Greeks,* 7th ed.. Trans. W. B. Hillis. New York: Harcourt, Brace, 1925.

Rousselle, Aline. *Porneia: On Desire and the Body in Antiquity.* Trans. Felicia Pheasant. Oxford: Basil Blackwell, 1988.

Rubenstein, Jeffrey L. *The History of Sukkot in the Second Temple and Rabbinic Periods.* Brown Judaic Studies 302. Atlanta: Scholars Press, 1995.

Russell, D. A. and N. G. Wilson. *Menander Rhetor.* Oxford: Clarendon Press, 1981.

Sanders, J. A. *The Dead Sea Psalms Scroll.* Ithaca, N.Y.: Cornell University Press, 1967.

Schenke, Ludger. *Die Wundererzählungen des Markusevangeliums.* Stuttgarter Biblische Beiträge. Stuttgart: Katholisches Bibelwerk, 1974.

Schreiber, Johannes. *Theologie des Vertrauens: Eine redaktionsgeschichtliche Untersuchung der Markusevangeliums.* Hamburg: Furche-Verlag H. Rennebach, 1967.

Schubart, W. "Das hellenistiche Königsideal nach Inschriften und Papyri." *Archiv für Papyrusforschung* 12 (1937): 1-26.

Schuller, Eileen M. *Non-Canonical Psalms from Qumran.* Harvard Semitic Studies 28. Atlanta: Scholars Press, 1986.

Scriba, Albrecht. *Die Geschichte des Motivkomplexes Theophanie: Seine Elemente, Einbindung in Geschehensabläufe und Verwendungsweisen in altisraelitischer, früjüdischer und früchristlicher Literatur.* Forschungen zur Religion und Literatur des Alten und Neuen Testaments 167. Göttingen: Vandenhoeck und Ruprecht, 1995.

Seely, Paul H. "The Firmament and the Water Above, Part 1: The Meaning of *raqia* in Gen. 1:6-8." *Westminster Theological Journal* 53 (1991): 227-40.

Segal, Charles. *The Theme of the Mutilation of the Corpse in the Iliad.*

Mnemosyne Supplements 17. Leiden, The Netherlands: E. J. Brill, 1971.

Sekki, Arthur Everett. *The Meaning of* ruah *at Qumran.* Society of Biblical Literature Dissertation Series 110. Atlanta: Scholars Press, 1989.

Selvidge, Marla J. *Women, Cult, and Miracle Recital: A Redactional Critical Investigation on Mark 5:24-34.* Lewisburg, Pa.: Bucknell University Press, 1990.

Shatzman, Israel. *The Armies of the Hasmonaeans and Herod: From Hellenistic to Roman Frameworks.* Texte und Studien zum Antiken Judentum 25. Tübingen, Germany: J. C. B. Mohr, 1991.

Sherwin-White, A. N. *Roman Society and Roman Law in the New Testament.* Oxford: Oxford University Press, 1963.

———. *Roman Foreign Policy in the East: 168 B.C. to A.D. 1.* Norman: University of Oklahoma Press, 1983.

Shimoff, Sandra R. "Hellenization among the Rabbis: Some Evidence from Early Aggadot concerning David and Solomon." *Journal for the Study of Judaism* 18, no. 2 (1991): 168-87.

Siker, Jefrey S. "Abraham in Graeco-Roman Paganism." *Journal for the Study of Judaism* 18, no. 2 (1991): 188-208.

Smith, Morton. *Clement of Alexandria and a Secret Gospel of Mark.* Cambridge, Mass.: Harvard University Press, 1973.

———. *Jesus the Magician.* San Francisco: Harper and Row, 1978.

———. "De Superstitione (Moralia 164E-171F)." 1-35 in *Plutarch's Theological Writings and Early Christian Literature,* edited by Hans Dieter Betz. Studia ad Corpus Hellenisticum Novi Testamenti 3. Leiden, The Netherlands: E. J. Brill, 1975.

Snyder, Graydon F. *Ante Pacem: Archaeological Evidence of Church Life before Constantine.* Macon, Ga.: Mercer University Press, 1985.

Speidel, Michael P. *Mithras-Orion: Greek Hero and Roman Army God.* Études préliminaires aus religions orientales dans l'Empire romain 81. Leiden, The Netherlands: E. J. Brill, 1980.

——— *The Religion of Iuppiter Dolichenus in the Roman Army.* Études préliminaires aux religions orientales dans l'Empire Romain 63. Leiden, The Netherlands: E. J. Brill, 1978.

Speidel, Michael P. and Alexandra Dimitrova-Milčeva. "The Cult of the Genii in the Roman Army and a New Military Deity." *Aufstieg und Niedergang der römischen Welt* ii/16 nr. 2 (1978): 1542-55.

Sperber, Daniel. *Magic and Folklore in Rabbinic Literature.* Bar-Ilan Studies in Near Eastern Languages and Culture. Ramat-Gan: Bar-Ilan

University Press, 1994.

———. "Some Rabbinic Themes in Magical Papyri." *Journal for the Study of Judaism* 16, no. 1 (1989): 93-103.

Stambaugh, John E. "The Functions of the Roman Temple." *Aufstieg und Niedergang der römischen Welt* ii/16 nr. 1 (1978): 554-608.

Stegner, William Richard. "Jesus' Walking on the Water: Mark 6:45-52." 212-34 in *The Gospels and the Scriptures of Israel*, edited by Craig A. Evans and W. Richard Stegner. Journal for the Study of the New Testament Supplement Series 104; Studies in Scripture in Early Judaism and Christianity 3. Sheffield: University of Sheffield Press, 1994.

Stern, Menahem. "Judea and Her Neighbors in the Days of Alexander Jannaeus." *The Jerusalem Cathedra* 1 (1981): 22-46.

Stinton, T. C. W. "*Si credere dignum est*: Some Expressions of Disbelief in Euripides and Others." *Proceedings of the Cambridge Philological Society* 202 [n.s. 22] (1976): 60-89.

Straten, F. T. van. "Gifts for the Gods." 65-121 in *Faith, Hope and Worship: Aspects of Religious Mentality in the Ancient World*, edited by H. S. Versnel. Studies in Greek and Roman Religion 2. Leiden, The Netherlands: E. J. Brill, 1981.

Swete, Henry Barclay. *The Gospel According to St. Mark: The Greek Text with Introduction, Notes and Indices*. London: Macmillan, 1898.

Tabeling, Ernst. *Mater Larum: Zum Wesen der Larenreligion*. Frankfurter Studien zur Religion und Kultur der Antike 1. Frankfurt am Main: V. Klostermann, 1932.

Tabor, James D. and Michael O. Wise. "4Q521 'On Resurrection' and the Synoptic Gospel Tradition: A Preliminary Study." *Journal for the Study of the Pseudepigrapha* 10 (1992): 149-62.

Tarn, W. W. *Alexander the Great*. Cambridge: Cambridge University Press, 1948.

Teixidor, Javier. *The Pagan God: Popular Religion in the Greco-Roman Near East*. Princeton, N.J.: Princeton University Press, 1977.

Teleford, W. R. *The Theology of the Gospel of Mark*. Cambridge: Cambridge University Press, 1999.

Theissen, Gerd. *The Miracle Stories of the Early Christian Tradition*. Trans. Francis McDonagh, edited by John Riches. Philadelphia: Fortress Press, 1983.

Thesleff, Holger. *An Introduction to the Pythagorean Writings of the Hellenistic Period*. Acta Academiae Aboensis Ser. A: Humaniora: Humanistiska Vetenskaper, Socialvetenskaper, Teologi 24, nr. 3.

Åbo: Åbo Akademi, 1961.

―――. "Notes on the Paradise Myth in Ancient Greece." *Temenos* 26 (1982): 129-39.

―――. *The Pythagorean Texts of the Hellenistic Period.* Acta Academiae Aboensis, Ser. A: Humaniora: Humanistiska Vetenskaper, Socialvetenskaper, Teologi 30, nr. 1. Åbo: Åbo Akademi, 1965.

Thom, Johan C. *The Pythagorean Golden Verses: With an Introduction and Commentary.* Religions in the Graeco-Roman World 123. Leiden, The Netherlands: E. J. Brill, 1995.

Todorov, Tzvetan. *The Fantastic: A Structural Approach to a Literary Genre.* Trans. Richard Howard. Ithaca, N.Y.: Cornell University Press, 1975.

―――. *Introduction to Poetics.* Trans. Richard Howard. Theory and History of Literature 1. Minneapolis: University of Minnesota Press, 1981.

Toorn, Karel van der, Bob Becking, and Pieter Van der Horst, eds. *Dictionary of Deities and Demons in the Bible.* Leiden, The Netherlands: E. J. Brill, 1995. S.v. "Terror of the Night," by M. Malul.

Toynbee, J. M. C. *Death and Burial in the Roman World.* Ithaca, N.Y.: Cornell University Press, 1971.

Tran Tam Tinh, Vincent. "Etat des études iconographiques relatives à Isis, Sérapis et Sunnaoi Theoi." *Aufstieg und Niedergang der römischen Welt* ii/17 nr. 3 (1979): 1710-38.

Tromp, Nicholas J. *Primitive Conceptions of Death and the Nether World in the Old Testament.* Biblica et Orientalia 21. Rome: Pontifical Biblical Institute, 1969.

Usener, Hermann. *Epicurea.* Sammlung wissenschaftlicher Commentare. Stuttgart: B. G. Teubner, 1887.

Vale, Ruth. "Literary Sources in Archaeological Description: The Case of Galilee, Galilees and Galileans." *Journal for the Study of Judaism* 18, no. 2 (1987): 209-226.

Vermeule, Emily. *Aspects of Death in Early Greek Art and Poetry.* Sather Classical Lectures 46. Berkeley: University of California Press, 1979.

Vernant, Jean-Pierre. *Figures, idoles, masques.* Paris: Julliard, 1990.

―――. *Mortals and Immortals: Collected Essays,* edited by Froma I. Zeitlin. Trans. Andrew Szegedy-Maszak. Princeton, N.J.: Princeton University Press, 1991.

―――. *Myth et pensée chez les Grecs: Études de psychologie historique.* Paris: Éditions la Découverte, 1985.

―――. *Mythe et société en Grèce ancienne.* Paris: Éditions la Découverte, 1982.

Versnel, H. S. "Beyond Cursing: The Appeal to Justice in Judicial Prayers." 60-106 in *Magika Hiera: Ancient Greek Magic and Religion*, edited by Christopher A. Faraone and Dirk Obbink. New York: Oxford University Press, 1991.

—————. "What Did Ancient Man See When He Saw a God? Some Reflections on Greco-Roman Epiphany." 42-55 in *Effigies Dei: Essays on the History of Religions*, edited by Dirk Van der Plas. Studies in the History of Religions (Supplements to *Numen*) 51. Leiden, The Netherlands: E. J. Brill, 1987.

Veyne, Paul. *Bread and Circuses: Historical Sociology and Political Pluralism*. Abridged ed. Trans. Brian Pearce. London: Allen Lane and Penguin Press, 1990.

Visser, Margaret. "Worship Your Enemies: Aspects of the Cult of Heroes in Ancient Greece." *Harvard Theological Review* 75, no. 4 (1982): 403-428.

Waszink, J. H. *Opuscula Selecta*. Leiden, The Netherlands: E. J. Brill, 1979.

—————. *Quinti Septimi Florentis Tertulliani De Anima: Edited with Introduction and Commentary*. Amsterdam: J. M. Meulenhoff, 1947.

Wegner, Judith Romney. *Chattel or Person? The Status of Women in the Mishnah*. New York: Oxford University Press, 1988.

Weinfeld, Moshe. "The Angelic Song over the Luminaries in the Qumran Texts." 131-57 in *Time to Prepare the Way in the Wilderness: Papers on the Qumran Scrolls by Fellows of the Institute for Advanced Studies of the Hebrew University Jerusalem, 1989-1990*, edited by Devorah Dimant and Lawrence H. Schiffman. Studies in the Texts of the Desert of Judah 16. Leiden, The Netherlands: E. J. Brill, 1995.

—————. *Social Justice in Ancient Israel and in the Ancient Near East*. Jerusalem: Magnes Press, 1995.

Weiss, Zeev. "Social Aspects of Burial in Beth She`arim: Archaeological Finds and Talmudic Sources." 357-71 in *The Galilee in Late Antiquity*, edited by L. Levine. New York: Jewish Theological Seminary of America, 1992.

West, Martin L. *Early Greek Philosophy and the Orient*. Oxford: Clarendon Press, 1971.

Westermann, Antonius. ΠΑΡΑΔΟΞΟΓΡΑΦΟΙ: *Scriptores Rerum Mirabilium Graeci*. London: Brunsvigae, 1839.

Widengren, Geo. *The King and the Tree of Life in Anient Near Eastern*

326 Bibliography

Religion (King and Saviour IV). Uppsala Universitets Årsskrft 1951, no. 4. Uppsala: A.-B. Lundequistska Bokhandeln, 1951.

Wiedemann, Thomas. *Emperors and Gladiators*. London: Routledge, 1992.

Wilson, Andrew M. and Lawrence Wills. "Literary Sources of the *Temple Scroll*." *Harvard Theological Review* 75, no. 3 (1982): 275-88.

Winter, Irene J. "'Idols of the King': Royal Images as Recipients of Ritual Action in Ancient Mesopotamia." *Journal of Ritual Studies* 6, no. 1 (1992): 13-42.

————. "The King and the Cup: Iconography of the Royal Presentation Scene on Ur III Seals." 252-63 in *Insight through Images: Studies in Honor of Edith Porada*, edited by Marilyn Kelly-Buccellati. Bibliotheca Mesopotamica 21. Malibu: Undena Publications, 1986.

Wissowa, Georg and Wilhelm Kroll, eds. *Paulys Real-Encyclopädie der klassischen Altertumswissenschaft*. Stuttgart: J. B. Metzler, 1905. S.v. "Daimon," by Waser; "εἴδωλον," by A. Körte, "Καταποντισμός," by Schulthess; "Λαῖλαψ"; "Manes," by Marbach; "Nekydaimon," by K. Preisendanz; "Nekromantie," T. Hopfner; "Paradoxographoi," by K. Ziegler; "Schiffahrt," by W. Kroll.

Woodman, Tony. "Nero's Alien Capital: Tacitus as Paradoxographer (*Annals* 15.36-7)." 173-188 in *Author and Audience in Latin Literature*. Cambridge: Cambridge University Press, 1992.

Wrede, William. *The Messianic Secret*. Trans. by J. Grieg. Library of Theological Translations. Cambridge: James Clake, 1971.

Wright, M. R. *Empedocles: The Extant Fragments*. New Haven, Conn.: Yale University Press, 1981.

Wyatt, N. *Myths of Power: A Study of Royal Myth and Ideology in Ugaritic and Biblical Tradition*. Ugaritisch-Biblische Literatur 13. Münster: Ugarit-Verlag, 1996.

Young, George W. *Subversive Symmetry: Exploring the Fantastic in Mark 6:45-56*. Biblical Interpretation Series 41. Leiden, The Netherlands: E. J. Brill, 1999.

Youtie, H. C. and Campbell Bonner. "Two Curse Tablets from Beisan." *Transactions and Proceedings of the American Philological Association* 73 (1937): 43-77.

Zertal, Adam. "The Roman Siege-System at Khirbet al-Hamam (Narbata)." 71-94 in *The Roman and Byzantine Near East: Some Recent Archaeological Research*. Journal of Roman Archaeology, Supplementary Series 14. Ann Arbor, Mich.: Cushing-Malloy, 1995.

Zlotnick, Dov. *The Tractate "Mourning" (Śĕmahot): Regulations*

Relating to Death, Burial, and Mourning. Yale Judaica Series 17. New Haven, Conn.: Yale University Press, 1966.

Zuntz, Günther Αἰών *in der Literature der Kaiserzeit.* Wiener Studien 17; Arbeiten zur Antiken Religionsgeschichte. 2. Wien: Österreichische Akademie der Wissenschaften, 1992.

————. *Persephone: Three Essays on Religion and Thought in Magna Greek.* Oxford: Clarendon Press, 1971.

Subject Index

Ancient Author and Title Index

Epictetus
Discourses, 119n32, 195
Eudemus of Rhodes, 98
Eupolemus
On the Kings of Judea, 220n16
Euripides
Helena, 168, 250
Herakles, 54n48
Hippolytus, 33
Orestes, 245
Eusebius of Caesara
Questionum evangelicarum libro, 92n50

Feriale Duranum, 138-39, 155n55, 211

Genesis Rabbah, 97, 144n10
Gilgamesh Epic, 102, 280
Golden Verses, 99, 132, 150n34
Greek Magical Papyri
PGM IV, 52n38, 105, 129, 146n17, 147n21, 165, 245, 246, 250, 260n33, 264n61, 265n64, 281
PGM V, 104
PGM VII, 264n61
PGM XIII, 17n19, 188
PGM XV, 129
PGM XIXb, 17n19

Heraclitus
Homeric Problems, 278-79
Herodas
Mimiambi, 235n11
Herodotus
History, 134, 251, 256n19
Hesiod
Theogony, 33, 98, 111n5, 299
Hieronymi et Hellanici Theogonia, 99
Homer
Iliad, 17n19, 29, 33-34, 54n48, 111n4, 134, 247, 255n13
Odyssey, 14n8, 54n48, 106,

111n4, 120n36, 122n44, 134, 236n21, 246-47, 255n13, 261n42

Instruction of Ankhsheshonq, 38
Isocrates
Philippus, 202n22

Josephus
Against Apion, 117n28
Antiquities, 32, 129, 209-210, 212, 216n2, 258n25
War, 130, 133, 159n70, 249-50, 251, 264n58
Juvenal
Satires, 232

Letter of Aristeas, 217n10
Livy
History of Rome, 46n7
Lucian
Alexander, 204n28
Lovers of Lies, 25, 114n17, 129, 189, 146n17, 180n27, 282
On the Death of Peregrinus, 203n23
Syrian Goddess, 117n29
True Histories, 25
Ludus, Johannes
On Portents, 45n4

Martyrdom of Pionius, 8-9, 16n13-15
Martyrdom of the Holy Apostle Peter, 45n2
Menander Rhetor
Progymnasmata, 148n28, 152n39, 237n27, 258n22
Mishna
Sanhedrin, 133
Šemahot, 144n10
Niddah, 176n12
Musonius Rufus
That Kings Should Also Study Philosophy, 217n4, 217n8

Modern Author Index

Greek, Latin, and Other Terms Index

Greek Terms

Latin Terms

Other Terms